IMAGINE

TECH FOR GOOD

SOLVING THE WORLD'S GREATEST CHALLENGES

Routledge
Taylor & Francis Group

MARGA HOEK

Designed cover image: Creative Studio Elise Laan

First published 2024
by Routledge
4 Park Square, Milton Park, Abingdon, Oxon OX14 4RN

and by Routledge
605 Third Avenue, New York, NY 10158

Routledge is an imprint of the Taylor & Francis Group, an Informa business

Research and editing: Theresa McCarty (chief researcher and editor), Lucy Wilde (deputy editor
and proof reader), Pascale Wojcik (assistant proof reader)
Project management: Rosalie de Kerf
Design and lettering: Creative Studio Elise Laan

British Library Cataloguing-in-Publication Data
A catalogue record for this book is available from the British Library

Library of Congress Cataloging-in-Publication Data

Names: Hoek, Marga, author.
Title: Tech for Good / Marga Hoek.
Description: Abingdon, Oxon; New York, NY: Routledge, 2024. | Includes bibliographical references.
Subjects: LCSH: Social responsibility of business. | Sustainable development. | Industry 4.0.
Classification: LCC HD60 .H6325 2024 (print) | LCC HD60 (ebook) | DDC 658.4/08--dc23/
eng/20230719
LC record available at https://lccn.loc.gov/2023027297
LC ebook record available at https://lccn.loc.gov/2023027298

ISBN: 978-1-032-49073-1 (hardback)
ISBN: 978-1-003-39206-4 (eBook)

DOI: 10.4324/9781003392064

TECH FOR GOOD

THE FILM

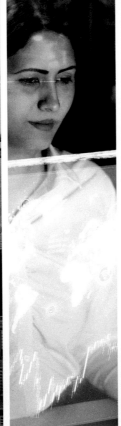
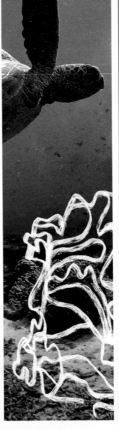

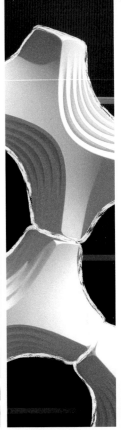

PREFACE

This is a book of hope. It sets us on an inspirational course at this pivotal moment in time. The hope of a bright and prosperous future steers us along our path and drives us to take positive action. Crossing over the threshold into the Fourth Industrial Revolution, we have a choice to make and a responsibility to decide how to use technology from here onward. My hope is that we will collectively choose to use technology for good.

When we use technology as a force for good, we will fundamentally solve our world's greatest challenges. Hope is the foundation for shifting our thinking and it gives us the motivation to act. Hope is the basis for catalyzing forward movement, enabling us to overcome fears that paralyze progress because it seems too hard.

President John F. Kennedy had hope and his message was clear: big things are achieved not because they are easy, but because they are hard. And now we have help in realizing these hopes. The help of technology is our greatest ally in achieving our biggest goals. Ethically and responsibly applied tech solutions are being scaled more quickly than ever before. Hope of technological advancement is far-reaching throughout the world, even in remote areas. Technology for Good, as I and many others word it, will be a defining factor of the next decades.

In writing this book, I discovered the world of tech to be far more expansive than I previously understood. I was amazed with the wide range of Fourth Industrial Revolution technologies and their abilities to contribute to a better world for us all. From administering medicines in remote areas to helping solve further biodiversity loss, from boosting our ability to mitigate climate change to reducing food waste, and from providing access to education to fostering greater equality, the list is long and touches all 17 Sustainable Development Goals.

By leveraging technology to solve our societal challenges, it has a true purpose. And as a consequence, our own purpose deepens as well. That purpose comes with a prize - a business prize - as I explained in my former book, "The Trillion Dollar Shift," how Business for Good is Good Business. And this applies even more to Technology for Good. With unprecedented access to a wide range of advanced technologies that will create real value, we will accelerate sustainable progress in a way we weren't able to before.

This book is the result of three years of extensive research, writing, editing, and rewriting. I can't express enough my gratitude to the team that has been committed to making sure we explain technologies in a way that is understandable and exciting. Identifying the impact advanced technologies will have on our global challenges sheds light on potential growth markets with vast business opportunities. There are 75 real-life business cases from companies all over the world, which are presented as exciting examples of opportunities on how to apply Tech for Good. My goal with this book is to expand your imagination through inspiration. My hope is that it will raise your confidence to act and to create positive impact on the world with the help of technology. My hope is that you will dare to appreciate technology and dare to imagine the possible, instead of dwelling on the impossible. It is my hope that you do not see all the challenges preventing you from action, but rather that you look at all the opportunities for success.

Einstein famously said, "the true sign of intelligence is not knowledge but imagination." So, join me in imagining what we can do. Imagine Tech for Good helping solve the world's greatest challenges. When we engage our mind, collaboration, investment and, most importantly, our perseverance, we shall overcome the hurdles along our way. This journey is more than worthwhile. Our planet and our people are at stake. And so is our business. By now, Tech for Good is a global movement. Neither businesses nor any other entities have any reason not to join.
I hope you will join me in the Tech for Good movement.

Marga Hoek

TECH FOR GOOD 1

TECHNOLOGY ITSELF IS NEUTRAL. IT IS THE IMPLICATIONS OF TECHNOLOGY THAT COUNT, RATHER THAN THE APPLICATIONS.
WE CAN DECIDE HOW TO USE TECHNOLOGY.
I SUGGEST WE USE IT AS A FORCE FOR GOOD.
TECH FOR GOOD.

IMAGINE

Imagine embarking on a journey into the Fourth Industrial Revolution. Along the way, we are surrounded with a wide range of amazing, advanced technologies that can help solve the world's greatest challenges like climate change, biodiversity loss and poverty, while improving global health and wellbeing. Imagine technologies transforming both business and the planet as we know it, realizing what was beyond our imagination not too long ago.

As we leave the Third Industrial Revolution behind, our world remains endangered and threatened. Global progress has come at a price; a huge price that the world cannot pay. We have overstretched our planet and face extreme consequences. The challenges we are up against are numerous, as the world battles climate risks, suffers societal inequalities, and experiences biodiversity loss.

We have learned, matured, and chosen a renewed course of action. This new pathway, one moving away from ever growing risks, points us in a direction steered by the steady compass of the Sustainable Development Goals. These 17 Goals, agreed upon by 193 countries, are the guiding principles that direct our journey in that new direction. Although there is movement toward a better future for all, we are progressing too slowly, on a long journey, with a vast distance that must be covered in so little time.

This book is about synergizing technology for global progress by employing it as a driver for sustainable growth. Businesses have taken on this challenge and are paving the way for a sustainable future. Companies with a positive impact can help lead the way. An astounding 69 of the world's 100 largest economies by revenue are companies, not countries. Business has the influence and power to lead, and therefore has the responsibility to do so. But how can we move faster to solve global challenges? How can we innovate and create solutions at scale?

Imagine, for instance, how technology can restore our planet's dying coral reefs. Advancements in 3D printing can help put a stop to it, and in some cases even reverse the damage inflicted on coral reefs. Although technology doesn't replace nature, it does achieve positive change. 3D printing coral reefs is but one example of how we can use technology to restore and create a better world. *Tech for Good* is your navigation into an exciting world. It provides you as a reader with a vision for technology's unprecedented potential to make business-positive impacts.

Tech for Good will take you on a journey all over the world, giving examples and providing insights on the most up-to-date global business innovations. *Tech for Good* sets out to inspire you across eight exciting technology groups, with a clear outlook on how to leverage tech to unlock new markets.

Technology itself is not meaningful. It is the implications of technology that count. As humans, and more specifically as business professionals, we have a choice to make. I suggest that we decide to use technology as a force for good. We must work to restore trust in technology by using it to the benefit of people and the planet. This vision is the foundation of Tech for Good.

Imagination is the key to discovering radical, new solutions. It does not mean we are naïve. It means that we have the ability to work with what has been created by former industrial revolutions. It means we can rise above, aiming truly to find solutions for the world's greatest challenges.

We have so many technologies to help us on this mission. The movement is already there. Join this global Tech for Good movement. Start your journey by reading this exciting book.

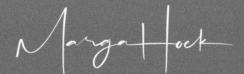

1
INTRODUCING
TECH FOR GOOD

The potential of the Fourth Industrial Revolution (referred to hereafter as 4IR) to address major global challenges, including poverty, climate change, nature loss, and inequality, is immense. Currently, we only tap into a fraction of this potential. The enormous promise of Tech for Good, both for the world as well as for business, is clear. While moving over the threshold into the 4IR, a wide variety of technologies emerges. These new tech applications make it possible to leverage sustainable impact at scale, and at the same time seize exciting market opportunities. With a purpose-driven approach to the way technologies are deployed, businesses will undoubtedly play a crucial role in perpetuating worldwide progress. While fostering a shared value business model and building trust in technological breakthroughs, businesses gain a competitive advantage.

Highlighting the 4IR as an unprecedented era, this chapter discusses the opportunities of the 4IR and sheds light on numerous tech solutions. This chapter reveals an overview of the eight groups of advanced technologies discussed in this book: Artificial Intelligence and Data, 3D Printing, Robotics, Advanced Materials, Extended Realities, Autonomous Vehicles and Drones, Blockchain, and Space Technologies. These techs are hugely important for business in the present and even more so in the future. The Internet of Things (IoT) is discussed, as it forms the foundation for these eight technologies. Offering a glimpse of what is yet to come, this chapter looks over the edge into the abyss of rapidly expanding, unknown new tech solutions.

HUMANS IN CHARGE OF TECHNOLOGY IN A CHALLENGED WORLD

As the downsides of former industrial revolutions and economic systems are becoming increasingly clear, humanity braces itself for tremendous changes that threaten to further destabilize societies and the ecology of the Earth. With a world experiencing more pressing circumstances than ever before, we need radical forward movement. The 4IR is the threshold of a universal shift marked by digital, physical, and biological worlds combining technologies that create possibilities for a better future. It also presents unforeseen risks.[1] The Earth has never faced so many challenges with such intensity at the same time. Shortcomings of industrialization and economic growth have led to irreversible damage to people and the planet. Although unprecedented progress was achieved, it came at a high price, and we are now living the aftermath in an "age of consequences."[2]

Severe ecological disruptions like climate change, biodiversity loss and resource scarcity stand to create an uninhabitable environment. These dire consequences leading up to the 4IR come with a staggering cost, as trillions of dollars and billions of lives are at stake. Climate change could be referred to as the greatest challenge of our time. It is not only an ecological problem, but equally a social and economic problem. The Intergovernmental Panel on Climate Change (IPCC), a group of experts convened by the United Nations, recently published Climate Change 2022: Impacts, Adaptation and Vulnerability.[3] In this extensive report, the IPCC doubled down on its warning to the global community: if temperatures continue to rise, many parts of the world could soon face increasing limits in how much they can adapt to a changing environment. The message is clear.

THE COST OF DISASTERS

According to the World Meteorological Organization (WMO) and UN Office for Disaster Risk Reduction (UNDRR), economic losses around the globe caused by severe storms and changing weather patterns increased sevenfold from 1970 to 2010, disproportionately impacting poorer countries and coastal regions. Climate change and extreme weather events have caused a surge in natural disasters over the past 50 years. Some estimates show economic impacts averaging anywhere from $49 to $383 million per day globally.[4] Out of the costliest ten disasters, three were hurricanes that occurred in 2017; they accounted for 35% of total economic disaster losses around the world from 1970 to 2019. In the United States, Hurricane Harvey caused what would be today's equivalent of approximately $96.9 billion in damage, followed by Maria in the Caribbean which cost $69.4 billion, and Irma which cost $58.2 billion in Cape Verde.[5]

As more and more people are at risk of suffering devastating losses and are being forced to flee their homes, dislocation is occurring on a global scale. Therefore, nations must act quickly to cut fossil fuel emissions and slow global warming. The produce, use and waste economy following the last industrial revolution, in addition to the ever-growing world population, with changing consumer behavior due to increased wealth in emerging economies, threatens life on land and in the oceans. More consumers mean more products and an increase in resource use. As much of what we produce is not reused, we continue to remain far away from turning our economy into a circular model. Many modern-day goods are made of plastic, yet this poses a problem when it takes up to 1,000 years for plastics to decompose.[6] Nearly 300 million tons of plastic waste are produced every year.[7] Yet about 91% of all plastic is not recycled and much of it ends up in our oceans.[8]

THE 'PLASTIC SOUP' CHALLENGE

Recent research reports that plastic waste in the Pacific Ocean now covers more area than France, Germany and Spain combined, and that area is growing rapidly.[9] Researchers estimate that the Atlantic's total plastic load alone is around 200 million tons.[10] China, Indonesia, the Philippines, Vietnam, and Sri Lanka together account for about 60% of all the plastic in the ocean, according to a 2015 study.[11] In 2016, the US alone generated 42 million metric tons of plastic waste, which was twice the volume produced in China that year. The US also generates the most plastic waste per capita, at an estimated 130 kilograms per person.[12] These numbers are rising each day, which causes a surge in plastics washing up on ocean coastlines and floating in the seas.[13] If this pace continues without serious action, the plastic will outweigh the fish in our oceans as early as 2050.[14] Currently, we only recycle 9% of the plastic we use.[15] Even if we bring that to 100%, we still have to solve the problem of existing plastic waste in the oceans that is killing the wildlife that consumes it, such as turtles, fish, and birds.

We suffer enormous social threats as well. Growing inequalities are experienced throughout local communities and across nations. The recent coronavirus has shone a glaring light on the lack of access to healthcare among regional and global populations. The COVID-19 vaccine availability around the globe has been plagued with inequality. In late November 2021, the number of vaccine doses administered per 100 people was more than 18 times higher in high-income than low-income countries, according to data from the World Health Organization (WHO) and the World Bank.[16] When the Omicron variant was discovered in South Africa and quickly spread across borders, the costs of this global vaccine gap became significantly clearer.

The growth of social movements such as Black Lives Matter prompts us to reflect more inclusively on the consequences of rising inequality throughout the world. Inequality endangers communities of color in innumerable ways, ranging from a lack of education and job opportunities to more vulnerable exposure to COVID-19. This harsh truth is evidenced in the data showing how Black Americans and Indigenous people have mortality rates from the coronavirus that are notably higher than all other races and ethnic groups.[17] In addition to health disparities, we still see gaping divides around the globe in financial inclusion, education, hunger, and environmental wellbeing. Although global economic systems in the decades behind us brought progress, the world has also experienced serious consequences where both humanity and the planet have suffered tremendously. That suffering is accompanied by a hefty economic price.

RAPID GLOBALIZATION IS DRIVING DEMANDS FOR MORE EFFECTIVE GOVERNANCE ALL AROUND THE WORLD.

Governance challenges are serious, and a threat to local and global stability. Rapid globalization is driving demands for more effective governance all around the world. With the rise of China, India, Brazil, and other fast-growing economies, economic interdependence has reached new levels. The interconnected nature of climate change and resource issues, economic crises, and national fragility risks are associated with several areas across society, such as the ever-growing salary divide, need for energy management, and biotechnology development.[18] Many of these issues involve interwoven domestic and foreign concerns that are highly problematic to navigate under current political and social structures.

Global challenges - ecological, social, and governance-related - have risen to such an extent that a new course of action is needed immediately. Even a resilient world like our planet and flexible species like humankind have their limits, and those limits have been reached. Not only does the health of the planet and its people suffer, but so does the stability of the economy when hit with severe setbacks. Revolutions are not always equal to progress. Although inventions and technological advancements are novel and exciting, we as humankind often overlook or ignore unforeseen consequences. We are now living with some dire residual effects of past industrial revolutions. Technology has ushered in incredible innovations and benefits, many of which we have yet to realize. However, along with these tech advantages come disadvantages that could be highly damaging if unchecked.

EVEN A RESILIENT WORLD LIKE OUR PLANET AND FLEXIBLE SPECIES LIKE HUMANKIND HAVE THEIR LIMITS AND THOSE LIMITS HAVE BEEN REACHED.

Yet, technology itself is not a problem. Technology has no overall meaning on its own. Its effects are driven by human choices and actions. Humans are still in charge of technological innovations and advancements, and thus have the power to direct the future of tech. We have the power to question our actions and motivations: What are our own individual values? What is our collective view on the purpose of technology? What do we see as progress? We have learned a lot since the former industrial revolutions. We know we need to implement a more sustainable business model and take full responsibility for our impact on this planet. There is only one Earth in the Solar System, and this place we call home will soon need to accommodate nearly ten billion inhabitants.[19]

There is a conscious choice to be made. Rather than providing great benefit and progress, technology could create the reverse effect. It has the potential to advance humankind in numerous ways, yet only if used responsibly and purposefully. Technology can provide solutions to even the greatest challenges on the planet. And we are in desperate need of technology to do so. With the wisdom to learn from the past and create a future we all want, the next industrial revolution simply must be a global movement toward sustainable progress. In this regard, solving the pitfalls of former eras, in addition to limiting additional harm, must be our top priority entering the 4IR. We as humans hold the key and responsibility to repurpose technology to create a better future for all. We need to aim for an ethical, positive impact-driven approach to technology instead of applying it in ways that are predominantly damaging people and the planet, or that serve no purpose at all.

TECHNOLOGY HAS THE POTENTIAL TO ADVANCE HUMANKIND IN NUMEROUS WAYS, YET ONLY IF USED RESPONSIBLY AND PURPOSEFULLY.

Unlocking new markets of all types with technology - even when it challenges the status quo and is not the easy path forward - will rejuvenate the economy. In addition, tech market innovations will help manage environmental, social, and governance challenges. Let's look at some examples. Take artificial intelligence, for instance: the algorithms behind deep fake technology, capable of misleading entire populations and disrupting democracy, can also be used to diagnose diseases such as cancer at an early stage, leading to better health outcomes. The expansion of the internet of things (IoT) could put jobs and personal data at risk, but if rolled out responsibly, it can revolutionize peoples' access to services regarding health, safety, finances, and daily planning. Powerful gene-editing tools could be used to engineer viruses capable of wiping out entire populations, but can equally be harnessed to save endangered species and eliminate debilitating hereditary diseases. This illustrates the importance of tech innovations to help unlock new markets.

THE SUSTAINABLE DEVELOPMENT GOALS:
OUR COMPASS TO A BETTER FUTURE FOR ALL

In 2015, two major events took place that effectively address the global challenges we are faced with. They have continued to provide a clear course of action. First, at the end of September 2015, all 193 United Nations member states came together in New York to commit to tackling 17 ambitious Global Goals – the Sustainable Development Goals (abbreviated as SDGs and referred to as Global Goals) – by 2030.[20] Second, that same year in December in Paris, 196 countries adopted a legally binding international treaty on climate change, later to be referred to as the Paris Agreement or Paris Climate Accords. From that year onward, these participating nations around the world embarked on a new blueprint for progress. These monumental events signified a moral compass for the world to follow and sent a strong message to the global community that change was needed.

A CLEAR CALL TO ACTION, THE SDGS PRESENT A PATHWAY FORWARD WITH THE UNDENIABLE TRUTH THAT BUSINESS AS USUAL IS NOT AN OPTION.

Although the world had already accepted the so-called ESG approach – referring to environmental, social, and governance sustainability aspects – the SDGs added great value in terms of clarity, definitions, and concrete targets while simultaneously incorporating the Paris Agreement objectives.

A BLUEPRINT FOR A BETTER FUTURE

The Sustainable Development Goals (SDGs) consist of 17 interlinked sustainability objectives designed as a blueprint to achieve a better and more sustainable future for all. These SDGs succeed the former Millennium Development Goals (MDGs) and include ambitions linked to beating hunger, tackling climate change, transforming production and consumption, and achieving gender equality. The framework to track progress consists of 17 goals, 169 underlying targets, and 232 indicators. In 2015, the same year in which 193 countries adopted the SDGs, a global Climate Agreement was reached. Each with concrete targets, these Global Goals are to be achieved by 2030 and function as the new roadmap to transform the world. With the potential for tremendous positive opportunities for business, the SDGs hold great promise. In that sense, the Goals need business as much as business needs the Goals. More information on the Global Goals and their impact can be found in the book The Trillion Dollar Shift.[21]

Figure 1
The UN
Sustainable
Development
Goals.[22]

While momentum to tackle the Global Goals has grown significantly, there is still a long way to go on this 'to-do list' for the world. Before the pandemic, progress was being made on implementing some important SDGs such as reducing poverty, improving maternal and child health, increasing access to electricity, and advancing gender equality. Several severe worldwide events have recently slowed progress on the SDGs. An increase in natural environmental disasters and the onset of the COVID-19 health crisis affect billions of lives and hit the global economy, bringing stark awareness to our collective vulnerabilities.

Although advancements have been made, in many instances they are not happening fast enough. Even today, the world is still not on track to meet its 2030 targets. In particular, the goals of eradicating poverty and providing safe access to drinking water are lagging far behind, as are combating climate change and human rights issues. The global pandemic has diverted financial and political focus from pressing development and climate mitigation, and instead toward the coronavirus response.

THE COVID-19 PANDEMIC BROUGHT LONG-STANDING, DEEP-SEATED DIVIDES IN OUR ECONOMIES AND SOCIETIES TO LIGHT.

For a clear picture of where we are and where we are going, robust and timely data are needed to monitor SDG progress. Even with more than five years since the adoption of the SDGs, considerable gaps in official statistics remain in terms of national coverage and timeliness for many of the Global Goals.[23] In particular SDG 4 (Quality Education), SDG 5 (Gender Equality), SDG 12 (Responsible Consumption and Production), SDG 13 (Climate Action), and SDG 14 (Life Below Water) lack comprehensive progress on the World Bank's Statistical Performance Index globally since 2015.[24] Further investments are needed to strengthen statistical capacities in many low-income countries and small island developing states. More policy analyses and trackers are also needed to assess implementation efforts on key SDG transformations, especially to monitor countries' actions on sustainable land use, diets, and responses to biodiversity loss.

We possess the human capacity to make progress and solve our universal problems. But with the rising global population, developing economies, and growing middle class, in addition to the setbacks suffered from the pandemic, we need to create solutions at a much larger scale and at a more rapid pace than we have up to this point. There is growing recognition that if we are to achieve these targets and build a better world for all by 2030, business-as-usual and continued incremental reforms will not be enough. To achieve this monumental progress, we need accelerating power that propels solutions at scale. This is where the power of the next industrial revolution comes in. Tech for Good enables the 4IR to help solve our most pressing global challenges.

LEVERAGING THE NEW TECHNOLOGICAL AGE: THE FOURTH INDUSTRIAL REVOLUTION

Entering the 4IR means entering a global era characterized by rapid advancements in new technologies and global connectivity. Artificial intelligence now forms part of our everyday activities – optimizing and customizing what we see, choose, and learn. Ubiquitous sensors are collecting more data than ever before, with connected devices simplifying our lives. Autonomous vehicles, drone delivery, and drone transport are set to transform global mobility. Even immersive reality-guided surgeries, 3D printing of body parts, and affordable biohacking are either here or on their way. These signify today's digital age as an age of unprecedented discovery and innovation.

IN BUSINESS

NAFHAM[25]

Initiative: K-12 Learning Management Platform
Headquarters: Cairo, Egypt

Egyptian households spend up to 17% of their budget on private tutoring as a supplement to formal learning. Nafham's free educational platform helps alleviate these expenses (SDGs 1,4,10).[26] All content is in Arabic, which presents wide scale possibilities across the world. This platform is especially valuable in insecure regions where education is interrupted, such as in Syria where conflict is forcing many people to leave their homes. Nafham's content relies on volunteer teachers, students, and parents that produce 5- to 20-minute globally available crowd-sourced videos which are revised by professionals (SDGs 9,11).[27] With more than one video for each subject, the platform provides alternative approaches for different learning styles. These videos are categorized by grade, subject, term, and academic schedule which makes the curriculum easier for students. Not only do students visit the platform, but mothers are also highly interested and active on Nafham's website both to enhance their own personal knowledge and to help their children (SDG 5).[28]

Tyro, an EdTech platform connecting students with qualified instructors through one-to-one and group sessions, acquired Nafham in 2021 under a share-swap agreement. "Both companies joining forces will technically make us the largest EdTech platform in the MENA region, providing both live online tutoring as well as recorded educational video content," says Mokhtar Osman, Tyro CEO.[29] "It is crucial to capitalize on both the technological capabilities and a solid customer base to be successful. With this merger, we are well-positioned to take the platform to the next level."

Nafham is now one of the largest online educational platforms in the Middle East, with six million annual users and over 150 million views garnered on their video content.

The tech revolution has started, and we are already experiencing incredible advancements. AI-augmented computing, for instance, is a revolutionary tech solution that helps doctors reduce medical mistakes, farmers improve yields and minimize inputs, teachers customize and spread education, and researchers unlock solutions for climate and weather modeling, or advanced material generation for clean fuels. Several companies all over the globe are taking advantage of technological innovations to enhance societies while also creating a competitive advantage in business. Nafham, a free online K-12 crowd-sourced educational platform, is creating a solution for the Middle East and North Africa (MENA) region's education deficit, and driving EdTech in Egypt, Syria, Saudi Arabia, Kuwait, and Algeria. Nafham's founders were inspired by Egypt's national educational crisis. The country's education system is overwhelmed by 2.2 million students annually, where a class initially designed for 40 students now hosts 60 or 70 students.[30]

As the underlying force powering the 4IR, technology has multifaceted potential to transform sectors rapidly and globally. Tech innovations will increase the productivity of systems while lowering emissions and waste; enable us to monitor and manage the Earth's surface and resources at a speed and scale we couldn't have dreamed of before; collect and harness vast amounts of data; and make breakthrough advances in several areas. These are still the early days of the digital age, but humanity stands at a critical juncture. It is essential to make drastic but informed decisions, and to put in place sound policy and governance architecture that has profound and lasting impacts on society and the planet. Collaboration and coordination internationally across multi-stakeholder groups will be critical as we enter the 4IR.

THE TECH REVOLUTION HAS STARTED, AND WE ARE ALREADY EXPERIENCING INCREDIBLE ADVANCEMENTS.

Tech companies, governments, industry, civil society, and researchers alike must be the catalysts for unlocking the potential of these technologies to effectively address the SDGs. Business is key for stimulating tech sectors to find new ways of investing money, time, and expertise into this agenda. If humanity truly wants to achieve the Global Goals, it must consciously propel progress by declaring an action-driven decade ahead, and maintaining a clear pathway forward. The SDGs come with a 2030 deadline and the world cannot afford to wait any longer. Accelerating the pace and scale of 4IR innovative tech breakthroughs will require us to go beyond celebrating a few brilliant cases. We must leverage the power that technology offers to speed up progress toward our Global Goals.

ADVANCED TECHNOLOGIES PROGRESSING THE GLOBAL GOALS

Technology, when harnessed for good, will accelerate progress on achieving the SDGs. The potential economic and societal impact of tech to meet these Global Goals is substantial. Recent studies show that existing AI applications across agriculture, energy, transport, and water could conservatively contribute up to $5.2 trillion to the global economy in 2030, a 4.4% increase relative to business as usual.[31] At the same time, these estimates indicate reduced global greenhouse gas emissions by 4%, an amount equivalent to 2.4 Gt CO_2e. This, for reference, is equal to the projected 2030 annual emissions of Australia, Canada, and Japan combined. This is one small aspect of the tech-SDG intersection.

The next page explores a few Global Goals, and offers the chance to consider how synergizing technology and sustainability works in practice.

ZERO HUNGER

Nutritional deficiencies and food shortages are global problems. According to the United Nations, consumers and retailers waste or spoil an estimated one-third of all food produced each year – equivalent to 1.6 billion tons worth over $1 trillion – due to poor transportation and harvesting practices.[32] Around 45% of deaths of children under five are linked to malnutrition, evidencing the challenge of world hunger.[33] Forecasts show that agricultural production needs to at least be doubled by 2050 to feed the growing population and prevent mass food shortages.[34] Businesses can contribute to solving these challenges, eradicating hunger, and improving food and agriculture systems. While implementing sustainable practices and partnering with other actors throughout the agricultural value chain, business solutions in tech such as empowering small farmers, increasing agricultural productivity and farmers' livelihoods, raising consumers' awareness, and increasing agricultural investment will be necessary elements to enhance food and agriculture systems. Biotech startups like NRgene are using machine learning and genetic sequencing to boost crop performance.[35] Phytech is another company optimizing crop production with insights and warnings it sends to farmers' smartphones.[36] As demonstrated in these use cases, AI and robotics hold great promise in improving crop productivity, boosting resilience, and optimizing food distribution.

GOOD HEALTH AND WELLBEING

There has been over $145 billion in investment in healthcare startups since 2010.[37] Improvements in a variety of technologies, including AI and blockchain, are advancing medicine, surgery, and healthcare data. Data management in medicine has become a major focus area for some of the largest tech companies including Alphabet, IBM, Amazon, Apple, and Alibaba. AI systems for earlier and higher-performance diagnostics for disease detection, from cancers to brain injuries or heart disease, and AI-enabled wearable devices, have proved to be lucrative endeavors in the healthcare sector. French startup Implicity creates a remote monitoring platform for patients with connected pacemakers and defibrillators.[38] This tech innovation boasts an AI module that determines the severity of each alert in accordance with the medical history of the patient. The platform analyzes and filters the data coming in from remote locations, thereby freeing up valuable time for medical professionals to focus on other essential tasks.

AFFORDABLE AND CLEAN ENERGY

A transition to clean energy demands a comprehensive transformation of the global economy. It will require approximately $100 trillion in additional capital spending over the next three decades.[39] There remain nearly 800 million people in the world without access to reliable and affordable electricity.[40] Rapid developments in AI, blockchain, and advanced materials for solar panels and battery technology are creating viable, low-cost solutions. More specifically, they have the potential to leverage renewable energy mini-grids to connect nearly 300 million people to power. Businesses can accelerate the transition to affordable, reliable, and sustainable energy systems by investing in renewable energy resources, prioritizing energy-efficient practices, and adopting clean energy technologies and infrastructure. With investment in Research & Development (R&D), businesses can pioneer new technologies that shift global energy systems to invigorate climate change solutions.

Powergen, with installed solar-powered mini-grid projects across Kenya and Zambia providing electricity to rural areas, is an example of an emerging technology with huge potential to accelerate electrification. It particularly targets areas with fewer centralized network power grids.[41]

In the advanced materials space, Cambridge-based tech startup Lambda Energy works to increase the efficiency of solar panel technologies through the development of a material that results in more efficient absorption of the sun and increased energy output.[42] National Grid Partners, the Silicon Valley-based investment arm of utility National Grid, has invested nearly $400 million in startups that have the potential to disrupt the future of energy through digital technologies.[43] More broadly, tech innovations are enabling a much greater proportion of renewables on centralized power grids, as well as optimizing decentralized energy systems worldwide. These solutions promise to improve efficiency, provide cleaner energy options for global market entry, and reduce costs.

INDUSTRY, INNOVATION, AND INFRASTRUCTURE

With the pace of digital transformation accelerating for nearly every industry, technology is more strategically important than ever before for businesses and their supply chains. Research shows that 64% of supply chain executives report that the pace of digital transformation for their organization is rapidly accelerating.[44] As a result of fast-paced digital transformation, investments in data, AI, and digital twin technologies to power supply chains are increasing. New sources of data and AI-driven models can be applied across companies' product developments, supply chains, and sales lifecycles to steer growth trends. Blockchain-driven innovations in the supply chain will have a considerable impact on the potential to deliver business value by increasing supply chain transparency, reducing risk, and improving efficiency and overall supply chain management.[45] Trade finance is projected to witness significant growth as well. Due to increased market disruption and advances in technology, enhanced digitized supply chain finance systems will become increasingly relevant. Skuchain is a tech company building blockchain-based business trade and supply chain finance products.[46] These are targeted toward the over $18 trillion global trade finance market that involves numerous entities including buyers, sellers, logistics providers, and banks.[47]

RESPONSIBLE CONSUMPTION AND PRODUCTION

New and enhanced materials are important tech innovations in areas surrounding consumption and production. The wood, paper, and paperboard recycling market is expected to exceed $29.7 billion by 2025.[48] Medium-density fiberboard is an example of an engineered wood product made by breaking down hardwood or softwood residuals into wood fibers, combining it with wax and a resin binder, and forming it into panels by applying high temperature and pressure. It is in the interest of business to find new solutions that enable sustainable consumption and production patterns.

Belgian tech startup Act&Sorb is capitalizing on how the recycling of treated and non-treated wood is becoming mandatory in many countries by bringing its disruptive technology to market.[49] Each year, millions of tons of wood residues are produced worldwide. With recycling options lacking, manufacturing cut-offs and end-of-life wood residues are incinerated or dumped in landfills. Act&Sorb's innovative recycling process counters this by creating value from bio-based wood residues. Its industrial potential will have significant positive energy efficiency, while helping furniture manufacturers and waste collectors contribute to the circular economy.

TRUST AS THE FOUNDATION

A firm foundation of trust is a prerequisite for the bold route toward a sustainable, technologically enabled future that is brimming with potential. Trust in technology appears to be low in many societies around the world, owing to cultural perceptions surrounding new innovations. Note that trust is not a unidimensional phenomenon. Trust has different sides to it, and the different forms of trust are important to distinguish so as to prevent jumping to conclusions and stereotyping. Academics Daniel Dobrygowski and William Hoffman provided us with a good framework to think about trust in technology. In their capacities as respectively head of governance and policy at the World Economic Forum's Centre for Cybersecurity and project lead for data policy, they distinguish mechanical trust from relational trust.[50]

Mechanical trust refers to trust in the outcome of technology itself, relating to the trustworthiness of the specific technology to function as it was intended. This is to be distinguished from relational trust, which considers the social norms and agreements behind the technology. Relational trust takes a philosophical step further to measure the impact of technology on complex systems across societies. Trust in technology itself, the "mechanical trust," seems to be growing rapidly. Yet only a few years ago, people were leery of trusting algorithms. In 2014, researchers at the University of Chicago Booth Business School and The Wharton School of the University of Pennsylvania, demonstrated that even when there was clear evidence algorithms could be trusted more than humans, people did the reverse and still trusted humans more, persevering in their resistance to trust technology despite the evidence.[51]

NOW, PEOPLE TRUST ALGORITHMS AND AI MORE THAN THEY TRUST HUMAN ADVICE, ESPECIALLY IN THE FACE OF COMPLEXITY.

This phenomenon was labeled "algorithm aversion." With widespread societal reliance on and engagement with algorithmic advice, it is highly counterintuitive that we would be skeptical of it. Extensive research on the concept of algorithm aversion has produced a definitive conclusion – algorithm aversion is costly.[52] But more recently, trust in algorithms has grown significantly and the trend has clearly shifted. Now, people trust algorithms and AI more than they trust human advice, especially in the face of complexity. For example, a new study mentions that with the uncertainty created by COVID-19 changing who and what to trust regarding medical and financial advice, 83% of Indian consumers and business leaders now trust AI-based tools more than they trust humans.[53] Interestingly, the same research study suggests 73% of business leaders trust AI bots more than themselves to manage finances.

The University of Georgia has also conducted novel research on the importance of algorithms in tech.[54] For their study, the team involved 1,500 individuals evaluating photographs. Volunteers were asked to count the number of people in a photograph of a crowd. The researchers then suggested a different number, either calculated by an algorithm or by a consensus of other people. Following that, each participant was asked whether they wanted to change their previous answer. The conclusion was that participants were changing their answers to match the algorithm output, whether it was correct or incorrect. In most cases, people were taking the average of their original answer and whatever the algorithm said. As the number of people in the photograph expanded, counting became more difficult. Significant insights lie in how people were more likely to adopt the algorithm-generated suggestion rather than count themselves or follow the "wisdom of the crowd."[55] These recent researchers have demonstrated that algorithms are indeed a reliable source that can be trusted. But does this mean people now trust computers more than humans? There may not be a conclusive answer, but widespread dissemination of Tech for Good will undoubtedly require both forms of trust. The business world specifically will benefit from being aware of the importance of trust. Not only is trust a necessity for businesses' license to operate from the public perception standpoint, it is also highly important for technology to be in the position to help solve our most pressing challenges.

TRUST IN TECHNOLOGIES' INTENTIONS, AND THE WAY THEIR POWER CAN BE USED, FELL TO AN ALL TIME LOW IN 2021.[56]

Unfortunately, relational trust has never been as low as it is now. Therein lies a challenge. Trust in technologies' intentions and impacts, and trust in the way this power will be used, fell to an all-time low in 2021.[57] Many stakeholders favor tighter regulations on tech companies to make sure technologies are used for good. Tech companies indeed have an extremely powerful influence, and according to many, they are too powerful. Pew Research Center recently found that in the US, 56% of Americans think major technology companies should be regulated more than they are now, and 68% believe these companies have too much authority and influence over the economy.[58] Many people are extremely worried about privacy, fake news, cybercrime, and more - especially in home devices.

A steady stream of controversies has dominated the conversation over how tech companies collect, manage, process, and share massive amounts of data. Even with a commitment to privacy and governance, the executives and founders of these companies have not convinced people that surveillance is not an omnipresent threat to their basic rights and freedoms. Mistrust of governments and corporations causes people to take pause and reconsider how much faith they should put in both leaders and services directing these quickly evolving technologies. More threatening instances are emerging, exemplifying people's trepidation. Even in the city of San Francisco — with a tech economy where high levels of enthusiasm for digital infiltration may be expected - facial recognition services are stringently controlled to "regulate the excesses of technology."[59]

In their impactful book Tech for Life, Jim Hagemann Snabe and Lars Thinggaard support the concept that technology must serve humankind. They state that, although the objective to improve people's lives and the planet through tech is valid, we must acknowledge that positive impact and "money-making" should at least both be addressed. But not only does the purpose of technology need to be refined, our entire public-private ecosystem around technology also requires repurposing. In this regard, we will have to face difficult questions and dilemmas. Some key inquiries in Snabe and Thinggaard's book include: How do we use data without losing privacy? How do we use platforms without creating monopolies? How do we use AI without losing control? Rightfully so, they conclude that to transform our world for the better, we need to encourage and inspire the responsible use of technology by finding a balance among profitability, sustainability, and trust.[60]

AT THE FOREFRONT OF OUR ACTIONS SHOULD BE THE GREAT IMPORTANCE OF SOLVING THE MAJOR CHALLENGES IN THIS WORLD.

If we direct the tremendous power of Tech for Good, we can tackle the challenges that plague the planet before it is too late. On our current trajectory, we are at great risk of doing too little, too late. Humanity must realize its role as a conscious actor of change while utilizing the instrument of technology as a force for good. Technologically enabled solutions can play a major role in creating a sustainable future for all, but only through rapid deployment that is much more effective at a larger scale and faster pace. The success of the 4IR will pivot on tech working for the economy, society, and environment. Ultimately, both business and the planet will thrive. Throughout the following chapters, we will provide you with a wide range of examples of how Tech for Good is for the benefit of all entities and systems around the globe.

THE POWER OF BUSINESS

Chief protagonists of change are businesses that seize market opportunities arising from tackling the Global Goals. Coalitions between diverse sectors and advanced technologies will inspire a new revolution. The global impact of business becomes abundantly clear when we consider that top corporations continue to accrue revenues far more than most governments. As mentioned above, 69 of the richest 100 entities in the world are corporations, not countries.[61] The top ten corporate revenues, including Walmart, Shell, and Toyota, all exceed $3 trillion.[62] It is relevant to note that today's largest companies are mostly tech or tech-driven. Colossal annual revenues of tech giants like Apple, Microsoft, and Netflix carry significant weight in the global marketplace. If Netflix was a country, it would be rated 126th on a list of wealthiest nations.[63] Tech-driven companies Tesla and Apple would respectively rank 125th and 47th in world GDP if they were countries.

CURRENTLY, 69 OF THE RICHEST 100 ENTITIES IN THE WORLD ARE CORPORATIONS, NOT COUNTRIES.

Now more than ever, power comes with an important responsibility. It is crucial that corporate boards, CEOs, and senior executives use their power as a force for good. Dominant companies need to be purpose-driven and action-oriented, employing the accelerating power of technology to solve prevailing socio-ecological challenges. All businesses, big or small, need to be involved and multi-stakeholder initiatives must come forth for cohesive and effective global action. It falls in the realm of possibility for all companies to employ the Tech for Good mindset. Influential business actors have the capacity to set and meet requirements in terms of time, volume, breadth, and prices for spurring effective large-scale technological change.

TECH GROWING THE SUSTAINABILITY PRIZE

All businesses need to strive for positive impacts on the SDGs, and this should be the core philosophy of all innovations. We need nothing less than comprehensive, interconnected, sustainable solutions. Fortunately, taking radical action toward a sustainable planet comes with a reward - a huge financial prize. New sustainable growth markets jointly represent at least $12 trillion in opportunities by 2030.[64] The Business and Sustainable Development Commission researched global markets and found that specific business opportunities arise within four domains: cities, food and agriculture, energy and materials, and health and wellbeing. The conclusion revealed that just 15 of the 60 largest opportunities account for half of the $12 trillion prizes. Thus, unlocking these markets also creates a projected 380 million jobs a year by 2030.[65]

FORTUNATELY, TAKING RADICAL ACTION TOWARD A SUSTAINABLE PLANET COMES WITH A REWARD - A HUGE FINANCIAL PRIZE.

The combination of sustainability and technology might seem an obvious business trajectory, but many companies have not fully realized this potential. Partnerships between sustainability and technology could prove more promising than anticipated, as they represent the possibility of novel markets that signify huge growth opportunities. The Ansoff Matrix, which was developed by H. Igor Ansoff and first published in the Harvard Business Review in 1957, is "a growth matrix that assists organizations in mapping strategic product market growth."[66] It is useful as a simple explanation of how the combination of technology and positive sustainable impact can create the highest value and the greatest opportunities for growth.

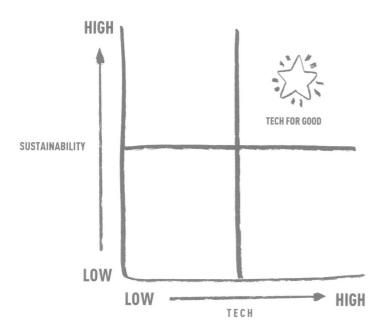

HIGH

SUSTAINABILITY

TECH FOR GOOD

LOW

LOW ——————→ HIGH

TECH

Figure 2
The Star Region: Tech + Sustainability.[67]
Author © 2023

Tech developments are not only limited to a specific sector. Fourth Industrial Revolution tech trends permeate across all elements of society. Lines between sectors blur as businesses become more tech-savvy and apply a variety of relevant advanced technologies. We see this amalgamation of progressive innovations in disruptive shapes and forms across sectors such as fintech, agritech, and carbontech. Yet, as presented throughout this book, along with incorporating the benefits of technology in every sector, we also want to do it in an ethical, purpose-driven way that creates more value for businesses, the planet, and people. This suggests that tech applications will be accelerated when the SDGs are at the forefront of business development.

Although many companies are aiming to make sustainable business leaps with internal leadership – within their own teams and balance sheets – one step forward would be thinking of partnerships and joint ventures. Business collaborations present opportunities to combine knowledge, competencies, and networks that merge sustainability and tech. Such collaborative systems would mean connecting with a larger, collective network that will operate at the scale, volume, and rate of change necessary to overcome global challenges. Currently, companies often either come from the tech angle or from the sustainability perspective, without integrating the two themselves from the start. Combining forces ensures positive results more rapidly and on a broader scale. The collaboration between Unilever and Google Cloud is a prime example. With an objective to reimagine the future of sustainable sourcing, these corporate giants are advancing sustainable business practices using technology to expand the use of data for eco-friendly decision-making.

IN BUSINESS

UNILEVER[68] AND GOOGLE[69]

Initiative: Sustainable Commodity Sourcing
Headquarters: London, UK and Mountain View, California USA

The two corporations are collaborating on the first commercial application of Google Cloud and Google Earth Engine for sustainable commodity sourcing (SDGs 10,17).[70] Combining tech and sustainability, they are harnessing the power of cloud computing with satellite imagery and AI to gain a more holistic view of the forests, water cycles, and biodiversity that intersect Unilever's supply chain (SDG 12). Not only does this enhance Unilever's brand value, but it also raises sustainability standards for suppliers. As a global industry giant that owns over 400 brands, with products that are used by 2.5 billion people every day, sustainability should be at the core of Unilever's business model. This sustainable sourcing initiative aims to achieve a deforestation-free supply chain by 2023. Unilever views this to be the first step, as the collaboration is being extended to more commodities in the future.

By combining the power of cloud computing with Google Earth's ability to map the planet via satellite imagery, Unilever will be able to store and understand huge amounts of complex data, as well as gain insights into any kind of impact on local environments and communities (SDGs 9,11). Along with greater accountability in the supply chain, cloud services will help Unilever to better detect deforestation and prioritize any areas of forests or habitats in need of urgent protection (SDG 15). This monitoring of sustainable sourcing brings the company a step closer to its goals of regenerating nature and ending deforestation in its supply chain by 2023.[71] It is a means to work with suppliers to increase transparency and take sustainable action wherever and whenever it is needed.

In 2019, Unilever reported that its purpose-led Sustainable Living Brands are growing 69% faster than the rest of the business and delivering 75% of the company's growth.[72]

CREATING SHARED VALUE

Originally an academic concept introduced in 2011, the idea of "shared value" was co-created by Harvard Business School professors Michael Porter and Mark R. Kramer.[73] As an approach to business and business models focusing on multi-stakeholder success, shared value captures value creation both in terms of beneficial societal impact and economic prosperity. This model is highly relevant in the Tech for Good context. Essentially, shared value is underpinned by the recognition that business results are improved by creating financial value while simultaneously creating value for society and the environment. This is the foundation of Business for Good, upon which Tech for Good is also built.

Shared value stems from the ambition to move away from reducing negative impact to creating a positive impact. The focus moves away from how to avoid doing harm to continually improving the human and planetary condition while prioritizing business gains. It is characterized by the principle that doing well and doing good are not mutually exclusive, but rather are connected in a positive way. In this context, in terms of markets, returns, stakeholder, and shareholder value, the model of shared value is becoming more and more important to core business practices. When companies operate sustainably and collaborate with partners, we all share in that success – environmentally, financially, and socially. Former DSM CEO Feike Sijbesma labeled the approach "purpose-driven, and performance-led," and in the case of DSM, it led to higher share prices and greater returns.[74] Addressing DSM's specialized solutions for health, nutrition, and bioscience, Feike Sijbesma's words demonstrated the sentiment of the shared value business model as a structure for sustained success.

THE ESSENCE OF THE SHARED VALUE APPROACH IS A POSITIVE ORIENTATION TOWARDS SUSTAINABILITY.

A key factor in the shared value approach is a positive orientation towards sustainability. It is not merely a strategy to limit negative impact, such as reducing the corporate ecological footprint. The approach centers on a comprehensive, positive impact that goes beyond one-dimensional concepts. For companies, the implementation of a shared value approach would mean a structural shift to mitigating risks and negative impacts throughout the entire business ecosystem to achieve net positive results. Reaching this outcome is often complex and requires a truly holistic transformation that places sustainability at the heart of business strategy. Yet, despite challenges, reorganization at all levels, from bottom to top, is indeed possible. When treated as a one-time investment and properly implemented, the rewards are lasting and immensely lucrative.

The paradigm shift we need is rooted in veering away from merely alleviating damage, but also toward embracing radical transformative change. A new paradigm is emerging, as the unlocking of business opportunities works to disconnect growth and negative impact. This disconnection of growth and negative consequences is a rising trend, with companies embarking on journeys to double their profits while simultaneously reducing their ecological footprint by half. Although this is a significant step, becoming net positive requires a more ambitious and long-term plan. Businesses are experiencing positive impact as they focus on sustainable, purpose-driven growth by employing a shared value approach.

BUSINESSES WITH NET POSITIVE IMPACT ON THE GLOBAL GOALS ARE A REAL FORCE FOR GOOD.

Interface is an example of a company that has achieved this positive impact through its Mission Zero.[75] Succeeding in bringing their plan to fruition earlier than anticipated, thanks to clear and precise business growth targets, the global flooring company successfully applies Tech for Good by using and developing new sustainable materials. In November 2019, Interface turned its full attention to its sustainability mission, Climate Take Back, which aims to reverse global warming.[76]

IN BUSINESS

INTERFACE[77]

Initiative: Climate Take Back
Headquarters: Atlanta, Georgia USA

In November 2019, Interface announced Mission Zero's success ahead of its original 2020 target and turned its full attention to its next mission, Climate Take Back, which aims to reverse global warming (SDG 13). As it looks to the future, Interface is working to become a carbon negative enterprise by 2040, and to develop processes and products that create a positive impact on the world.

With its Climate Take Back mission, Interface aims to overcome the biggest challenge facing humanity and reverse global warming.[78] The progressive company believes it is no longer enough to limit the damage humans inflict on the planet, but that we should collectively move towards reversing it. Interface wants to restore our planet and leave a positive impact. Climate Take Back moves the company forward from eliminating any negative impact to producing a positive impact. Interface's positive mission is based on four principles and points of attention:

Live Zero: Making sure no more carbon is put into the atmosphere.
Love Carbon: Using the carbon that is already in the atmosphere as a building block to make products and resources.
Let Nature Cool: Running their business in such a way so as not to interfere with nature's ability to cool itself.
Lead the Industrial Re-revolution: Sharing what they are learning, and have learned, to change how business is conducted.

Currently, 76% of energy used at Interface's manufacturing sites is renewable (SDG 12); they have a 96% reduction of market-based GHG emissions at carpet manufacturing sites (SDGs 7,13); 85% of their waste sent to landfills from global manufacturing sites is down since 1996 (SDGs 12,13); and 50% of the company's materials in the flooring products are recycled or bio-based (SDGs 3,11,12).[79]

Included in the business shared value approach is the use of technology as a driver for value creation. Not only should companies find shared value opportunities within societal challenges, but they must also leverage assets, expertise, and capital to support the proliferation and dissemination of technology to drive sustainability objectives in a profitable and responsible manner. Advanced technologies are a significant agent of value creation and present unprecedented opportunities for both society and business. There is great potential to augment companies' assets, expertise, and capital when applying the Tech for Good shared value model.

ACROSS TECHS FOR GOOD

A better understanding of Tech for Good applications entails sufficient knowledge about developing technologies, in addition to pursuing evidence of how companies are globally applying these advanced techs for good. The 4IR will seed a range of new technologies, with new variations being developed every day. Distinguishing among these technologies, while also recognizing their interconnectedness, brings up the question: which tech solutions are important for sustainable business solutions and why? To answer this question, we identify the most prominent Fourth Industrial Revolution technologies that are being implemented today. Each technology is extensively discussed in the following chapters.

The prominent characteristic of technologies to be relevant for Business for Good is their potential to be impactful across the SDGs. Interesting analyses seek to match technologies with their beneficial impact on the SDGs. The World Economic Forum (WEF) found that across the Global Goals and their 169 targets, 70% of the targets could be enabled by 4IR tech applications already in deployment.[80] Research also indicates that technology has a high impact across 10 of the 17 SDGs.[81]

THE WEF FOUND THAT ACROSS THE GLOBAL GOALS AND THEIR 169 TARGETS, 70% OF THE TARGETS COULD BE ENABLED BY 4IR TECH APPLICATIONS.

Furthermore, it is also significant that many technologies are being applied already, and thus the business solutions that incorporate them are ready to be further scaled. With businesses primed for the tech revolution, enhancing and unlocking new business opportunities will become more prevalent. Although there are many new and transformative upcoming technologies, they are still not all at market-ready application stages. In some cases, business integration continues to remain a long way off. Prioritizing current business applications, this book highlights feasible technologies that can be rapidly applied with beneficial impact and economic success.

Each of these eight technology groups have their unique benefits, as well as their collective uses, that work to address global challenges. In other words, not only is each tech impactful on its own, but all of them are interconnected.

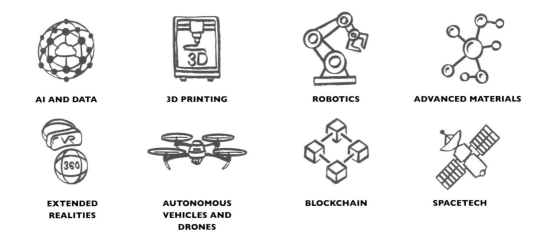

AI AND DATA

3D PRINTING

ROBOTICS

ADVANCED MATERIALS

EXTENDED REALITIES

AUTONOMOUS VEHICLES AND DRONES

BLOCKCHAIN

SPACETECH

ARTIFICIAL INTELLIGENCE & DATA

From general applications like mobility, communication, and medicine, to more technical uses such as game playing, knowledge reasoning, and robotics, artificial intelligence (AI) and data are altering our lives. AI's ability to transform vast amounts of complex, ambiguous information into real-world insights has the potential to assist in solving some of the world's most enduring problems. The tech is primed to undertake tasks with greater efficiency and scale than a human could. Elimination of human intervention allows AI to carry systems beyond finite human skills and create relentless advances and unprecedented breakthroughs in data management. In 2020, the global AI market size was valued at $93.33 billion and is expected to reach $997.77 billion by 2028, with a CAGR of 40.2%.[82]

In terms of the SDGs, this technology can enhance patient diagnosis with accurate data, personalize learning through AI-powered education, and employ greater renewable energy efficiently using AI real-time analysis. There are many ways in which AI and data can be used for good throughout various sectors in a financially profitable way.

3D PRINTING

3D printing, also referred to as additive manufacturing, is an advanced technology that can construct three-dimensional solid objects layer by layer from a digital file. This tech's decentralized, low threshold production and manufacturing unlocks a wide range of benefits across at least 9 of the 17 Global Goals. Over the past few years, the world has been experiencing unparalleled growth in the 3D printing market. In 2020 alone, the value of the global 3D printing market rose by 21% compared to 2019 to an estimated value of $12.6 billion.[83] 3D printing supports the reduction of waste during production, enables cheaper and easier repairs, spurs increased economic productivity, and lowers transportation costs and carbon footprint.

Signifying an exciting shift in global supply chains, 3D printing is set to replace and disrupt traditional manufacturing methods in many areas. Gone are the days of the conveyor belt, which once was an exceptionally advanced technology. Already seeing unprecedented adoption rates, as well as aftermarket supply chain growth, 3D printing has possibly the most impact out of all tech advancements in new product development applications across multiple industries.

ROBOTICS

Robots themselves design advanced software and algorithms (including artificial intelligence) to interpret the data collected and further enhance processes, thus helping reduce the number of human operators required. These automated production systems are becoming increasingly flexible and intelligent, continuously adapting their behavior to maximize output and minimize cost per unit. By taking over the monotony of repetitive tasks, in addition to removing people from any danger due to perilous labor, automation displaces menial human labor and enables more thought-provoking and challenging work. The global robotics market was valued in 2020 at $27.73 billion, and projections claim it can reach $74.1 billion by 2026.[84]

Modern generation robots are improving accessibility - in healthcare, for instance - by delivering medical supplies around remote hospitals. In agriculture, they enhance monitoring of environmental impacts of farming operations and reduce the use of excess water. Industries and companies are finding ways to utilize robots to improve their processes, allowing businesses to be more efficient. It is becoming more and more evident that robotics enhances sustainability efforts across sectors. Robots in today's world are helping fight climate change, manage recycling, streamline healthcare, boost manufacturing, and much more.[85]

ADVANCED MATERIALS

The current age and technological era enable products and functions that are lighter, tougher, thinner, denser, and more flexible or rigid, as well as heat and wear resistant. New and advanced materials go beyond utility, focusing on design, ergonomics, economics, and the ecology of a substance. Many new materials being researched today offer the promise of decreased energy usage, better performance at lower costs, and less dependence on traditional raw materials. New materials market forecasts state the industry can reach $2.1 trillion by 2025, recording a 10% CAGR globally from 2019 to 2025.[86]

Materials science, including engineering, research, and financing mechanisms, is rapidly moving forward to address the SDGs. New materials – such as light-absorbing building materials – could have major beneficial impacts like aiding in combating global warming. Some examples of new and advanced materials business cases that are making a difference include applications for less expensive solar power, electric-car batteries that can go longer between charges, lightweight and portable electronic devices, implantable medical devices for personalized medicine, lifesaving pharmaceuticals, more streamlined industrial manufacturing processes, and cleaner, more efficient energy usage. The potential for research and development of advanced materials to create a better world is truly limitless.

EXTENDED REALITIES

This widely integrated tech involves computer-generated digital imaging superimposed onto our real world. Falling into three categories, Extended Realities (XR) constitute Augmented Reality (AR), Virtual Reality (VR), and Mixed Reality (MR). Unprecedented IoT design and development of products and services becomes possible through XR. Those affected by mental health and those most developmentally deprived largely benefit from AR/VR devices. Commercially, the value of the XR market stood at $26.05 billion in 2020 and is expected to reach $463.7 billion in 2026.[87] XR experiences aid in diverse applications, from fostering relaxation during surgical operations with MR systems to AR/VR-optimized infrastructure planning to gender equality promotion through VR media.

With technological advances in network capability and computing potential, it is now possible to use these XR technologies in almost all domains and locations. This flexibility provides an unprecedented opportunity to create applications that have a broader impact on society. Diverse sectors across the world today including healthcare, environment, and education can all benefit from this tech to solve widespread societal challenges.[88] XR presents an opportunity to create an enhanced experience to reach the SDGs and expand tech usage for the benefit of the world. There is untapped potential to boost productivity and safety in several industries using XR.

AUTONOMOUS VEHICLES & DRONES

Autonomous vehicle (AV) tech ranges from autonomous road vehicles and driverless cars, to buses and trucks, to ships and drones. The global commercial drone market size is expected to expand at a CAGR of 57.5% from 2021 to 2028,[89] while the global AV market size is projected to grow to $556.67 billion by 2026, a CAGR of 39.47%.[90] AVs and drones address the SDGs in several areas, including agricultural monitoring using drones and delivery bots aiding in underserved or disaster-affected areas. Tech applications span a variety of industries and aid in scaling innovations across sectors and societies. AVs and drones can manage and reduce ocean waste and marine threats, as well as elevate cities to sustainability status with gained control over traffic congestion and prevention of human-error based dangers.

In addition to saving lives through rescue operations, AVs and drones bring a spike in safety too. Data suggest that self-driving cars will ultimately make roads safer.[91] Fully autonomous vehicles could nearly eliminate human error from the equation, thereby making our roads safer for drivers, passengers, cyclists, and pedestrians. Drones also present novel mapping and surveillance functions, which include patrolling forests to monitor environmental and ecological changes. This saves time to gather data that human manpower would require, as well as reduces the cost of clearing a pathway for human entry.

BLOCKCHAIN

Blockchain is a disseminated network comprising computer systems and the internet that keeps account of transactions. Within a blockchain, one record is dispersed and protected across the system while every computer involved individually approves the exchanges. In a world where data security and accountability of operations are at risk, blockchain boosts the traceability of information. The global blockchain technology market size was valued at $3.67 billion in 2020, and is expected to expand at a CAGR of 82.4% from 2021 to 2028.[92] Blockchain contributes to poverty management for farmers who have been exploited for their crop pricing in the market. Vulnerable populations gain security from blockchain's payment services. It also ensures data safety, whether it is personal health data or education records.

Because blockchain technology eliminates the role of intermediaries, central authorities, or third-party assurance providers to validate transactions and processes, it presents a new level of organizational transparency and trust.[93] This means that a business entity's full potential can be brought to bear when making more informed decisions, without the common financial risk. In this regard, there are expectations for the tech to unlock financing mechanisms to deliver on core business missions. The impact and potential of blockchain today to address the SDGs is recognized across regions and industries, spanning from the financial and the business sectors with cryptocurrency transactions to the retail and the agricultural spaces with product traceability.

SPACETECH

SpaceTech is currently used to explore other planets, study the universe, and provide communication and navigation services to support human activities.[94] This tech solution encompasses a wide range of concepts, including instruments such as satellites and human aspects of space travel like astronautics, physics, and chemistry. SpaceTech also covers research and development of new technologies, new applications for existing technologies, and improvement of technologies for existing space systems. More specifically, SpaceTech is a broad term used to describe any technological advancement or tool that is designed directly for use in outer space, whether it be for communication, navigation, exploration, or some other purpose.

Billions of dollars from some of the world's biggest investors and companies are being allocated to SpaceTech. Investments in SpaceTech-focused companies globally in 2020 reached $132.2 billion.[95] As the new space economy develops, it increasingly overlaps with sustainability in areas such as Earth observation, energy, and communication. These developing technologies from both public and private companies are becoming a new avenue for investors interested in pursuing breakthroughs in both sustainability science and space-enabled markets. The United Nations acknowledges the importance of space-based technologies to be crucial in understanding climate change and the full disaster management cycle.[96] Not only does SpaceTech help to address these environmental and social impacts, it also creates business value and presents unprecedented opportunities for businesses to do good while also building competitive advantage. Space technologies have positive impacts on every single SDG.

IOT AS AN UNDERLYING FOUNDATION FOR EIGHT TECHNOLOGY GROUPS

The Internet of Things (IoT) forms the foundation for the eight technology groups explained in this book. This foundational system gives life to advanced technologies and plays an important role in connecting all 4IR technologies. IoT is the network of physical objects – "things" – that are embedded with sensors, software, and other technologies. These objects are connected and exchange data between devices and systems using the Internet. IoT thus fuses the digital and the physical worlds. Devices and objects that use IoT can not only be ordinary household objects, but also sophisticated industrial tools. According to WEF research, the Internet of Things plays a role in 33% of top tech applications.[97] By way of low-cost computing, the Cloud, big data, analytics, and mobile technologies, physical things can share and collect data with minimal human intervention. As IoT has become one of the most important technologies of the 21st century, it is expected that the market for IoT devices will grow to $22 billion by 2025.[98]

Seamless communication is now possible among people, processes and things, as low-cost computing allows data to be collected with minimal human intervention. The next page demonstrates the role IoT has as a foundation for each of the eight tech groups discussed in the book.

AI AND DATA
- IoT, AI, and data form an ecosystem of automation.
- IoT devices provide data that can be used to teach AI systems.

3D PRINTING
- IoT-enabled 3D printing helps decrease material consumption and improve process efficiency.
- IoT-based automation technology allows for 3D printing market growth by reaching new target audiences.

ROBOTICS
- IoT enables interaction between and among robotic things and devices.
- IoT enables robots to recognize events or changes in their surroundings and autonomously have an appropriate response.

ADVANCED MATERIALS
- IoT and Cloud computing are used in high-volume manufacturing solutions to enable the accelerated adoption of new material technologies at an industrial scale.

EXTENDED REALITIES

- IoT helps make XR scalable through efficient object-centric and location-based data management.
- XR taps into refined environment information which IoT networks make available.

INTERNET OF THINGS

BLOCKCHAIN

- IoT and Blockchain technology together enable machine-to-machine transactions.
- Direct communication between devices is key in blockchain technology, IoT can track individual devices as well as interactions between devices.

AUTONOMOUS VEHICLES AND DRONES

- IoT helps address issues such as automotive safety, transportation efficiency, monitoring capabilities, and infrastructure challenges through effective data analysis.

SPACETECH

- Satellite communications are needed to create IoT networks.
- Intersatellite connections can be supported and developed using IoT.

IN BUSINESS

SMARTCULTIVA[99]

Initiative: IoT-based Smart Farming
Headquarters: Miami, Florida USA

The agricultural sector is a prime example of industry using IoT-enabled tech in sustainable business. IoT-based smart farming presents solutions to global food security challenges; Smartcultiva is just one startup harnessing the tech to address this issue.

Agricultural producers in cities must track several parameters daily to ensure high quality indoor or enclosed crops (SDGs 2,11). IoT sensors assist in mitigating this challenge by mining data about important farm factors such as soil, air, water, and climate for forecasting and analysis (SDGs 14,15).[100] In addition, IoT-based smart farming systems automatically adjust farm equipment to the changing conditions and allow for remote control.

The USA-based startup Smartcultiva delivers a set of sensors, connected devices, and software for farm management (SDG 9). The tech solution measures humidity, air and water temperatures, light intensity, carbon dioxide levels, and soil moisture before transferring these data into cloud based IoT applications using various network protocols. These data are accessible on both mobile and web applications. The advanced nano sensing IoT devices are integrated with proprietary AI software capabilities to monitor and control the indoor farming environment, targeting micro farmers, agro businesses, and indoor controlled space farming for the future (SDG 12).

INNOVATION FOR TRANSFORMATION

Tech for Good is all about innovation, both at a company level as well as at a country level. The 2019 Sustainable Development Report[101] and Global Innovation Index[102] used a PwC analysis to inform findings that, at the country level, there is a strong relationship between nations' abilities to innovate and their progress on the Global Goals. Countries that have strong innovation capabilities and capacities often make the most progress on the Global Goals, whereas countries with lower innovation potential have generally fared less well. But it also must be noted here that many developing countries still lack access to the basic requirements that innovations need. Another reason for urging to support developing countries that still fall behind on making progress toward the Global Goals, like poverty and health, is to make sure they have a digital connection. As of 2021, 2.9 billion people were still offline, of which 96% live in developing countries, despite strong global growth in the use of the internet.[103]

AN ESTIMATED 37% OF THE WORLD'S POPULATION – 2.9 BILLION PEOPLE – HAVE NEVER USED THE INTERNET.[104]

Further supporting this notion, research focusing on a company level recognizes the existence of a positive and strong relationship between innovation and sustainability performance. A recent study of the relationship between innovation and sustainability found that innovation positively impacts sustainability, and evidence of innovation size or degree has a direct effect on sustainability performance.[105] This is to say that innovation drives sustainable progress, yet for it to have a significant impact, we must steer the application of technology in the right direction. A diverse spectrum of innovative ideas will be required for true transformation to achieve this huge global shift to a sustainable economy and world. Let's distinguish incremental innovation from radical transformation.

Incremental innovation can be qualified as "change as usual." This refers to a series of improvements made to a company's existing products or services. The incremental strategies are very relevant and useful, but only if achieved at scale. If large companies improve their current business models and processes in such a way that their negative ecological footprint is reduced by technologically fueled efficiency measures, this will have a tremendous impact on a large scale. Yet, to really address the world's challenges and solve our most pressing problems, another type of innovation is needed. We need radical innovation. Radical innovation drastically transforms the way businesses use resources to manufacture, distribute, consume, and recycle products. Advanced technologies can support incremental innovation, but their true value is realized through radical innovation that breaks away from the status quo and catapults us into a new era of sustainable progress.

SOLVING CLIMATE CHANGE MAY BE THE GREATEST MOONSHOT CHALLENGE OF OUR TIME.

A specific, fascinating form of radical innovation is "moonshot" thinking. Moonshot innovations refer to the approach of choosing huge, seemingly insurmountable problems and proposing radical solutions using disruptive technologies.[106] The concept of the moonshot derives from the Apollo 11 spaceflight project that landed the first human on the moon in 1969. Mostly in the conceptual or prototype phase, moonshots are theoretically grand and "shoot for the moon." Moonshot thinking is a visionary way of addressing business challenges and the world's largest problems. It is the starting point from which impactful solutions are imagined and created. The world needs more moonshot innovations and more companies with moonshot vision to achieve our Global Goals.

Moonshot ambitions unlock big-picture inspiration and motivation for forward-thinking companies. In business, moonshot thinking empowers people to look for unconventional solutions, with a high probability of success. While organizations go beyond established ways of doing things and assume that everything is possible, teams can use fast-paced experimentation to continuously learn and improve.[107] Allowing moonshot ideas to be expressed throughout businesses lessens the fear of failure and helps teams focus on success. However, making these quantum leaps in innovation is uncharted territory, and setting such grand ambitions demands a lot of courage. Solving climate change, hunger, poverty, and the other Global Goals are the ultimate moonshot challenges of our time; they need radical solutions in the form of moonshot innovations.

Many purpose-driven startups and tech giants are aiming toward moonshot solutions. Consider Microsoft as a leader in implementing moonshot thinking as the company is now striving for a net positive impact across its operations. While other corporate heavyweights, such as Amazon and Walmart, pledge to go carbon neutral in the same timeframe, Microsoft vows to go even further to be carbon negative by 2030.[108] In doing so, they endeavor to remove more carbon from the atmosphere than they produce. This next-level ambition is exemplary of moonshot innovation, since the business reasons for the end goal, such as beating climate change, primarily aim to find radical solutions for the good of both the company and the world.

MOONSHOT INNOVATIONS COMBINE ALL TECH SECTORS, NEW TECHS, AND NETWORKS TO REINVENT SOLUTIONS THAT BENEFIT PEOPLE, PLANET, AND PROFIT.

Radical solutions need breakthrough technologies. Alphabet's X lab, a former Google division, is an example of an entity with moonshot vision. Its mission is "to invent and launch moonshot technologies that can make the world a radically better place."[109] Specifically, X's business solutions span from the launch of the Waymo self-driving car unit to a computational agriculture project called Mineral. One of its most prolific and innovative moonshots with broadscale implications was to supply a foundational internet network for everyone on Earth as a condition for enhancing the value of the 4IR.

Moonshots are not necessarily disruptive. This is only the case if innovations push older, existing business models and technologies out of the market. Moonshot innovations, however, typically unlock new markets since they bring about radical new solutions, often with new business models in a new market. Even when industry shifts happen overnight, full market disruption is not typically experienced until after a long process of development with a moonshot innovation preceding it. Radical moonshot innovations, disruptive or not, in addition to more incremental movements, are important in the shift to a more sustainable world. This is what the 4IR's technologies set out to do. They enable businesses to "shoot for the moon" to achieve radical technological breakthroughs that go far beyond what we could imagine.

5 IN BUSINESS

ALPHABET X[110]

Initiative: Project Loon
Headquarters: Mountain View, California USA

Alphabet X is a diverse group of inventors and entrepreneurs who build and launch technologies that aim to improve the lives of billions of people. It calls itself "the moonshot factory." However, the groundbreaking tech company also found that moonshot innovations are very challenging, as the path to both technical and financial success after the drawing board phase is both nonlinear and tough. One of their moonshot innovation projects, Loon, which was shut down after nine years, sought to address the issue of 50% of the world's population that does not yet have internet access (SDGs 10,11).[111] This was an important, even crucial, mission because if people have no access to the internet, they cannot benefit from the value of advanced technologies (SDG 12).

X also found how difficult moonshot innovations really are, as its mission was not accomplished due to the fact it failed to find a sustainable business model and partners necessary to continue operating with Loon. Alastair Westgarth, CEO of Alphabet X's Project Loon, said: "We haven't found a way to get the costs low enough to build a long-term, sustainable business. Today, I'm sad to share that Loon will be winding down."[112]

Although many moonshot innovations fail, they often inspire new variations that become successful in the end. When the project ended, X pledged a fund of $10 million to support nonprofits and businesses focused on connectivity, the internet, entrepreneurship, and education in Kenya (SDG 17).[113] This ensures that all parties will not lose anything in the end.

WE HAVE

IMAGINED

From here onward, the eight technology chapters will spark your imagination, allowing you to imagine how technology can fast-forward achieving the SDGs while creating good business at the same time. Imagination is the key to solutions. When we envision a better world, the realization of that world becomes our purpose.

The following pages expand on the nature of these eight techs, their market size, and the Global Goals they affect. Most importantly we touch on how these technologies are being applied for good in different business sectors. The chapters ahead are bursting with ideas, aimed at creating a better world for everyone, through radical tech innovation. We do this without being naïve or losing sight of the possible downsides and risks associated with these techs. To make better use of 4IR technologies, all stakeholders must jointly overcome hurdles and be cautious of relevant risks while moving in a new direction.

Tech for Good is a growing global movement. A better future for us all, which we create together, awaits. Join the Tech for Good movement.

Together we can solve the world's greatest challenges.

TECH FOR GOOD

THE FILM

ARTIFICIAL INTELLIGENCE AND DATA

2

AI IS NEITHER GOOD NOR BAD.
IT'S A TOOL WE MUST USE RESPONSIBLY,
TO PROMT GROWTH AND HEIGHTEN EFFICIENCY
IN MANY INDUSTRIES.

WE ONLY NEED TO

IMAGINE

Imagine finally finding a way to curb world hunger. Imagine overcoming global food shortages by enhancing and automating crop yields. Picture the year 2050. The global population is at its peak. Communities that were once deprived of basic sustenance now have all their nutritional needs met. It would be a prosperous world, wouldn't it? By efficiently sowing fertile fields and harvesting rich produce, our planet could achieve an enhanced food production model.

It is possible to materialize this future using the power of technological advancements in artificial intelligence (AI) and data. Through sound and deliberate management of these technological applications, we have the power to balance out inefficiencies and sustainably manage resources. As one of the most pressing global issues, world hunger needs to be addressed by way of business and scientific innovations. Food shortages stem from both socioeconomic and environmental pressures, thereby creating failure in the market mechanism to balance supply and demand. Because there is no greater mission of the human condition than supporting basic survival needs, it is logical that tech entrepreneurs, CEOs and government officials make agricultural advancement a priority.

The power of AI and data analytics can give rise to a world without fear of hunger and food shortages. Following business trends, the agricultural industry is maximizing efficiency by turning to AI and data management technologies. Farmers are increasingly using precision agriculture AI systems to improve harvest quality and accuracy for crop management by creating probability models for seasonal forecasting.

It is exciting that we can now enable automated maintenance of farms with minimal human intervention. That which once required environment-dependent conditions on the field can now be replicated in the greenhouse, resulting in excellent crop yields in terms of quantity and quality. With an AI-based system for data collection, we are automating the labor-dependent process to transform food production forever. Scientists and businesses are now applying AI and data management to the agricultural production process of farming – the most ancient industry is joining forces with the latest in technology. From weather pattern predictions to pest control monitoring, satellite data enables farmers to tap into and integrate massive sources of information into their daily practice. AI brings the data together and synthesizes analytics to provide recommendations to farmers about how they can increase crop production on their land.

The Earth's ecosystems are highly complex. Everything is connected through cyclical interactions, and it is nearly impossible to isolate our actions or assess individual impacts. Yet, even through these highly evolved natural systems, AI and precise data analytics are breaking through to assist in creating business value and sustainable growth. Market research predicts the number of data points gathered on an average farm will grow from around 190,000 today to 4.1 million in 2050.[1] This volume of crop analytics is advancing rapidly, and has become too abundant for humans to process. Therefore, farmers and agricultural technology workers are turning to AI to help analyze data points. As a result, the value derived from these data sources is greatly enhanced.

Despite all the benefits that AI and data could bring to agriculture, the way this tech is sometimes portrayed in the media raises suspicions. Concerns arise of a dystopian world where intelligent robots seize human jobs and people's privacy is put at risk due to invasive high-tech surveillance. This viewpoint considers a future with AI dominating humanity in various contexts. Ethical questions posed by the development of autonomous machines or weapons analyze the misuse of data for destructive operations. But are AI solutions and data management applications really all that bad? Evaluating such concerns entails a critical understanding of what AI and data really are, and the extent of their capacity to influence human lives. The sustainable dimension of this capacity has the unprecedented potential to bring about viable solutions.

Breakthroughs in the AI and data tech space are opening new business opportunities and economic potentials. A leading objective of modern science is to enable machines to function as intelligently as humans. Although technology has not yet arrived at this level, we could potentially experience machines adopting human cognition and instincts in the near future. With sensors that supply data, and advanced machine learning systems that build algorithmic models based on that information, tech is emulating agricultural ecosystems and facilitating the understanding of food networks like never before. Sensors that operate continuously can be installed in farm machinery to gather useful data such as temperature, humidity, light levels, fertilizer composition, and other parameters. Analytics models have the capacity to look months ahead and use previously collected data to provide farmers with base predictions for the season's most suitable crop varieties, ideal planting times and fertile soil locations.

Imagine how we can use models and calibrate machines to improve soil conditions, consequently boosting crop production to optimize farm management. The possibilities here are endless. With tech-assistance in determining aspects of irrigation or fertilizer use, AI-based smart farming can automate processes that accelerate and streamline agricultural activities. Emerging as a force for good that could change the way we lead our lives forever, AI and data can have a truly transformational impact on world hunger alleviation.

Marga Hoek

2 EXPLORING
AI AND DATA

Tech innovations are permeating all aspects of our lives. The digital environment, including AI and data technologies, is experiencing rapid progress. This chapter uncovers the transformative capabilities of these tech solutions to address some of the world's most pressing issues. With a universal reach that touches vast areas of our daily lives and beyond, AI and data will have profound implications for business growth in nearly all industries including agriculture, automotive, environmental, textiles and education.

Many SDG sectors will benefit from AI and data proliferation in the coming years. The following pages explore business opportunities in the field of education, where many students with relatively serious learning needs can rely on AI and data for academic accessibility and capacity building. Tech applications addressing affordable and clean energy are also touched on in the context of machine learning, heat maps, and smart meters. Data analytics is also an important aspect for growth in many industries. Further refining algorithms to track and monitor our consumption patterns, the tech is disrupting markets for business success and benefitting the environment alike.

In an ideal scenario, AI and data offer task completion and operability at scale, while also enabling a high degree of efficiency that surpasses the human dimension. Such advanced technology that infiltrates every aspect of our lives also presents risks and challenges. AI and data specific issues and how to mitigate these are addressed at the end of this chapter.

THE TECH

From general applications like mobility, communication and medicine, to more technical aspects such as gaming, reasoning, and robotics, AI is transforming our world. It is touching and revolutionizing the very essence of our daily lives. AI's ability to transform vast amounts of complex and ambiguous information into actionable insights allows us to solve some of the world's most enduring problems. Data collation and management is now performed with greater efficiency and at a broader scale than humans could ever do manually. As the constructive amalgamation of computers, algorithms and robots that mimic the intelligence observed in humans, AI's capabilities span knowledge learning, problem-solving, and rationalizing. Specifically, AI comprises a set of processes including data analytics, enabling technology, applications, and software that make existing computing smarter. In addition to its predominant Science, Technology, Engineering and Mathematics (STEM) learning and research uses, AI possesses other salient qualities in the field of social sciences, bringing together components of humanities such as psychology and philosophy. Thus, unlike traditional computing, AI can make decisions on its own, in a range of situations, without any pre-programing or human intervention.

Data access and collection are integral to AI operation. As a process of gathering and measuring information from countless different sources, data collection is to computers what socialization is to a child. To learn and adapt to the surrounding world, both children and computers need awareness of existing information, norms, standards and practices. Ideally, data accessed and collected are used to develop practical AI and machine learning solutions. For optimal results, only those data that are appropriate for the business problem at hand are collected and stored. While data collection entails the gathering of large swathes of information, there must be standards in place for AI to capture the most optimal range of necessary data.

The ultimate economic potential of AI and data is based on the principle of expanding technological possibilities that were previously impossible. This is precisely the quality that underscores AI's economy-wide application and power as an efficiency multiplier. Rather than augmenting or accelerating existing capabilities, this tech can and should aim to change the game and disrupt markets, industries and the entire commercial foundation on which societies are built. Existing applications include self-driving cars, human speech and translation, and more efficient supply chains. Currently, AI taps machine learning using large amounts of data and powerful algorithms to develop increasingly robust predictions about the future.

The majority of AI is centered on systems that can learn and evolve through information and experience, often to carry out specialized tasks such as driving, playing strategy-based games, or making investment decisions. This subset, also referred to as cognitive computing, needs to be trained by learning from experts. AI deals with developing computing systems capable of performing tasks that humans are very good at, for example recognizing objects, processing speech and making decisions in a constrained environment. By concentrating on these current abilities, the focus for the future centers on creating an Artificial General Intelligence (AGI) that can apply itself to a broad range of tasks in a much less structured way. In other words, AGI will function in a more human way, considering areas of greater uncertainty rather than making binary decisions.

With the wave of automation gaining momentum, we are observing widespread and rapid adoption of early AI technologies that are transforming industries across every sector. This will have wide-ranging implications for organizations, countries and ultimately the global economy. Nothing but acceleration awaits as parallel technologies such as the Internet of Things (IoT) unlock more AI opportunities. Today, AI and data processes empowering organizations, governments and communities are not novel phenomena. The growing practice builds a high-performing ecosystem to serve the entire world. The tech's profound impact on human lives is solving some of today's most critical challenges.

SOUND FOUNDATIONS

Since the mid-1950s, AI has been one of the most revolutionary developments in human history. Now, more than half a century later, the world is witnessing the tech's transformative capabilities that are powering some of the most cutting-edge solutions in the modern era. In recent years, software-driven advancements such as cloud computing and groupware have allowed AI to progress at a rapid pace. Artificially intelligent machines are able to sift through and interpret massive amounts of data from multitudinous sources to execute a wide range of tasks. To augment human capabilities with expertise, AI and data solutions are emerging in a variety of sectors.

AI's self-learning nature is the foundation of the tech's evolution to produce extraordinary breakthroughs. For instance, IBM's Watson supports medical professionals by providing analysis of a breadth of research that human doctors are not able to read. In addition, AI has beyond-human capabilities to analyze high-resolution images from satellites, drones or medical scans. These in turn have the potential to beneficially impact responses to a wide range of global challenges such as humanitarian emergencies, agricultural scarcity and climate impacts.

Technological capabilities unique to AI and data processing allow for unprecedented business growth. Machine learning is a form of AI that uses algorithms that allow computers to self-learn by processing data and running models based on internal examples rather than relying on human programming. For example, a machine learning technique called deep learning, inspired by biological neural networks, can find and remember patterns in large volumes of data. These deep learning systems execute tasks automatically without being programmed and generally outperform traditional machine-learning algorithms in terms of time and efficiency.

MARKET SIZE OF AI AND DATA

AI has seen enormous growth in recent years. The market growth is driven predominantly by the increasing adoption of cloud-based applications and services, as well as a rise in the connected device market.[2] The global AI market size is expected to grow from $44.51 billion in 2021 to $56.89 billion in 2022, at a compound annual growth rate of 27.8%.[3] In terms of the projected growth rate, the global market saw an increase in published patent applications involving AI at a monumental scale of 283% from 2010 to 2016.[4] By 2025, the market is expected to surge to $126 billion.[5]

IN 2021 THE GLOBAL AI MARKET SIZE WAS VALUED AT $93.5 BILLION AND IS PROJECTED TO REACH $1.82 TRILLION BY 2030 WITH A CAGR OF 38.1%.[6]

AI will enable a range of disruptive business models.[7] This entails developing a more personalized set of products or services based on deep customer insight from multiple datasets and learning preferences over time. Moreover, a closed-loop process making room for more effective and efficient production and consumption is expected to be designed and managed by AI tech at a scale and complexity that is beyond existing approaches. On an organizational level, agile and adaptive behaviors will come into play to make more sense of customer-focused data, markets and operations. They will anticipate the best strategies to adapt and respond to changing needs.

BUSINESS OPERATIONS MIGRATING TO THE PUBLIC CLOUD CAN REDUCE TOTAL IT CO_2 EMISSIONS BY NEARLY 60 MILLION TONS PER YEAR, WHICH EQUATES TO TAKING 22 MILLION CARS OFF THE ROAD.[8]

Many compelling examples exist of how AI and data are being used for good across many industries. One primary area of focus is smart city design. Business leaders are exploring the capacity of AI within cities to improve design, enhance quality of life and optimize operations. Using this technology urban planners can produce design solutions that transform public spaces with possibilities that include tracking resident wellbeing and analyzing social behavior. Advanced sensors on buildings that generate pertinent data regarding how people interact with a property or move around a space can track efficiency and accessibility. Not only does this tech solution save both money and energy, but it also ensures citizen satisfaction. The smart building market was valued at approximately $83 billion in 2020 and is expected to reach over $229 billion by 2026, at a CAGR of over 11.33%.[9]

THERE IS A $14 TRILLION ESTIMATED ECONOMIC INCREASE OF ADDITIONAL GROSS VALUE ADDED BY AI IN 2035.[10]

Significant investment in 5G technology is also playing a key role in AI market development, as is an increase in demand for intelligent virtual assistants. For instance, in March 2019, Apple acquired the machine learning startup Laserlike of Silicon Valley. This move strengthened Apple's AI efforts including upgrading virtual assistant Siri.[11] Key AI market opportunities include the potential for improving operational efficiency in the manufacturing industry and customer service in the retail sector.[12] Further, the increasing implication of machine learning applications in manufacturing industries is anticipated to power the market.

AI-POWERED ROBOTS

Over the past decade, a salient rise in demand has been observed in developed countries for a crucial component of AI: customized robots. Countries have been focused on manufacturing and supplying AI-powered industrial robots. For instance, in 2016, China exported around 87,000 industrial robots worldwide.[13] Similarly, in 2016 South Korea and Japan supplied around 41,400 and 38,600 of these robots, respectively, that all require an AI platform to function.

Investment banking and high-frequency market trading are sectors that employ many of the algorithms used to develop AI. AI allows investors to collect and analyze more information than ever before when accounting for environmental, social and governance risks and opportunities. With AI robo-advisers that analyze millions of data points and execute trades at the optimal price, the tech can help investors process large volumes of data that hold essential information for sustainable investing decisions. This enables analysts to forecast markets with greater accuracy while trading firms efficiently mitigate risk to provide higher returns.

Underscoring these tech benefits, electronic trades account for almost 45% of revenues in cash equities trading.[14] Future examples where AI and data could be applied to sustainable investing include the optimization and balancing of energy usage, both in consumer and industrial settings, and the potential for reduced waste and fuel usage. To help financial services firms and individual investors navigate the evolving world of sustainability investing, Lab49 has partnered with Databricks to develop a novel AI and data solution to the increasingly complex market sector.

IN BUSINESS

LAB49[15]

Initiative: Empowering Sustainable Investing with AI
Headquarters: Dublin, Ireland

Lab49 is a specialist consultancy that designs and develops innovative technology solutions in partnership with key participants in financial markets. Despite the increase of the sustainable investing market segment and its rate of growth, standards for reporting on and tracking the ESG performance of investments have been slow to emerge. Many specialized ratings companies and data providers now exist, but consensus around benchmarks, attributes, or what should be tracked is lacking.

As demand and investor sophistication continue to grow in the coming years, new standards and techniques are needed for financial institutions to serve their customers more easily and fairly. Firms today are faced with the rapid proliferation and fragmentation of data, much of which comes in an unstructured form requiring sophisticated techniques for analysis. Third party data sources are also only updated on a periodic basis, creating time lags that can negatively impact decision making and tracking as well as mismatches between sources. Further, investors do not all share the same concerns and need better tools to assess potential investment portfolios.

Working with San Francisco-based AI and data company Databricks, Lab49 seeks new solutions to these investment challenges (SDG 17).[16] Databricks' data driven ESG industry solution creates more timely analytics around sustainability performance from publicly available sources. Lab49 and Databricks have developed an end-to-end proof of concept for delivering analytics and aim for a high-quality user experience. The tech solution enables all levels of investors or financial advisors to interact with the data and make informed decisions (SDG 10). "The novel tech solution demonstrates how financial services firms can improve their capabilities around data, analytics and customer-facing applications to respond to clients' evolving needs related to ESG and investing in general," says Lab49 Director of Operations Ashley Whitney.[17]

The Databricks solution gathers sustainability reports from individual companies, combining them with publicly available media aggregated from numerous sources to measure the broader market's view of the same companies. This is achieved via the application of natural language processing (NLP), as well as AI and machine learning techniques.[18] The combination of analytics from these two sources creates a broad dataset for comparing the areas companies are choosing to put emphasis on publicly versus how the market perceives their behavior and the outcomes of their actions (SDGs 9,12). This amalgamates a vast array of additional data sources including ESG ratings from third parties, derived from other alternative data sources, and economic performance to drive investment decisions.

In the medical sector, AI is also making an impact. Nvidia, one of the largest chip makers on the planet, is a serious investor in AI technology and its chips are key to pushing the technology forward.[19] Because AI requires more computational power than traditional algorithms, heavy investment in new chip designs is an industry imperative. So far, Nvidia has concentrated its AI investments in the technology's use in the automotive, robotics, construction and healthcare industries. Nvidia has partnered with computer software company Nuance to use deep learning chips and a platform to bring AI to medical imaging. Nuance's ambient clinical intelligence technology is an example of how it is accelerating the development of solutions for urgent problems in the US healthcare system by training its automatic speech recognition (ASR) and natural language processing (NLP) models using Nvidia's chips. Nuance has realized a 50% speedup in ASR and NLP model training on Nvidia products without loss of accuracy, helping to reduce their time to market.[20]

LABOR PRODUCTIVITY IMPROVEMENTS ARE EXPECTED TO ACCOUNT FOR OVER 55% OF ALL GDP GAINS FROM AI FROM 2017 TO 2030.[21]

Projections for the benefits of AI show massive financial potential. AI techniques cited by McKinsey can potentially create between $3.5 trillion and $5.8 trillion in value per annum across nine business functions in 19 industries.[22] This constitutes about 40% of the overall $9.5 to $15.4 trillion annual impact that all analytical techniques could potentially enable. The market is projected to grow due to the rising availability of high-quality and personalized AI-enhanced products and services.

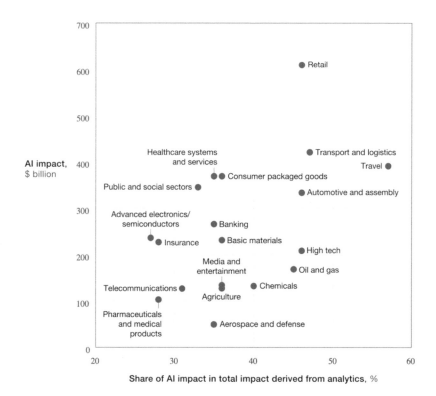

Figure 3
AI value creation across sectors, derived from McKinsey & Company. [23]

Other areas where AI has a sizable impact on business are retail and marketing. Considered to derive the most significant potential value from AI, these business sectors rely on the tech for product pricing, promotion, and customer service management. Not only does this aspect of AI respond to the SDGs related to industry and manufacturing, but it also drives economic growth and consumer satisfaction. Using customer data to personalize promotions, for example including tailoring individual offers every day, is an example that could lead to a 1% to 2% increase in incremental sales for retailers alone.[24]

$387.45 billion 2022 global AI market size.[25]

$1.82 trillion 2030 global AI market projection.[26]

$189.56 billion 2030 expected global advanced data analytics market.[27]

AI AND DATA FOR GOOD

If implemented correctly, AI and data are powerful examples of tech for good. Global agencies note that anticipated benefits of AI are widespread, ranging from peace to prosperity. The 2017 UN Artificial Intelligence Summit held in Geneva identified AI as one of the most important global initiatives for its potential to accelerate progress towards a "dignified life."[28] Not only businesses, but also individuals and societies as a whole stand to reap substantial value from the unprecedented comprehensive applications of this technology.

AI is responsible for many common elements in our daily lives we may take for granted: self-driving cars and voice/face recognition in smartphones; sustainable development and assisting global efforts to eliminate poverty and hunger; protecting the environment and conserving natural resources. The pervasive nature of this technology means that humankind will experience it in all aspects of life across all sectors. Forward-looking companies are seeing the business benefits and the global community is responding by implementing the tech into sustainable initiatives. Fortunately, AI and data have capabilities that are being harnessed to tackle societal moonshot challenges.[29] Breakthroughs in cancer research and climate science, for instance, are two monumental contributions from AI and data technological advancements.

More than ever before, businesses are employing strategies to inspire innovative solutions and new ideas for managing complex systems in the transition to a sustainable future. Big and little data are crucial to the success of this shift. Increasingly sophisticated AI algorithms that function without human intervention fine-tune existing business models at a faster pace. Tech companies like Google, Amazon and Microsoft are offering software development platforms that aid in this innovation. Using their corporate stance for good, these corporations help automate the process of building machine learning systems, which lowers barriers and greatly expands the number of software developers capable of accessing these innovative tech tools for mission-driven organizations and cost-reduction.[30]

Sustainable solutions featured with strong representation in the corporate context translate to more sustainable profits for businesses. Recent large investments reveal a burgeoning AI market, where businesses with heavy ecological footprints experience firsthand how they can implement the tech to shift their activities to be more environmentally conscious and socially responsible. One example is IBM using AI for improved weather forecasting, which is improving predictions for 30% more accuracy. [31] Not only does this benefit IBM's business, but it also helps renewable energy companies that use the tech giant's products to better manage their operational plants. In this regard, businesses will maximize renewable energy production while reducing carbon emissions.

Although making institutional changes on a large scale is potentially daunting, the ultimate reward is well worth it. With the capacity to be more capable and successful than ever before, businesses are anticipated to flourish. The infinite possibilities of AI and data present unprecedented potential and the applications are truly unlimited as AI and data continuously develop to build on their own capabilities by way of a self-learning structure. Google for example created an AI that teaches itself to reduce the energy it takes to cool the company data centers, which ensures a 40% reduction in energy used for cooling and a 15% reduction in overall energy overhead.[32] There are many ways in which AI and data can be used for good, while also being profitable throughout various business sectors. Tech leaders including Microsoft, IBM and Google have business initiatives specifically dedicating resources to build AI solutions for good and supporting developers who do as well.[33]

84% OF C-SUITE EXECUTIVES BELIEVE THEY NEED TO LEVERAGE AI TO ACHIEVE THEIR GROWTH OBJECTIVES.[34]

While challenges and concerns persist regarding how AI technologies and data analytics are being detrimentally used around the globe, there are numerous ways in which this tech is benefiting societies and businesses. Many of these initiatives include advancements in the following sectors: agricultural, healthcare, climate, finance, education, infrastructure and environment. From assessing the learning capabilities of students and helping people with disabilities to managing agricultural output and creating sustainable cities, AI and data are being used to implement major changes for good all over the globe. On the next page we highlight how tech superpowers Google and Microsoft are using their vast resources to leverage AI for good to take on global warming and climate impacts.

IN BUSINESS

MICROSOFT[35] AND GOOGLE[36]

Initiative: AI for Earth and AI for Social Good
Headquarters: Redmond, Washington and Mountain View, California USA

When organizing large datasets for climate modeling and developing more sustainable spaces, AI has unprecedented potential to employ its capabilities. Microsoft's AI for Earth[37] and Google's AI for Social Good[38] initiatives lead the way for big businesses tackling climate issues (SDG 13). "AI is one of the most important things humanity is working on. It is more profound than electricity or fire," says Google CEO Sundar Pichai.[39]

Microsoft's AI for Earth program supports a range of innovative solutions for those working to solve global environmental challenges, including agrimetrics (comprising heightened connectivity and automation across the food and farming sectors), cloud agronomics (remote-sensing tech and AI to monitor forest and crop health through analytics) and breeze technologies (developing compact air quality sensors to create hyperlocal maps) (SDGs 2,9,12,15).[40] Some AI for Earth projects also include a government think-tank in India working to develop AI applications for small-scale farming.[41] China, too, has launched a pilot program to develop automated farming technologies such as unmanned combine harvesters or robotic tractors.[42]

In 2018, Google issued an open call to organizations promoting ideas for how AI can address societal challenges. Google received over 2,500 applications from 119 countries across six continents with diverse projects that ranged from environmental to humanitarian. Of these, one of the most notable was a research team from the Department of Computer Science at Makerere University in Uganda that was concerned with the disproportionate effects of air quality issues in low-income countries (SDGs 1,13,16). A solution called AirQo was developed- an initiative that combines human ingenuity, AI models, and boxes packed with air monitoring technology to predict pollution patterns in Kampala.[43] Air sensors placed on buildings and taxis collect massive quantities of pollution data in the city, while cloud-based AI software performs data analysis (SDGs 9,11). The tech passes data on to government agencies working to improve air quality and reduce the risk of exposure within local communities (SDGs 3,10).

AI FOR GOOD

With a universal reach that will touch all sectors, AI has the potential to help make decisions about SDG impacts in areas such as agriculture, water, energy, and transport. These could add more than $5 trillion to the global economy over the next decade.[44] AI and Data management can help businesses bridge perceived gaps between profitability and sustainability. There is ample opportunity for AI to drive positive change on these two fronts across many sectors. By measuring sustainability and economic metrics in various business applications, AI can help reduce waste and enhance productivity.

$6.6 TRILLION OF AI'S CONTRIBUTION TO THE GLOBAL ECONOMY BY 2030 WILL LIKELY BE THE RESULT OF INCREASED PRODUCTIVITY.
AN ADDITIONAL $9.1 TRILLION IS PROJECTED TO STEM FROM CONSUMPTION PATTERN CHANGES.[45]

In the global retail sector for example, using AI to measure the probability of need, demand and consumption addresses profit losses from products expiring and avoids holding on to products that become redundant due to seasonal trends. In other industrial business trends, the circular economy of plastics requires a comprehensive approach to production and extended use to conserve resources and protect the environment. Companies can improve profitability and reliability with solutions that leverage insights enabled by AI and machine learning, all the while reducing capital investments.

Renewable energy systems that are AI-enhanced – including bioethanol, biodiesel, carbon capture, solar and wind initiatives, as well as carbon capture from industrial operations - continue to grow in popularity to help mitigate climate change. The tech is developed as an approach that greatly increases model accuracy, quality, and performance across the entire industrial asset lifecycle. Forward-thinking companies like AspenTech are optimizing assets and are investing significant resources in developing highly effective embedded AI modeling applications to support the design and commercial scale-up of carbon capture technology.[46]

"TO DEVELOP AI IN A RESPONSIBLE WAY, IT IS CRITICAL THAT YOU HAVE THE PROPER GOVERNING APPROACH AND MAKE SURE DATA ARE ALL ANONYMIZED."[47] - ERICSON CHAN, CEO OF PING AN

The International Union for Conservation of Nature (IUCN) – the largest association of nature conservation groups – drafted its program for the 2021 to 2024 period identifying AI as one of the main enablers to achieve its goals related to core program areas. Within AI, the IUCN considers the use of big data and machine learning as the most important enablers in the organization's future programs.[48]

DATA FOR GOOD

AI technologies are closely associated with data science and analytics. Upcoming advancements in these tech applications have unparalleled potential to solve problems that humans and current systems cannot. While AI improves the efficiency and speed of business models by taking on responsibility for more routine work at a lower cost, data analytics techniques reveal trends and metrics that can be used to optimize business processes and increase efficiency. Data monitoring and tracking are essential for making progress. Businesses that are able to utilize and respond to data in a way that most efficiently targets their bottom line will be the most successful.

BIG DATA AND AI CAN HELP ADDRESS SOME OF THE WORLD'S GREATEST CHALLENGES IN WAYS THAT HUMANS AND CURRENT SYSTEMS CANNOT.

Organizations such as Data for Good serve as a type of global progress tracker, which allows stakeholders to easily visualize the progress being made by change agents all over the world.[49] As a sort of global control center, Data for Good tracks business progress at various levels: per SDGs, per country, per organization, per mission, and per project. The platform efficiently coordinates mobilization for stakeholder engagement in achieving the 17 SDGs. With a stakeholder engagement model that focuses on collaboration, Data for Good's mission is to create an ecosystem for change. It is the first platform of its kind to portray global sustainability data into easy-to-understand dashboards to track progress.

This is where big data comes in. It refers to large datasets that are computationally analyzed for patterns and trends.[50] It is also being used together with AI to generate new forms of information to address some of the world's biggest challenges. Automated business processing companies like Salesforce and Intuit draw upon the data of many customers, creating new insights and patterns that help businesses respond to customer and societal needs. As another example, larger and better-curated government and third-party datasets are also being used to access information for good.

THE POSSIBILITIES ARE LIMITLESS. NOT ONLY BUSINESSES, BUT NONPROFITS CAN UTILIZE DATA TO ACHIEVE THEIR GOALS.

Beyond corporations and governments, the nonprofit sector also benefits from AI and data. The forest monitoring project Global Forest Watch[51] and the technology nonprofit Rainforest Connection[52] use machine learning to identify factors that contribute to forest losses in the Congo and the Amazon. Other examples include the sustainable fisheries initiative, Global Fishing Watch, which analyzed approximately 22 billion messages from fishing boats to uncover illegal industrial fishing vessels.[53] To access external data sources, organizations can also use data analytics solutions such as Tableau and Alteryx, which both have programs to help mission-driven organizations use their platforms.

If we take a natural resources standpoint, data are presenting a high degree of ecological value. Tropical forest regions, seascapes and mangroves are all areas where big data has been informing larger AI projects to help monitor biodiversity and track individual and communal behavior for improved resource management. From the business perspective, AI in this context will acquire data and set rules about the access to nature by communities, including decisions about where, when and how to intervene for conservation initiatives if necessary. Such examples show that stakeholders from both the private and public sectors have essential roles to play in ensuring that AI and data can achieve business goals for the betterment of society and the planet. How data are collected and generated will be pertinent for enhancing business practices.

THE ECOLOGICAL VALUE OF DATA COLLECTION MUST BE HARNESSED.

THE AI4SDGS COOPERATION NETWORK

The AI4SDGs Cooperation Network aims to advance the SDGs and digital cooperation through AI innovation and partner networks with AI related institutions, universities, and industries all over the world. It will collectively promote the realization of the SDGs through AI and advance the development with beneficial use of AI while avoiding the negative impacts.[54] The AI4SDGs Cooperation Network will especially support underdeveloped countries and regions and promote the realization of leaving no one behind.

AI AND DATA PROGRESSING THE GLOBAL GOALS

AI and data are looking to make exciting technological breakthroughs in spaces that can enhance business productivity and shift economies to new heights. Recent studies show that AI and data can potentially act as catalysts for addressing 134 targets, or 79% of initiatives across all the SDGs.[55] The benefits are endless and beyond what the world could have expected a few decades ago, as some examples of areas of application across a wide variety of sectors demonstrate below.

GOOD HEALTH AND WELLBEING

This can be addressed by combining various types of alternative data sources such as geospatial data, social media data, telecommunications data, online search data, and vaccination data. These datasets can thus help predict virus and disease transmission patterns, as well as be highly relevant in optimizing food distribution networks in areas facing shortages and famine. From a healthcare standpoint, supporting diagnosis in areas such as detecting small variations from the baseline in patients' health data or comparing similar patients could generate business opportunities for lifesaving tech solutions. United Kingdom based AI startup Okra Technologies has launched a new software platform that regulates the price that can be charged for new medications years ahead of when these pharmaceuticals are launched.[56] Not only does it create business value, but this platform uses AI to dramatically free up the time spent on crunching datasets, modeling scenarios, and building price predictions.

QUALITY EDUCATION

Scholastic tech programs can make an impact on improving student outcomes dramatically. AI is being used in student homework programs to respond and adjust to their learning needs, resulting in a tailor-made curriculum. In addition, advanced facial recognition technology gives certainty to education authorities that the correct students are sitting their exam papers. Capability building can also help augment academic initiatives through a focus on accessible education opportunities such as online courses and freely available guides, as well as contributions of time by organizations such as technology companies that employ highly skilled AI talent.[57] One of the renowned online learning platforms, Coursera, has AI-produced granular information for effective learning. Owing to the big data analysis system Coursera offers, the graduation rates of low-income and first-generation college students have risen by 30% and warning signs have been identified before dropout to allow targeted interventions.[58]

AFFORDABLE AND CLEAN ENERGY

This is another area where AI has shown promising results. Disseminating power capabilities in Nigeria, Renewable Africa 365 and Omdena have developed a grid coverage analysis and machine learning heat maps to identify sites that are most suitable for solar panel installation.[59] AI's contribution in this pursuit could bring renewable energy to 100 million people living in communities lacking access to the national grid.[60] Smart meters are another ground-breaking technology solution using AI for success. Helping customers tailor their energy consumption to personal needs, smart meters pave the way for reduced costs through more customized tariffs and more efficient supply.[61] Machine learning techniques such as these offer broad applications when predicting renewable energy efficiency and costs, thereby opening a massive source of data that could be used to predict usage patterns and inform sound recommendations.

INDUSTRY, INNOVATION AND INFRASTRUCTURE

AI contributes to this category across a broad spectrum, especially through tech giants like Google. One of Google's missions is to organize the world's information and make it universally accessible and useful. Whether searching for photos of loved ones, breaking down language barriers in Google Translate, typing emails, or getting things done with the Google Assistant, AI is enabling this in exciting new ways.[62] Streaming and content providers are increasingly turning to iSize, a London-based company specializing in deep learning to optimize video streaming and delivery to address the challenge of delivering a reliable and high-quality video experience while managing the financial and environmental costs.[63] The tech company has pioneered deep-learning solutions that optimize video streaming quality while reducing bit rate requirements, which allows for a significant reduction in data and energy consumption.

REDUCED INEQUALITIES

AI responds to this goal by providing populations from various regions and economic backgrounds with new ways of looking at existing problems. From rethinking healthcare to advancing scientific discovery, developing nations are designing AI sustainability business models to increase the communication capacity of their urban and rural communities while being economically competitive in international business. Ping An Technology, part of China's Ping An Insurance Group, is one of the world's largest insurers that invests 1% of its revenues into technology development. The insurer advocates AI as a disruptive tech solution and endeavors to employ it for the benefit of both their business and society. Predicting and preventing many kinds of risks, AI improves day-to-day business operations. By collecting and analyzing data to understand patterns based on the apps people use, Ping An's credit team can make more accurate decisions about customer credit which lowers the risk of credit loss for the company.[64]

RESPONSIBLE CONSUMPTION AND PRODUCTION

AI brings huge value for monitoring and managing consumption and production patterns. The technology is yielding optimal consumption and production levels, eliminating waste and vastly improving resource efficiency. Annual estimates of food waste due to poor transportation, inefficient harvesting practices, processing, and natural spoilage are all capacities AI can support.[65] A startup called Wasteless developed an AI-powered system for automatically reducing the price of perishable food items, which is reflected in the price tags on grocery stores shelves. Wasteless helps reduce food waste in grocery stores by at least 40%, and the company believes it can increase that number to 80% as they further refine this technology.[66] AMP Robotics, based in Denver, Colorado, is a startup that employs robotic systems to sort recyclable material. AMP has processed over a billion recyclables across installations in over 20 states, which translates to a reduction in greenhouse gas emissions of approximately half a million metric tons.[67]

CLIMATE ACTION

AI and its innovators also address one of the most pressing issues the planet faces today. Developers are finding ways to apply the technology to help understand and fight climate change through simulations, monitoring, and measuring for resource management. In addition, AI has been deployed in conservation biology. It aids with more accurate and streamlined wildlife monitoring and data collection made possible using drones and sensors. AI has the potential to help diverse global businesses fulfill 11% to 45% of the "Economic Emission Intensity" targets of the Paris Agreement by 2031.[68] We find several climate intelligence startups emerging that offer predictive analytics platforms to enable a range of businesses to anticipate and prepare for extreme weather events. For example, One Concern is developing a digital twin of the world's natural and built environments. It aims to dynamically model the effects of climate change, offering its customers what it terms Resilience-as-a-Service.[69] The company operates primarily in the Japanese market. Other global startups in this space include Cervest, Climavision, Gro Intelligence, ClimateAI, Jupiter Intelligence and Terrafuse AI.[70]

AFFORDABLE AND CLEAN ENERGY

- Employ more renewable energy by increasing efficiency through AI real-time analysis.
- Reduce global energy poverty by using AI agents to propose energy deals.
- Cut CO2 emissions with advanced data analytics, by enhancing energy efficiency and reducing environmental impact.

GOOD HEALTH AND WELLBEING

- Analyze healthcare records to improve treatment quality and efficiency.
- Assist in patient diagnosis.
- Reduce pressure on staff by using robots in healthcare, speeding up the development of new drugs.

CLIMATE ACTION

- Implement climate change data analysis and climate modeling to predict climate-related problems.
- Enable sustainable AI and data solutions as a response to rising energy demand.
- Make informed business decisions to mitigate climate change through improved modeling and data analysis.

INDUSTRY, INNOVATION AND INFRASTRUCTURE

- Help retailers use deep learning to predict customers' orders.
- Help employees improve decisions using analysis of complex datasets.
- Accelerate innovation cycles, enable faster production, and improve time through machine learning.

AI AND DATA

QUALITY EDUCATION

- Personalize learning through AI-powered education using analytics.
- Improve graduation rates of low-income and first-generation college students.
- Provide virtual mentors for learners by integrating modeling, classroom simulation, and knowledge representation.

RESPONSIBLE CONSUMPTION AND PRODUCTION

- Generate optimal consumption and production levels through data management, waste elimination, and resource efficiency.
- Manage data with greater efficiency using fewer resources to improve product quality.
- Create carbon-neutral business models.

REDUCED INEQUALITIES

- Design AI sustainability to increase the communication capacity of urban and rural communities in developing nations.
- Use data applications and business models to spot inequalities in legal practices.
- Use AI-inspired devices to correct disabilities, yielding a more equal and inclusive society.

ENHANCING BUSINESS MODELS

Global communities are increasingly recognizing and utilizing AI and data capabilities. The business applications emerging for this tech are expanding with new opportunities presenting themselves. In the most advanced stage, AI and data function without human intervention. Moving beyond our finite human abilities and skills, advanced iterations of AI and data present continual updated versions and breakthroughs the world has not seen before. Through organized and responsible management of AI and data implementation, we have before us the emergence of a new business strategy. Capturing valuable data will be at the core of the AI revolution and harvesting data about consumer and societal behavior will be the cornerstone of AI business for good.

44% OF EXECUTIVES BELIEVE THAT FAILURE TO IMPLEMENT AI WILL ADVERSELY AFFECT THEIR BOTTOM LINE IN THE YEARS TO COME.[71]

But how can businesses use AI and data to be both profitable and sustainable? The answer may lie in how the tech's applications enable organizations to create agile and adaptive business strategies. These would be strategies that learn and adapt to the rapid evolution of customers and markets. Through the tech's unique ability to learn, unlearn, relearn and self-adjust to modify strategies, autonomous operations for greater efficiency are becoming possible. Businesses are beginning to move in tandem with the technology's developments as they are observing benefits of the evolving AI-driven automation ecosystem. Although the projected rapid pace of AI-driven automation evolution in the coming years will present each business with challenges, the lucrative market opportunities expected to come to the forefront and dominate the tech space will be vast as well.

OUR WORLD IS CONSTANTLY CHANGING AND WE MUST LEARN HOW TO ADAPT IF WE ARE TO KEEP UP. AI OFFERS US A PATH TO ACHIEVE THIS.

Our world today reveals that as we become increasingly connected, businesses have the chance to collect more data, process targeted insights and innovate at a faster rate. This denotes that the evolution of markets will be inevitable, featuring marketplaces with lean operations, vibrant businesses, growing profits, informed consumers and dynamic businesses.[72] AI will ultimately allow organizations to make more sense of the data they have about their customers, markets, and operations and to anticipate how best to adapt and respond to changing needs.

AI AND DATA PROVIDE UNLIMITED OPPORTUNITY FOR GROWTH. THE ORGANIZATIONS THAT ACT QUICKLY WILL THRIVE.

In a world where tech disruptions are continually raising the stakes, organizations that act quickly and reinvent themselves digitally will thrive. Data and AI provide unlimited opportunity for sustainable business growth and the resources for major competitive advantage. From scheduling conferences and team meetings to supporting decision-makers, AI can help to assist with business management activities. Avanade's cloud-based solution is utilized by businesses of all sizes to help operations run smoothly.

IN BUSINESS

AVANADE[73]

Initiative: Accelerating Business Transformation and Innovation
Headquarters: Seattle, Washington USA

Avanade is a joint venture between Microsoft and Accenture. It leverages the Cortana Intelligence Suite along with other solutions for predictive analysis and data-based insights for business. Avanade uses AI and data analytics to help advise companies on the development of new products by understanding behavior and trends, which assists businesses smoothly transition to AI platforms (SDGs 4,9). From process automation to business analytics to predictive data visualizations, the company brings unprecedented insights to its clients and maximizes the value of data and business impact. Elisabeth Brinton, Corporate VP for Sustainability at Microsoft, states: "Avanade's new services for the Microsoft Cloud for Sustainability will help organizations use technology to run the execution of their sustainability commitments and reduce emissions faster."[74]

Avanade believes that data analytics and AI are great equalizers, where "smaller organizations can create a big presence, and big companies can create intimate connections" (SDGs 10,11). After conducting a study, Avanade found that 97% of organizations are already evaluating the work AI could do – or augment what humans can do. The opportunity for AI and data at a large scale to grow business profits is truly limitless and provides a major competitive advantage (SDGs 8,12). Avanade helps businesses realize this potential and incorporate this tech successfully into core business practices.

AI and data analytics offer businesses an automated, closed loop and multi-style integration strategy. Powered by AI data inputs, this closed-loop strategy employs real-world operational data that feed the AI to make smoother integrations and transitions. Embedding these evolving AI integrations into core operations, businesses can swiftly pivot their sustainability initiatives and financial investments to respond to their company-specific datasets.[75] Closing the loop through AI functions will help identify internal inefficiencies more quickly. As a result, effective and efficient production and consumption can be researched, designed and managed at a scale and complexity that goes beyond existing approaches.

SMALLER ORGANIZATIONS CAN CREATE A BIG PRESENCE AND BIG COMPANIES CAN CREATE INTIMATE CONNECTIONS.

With its ability to hone and learn preferences over time, industries are witnessing the emergence of deep insight into consumer preferences with regards to highly personalized products and services. In this sense, AI and data help businesses make money while utilizing their great potential to do good. Businesses can enhance personalized product and service commerce by supplementing both sales and marketing with advanced and intelligent analytics. Not only does this supply actionable intelligence for businesses about customer buying patterns and other trends, it also steers company resources in a profitable and sustainable direction.

BUSINESSES CAN USE AI AND DATA TO MAKE MONEY WHILE UTILIZING THEIR GREAT POTENTIAL TO DO GOOD. PREDICTING SUPPLY CHAIN MOVEMENTS IS WITHIN OUR REACH TOO.

Machine learning algorithms aid retail and other businesses in managing their inventory more efficiently. Major AI players like IBM Watson are heavily investing in supply chain management to help automate the transformation of natural resources, raw materials and components. By optimizing production through turning over inventory management and supply chain decisions to AI-based apps, companies can free up workforce talent to engage in other tasks. TransVoyant is combining machine learning and the Internet of Things to create applications that predict supply chain movements.

IN BUSINESS

TRANSVOYANT[76]

Initiative: Comprehensive Data Fusion, Business Analytics, and Insights
Headquarters: Alexandria, Virginia USA

From terrestrial, near-space and space-based sensors, TransVoyant collects, organizes and fuses over one trillion global behavior events each day, which is the largest repository of real-time big data in the world. Proprietary algorithms and unique learned behavior models give the company vast expertise on how to continually understand the end-to-end global flow of commerce (SDGs 9,12). These behavior models enable TransVoyant to help clients and businesses to predict lead times, variability, disruptions, and opportunities as well as initiate prescriptive actions that increase revenues, reduce costs and improve customer service.

TransVoyant provides the capability to rapidly solve, innovate, and provide fully measurable outcomes for a business's bottom line. It also helps companies troubleshoot challenges through AI by offering solutions such as continuously fused, organized and normalized live-streamed data across the entire enterprise; machine learning and AI-enabled advanced analytics that allow businesses to understand the past, present, and future of their business ecosystem; and a platform with modern architecture, easily configurable to specifications, and extensible to unique business needs.

TransVoyant CEO and Co-Founder, Dennis Groseclose, discusses the company's benefits to sustainable business: "Today our business helps Fortune1000 brands like the HPs and IBMs to know exactly where their products are along the supply chain in real time. TransVoyant is really focused on present and future behaviors of businesses, and how we can produce useful information enabled by AI and big data."[77] TransVoyant's primary purpose is to provide solutions that can transform complex global supply chains into a competitive advantage for businesses (SDGs 8,9,10). The company has a number of customers that are embracing the fast-changing digital world to enhance their client services, reduce and avoid high costs, and are looking for opportunities for improvement.

GLOBAL GOALS' GROWTH OPPORTUNITIES

History proves that technological progress drives long term economic growth and business success. Current trends point to AI and data being a driving factor in increasing overall productivity, resulting in a surge in income and consumption patterns. In this regard, technological progress promises the rise of a sustainable economy and the future of business is filled with immense possibilities. Global businesses are intrinsically reliant on performance metrics, as success in the marketplace is dependent on how data is organized and analyzed. As a basis for business applications, AI is evolving into a necessary component to core business practices, allowing for vast amounts of data processing at record speed.

AI INCREASES PRODUCTIVITY. THE TECH PROMISES A SUSTAINABLE ECONOMY AND SO MUCH MORE.

Not only does the tech give management teams freedom to make more rapid decisions that potentially position them to be competitive in real-time, but it also enables companies to use machine algorithms to identify important trends and insights. Companies are growing in several existing and new SDG markets such as health and wellbeing, security and safety and education and training. All of this is thanks to AI and data.

The main SDG domains AI and data address in terms of business opportunities include healthcare and hunger, education and skills training, security and safety, and resources and ecology. These broad areas may increase AI and data's potential for good in terms of both business opportunities and the planet.

NOURISHING FOOD AND SUPPORTING HEALTH

Several areas within the healthcare sector experience unprecedented benefits that AI advancement and data science offer. One of the ways in which AI is significantly enhancing healthcare is through aiding in diagnosis and detecting illness and disease before medical professionals are involved. The tech ultimately saves time, lives and efficiency of processes within its application in healthcare systems.

AI and data are being used as vital components in medical advancements of drugs and pharmaceuticals. The unreliability, cost and time-consumption of traditional methods of drug discovery have led biopharmaceutical companies to collaborate with AI-based tech firms to improve processes from the development phase to the dissemination point. The cost to develop a new drug has risen to nearly $3 billion and can take an average of 12 years for each new product.[78] Over the last decade though, AI has enabled more affordable drug development and more intelligent use of data to smoothly run the timelines that are associated with bringing a new drug to market.

AI HAS THE POTENTIAL TO PROVIDE OVER $70 BILLION IN SAVINGS FOR THE DRUG DISCOVERY PROCESS BY 2028.[79]

Beyond the use of AI to develop innovative drug therapies and customized medicine, data management has emerged that is spurring robotics innovations to support surgeries now too. Also relevant, AI-enabled wearable devices are detecting potential rudimentary signs of diabetes through heart rate sensor data with 85% accuracy.

The scope of this tech goes beyond helping more than 400 million people afflicted by the disease worldwide if made sufficiently affordable.[80]

AI TECHNOLOGY HAS BEEN IMPLEMENTED TO HELP YIELD HEALTHIER CROPS, REDUCE WORKLOADS, ORGANIZE DATA, AND IMPROVE A WIDE RANGE OF TASKS IN THIS $5 TRILLION INDUSTRY.[81]

The innovative Danish startup Corti proves another interesting way that AI technology is supporting global health.[82] This novel approach listens in on emergency calls and analyzes conversations in real time. Utilizing machine learning, Corti helps medical dispatchers diagnose illnesses and provides prompts for effective action. The company's highly effective technology eliminates human error and saves over 20% more lives as human dispatchers manage to recognize about 73% of cardiac arrest calls while the Corti AI correctly analyzes nearly 95% of the calls.[83]

AI HAS BEEN EMPLOYED TO BOOST AGRICULTURAL YIELDS AND MINIMIZE WORLD HUNGER.

AI helps combat global hunger too and Microsoft is a major influencer in this important endeavor. The tech giant has partnered with various innovative scientists, conservationists, farmers and other groups as part of its $50 million AI for Earth program to explore the implications of AI technologies on agricultural efforts. For example, the nonprofit International Crop Research Institute for Semi-Arid Tropics (ICRISAT) is working with Microsoft to enable farmers to increase yields using AI. The sowing seed application they developed together draws on climate data and weather information while using sophisticated forecasting models powered by Azure AI to determine the optimal time to plant, the ideal sowing depth, and how much manure to apply to the soil. The information is shared with rural farmers through text messaging technologies on a basic feature phone.[84]

IN BUSINESS

AZURE FARMBEATS[85]

Initiative: Microsoft AI, Edge and IoT for Agriculture
Headquarters: Redmond, Washington USA

Azure FarmBeats is a Microsoft product for agri-businesses that uses low-cost sensors, drones, satellites and image-based machine learning algorithms to increase the productivity and profitability of farmers.[86] Cloud-based AI models provide a precise, instant picture of the conditions on the farm, down to the square meter that enables farmers to make targeted decisions about crop management (SDGs 2,3,12). Since this tech does not require internet connectivity or complicated systems to use, it is saving labor, reducing costs, and improving output by developing strong seed varieties and automating laborious tasks (SDGs 8,9). It also detects crop disease or issues for earlier interventions, applies herbicide precisely and generally maximizes crop production so that there are more profits and fewer losses.[87]

FarmBeats system has been deployed worldwide, including in locations like the United States, India, Africa and China. Most data driven agriculture solutions that are available today are too expensive for the average farmer. Sensors can cost $350 or more and with over 500 million small-holder farmers across the world, this is more often than not unattainable.[88] Thus, it is crucial that the overall cost of the IoT deployment is affordable for all farmers without compromising quality of data (SDGs 10,11). Ranveer Chandra, Principle Researcher at Microsoft explains: "We want to enable data-driven farming. The first goal is to give a real-time view of the farm, a real-time pulse of the farm to the farmer. Connectivity is cheap through our product, so farmers can now have many more sensors. Once farmers have all this data, they can analyze the data and predict what the future will look like."[89]

Solar panels power the entire system and then farmers place a few sensors – one every couple hundred meters or so – in the ground (SDG 7). A smartphone with the camera is then attached facing down to either a drone or a lower-cost helium balloon. Farmers have reported vast savings using this tech – 30% less water for irrigation and 44% less lime to control soil pH.[90] The data gathered on soil temperature and moisture levels help farmers maximize their planting time for more productive time management and harvest. Further, FarmBeats enables a better plan for a farm's planting structure via its aerial imaging capabilities that precisely document flooding patterns (SDG 15).

UPSCALING SECURITY AND SAFETY

Companies and cities worldwide are implementing AI to reduce and prevent crime, and respond more quickly to crimes in progress. This was considered technologically impossible a few decades ago, but recent developments in machine learning have revolutionized security and justice. The United States spends over $80 billion a year on incarcerations at the state, local, and federal levels with an astounding total of more than $100 billion per year on law enforcement.[91] Although this issue is a deeper societal problem, businesses can leverage AI and data technologies to address SDG concepts of national and global security.

WITH AI-ENABLED CAMERAS, SAFE CITIES CAN BE THE NORM.

Companies are using AI-enabled cameras to watch for crime. Hikvision, a Chinese security camera producer, uses chips from Movidius (an Intel company) to create cameras able to run deep neural networks.[92] This new camera has advanced capabilities to better scan for license plates on cars, run facial reconition to search databases for potential criminals, and automatically detect suspicious anomalies like unattended bags in crowded venues. Achieving 99% accuracy with their advanced visual analytics applications, Hikvision has grown significantly with a 2021 revenue of $11 billion and year-over-year growth of 39.68%.[93] Not only does this AI tech company keep cities safer, but it also has the potential for huge market growth.

THE POTENTIAL OF AI AS A SOCIAL EQUALIZER COULD TRANSFORM LIVES.

AI is also used to redesign city borders as a social equalizer. There is ample opportunity for the tech to tap into the smart building market, which is expected to reach $229 billion by 2026.[94] Mass-produced housing for instance considers the design and layout of development to keep efficiencies high and maintenance costs low as a method to build more secure communities. Innovative AI and data initiatives are protecting the natural environment too. The Rainforest Connection built RFCx, a poaching and deforestation detection system that monitors audio recording devices in rainforests.[95] As economic losses of GDP $2 to $5 trillion per year are attributed to downgrading rainforest to pasture and less productive land use, these alert systems designed to catch poachers have a huge economic impact and business opportunity.

ADVANCING EDUCATION AND TRAINING

AI and data are poised to have a big impact on education all over the world. More than 1.5 billion students around the globe will benefit from adaptive learning technology, which structures content for students based on individual abilities.[96] A key challenge for education services is the lack of reliable and up-to-date metrics for statistical analysis to make curriculum improvements. As educators need to customize learning for each student and reach performance benchmarks, AI supplies valuable tools that can support learning in and out of the classroom.[97] For students, personalized learning platforms are becoming increasingly important.

There are several examples of AI providing customized teaching for each student using AI. Offering free education to thousands of children in over 1000 learning centers across China, for example, tech company Squirrel measures learning levels to provide students with optimal learning content and speed.[98] Another business, Quill.org, was founded by a group of educators and technologists and is helping students become better writers and critical thinkers. This tool is to help students identify the different parts of a sentence, with a focus on real-time feedback. More than 200,000 students – 62% from low-income schools – have used Quill, and 2.8 million students have written 403 million sentences on the Google platform.[99] These learners have collectively answered 20 million exercises, along with personalized services for writing instruction that has helped them master core writing skills.

IN BUSINESS

CAPGEMINI[100]

Initiative: Preserving the Mojave Desert
Headquarters: Paris, France

Capgemini, a multinational IT services and consulting company, has partnered with The Nature Conservancy (TNC) in Nevada to develop an artificial intelligence solution that could help restore the natural balance of the Mojave Desert.[101] This rich landscape with a vast variety of wildlife spreads across 20 million acres of the US, spanning California, south-western Utah, southern Nevada, and north-western Arizona.[102] The Mojave's open, sandy plains are also a popular location for off-roading vehicles, which, when driven illegally, pose a threat to its fragile ecosystem. Across such a huge expanse, it can be almost impossible to locate off-roading trails. For millions of years, tortoises, golden eagles, insects, and unique cacti have called this desert their home. It is therefore important to know where to intervene in an effort to prevent ecosystem degradation, as the Mojave creates upwards of $45 billion in economic benefits annually (SDG 11).[103]

Capgemini convened an integrated team of AI specialists, earth scientists, and project managers to create a system that will gauge impact of landscape and ecosystem degradation indicators across the Mojave Desert (SDGs 13,17). Using AI and machine learning that develop aglorithms to trace the paths and erosion rates of off-road trails remotely, TNC is better equipped to identify off-road trails in specific areas. Specifically, Capgemini's tool studies satellite imageries and also monitors the off-road vehicles and trails to determine the impact on the landscape and wildlife ecosystems (SDGs 8,12). These data are then compared to other relevant information such as the positions of nesting sites, migration routes, and individual communities of protected species like the Mojave Desert tortoise (SDGs 10,15).

Although Capeskin's solution has been initially monitoring just a portion of the Western Mojave, the solution has the possibility of surveying degradation of the desert at scale (SDG 16). "Gemini brings deep AI and data science expertise, and our innovative solution can help find and monitor land decorations in the Mojave Desert," says Jerry Kurt, Head of Insights and Data at Gemini in North America.[104] "We're very hopeful that we will be able to apply this solution to a wide range of conservation efforts that help protect at-risk natural environments around the world." In the future, the initiative will tailor AI solutions with particular species in mind. The innovative team tech effort is facilitating coexistence of humanity and nature in this unique part of the world.

AI+SDG LAUNCHPAD

The AI+SDG Launchpad is an innovative business proposition that allows any school, college, university, or research institute to easily create and manage a curriculum that bridges the gap between data-enabled sciences and the United Nations' Sustainable Development Agenda for 2030.[105] The Launchpad serves as a blueprint for single or multi-semester courses that allow students to engage with global challenges, they are passionate about in a structured way. The Launchpad programs have reached more than 500 students in five countries, with collaboration on a range of SDG topics, from carbon sequestration and curtailing media bias to ocean health and predicting refugee migration.

Top management schools see the immense value of tech in the business world. Highly ranked business schools are increasingly offering courses and training on how to utilize AI and data to improve corporate strategy and transform organizations into innovative, efficient, and sustainable companies of the future. MIT Sloan School of Management for instance offers a course named Artificial Intelligence: Implications for Business Strategy for students and business executives to learn how to capitalize on the value automation could bring to business. The course discusses how companies can gain important core competencies including AI, machine learning, and data management in their business strategies.[106]

"I THINK INFORMATION TECHNOLOGY IS ONE OF THE MOST IMPORTANT FACTORS CAUSING CHANGES IN BUSINESS TODAY."[107] - THOMAS MALONE, FOUNDING DIRECTOR MIT CENTER FOR COLLECTIVE INTELLIGENCE

Cognii is a provider of AI-based educational technologies, working with organizations in the K-12, higher education, and corporate training markets to help deliver cost-efficient learning outcomes.[108] Its products include the Cognii Learning Platform, Virtual Learning Assistant, and Assessment Engine. The company offers a suite of products powered by AI for better assessment and real-time tutoring. The Cognii Virtual Learning Assistant engages students in personalized tutoring conversations, providing immediate scoring and feedback on written answers to questions. Netex Learning is another company utilizing AI and data to implement education sector business opportunities.

IN BUSINESS
NETEX LEARNING[109]
Initiative: Netex Knowledge Factory
Headquarters: A Coruña, Spain

Netex is creating smart digital content platforms, complete with content delivery, practice exercises and real-time feedback and assessment for a range of educational purposes (SDG 4). Educators can use this AI solution to design digital curriculum and content across devices, integrating diverse media like video and audio, along with self- or online-instructor components. Netex also provides a personalized learning cloud platform designed for the modern workplace (SDGs 9,10). Design possibilities include customizable learning systems with apps; gamification and simulations; virtual courses; self-assessments; video conferencing; and other tools. Learning platforms for businesses are designed to allow employees to master additional skills and receive continuous and automated feedback (SDG 8). This tech solution helps improve performance and increase production (SDG 12).

Valencia International University (VIU) is one of the leading online universities in the Spanish-speaking world. Netex enhances VIU's bachelor and master's degrees subject catalog for more than 250 subjects in arts and humanities, science and technology, education, business, legal, and more.[110] Results of the program thus far include over 160 curriculum authors, more than 33,000 pages of courses developed and hundreds of e-learning units scripted and disseminated.

REJUVENATING RESOURCES AND ECOLOGY

Resource scarcity entails energy and water availability deficits which is a growing concern among businesses and corporations. AI-powered data analytics can assist in resource scarcity management. The tech is speeding up expansion by way of reducing the chance of human error in energy sourcing, storage, and dissemination. AI and data management is a critical tool for companies looking to reduce costs, expand access to renewable power and preserve the natural environment.

AI and data technologies have great possibilities for improving predictability in the renewable energy sector. They promise to lead industry wide improvements that make renewable sources of energy viable solutions on a wider scale. Utility companies are leveraging AI and data to manage diverse factors that are affecting renewable energy generation. Not only is it helping to cut costs, but it is also enhancing profits and consumer satisfaction. AI can improve solar and wind power reliability by analyzing enormous amounts of meteorological data and use this information to make predictions. Utility companies will then be able to better serve customers by utilizing AI to integrate microgrids and manage distributed energy.

AI TECHNOLOGIES HAVE GREAT POSSIBILITIES FOR IMPROVING PREDICTABILITY IN THE RENEWABLE ENERGY SECTOR.

Businesses globally can take proactive and cost-effective action by accelerating the adoption of the most technologically advanced renewable energy systems. When energy generation technologies are added from local and community levels to larger grids, AI manages energy flow instability through capabilities such as analyzing grids before and after they absorb smaller units while working to reduce congestion. EleXsys Energy is employing cutting edge tech solutions that advance renewable energy deployment all over the world.[111]

Several energy companies currently use AI to facilitate and intelligently improve their internal systems. Sentinel Solar by Nnergix, for instance, developed a business model that leverages AI to pool data from the energy industry to make predictions and develop weather forecasts for improved accuracy. The innovative company coordinates and controls renewable energy reserves through load management by analyzing sensor data to make power available as soon as needed.[112] It is the first of its kind platform to manage solar self-consumption portfolios that allows efficient monitoring and management of photovoltaic portfolios. With over 9,000 self-consuming owners, the Barcelona-based company's use of AI and data reduces time and personnel costs.[113] In 19 countries with over 11,000 sites, the company has generated significant energy savings for its customers all over the world.

COMPANIES MUST BE PROACTIVE TO ACCELERATE THE ADOPTION OF AI.

AI also serves as a beneficial tool for water management. The tech can help reduce water wastage through leakages. It is estimated that around 40% of piped water in India is lost to leakage.[114] In the US, an average family can waste 180 gallons of water per week, or 9400 gallons of water annually from household leaks, which is equivalent to the amount of water needed to wash more than 300 loads of laundry.[115] Implementing AI to analyze real-time water loss and automating pipes to shut off whenever there is a leak can improve the amount of water wastage.

AI can predict leaks, help detect pollutants, and integrate various systems across a city or area for cost-effective and sustainable water management. In terms of wastewater treatment, the tech helps implement monitoring algorithms that can monitor water quality and reduce contaminating pollutants. The process of water management is streamlined with advanced tools like data analytics and regression models, often exhibited in smart irrigation AI systems to both minimize and optimize the use of water resources.[116]

ADDRESSING RISKS AND CHALLENGES ON THE ROAD AHEAD

While the widespread adoption of AI and use of data have profound positive implications for many businesses of all sizes and societies at large, there are also associated risks, challenges, barriers, and disadvantages. Creating a machine that simulates human intelligence requires a lot of time and financial resources. Further, AI needs to operate on the latest hardware and software to stay updated and meet digital requirements, which further raises the cost. Another major disadvantage of AI is its difficulty learning to think for itself. It is dependent on its restricted operating system capabilities, which makes its utility limited. AI is capable of learning over time based on pre-introduced data and past experiences, but the tech is not yet capable of being creative in its approach.

THE RAPID GROWTH OF AI HAS GENERATED CONCERNS ABOUT UNCONTROLLABLE TECHNOLOGY.

As with other technologies mentioned throughout the book, probably one of the biggest disadvantages of AI is its perceived risk to employment. Slow replacement of repetitive tasks with bots entails a reduction in the need for human labor. Studies predict that AI will replace at least 30% of human labor by 2030.[117] Addiction to AI due to excessive reliance on the tech could also cause problems for future generations in terms of work ethic and cognitive function. Ethics and morality then become increasingly important human features that can be difficult to incorporate into AI developments. The rapid progress of AI has raised concerns about the technology growing uncontrollably and eventually wiping out humanity. This moment is referred to as the AI singularity.[118]

Data availability in the realm of AI can also be a challenge. Big data analytics are very useful to businesses in many sectors, but the downside is that the average IT personnel without the necessary knowledge may be at a loss when tasked to glean data to make decisions. Companies will need specialized information scientists who know how to interpret results from these datasets. This can pose a financial dilemma as these experts require large salaries that most small-to-medium-sized businesses cannot afford. If businesses do not have the in-house skills available or staff who understand this information, then utilizing data for business success is not a cost-effective endeavor. In fact, when mismanaged it can jeopardize competitive advantage. Companies that decide to embrace the idea of AI and big data will need to change their entire organizational structure to maximize the tech's benefits.

COMPANIES MUST BE ALERT AND READY TO DEFEND THE SECURITY RISKS AI COULD POSE.

AI and data management also provide a number of security risks. Most of the information that companies collect using AI capabilities includes sensitive data that require a specific level of protection. Having access to these analytics, organizations become an attractive target for potential cyberattacks. A data breach is often the single greatest threat that a company faces when trying to implement this tech throughout the corporate or organizational structure. Since AI technologies are unique in that they acquire knowledge and intelligence to adapt accordingly, criminals leverage these capabilities to model adaptable attacks and create intelligent malware programs. As hackers become more advanced, data attacks are harder to detect. The same capabilities that enable AI and data to be used for good are employed for its downsides and security risks.

WE HAVE
IMAGINED

AI and data technologies are poised to alter the foundational structure of business globally. Although there are challenges and barriers to overcome, as well as security risks to consider, AI and data have an unprecedented opportunity to be implemented as a force for good. Self-maintained indoor farming with enhanced operational data analytics or AI-enabled monitoring for increased crop yields are just the beginning.

These tech solutions lead to an altogether new lifestyle and outlook concerning the availability of nutrients. Beyond an effective solution for addressing global hunger, business opportunities include other sustainable initiatives such as self-driving vehicles that reduce pollution and limit traffic deaths. Across markets, AI and data present a pathway towards new and intelligent automated supply chains.

AI and data provide advances and economic opportunities in a wide range of markets. From medical research, resource management, and energy technologies to automation in monitoring and satellite imagery analysis of the environment, AI and data have profound effects on all facets of global business. Imagine all the ways these technologies will offer promising solutions that serve as integral components of the 4IR, supercharging the economy and supporting sustainable business.

We have imagined AI and Data as Tech for Good.

3D PRINTING 3

3D PRINTING CAN PROPEL INNOVATION TO PROTECT OUR PLANET IN INFINITE WAYS. EVEN SAVING WILDLIFE FROM EXTINCTION IS WITHIN REACH.

WE ONLY NEED TO

IMAGINE

Imagine not only saving our coral reefs but fortifying them like never before. It's a beautiful thought, isn't it? Where our oceans aren't simply surviving, but thriving. The bright architectural beauty of our oceans' coral reefs is fading. These aesthetically appealing natural organisms are dying, but we have the power to save them. Reefs contain staggering biodiversity that illuminates our seas with life and color.

Photosynthesis is integral to this vibrant underwater habitat, as the sun provides food for marine life and is vital for the survival of these aquatic creatures. However, photosynthesis only occurs near the ocean's surface. This is where coral reefs come in. These large, amorphous protrusions, making up underwater colonies of brilliant colors, provide sanctuary and food to small marine animals, who spend the majority of their life cycles in the coral reef. Coral reefs, thus, are an essential source of sustenance. They provide key nutrients and proteins for not just sea life, but for one billion people, too.[1] In addition to protecting our coastlines and serving as an attraction to visiting ecotourists, scientists speculate that coral reefs may extend broad benefits to industries like manufacturing and pharmaceuticals.[2]

Yet this fruitful beauty of our earth is under threat. Aspects of climate change such as the warming of waters, pollution, ocean acidification, overfishing, and physical destruction are killing coral reefs worldwide. Recent studies reveal that 50% of the globe's coral reefs have already been destroyed, and another 40% could be lost over the next 30 years.[3] The death of the coral reefs spells an end for most of our oceans' ecosystems, which is bound to have direct, negative effects on humankind. Advancements in 3D printing can help put a stop to, and in some cases even reverse, the damage inflicted on coral reefs. While maintaining the sentiment that technology does not replace nature, but rather affects positive change within it, we can use 3D printing to help repair and retain elements of our environment. 3D printing companies XtreeE and Seaboost present a novel example.[4] These organizations specializing in the ecological design of marine structures collaborated to create the X-Reef, which mimics the ecosystem of the Mediterranean. Consider that a coral reef organically grows over the course of several hundred years. Now, as exemplified by X-Reef, that process can be accelerated to a handful of hours, mere "printing time." 3D printing can also be used to prevent loss and protect existing, vulnerable reefs. SECORE International is an exemplary initiative seeking to reduce the costs of coral restoration by using 3D-printed settlement substrates.[5] The organization refers to them as "seeding units" because they self-attach to reefs and provide an attractive habitat for coral larvae. This setup increases the survival rate of wild coral.

These man-made corals are designed in special ways to allow the surrounding fauna to make homes in the structures, just as though they were native. As experiments have successfully demonstrated, the coral itself grows thanks to transplantation. Either by directly transplanting living coral or replicating coral cells into the material, scientists prime the 3D structures to host plant life on their surfaces. In this regard, the underwater wonders that are coral reefs grow further with the aid of 3D printing.

Imagine, 3D printing transforming regeneration opportunities for reef-building corals of the underwater ecosystem. This technology turns the tide for one of the most beautiful and important wonders of sea life by providing a base for the coral to grow and flourish. This practice does not fix the underlying problem that human activity is destroying coral reefs. It does, however, buy coral reefs and our oceans some valuable time and hope for restoration.

Imagine making up for lost time. This is 3D Printing for Good.

Marga Hoek

3

EXPLORING
3D PRINTING

This chapter explores the advancements in 3D printing technology, weaving its historical development with its current potential in sustainable business. The tech, also referred to as additive manufacturing, can be used to produce many different types of products. Discussing these innovations, the pages ahead illuminate how 3D printing is used for good.

The ways in which this exciting technology positively impacts sustainable economic growth across business sectors are highly relevant. With this in mind, the 3D printing tech market promises inspiring opportunities. This potential is illustrated throughout the chapter, illuminating how businesses employ 3D-based strategies to inspire innovative solutions. In this regard, the Global Goals present an opportunity for additive manufacturing to play a major role in creating shared value solutions. With large-scale adoption, along with forward-moving research and development, the 3D printing market is expanding rapidly.

Several cases are presented throughout this chapter, including AI and data applications of 3D printing. Complementing these initiatives by taking advantage of Global Goals growth markets, the performance of businesses can be enhanced in many sectors. Various developments are discussed in the areas of health and wellbeing, cities and infrastructure, and food supply chains. Potential adaptation and mitigation strategies for the challenges and risks that come with 3D printing are addressed near the end of this chapter. This following pages reveal the multidimensional stories of several organizations that implement 3D printing as a Tech for Good.

THE TECH

At its simplest, 3D printing, also known as additive manufacturing, is the production of a three-dimensional solid object rendered from a digital file. 3D printing is a great example of a 4IR technological solution, as it blends the digital and the physical worlds. As opposed to traditional manufacturing technologies, additive manufacturing builds 3D objects layer by layer, using computer-aided design (CAD) and a wide range of materials such as metal, plastic, concrete, or paper. While the terms "additive manufacturing" and "3D printing" are often used interchangeably, additive manufacturing is a broader term including several technologies. 3D printing is one of such technologies and generally refers to non-industrial applications.

ADDITIVE MANUFACTURING IS ONE OF THE MOST DISRUPTIVE TECHNOLOGIES OF OUR TIME.

On a more technical level, 3D printing enables decentralized, low-threshold production and manufacturing, and unlocks a wide range of positive impacts and business opportunities globally. Not only is 3D printing becoming faster and producing much larger objects, but scientists are also coming up with innovative ways to print by developing stronger source materials such as harder metals. Soon, 3D printers will likely make their way into homes, businesses, disaster sites, and even outer space. Additive manufacturing is already used for the construction of large structures and objects including bridges, houses, and aircraft propellers. The possibility of completely 3D-printed cityscapes may not be far off.

The variety of sizes of 3D-printed items is vast. The smallest 3D XS printed objects are the nano sculptures created by artist Jonty Hurwitz. His notable sculpture "Trust" has a size of 80 x 100 x 20 microns and, as of October 2014, was "the smallest creation of the human form in history."[6] The largest 3D XL printed forms comprise a range of objects, such as boats. One called the 3Dirigo was printed by the University of Maine Advanced Structures and Composites Center. It measured 7.62 meters long and weighed 2.2 tons.[7]

3D PRINTING IS ENVIRONMENTALLY EFFICIENT, PRODUCES ZERO WASTE, AND COSTS LESS THAN TRADITIONAL MANUFACTURING. IT IS EXPECTED THAT BY 2025, THE GLOBAL 3D PRINTING AND SERVICES MARKET WILL REACH $50 BILLION.[8]

Although the equipment required for 3D printing can be expensive, prices are dropping as scientists and engineers invent more efficient printers and the tech's penetration of the manufacturing market grows. Since business models are also evolving, we can expect to see a rapid expansion of the technology's applications in both industrial and consumer uses. For instance, the on-demand manufacturing business model emphasizes speed in delivery and the ability to produce parts at the point of need. 3D printing makes on-demand manufacturing possible, as no tooling is required and lead times for small batches can be significantly shortened. Using 3D printing to manufacture end-use parts in-house reduces supply chain complexities. In reducing production complications, manufacturers' exposure risk in supply chain disruptions may decrease.

The tech also enhances mass customization by allowing companies to explore this business model through providing viable solutions to manufacturing customized products. Unlike other conventional techniques, which require substantial investment in tooling for customized parts, 3D printing only requires uploading digital designs of a product or its parts. Companies, such as FitMyFoot, already leverage the mass customization provided by additive manufacturing. FitMyFoot uses additive manufacturing to produce sandals with custom-fit 3D-printed insoles.[9] The technology, which digitally maps each foot with over 200 points, creates a 3D-printable file of an insole that is unique to every consumer.

Other initiatives advancing the tech include simulations for how 3D printing processes would play out in outer space for constructing components and predicting part quality. 3D printing is critical to NASA's plans for deep space exploration, notably its mission to Mars. This trajectory is backed by several additive manufacturing-related initiatives through NASA in recent years.[10] Advanced modeling software developed by Cornell University has been successfully deployed and tested on the International Space Station (ISS). As part of a collaborative experiment conducted with NASA, the ISS US National Laboratory, and HP, Cornell's modeling software was integrated into HP's Spaceborne Computer-2. In addition, NASA partners with space tech companies Launcher[11] and VELO3D[12] to explore the manufacturing of 3D-printed rocket engines. 3D printing is also integral to designing and testing elements for an AI-powered lunar rover that may be deployed during NASA's return mission to the moon and in the production of a habitat that accurately resembles the conditions that future astronauts will experience on Mars.

As highlighted, the capabilities of 3D printing and additive manufacturing have not yet seen their full potential. The tech is currently primarily used in manufacturing and medical industries. Additionally, sociocultural sectors apply 3D printing for commercial purposes. The tech boasts a plethora of applications that have yet to be realized. Predominant research institutions are also supporting and promoting the broad range of additive manufacturing research, educational, and professional training activities. With several affiliated faculty from departments such as engineering and medicine, the Additive Manufacturing Institute of Science and Technology (AMIST) at the University of Louisville (UofL) is an example of a leading research university working on 3D printing Tech for Good applications.[13] UofL's AMIST combines the expertise of its professional staff with strategic partnerships in additive technologies to focus on integrating 3D printing to devise new solutions to real-life problems in healthcare, energy, the environment, communications, and security.

SOUND FOUNDATIONS

A lot can be expected for the future of 3D printing, but first, let's review the history and the current landscape of this tech solution. Additive manufacturing was first conceptualized in the 1980s and applied as "rapid prototyping." At present, its uses are diverse. The technology is now available through off-the-shelf printers and is increasingly integrated with conventional production technologies for industrial applications. The tech has been growing and evolving over the years. It is becoming more efficient and accessible globally. As early as 1989, the aerospace and defense sector was one of the first adopters of 3D printing. The scope and implementation of the technology has since grown substantially.[14]

3D PRINTING AS A FOURTH INDUSTRIAL REVOLUTION TECHNOLOGY CAN ALTER HOW COMPANIES CONCEIVE, DESIGN, PRODUCE, DISTRIBUTE, AND REPAIR.

In the 1990s, many companies and startups began experimenting with the different additive manufacturing technologies. The early 2000s were marked with high-tech devices being difficult for the public to access, while it was predominantly big global companies and major research universities that had use of 3D printers. These first prototypes were extremely large and expensive, as was the case with the first commercial computers. With innovations progressing steadily, as well as discoveries, methods, and practices refined and invented consistently, we now have computers with processing speeds a thousand times faster than the early models. Instead of the big machines of the past, the present enables devices that fit in our palms. In 2005, open-source software altered the 3D printing landscape, giving people increased access to this technology. The patents expired on the first wave of 3D printing and researchers developed a 3D printer that could print itself and release the designs with open-source licenses on the web. The RepRap Project, which was created as an open-source initiative, devised a 3D printer that could build another 3D printer along with a number of 3D printed objects.[15] Quickly hacked and improved upon by engineers around the world, the enhanced designs spread rapidly. Because of these innovative updates and subsequent market integration, the tech has become more accessible. Although 3D printers used to be expensive, affordable off-the-shelf printers now exist in the mainstream market. Today, people can buy a 3D printer for as little as $250 to $550.[16] In addition to the lowered cost, progress can also be seen from a product development standpoint. Advancements in additive manufacturing give rise to consumer options and allow for diversity in design. Simultaneously, more sophisticated printers are appearing, enabling more diverse manufacturing possibilities across sustainable business sectors. Given the shifting trend in 3D printing applications from prototyping to functional manufacturing, a rapid expansion of the technology's application throughout manufacturing will make its way into business and consumer markets.

AFFORDABLE OFF-THE-SHELF PRINTERS NOW EXIST IN THE MAINSTREAM MARKET.

The input materials for additive manufacturing have evolved over time as well. Currently, a variety of plastics and filaments are widely available. Materials such as carbon fiber and glass fiber, as well as edible materials like chocolate or pasta, can also be 3D printed.[17] In 2019, robotic construction company Apis Cor used its technology to build the world's largest 3D-printed building, a two-storey office in Dubai.[18] The tech is now consistently used in developing products for many industries and sectors that have adopted the technology into their everyday workflow.

3D PRINTING MARKET SIZE

Over the past few years, the world experienced unparalleled growth in the 3D printing market. The global 3D printing market grew by 21% in 2020 as compared to 2019 to an estimated value of $12.6 billion.[19] Transition from traditional manufacturing technologies was likely accelerated due to the COVID-19 lockdown. Businesses saw an accelerated adoption of additive manufacturing throughout 2020, with 65% of engineering businesses increasing their usage of 3D printing compared to 2019.[20] The 3D printing market is predicted to more than double in size over the next few years, ultimately reaching an estimated value of $37.2 billion in 2026.[21] A number of reasons explain this rapid growth, including: costs of the printing machines lowering significantly; machines becoming more efficient; more printing materials becoming available; and the rise in product variety.[22]

The venture capital market raised huge funds of over $1.1 billion for 3D printing startups in 2019 alone.[23] Since the start of the COVID-19 outbreak, the additive manufacturing market has continued to grow with many 3D printing equipment manufacturing companies at the forefront of the solution. Rapidly producing personal protective equipment, nasopharyngeal testing swabs, and even emergency-use medical devices. This agile manufacturing technology offers benefits that allow for a quick pivot of production lines.

"FIVE YEARS FROM NOW, YOU'LL SEE A LOT OF CONTRACT MANUFACTURERS THAT HAVE SCALED UP CONSIDERABLY AND HAVE HUNDREDS OF THESE SYSTEMS."[24] - ZACHARY MURPHREE, VP OF TECHNOLOGY PARTNERSHIPS AT VELO3D

Aside from pandemic-driven applications, the additive manufacturing market grew even further in 2020 and has been coming into play through 2023 as a solution to disrupted supply chains. Decentralizing production reduces the strain of global logistics, as additive manufacturing allows for manufacturing to take place on any site with the appropriate 3D printer and post-processing setup.[25] All these aspects have driven significant growth in the additive manufacturing industry. Although the technology has not yet achieved widespread mainstream use, we are witnessing a gradual upscaling of 3D printing consistent with the common pattern that arises with each new technological innovation.[26]

Additive manufacturing is expanding in many sectors and the market is responding. The industry grew by 7.5% to nearly $12.8 billion in 2020.[27] In 2020, while access to traditional manufacturing technologies was limited, 65% of engineering businesses used additive manufacturing more.[28] It is predicted that the tech will no longer be considered only as a rapid prototyping mechanism with 54% of engineering businesses increasing their usage of 3D printing for functional end-use parts in 2020.[29] At 73% of engineering businesses estimating they will produce or source more 3D printed parts, the annual growth of 3D printing is scheduled to be 21% between 2021 and 2030.[30] The 3D printing medical devices market is a major growth area and is projected to reach $5.1 billion by 2026 from $2.4 billion in 2021 at a CAGR of 16.3% during the forecast period.[31]

THE FORECASTED 3D PRINTING MARKET SIZE WORLDWIDE WAS $37.2 BILLION IN 2021, DOUBLE WHAT IT WAS IN 2016.[32]

THE GLOBAL ADDITIVE MANUFACTURING MARKET SIZE WAS $15.2 BILLION IN 2021 WITH A CAGR OF 21.75% FROM 2022 TO 2028.[33]

THE FORECASTED 3D PRINTING MEDICAL DEVICES MARKET SIZE WORLDWIDE WILL BE $5.1 BILLION IN 2026, COMPARED TO $2.4 BILLION IN 2021.[34]

PURSUING MANUFACTURING BREAKTHROUGHS

This innovative technology is already transforming business models across global manufacturing. As mentioned, we have only seen the beginning of the tech's influence. Ultimately, the full digital and physical blend of the 4IR could alter how companies conceive, design, produce, distribute, and repair products. Traditional manufacturing and 3D printing differences are a matter of choosing between subtractive or additive production methods. Additive technologies create from the bottom up rather than subtracting material that is then discarded. These technologies reduce materials cost by 90% and cut energy use in half. [35] More and more major manufacturers are turning to 3D printing, and suppliers are noticing these changes as well.

Additive manufacturing technologies reduce material costs by 90% and cut energy use in half.[36] Entrepreneurs and companies can profit from this trend as they innovate and improve manufacturing. They do this by either growing 3D businesses or implementing 3D printing in production and throughout supply chains. Signifying an exciting shift in global supply chains, 3D printing is set to replace traditional manufacturing methods in many areas. It is already seeing unprecedented adoption rates as well as aftermarket supply chain growth. 3D printing possibly has the highest impact out of all tech advancements in new product development applications across multiple industries.

"3D PRINTING IS GOING TO CONNECT US WITH OUR HERITAGE, AND IT'S GOING TO USHER IN A NEW ERA OF LOCALIZED, DISTRIBUTED MANUFACTURING THAT IS ACTUALLY BASED ON DIGITAL FABRICATION."[37]
AVI REICHENTAL, CEO OF 3D SYSTEMS

The COVID pandemic and its reverberating economic impact highlighted vulnerabilities in global supply chains across every major industry. Governments, institutions, and businesses around the world have been working to increase resilience in supply chains. Recent developments in this regard include the Biden Administration's joining of several large American companies to launch Additive Manufacturing Forward.[38] This voluntary, public-private compact was signed in May of 2022 and is comprised of founding companies GE Aviation, Siemens Energy, Lockheed Martin, Honeywell, and Raytheon Technologies.[39] It seeks to broaden 3D printing usage among US-based small and medium sized suppliers.

We have discussed the potential for 3D printing to aid in rebuilding coral reefs. The transition to this tech-based production model in sectors like healthcare and medical, buildings and infrastructure, and food and agriculture offers a wide range of beneficial impacts and business opportunities. Additive manufacturing solutions unlock vast possibilities in mobility systems in an array of industries such as automotive, aerospace, railway, and maritime. Siemens Mobility, for instance, is seizing these opportunities. Capitalizing on this business solution illustrates how Siemens' ability to 3D print tools and parts transformed their supply chain.

Many industries have taken advantage of 3D printing for manufacturing benefits. The tech is used alongside, or in place of, Computer Numerical Controlled (CNC) machining to produce precise iterations of complex, custom manufactured parts. 3D printing and CNC machining will be deployed throughout manufacturing chains, cutting the cost for making mid-to-large units of products, or one-off prototypes.[40] The additive manufacturing process can also cut down on waste, making for a more sustainable manufacturing process for any industry and reducing the carbon footprint for one of the most wasteful aspects of any industry.

IN BUSINESS

SIEMENS[41]

Initiative: Siemens Mobility with Stratasys 3D Printer
Headquarters: Munich, Germany

Meeting increased customer demand for customized parts, Siemens Mobility division required an alternative manufacturing solution to overcome the time and cost barriers associated with traditional low volume production (SDGs 9,12). This was exemplified during a recent project for the German transport services provider, the SWU Verkehr GmbH. With the integration of a Stratasys Fortus 900mc 3D printer into its production process, Siemens was able to address these challenges by 3D printing on-demand, customized parts rapidly and cost-effectively, on-demand. (SDG 17).[42] The collaboration reduced inventory costs for both the company and customers. As a result, the Mobility division is now able to respond more quickly to low volume customer demands while boosting its manufacturing flexibility. This has helped increase client satisfaction.

The company started printing spare parts and tools and opened a digital rail maintenance center in 2018 where hundreds of trains enter every month. The high volume puts pressure on the supply chain and requires robust manufacturing solutions to fulfill the wide-ranging needs of customers quickly and cost-effectively. By 3D printing on demand, Siemens is able to cut down manufacturing time up to 95%, lowering a typical six-week production cycle to only 13 hours, and reducing costs significantly at the same time (SDG 8).[43] The rail service center also leverages additive manufacturing to increase its tooling capabilities and overcome the lengthy lead times of traditional production methods. Michael Kuczmik, Head of Additive Manufacturing for Siemens Mobility GmbH Customer Service claims: "The ability to 3D print customized tools and spare parts whenever we need them, with no minimum quantity, has transformed our supply chain."[44]

3D PRINTING FOR GOOD

3D printing has a transformative impact on people and the planet. This will prove increasingly relevant both socially and economically. As one of the major emerging fields and technologies, businesses can employ this additive manufacturing tech as a force for good in a profitable way. Additive and 3D printing capabilities allow us to visualize a reinvented future of manufacturing, where unlocking new possibilities to create shared value is becoming more prevalent all around the world. This includes remote and hard-to-access regions.

With great prospects for the positive impact 3D printing can have on the environment, there are several benefits for good, including how the tech reduces manufacturing waste, lowers carbon footprints, and supports the circular economy. A defining feature of additive manufacturing (layer-by-layer) processes is reduction of manufacturing waste. By optimizing raw materials, 3D printing uses only the amount needed to build a product. Less manufacturing waste means that businesses save considerable amounts of resources. The tech also has the unique potential to democratize the production of goods, from food to medical supplies, to great coral reefs.

IN THE FUTURE, 3D PRINTING MACHINES COULD MAKE THEIR WAY INTO HOMES, BUSINESSES, DISASTER SITES, AND EVEN OUTER SPACE.

Because it does not rely on complex manufacturing and assembly supply chains, 3D printing facilitates localized production and reduces the need to transport goods manufactured in off-site locations. Empowering the circular economy, the production of printing filaments made from recycled materials as additive manufacturing inputs is becoming increasingly popular. This process adds value in terms of environmental benefits. The tech allows consumers to repair broken products by self-manufacturing spare parts on home printers or at local 3D printing centers. These services lengthen the life of original products, either by transforming them into a new raw material or by repairing and reusing them.

In addition to business growth in 3D printing tech applications, the support of governments and foundations is imperative. As the technology spreads, it continues to connect marginalized and difficult-to-reach populations with essential products. That said, this emerging technology has the potential to transform societies and the development sector. 3D printing carries huge promise for the future and, with the potential to make a further impact, is being deployed to progress many of the Global Goals.

3D PRINTING PROGRESSING THE GLOBAL GOALS

3D printing will undoubtedly accelerate achieving the SDGs in many ways, across a variety of sectors. Starting off with SDG 1 - No Poverty, 3D printing aids by significantly reducing the cost of buying products and components. It also enables cheaper and easier repairs through localized, inexpensive production of spare parts. Local production in poor areas of the world has several benefits. Not only does it give people access to print things they need, but implementing additive manufacturing capabilities on a small scale also makes it easier for those populations to upcycle waste. New Story, a Silicon Valley-based nonprofit that builds safe housing for those living in extreme poverty, worked with Icon, a construction tech company, to create a 3D printer that can build a house in a day for under $4,000.[45] The next page demonstrates that 3D printing has a significant impact on at least 9 of the 17 global goals.

ZERO HUNGER

This technology has great meaning, primarily in reducing food waste. Research suggests that humans waste approximately $1 trillion worth of food across the world annually.[46] Additive manufacturing and 3D printing meals play a part in reducing heaps of wasted food production through lowering costs and increasing availability.

One example of a company printing food is Novameat, a Barcelona-based startup that has created a ribeye steak alternative out of a blend of water, vegetable fat, and plant proteins using a 3D printer. This company is aiding the world in reducing greenhouse gas emissions while offsetting the massive water waste that results from the 346.14 million tons of meat that humans consume globally each year.[47] We will talk in more detail about 3D printing food to feed the world further along in the chapter.

GOOD HEALTH AND WELLBEING

Currently, 3D printing is a largely untapped market for healthcare. It is predicted there will be huge potential through additive manufacturing innovations to transform the quality and accessibility of healthcare around the world. By providing access to customized medical devices and prosthetics, medical services are improving the quality and comfort for users while reducing the costs of manufacturing them. In the most advanced utility, 3D printing is being developed to manufacture internal organs, meaning patients would no longer need to wait for a suitable donor. This concept is in development, but printing complete organs is highly complex and there are matters of ethics that will need reviewing.

3D bioprinting is the automated fabrication of multicellular tissue that is growing in use. For instance, $44 million US-based 3D bioprinting startup Organovo designs and creates functional human tissues with reproducible 3D tissues that accurately represent human biology.[48] Additive manufacturing companies, such as Markforged, enable businesses to design, manufacture, and fabricate innovative components. The Digital Forge - Markforged's industrial platform of 3D printers, software, and materials that enables manufacturers to print parts at the point-of-need – produces parts for a range of industries.[49] From prosthetics to prototypes, the core business model for the medical sector is to ensure healthcare professionals are supplied with specialized emergency medical devices and parts faster than ever before.

HEALTHTECH: 3D PRINTED VACCINES

There has also been serious movement towards printing vaccines. For instance, MIT invented a 3D printed vaccine which offers several immunizations at once.[50] The particles containing the immunization were constructed from a biodegradable material. This project will improve immunization rates for people without regular access to healthcare. The initiative has several benefits, such as allowing babies to take all their immunizations at once for the first two years of their lives.

Scientists at Stanford University and the University of North Carolina at Chapel Hill have created a 3D-printed vaccine patch that provides greater protection than a typical vaccine shot. Applying the vaccine patch directly to the skin allows vaccines to target the immune cells. In practice, the resulting immune response from the vaccine patch was ten times greater than a vaccine delivered into an arm muscle with a needle jab.[51] "In developing this technology, we hope to set the foundation for even more rapid global development of vaccines, at lower doses, in a pain- and anxiety-free manner,"[52] said lead study author and entrepreneur in 3D print technology Joseph M. DeSimone, professor of translational medicine and chemical engineering at Stanford University and professor emeritus at UNC-Chapel Hill.

DECENT WORK AND ECONOMIC GROWTH

Additive manufacturing makes local production possible, which lowers transportation costs and prevents the pollution that typically comes with transportation. The tech also enables remote areas and developing economies to create labor and entrepreneurial opportunities for local production and needs. Not only do these benefits enable supply chain movement with greater ease, but they also suggest the technology stimulates economic activity. We find an example of this with the additive manufacturing consultancy firm The Barnes Group Advisors (TBGA). The firm constructed an additive manufacturing production campus for the Pittsburgh International Airport, known as Neighborhood 91. It is the first development in the world to condense and connect all elements of the additive manufacturing and 3D printing supply chain onto one campus. Pennsylvania Senator Devlin Robinson stated in 2021, with regards to economic advancement, that "Neighborhood 91's ability to foster local employment while lowering costs and boosting production is one of a kind."[53] Specifically, the impact of this tech campus could lead to benefits of nearly 30% decrease in production costs for parts, and can also potentially reduce manufacturing lead times by 80%. [54] Neighborhood 91 may also have a positive impact on R&D productivity and innovation by allowing for a greater reduction in learning curves and under-utilized equipment.[55]

INDUSTRY, INNOVATION, AND INFRASTRUCTURE

Improving the share of GDP derived from industry, 3D printing provides an increasing number of economies access to the tools necessary to manufacture complex products. It also increases access for small-scale producers by dropping the capital cost of manufacturing complex products. Furthermore, the tech boosts innovation – spurring the development of more intricate designs and encouraging innovation in the materials used in product creation. Laser Melting Innovations (LMI) launched its highly economical laser-based 3D printer, Alpha 140, in 2018. LMI aims to overcome existing barriers to 3D printing adoption by making the technology easier to use through integrating its system with more cost-effective components, subsequently reducing a business's equipment investment. Because of these innovations, the company has been able to lower the price of its machine to under $118,500.[56] These compact metal 3D printers, due to functionality and low price, are a source of intrigue for research institutions and small businesses seeking to adopt metal 3D printing.

SUSTAINABLE CITIES AND COMMUNITIES

A shift toward 3D printing would allow more localized production. On-site product creation capability greatly cuts transport needs, and therefore simultaneously reduces air pollution and congestion in cities. The New Raw, a Rotterdam-based research and design studio, and Zero Waste Lab in Thessaloniki, a recycling facility that operates under The New Raw and Coca Cola's Zero Waste Future Program, partnered to turn plastic waste into 3D printable products and installations.[57] Recently, the group expanded its "Print Your City" initiative by inviting citizens to contribute their plastic waste and help design 3D printable street furniture to be placed around their city. Not only does this engage citizens in reusing their household plastic waste, it also helps in constructively transforming public spaces within cities. This business partnership aims to grow profits while at the same time involve participants in the recycling process by teaching them about the benefits of a circular economy.

RESPONSIBLE CONSUMPTION AND PRODUCTION

Sustainable 3D printed buildings are also a response to the realization of sustainable construction. Given its structural profile and closed-loop process that is additive rather than reductive, additive manufacturing produces less waste during production than more traditional manufacturing models. It also promotes the use of local products and the recycling of materials to create new products.

Shapeways, a leading global digital manufacturing platform with proprietary software in 3D printing, is a platform where 3D printing service providers can register and find potential customers while making a profit.[60] Designers with consumer and market expertise are also available to create custom models on request. Valued at $410 million, Shapeways is a novel service where businesses may start with nothing and end up with fully printed products.[61]

IN PROPTECH: 3D PRINTED PROPERTY - ARCHITECTURE AND BUILDINGS

Chinese company WinSun specializes in 3D printing architecture and the production of new building materials.[58] WinSun's 3D printing technology uses industrial solid waste to replace cement in the production of a new type of low-carbon building. With 17% annual growth of China's large construction industry, WinSun's mission is to use 3D printing to produce more than 22 million square meters of prefabricated building materials from industrial solid waste.[59] The "ink", or printer additive, is made from 100% recycled materials, saving 18,000 tons of cement in 2016 alone. The structures are highly energy-efficient, can withstand magnitude 9 earthquakes, and save significant time and resources during construction, with less waste and pollution of the environment.

TECH FOR GOOD

THE FILM

RESPONSIBLE CONSUMPTION AND PRODUCTION

- Reduce waste during production.
- Enable local production.
- Recycle and upcycle materials for reuse and new product development.

SUSTAINABLE CITIES AND COMMUNITIES

- Automate 3D-printed infrastructure and buildings.
- Facilitate quick printing of disaster housing and homeless shelters.
- Reduce transport needs and pollution.

INDUSTRY, INNOVATION AND INFRASTRUCTURE

- Increase access for small-scale producers.
- Allow more flexible, local on-demand manufacturing in remote areas.
- Boost innovation through optimized product design and packaging.

NO POVERTY

- Reduce the cost of making advanced products and components.
- Enable cheaper and easier repairs.
- Offer the opportunity of turning waste into products.

3D PRINTING

ZERO HUNGER

- Reduce the quantity of food wasted during production.
- Help to lower food costs and increase availability.
- Offer greater accessibility to printed foods.

DECENT WORK AND ECONOMIC GROWTH

- Increase global resource efficiency.
- Pioneer increases in economic productivity and localized production.
- Allow local production and repair.

GOOD HEALTH AND WELLBEING

- Provide access to customized medical devices, prosthetics, vaccines, and medications.
- Enable cheaper, customized, and faster bone-printing.
- Bioprint human tissue and organs that currently rely primarily on donors.

ENHANCING BUSINESS MODELS

3D printing is enhancing business models across industries and sectors. We are already seeing the tech's potential to significantly reduce costs, while at the same time enable sustainable and localized production. With the unparalleled ability to increase speed-to-market, lower costs and customize specialty parts, 3D printing is driving innovation and new technologies. Shifting the manufacturing landscape, this tech offers numerous benefits to 4IR businesses. Given the wide variety of materials that can be used in additive manufacturing, this technology can be catapulted forward as a positive force disrupting business models. Many currently established business sectors, including but not limited to food, healthcare, pharmaceuticals, industry, construction, and infrastructure, will benefit from implementing 3D printing capabilities at scale.

For small-scale businesses, the threshold for market entry with an impactful disruptive business model is significantly lower since there are likely no extra machines or input materials needed. For large companies, the 3D breakthrough means eliminating excess inventory, reducing warehouse costs, and minimizing wasteful overstocking. Throughout the entire supply chain, opportunities for shared value are present. Additive manufacturing enables the creation of tailored, personalized products and services by allowing new offerings to be both sustainable and customer-centric. We can view these possibilities as paving the way for creating additional business value.

Products can be programmed down to the particle and made specifically for both companies and individuals. The possibility for personalization, as well as mass production, is stronger than ever. With this trend growing, 3D printing serves as a cornerstone for businesses to seize value creation. One notable example is MetalFuse, recently launched by leading metal manufacturing company Raise3D, which allows for faster and more cost-effective 3D printing of customized metal parts.

BUSINESS ADVANTAGES OF 3D PRINTING IN MANUFACTURING FOR GOOD

Of the many advantages of 3D printing as a Tech for Good in business, a significant feature is rapid prototyping. Rapid prototyping is the ability to design, manufacture, and test a customized part in as little time as possible. This implies that the speed with which additive manufacturing capabilities enable production has significant business advantages. Also, if needed, the design can be modified without adversely affecting the speed of the manufacturing process. Not only does rapid prototyping speed up the product development process, it also spurs innovation. Designers can employ it to create complex and intricate models that greatly reduce the time between initial design and analysis.

With 3D printing techniques, a business can design parts, manufacture them in-house on a professional 3D printer, and test them – all within a short time. For both small and large businesses, this makes a significant difference. There are no long lead times typically associated with outsourcing complex manufacturing projects. This presents businesses with freedom and flexibility, allowing the inclusion of multiple materials into a single object and enabling mechanical properties to be used together. 3D printing enables quick and easy modification through product adaptation based on a constant stream of feedback. With the use of CAD and a 3D printer, this automated process not only uses the exact amount of material needed to develop a precise prototype, but it also mitigates the risk of making costly mistakes which saves money and time.[62]

In addition to the speed and flexibility of 3D printing, cost reduction is also a major bonus. For small production runs and applications, 3D printing is the most cost-effective manufacturing process.[63] Traditional prototyping methods like CNC machining and injection molding require various expensive machines. Further, they have much higher labor costs, as they require

IN BUSINESS

RAISE3D[64]

Initiative: MetalFuse
Headquarters: Irvine, California USA

Raise3D is a manufacturer of industrial-grade 3D printers. With flexible manufacturing processes, the tech company creates 3D printing products, services, and solutions that consistently serve small, medium, and large enterprises throughout the world. In mid 2021, Raise3D launched MetalFuse at leading 3D printing and additive manufacturing event TCT Asia in Shanghai, China.[65] MetalFuse is an end-to-end Metal Fused Filament Fabrication (FFF) tech solution that enables faster and more cost-effective 3D printing of metal parts (SDG 12).[66] In the process of MetalFuse development, the company compared its solution with various FFF printers for print accuracy, print size, repeatability, stability, and slicing software support optimized for Metal FFF. Raise3D thus improved the accuracy and mechanical properties of the printed samples (SDG 9).

This tech innovation enables local customers to produce tailor-made metal parts requiring far less time and at greatly reduced cost (SDGs 8,10). Edward Feng, Global CEO of Raise3D, said: "Our Raise3D MetalFuse system offers a solution to additive manufacturing of metal parts that is easier, safer, cleaner, cheaper, and faster than the current AM metal parts productions, making it accessible to everyone using those solutions."[67] Also in 2021, Raise3D announced the closing of a funding round raising $15.81 million, and plans to continue to launch the large-scale delivery of commercial MetalFuse systems through 2022 onward.[68]

experienced machine operators and technicians to run them. This contrasts with the 3D printing process where generally only one or two machines and fewer operators are needed to manufacture a part. There is far less waste material because the part is not carved out of a solid block as in subtractive manufacturing. The "ink" or material within the printer builds the part without any required additional tooling.

Because of the speed and lower costs of 3D printing, production processes are reduced, thereby leading to competitive advantage. Businesses can improve and enhance production, allowing them to deliver better products in a shorter amount of time. Further, 3D printing also allows for cost-effective market testing. Obtaining feedback from potential customers and investors on a tangible product eliminates the risk of large upfront expenditures for prototyping.[69] The nature of 3D printing promotes step-by-step production which guarantees enhancement of the design and potential for higher quality products. That is, parts are printed in succession, thereby enabling each successive individual part to be monitored and ensuring errors are caught in real time. Beyond the reduction in wasted materials, the tech also increases the consistency of quality of the parts produced. Because of these advantages of quality and consistency, 3D printing allows businesses to mitigate risks in manufacturing.

3D PRINTING TECHNOLOGY AFFORDS PRODUCT DESIGNERS THE ABILITY TO VERIFY PRODUCT PROTOTYPES BEFORE MAKING SUBSTANTIAL INVESTMENTS IN MANUFACTURING THAT CAN BE POTENTIALLY COSTLY AND INEFFICIENT.

These factors make 3D printing systems far more accessible to a wider range of people than traditional manufacturing processes. With 3D printing, fewer parts need outsourcing for manufacturing. This equals truly sustainable manufacturing through reduced environmental impact. Additional sustainability benefits include input materials used in 3D printing being generally recyclable.[70] For small production runs, localized prototyping, small business, and educational use, 3D printing often proves vastly superior to other industrial methods. This type of on-site 3D printing transforms the way companies develop and produce parts and prototypes, as exemplified by BCN3D's collaboration with Spanish shoe company Camper to innovate and recreate in response to market trends.

The technology is enabling Manufacturing as a Service (MaaS) and enhancing service-based business models. 3D printing allows parts to be produced from a digital file, and most of the workflow is data driven. Professor Ian Campbell at Loughborough University illuminates the potential of 3D printing compared to traditional manufacturing: "Additive manufacturing can do some incredible things in terms of creating complex geometries, but to expect one person or even a team of people to sit down and create those sorts of geometry would create a real bottleneck if it was all being done using conventional tools."[71] This superior network approach that eliminates tooling allows for much more efficient production, with a reduced ecological footprint in resources, waste, and emissions because of the local production aspect and a sharing economy business model. When developed and implemented correctly, 3D printing could turn out to be a potential solution for many of our current global challenges.

GLOBAL GOALS' GROWTH OPPORTUNITIES

At present, additive manufacturing solutions are used throughout many sectors. The tech's transformation has taken off and the potential for market integration is growing. However, the debate on conceptualization and implementation remains, with the main setback for 3D printing being that it is still not implemented on a large scale. Yet, this is changing rapidly.

IN BUSINESS

BCN3D[72]

Initiative: Camper In-house 3D-printed Footwear Design
Headquarters: Barcelona, Spain

Spanish shoe company Camper employed its technical department to streamline their process of developing new collections by integrating desktop 3D printers (SDGs 9, 12). In-house 3D printing has significantly increased the pace of Camper's design process, allowing for more creative freedom and accelerating their workflow while keeping costs down (SDGs 8, 10).[73] The design team typically has a three-month deadline to create each new collection, giving them little time to prepare. Therefore, 3D printing offers a fast and cost-efficient solution which allows for testing a product and maintaining high-quality standards before it goes to market. Before the company started working with in-house 3D printing, they were out-sourcing the production of physical models.

This process was slow and expensive, taking up to two weeks to receive a proto-type, reducing iteration to the minimum, with most of the work being done through 2D digital designs limited to a screen. With various 3D printers on-site, including the incorporation of several BCN3D Sigma and Sigmax 3D printers, Camper has new designs immediately.[74] This is a huge advantage for designers, because they can print a shoe model in 3D the next day. "With various 3D printers on site, Camper's designers now have new designs literally in the palms of their hand,"[75] said Xavier Martínez Faneca, CEO of BCN3D. Enhancing creative possibilities for Camper, this tech offers a significant acceleration of new product development and a cost-efficient solution for the company's iterative design process.

The impressive market numbers mentioned earlier in this chapter indicate this shift. Some SDG growth markets - market segments that will unlock and provide new and fast-growing market opportunities - are driving the circular economic business model. 3D printing is enabling the circular economy throughout a wide range of business sectors, including healthcare, construction, infrastructure, and food. We'll shed some light on the opportunities for these markets now.

IMPROVING WASTE MANAGEMENT SYSTEMS

Globally, there was initially the straight economy model. Simply put, in this frame, the product was contrived, traded, and then discarded when it reached its expiration date. In contrast to that model, we have the circular economy that is centered on renewable, recyclable, and reusable products. Additive manufacturing creates a range of innovative opportunities to seize the immense value of the transition from a straight to a circular economy. The global opportunity for a shift to a circular economy is predicted to be approximately $4.5 trillion per year in the next decade, and as much as $25 trillion by 2050.[76] In Europe alone such an approach could boost resource productivity by 3% to the year 2030, which would save in monetary value up to $710 billion a year, and $2.1 trillion more in other economic benefits.[77]

WHAT IS A CIRCULAR ECONOMY?

A circular economy refers to an economic system that eliminates waste and aims for continuous use of resources. William McDonough popularized the concept with his book "Cradle to Cradle," after which it grew rapidly in use.[78] The circular economy concept emulates the cyclical systems of the natural environment. Thus, humans should take note of this natural process and engage anew, adopting nature's cyclical flow – hence the word circular economy.

Worldwide business operations are aiming to reduce their ecological footprint in terms of resources and waste. Companies that bring forward solutions endeavor to do so by using 3D printing in a smart way – by tapping into lucrative growth markets across business sectors. For instance, the tech solution dramatically reduces the production of scrap waste – sometimes by as much as 90% compared to conventional manufacturing.[79] This percentage can further improve if scraps from the production process are reused. As a result, we have in our hands maximum impact with the additive manufacturing process, as production uses waste and secondary materials rather than virgin materials.

THE 3D PRINTING PROCESS ALONE CAN HELP SLASH GLOBAL CO2 EMISSIONS BY AS MUCH AS 5% BY 2025.[80]

Thanks to the advancement of 3D tech, the intensive process of decomposition, such as that of plastic water bottles, can now be made easier. We have 3D printers today, including the ProtoCycler[81] from ReDeTec and the Filabot Reclaimer,[82] that efficiently break down single-use plastics. A decomposition process that took 450 years carries less weight as it has, since advanced technology now enables bottles to be transformed into the raw materials for additive manufacturing to build its 3D prints. In this way, we upcycle waste into valuable materials. The

IN BUSINESS

REDETEC[83]

Initiative: ProtoCycler, 3D Printing Waste Reducing Machine
Headquarters: Toronto, Ontario Canada

ProtoCycler is an all-in-one recycling system for 3D printers, which allows businesses to make their own filament from recycled waste and virgin plastic pellets. The ProtoCycler machine reduces the amount of waste associated with 3D printing (SDG 12). To eliminate waste after printing, this company created an additive manufacturing solution that is also a recycling system with the ability to recycle the majority of the most commonly used plastics and other additive materials on the market. It is the only 3D printer on the market that has a grinder included, which recycles 3D printer waste and turns it back into filament. ReDeTec also uses its own patented extrusion technology, with fully automatic built-in diameter feedback that produces exact 3D printer filament for every use (SDG 9). By allowing users to create their own spools from virgin plastics, businesses can reduce the cost of 3D printer filament spools by up to 80% (SDG 16).[84] This saves hundreds or thousands of dollars per year on printing costs. For the purposes of eliminating waste, the technology has the potential to be widely used across communities and in sectors ranging from education to aerospace (SDGs 11,17).

MEDTECH3D[85] AND AXIAL3D[86]

Initiative: A Catalogue of 3D Printing Healthcare Services for Practitioners
Headquarters: Belfast, Ireland and Durban, South Africa

MedTech3D and Axial3D are two medical technology companies who partnered to distill focus on 3D printing in association with healthcare, while bringing affordable medical imaging and 3D printing to clinicians in South Africa (SDG 17).[87] One of their main applications, and an industry they have impacted using the technology, is surgical planning (SDGs 3,9). This helps in converting medical images like CTs or MRIs into 3D models and printed as patient-specific anatomical models. Risk is reduced and surgeons perform an operation more efficiently by using a patient-specific model to plot surgical procedures (SDG 10). Such models are provided by the UK-based Axial3D which offers clinicians patient-specific 3D printed anatomical models derived from their medical images. The company's unique platform allows for these models to be transformed and produced at rapid rates of under 48 hours. [88] Hospitals are benefitting from these patient-specific prints, especially for their emergency surgical procedures.

ProtoCycler machine, developed by Canadian company ReDeTec, reduces the amount of waste associated with 3D printing. To reduce wastage after printing, this company created an additive manufacturing solution that also serves as a recycling system. More specifically, it recycles most of the commonly used plastics and other additive materials on the market, birthing a unique business model for 3D printing.

One cannot underplay the importance of recycling plastic. At present, we only recycle 8% to 9%, and plastics continue suffocating our oceans as well as land.[89] If humans continue this cycle, we will have more plastic swimming in our seas than fish by 2050.[90] Taking bold action is more necessary than ever. Dutch company 3Devo has launched a machine that allows businesses to create filament directly from this plastic waste, boosting the circular economy system that empowers users to create their own 3D printing material.[91] 3Devo's innovation, the SHR3D IT machine, is capable of transforming plastic waste into 3D printable granules.[92] In just one hour, SHR3D IT is able to recycle 5.1 kilograms of plastic. In addition to this innovative system, 3Devo launched the Filabot Reclaimer machine that benefits businesses by creating filament directly from these granules. In this way, the startup gives a boost to a complete circular economy system that allows users to create their own 3D printing material.

3D PRINTING CAN ADDRESS THE UP TO 1.3 BILLION TONS OF FOOD WASTE ENTERING THE WASTE STREAM THAT CAUSES ECONOMIC LOSSES OF OVER $750 BILLION.[93]

3D printing can also address food waste. Globally, we either lose or waste one-third of the food produced, which adds up to 1.3 billion tons to the waste stream and causes economic losses of over $750 billion.[94] One technological innovation worth mentioning is Uprinting Food, spun into the Dutch company of the same name. Uprinting Food creates an innovative way to use residual food flows and create delicious-tasting and looking meals. By blending and combining the different ingredients from residual food flows, purees are created, which then are used to 3D print solid meal options. These prints are baked and dehydrated for crunch and longevity. This Dutch Tech for Good initiative aims to help restaurants analyze and reuse food waste by 3D printing it into tasty snacks.[95] Additive manufacturing further has the potential to eliminate the need for extensive transport, storage, and travel required by traditional food production.

FOSTERING HEALTH AND WELLBEING

From a medical perspective, the business of 3D printing to create value for SDGs 1, 3 and 11 is a vast and largely untapped market. Additive manufacturing tech advancements allow healthcare professionals to attain instant access to prosthetics, organs, and tissues for patients. 3D printing for medical procedures, also known as bioprinting, combines 3D printing tech and biomaterials. Replicating parts that imitate natural tissues, bones, and blood vessels in the body, bioprinting is still a relatively recent concept. It has been used in medicine since around 2007 and has been employed to help study or recreate almost every tissue, cartilage, and organ in the body.[96] If this is our present, imagine the future.

3D PRINTED BONE GRAFTS AND BONE SUBSTITUTES ARE SET TO MAKE UP $4.15 BILLION OF THE SURGICAL MARKET BY 2026.[97]

Burn victims who do not have enough undamaged skin to harvest can find some relief with bioprinter-enabled wound care and healing. Bioprinters gather a patient's wound and cell information from a scanner, then create new skin that can be grafted onto the patient.[98] Human bone technological advancement is in high demand in global healthcare as well, and we have reached the point where one bone graft is performed by a surgeon on patients every minute of every day.[99] Back and knee surgeries alone account for thousands of bone grafts annually, and the numbers are rising. In global terms, bones are set to make up $4.15 billion of the surgical market by 2026. If we bring 3D printing into this equation, it becomes a game-changing market solution and generates healthy profits for healthcare investments.

Among the extraordinary benefits for 3D printers are the ways in which they also incorporate business success into practical use for customers. For example, Fasotec, a Japanese 3D printing company, and Tokyo's Hiroo Ladies clinic began a service that produces replicas of fetuses by scanning a pregnant woman's abdomen.[100] The fetus is printed with clear filament to model out the semi-formed baby inside, rather than the typical ultrasound photos. A 3D printer is then used to construct the model. The baby's position, posture, and appearance look exactly as it does in the mother's uterus. Fasotec is only one example. There are several other important business opportunities for medical 3D printing. Large players such as Stratasys and 3D Systems are certifying an end-to-end process for producing medical parts with newly developed materials. They are using their printing technology and offering printing services to customers such as hospitals.

MAXILLOFACIAL PROSTHETICS ARE TRADITIONALLY VERY LABOR-INTENSIVE AND EXPENSIVE TO PRODUCE, AND 3D PRINTING OFFERS A WAY TO LOCALIZE THE PROCESS AS WELL AS CUT COSTS.[101]

3D Systems Precision Healthcare Solutions in another HealthTech business founded on the ability to create highly personalized 3D printed medical devices and patient-specific surgical simulation.[102] This tech solution features direct printing of individualized implants and customized instrumentation, while creating healthcare market shifts that are taking place throughout the world. Not only increasing speed and reducing cost, the company's 3D printed medical products also transform and enrich lives for a healthier population. 3D Systems partners with surgeons, healthcare professionals, medical device manufacturers, and medical teaching staff to offer a range of precision healthcare solutions. These services include virtual reality simulators, 3D printed anatomical models, virtual surgical planning, patient-specific surgical guides, instrumentation, and implants. Helping patients all over the world through technological advancement for good, 3D Systems generates products that assist a variety of critical health concerns.[103]

THE 3D PRINTING IN HEALTHCARE MARKET IN THE MIDDLE EAST AND AFRICA IS EXPECTED TO REACH A VALUE OF $1.97 BILLION BY 2023, EXPANDING AT A CAGR OF 21.82% FROM 2018 TO 2023.[104]

It is worth marveling how a number of orthopedic implant surgeries including hip replacement, shoulder replacement, knee replacement, and spinal implant procedures are becoming increasingly significant across the world. Predictions state that the global orthopedic 3D printing devices market will register a compound annual growth rate of nearly 26% between 2019 and the end of 2023.[105] Because of this large market growth, several vendors are now offering 3D printing technologies to meet the increasing demand for orthopedic implants. This process enables hospitals to use patient-specific prints for emergency surgical procedures.

Kenya is another country that has been excelling in terms of growing and developing with 3D printing technology. A 20-year-old electrical engineering student from Nairobi University, Alois Mbutura, developed a minuscule vein finder in the hope of addressing infant mortality and improving vaccination services. This tiny device was 3D printed using a MakerBot 3D printer. Medical startup Kijenzi Medtech is also using 3D printing technology to provide medical solutions to Kenya's very rural, remote clinics. This inspiring endeavor is looking at training nursing staff to print components on-site by downloading files and sending them to the printer. [106] Micrive Infinite is doing its part to spur more homegrown medical solutions to help and improve healthcare in Kenya as well.

IN BUSINESS
MICRIVE INFINITE[107]
Initiative: Homegrown Medical Solutions
Headquarters: Nairobi, Kenya

Micrive Infinite is spearheading localized medical solutions to improve healthcare in Kenya (SDGs 3,9). The company is integrating engineering, 3D printing technology, and medical research to transform surgery, treatment, and patient rehabilitation. The business model is based on 3D printing prototypes that help surgeons understand a patient's medical issues before surgery can be done. It is a type of "compass for surgeons" planning for accurate execution of surgeries that can help patients heal faster as well as ease costs (SDG 4). Although started with only an idea, the business has grown since 2017 and grossed 25 million in Kenyan shillings (approximately $220,000 to 230,000).[108] The business now has four employees handling various tasks, from sourcing for business to making the prototype that is delivered to surgeons (SDG 12).

FRAMLAB[109]
Initiative: Homed, Shelter for the Homeless
Headquarters: Brooklyn, New York USA

Issues have arisen due to the reduction in the budget allocated for investments in building and preserving affordable housing in New York City (SDG 11). Over 60,000 people are seeking refuge in homeless shelters every night (SDGs 3,10).[110] To address this urban issue, Framlab proposed the innovative Homed scheme to accommodate the growing number of people without shelter in NYC (SDGs 1,12). The limited number and expensive cost of available land has led Framlab to utilize what they have termed "vertical lots," formed by building walls to create temporary shelters. "Although almost every square foot of space in NYC has been claimed and utilized, there still manages to exist an abundant amount of "vertical lots" sitting idle," explains Andreas A. Tjeldflaat, Founder and Design Director of the agency behind Homed. [111] "These are the blank sidewalls of buildings that emerge and disappear as new developments come and go." This system is constructed of scaffolding onto windowless facades across the city, and fashioned into hexagon-shaped modules. Each pod houses one person, in order to maintain their privacy and safety, compared to conditions in the communal facilities often provided by shelters. As a single-person housing system, the 3D-printed modules allow furniture, storage, lighting and appliances to be integrated into the structure – resulting in a minimal space, tailored to the specific needs and desires of its residents (SDG 9).[112] A viable solution to New York City's shelter challenges, Framlab's Homed has the potential to save millions of dollars.

CITIES AND INFRASTRUCTURE SOLUTIONS

We have entered an unprecedented era where a variety of buildings and houses can now be printed. House printing has in fact already been demonstrated as a solution for low-income needs. Companies such as ICON and New Story have promoted a low-cost 3D printed house for only $4,000.[113] Beyond this 3D printing technology being inexpensive, it is also time effective. It boasts capabilities of constructing a single story, 600 to 800 square feet home in under 24 hours. In contrast, traditional manual labor construction would extend this period to anywhere from four to seven months.[114] Imagine how we can combat homelessness via this low-cost housing tech. In developing areas of large cities, planners will establish 3D printing business opportunities to combat homelessness. And what is more, undertaking projects like these has already become a reality. Considering these housing heroics, we can call 3D printing, when applied for good, a truly life-saving technology.

WE CAN CALL 3D-PRINTING, WHEN APPLIED FOR GOOD, A TRULY LIFE-SAVING TECHNOLOGY.

A prime example is the creative design agency Framlab that developed 3D printed pods to shelter New York's homeless.[115] The company is taking action to address housing constraints in New York City. Spending on homelessness more than doubled to $3.2 billion between fiscal years 2014 and 2019, and homeless shelter operations during that same time period went from $326 million to $666 million.[116] It is further predicted the city will need at least $260 million more in funding annually beginning in 2024 to support homeless shelters, outreach, and housing vouchers.[117] Framlab's pod project, called Homed, is a tech solution consisting of a prefabricated outer aluminum shell with 3D printed polycarbonate interior modules and tailored with a customizable range of amenities.

The US company ICON produced the first 3D-printed tiny house. This 400 square feet home, printed in less than 48 hours, is rented for only $300 a month.[118] The company's Community First! Village in Texas provides financial support programs for residents and aims to house 40% of Austin's homeless population.[119] ICON has delivered over two dozen 3D printed homes and structures to date across the US and Mexico, the most completed by any tech construction company.[120] Numerous projects are underway to deliver 3D printed social housing, disaster relief housing, and mainstream housing developments. In the future, there is hope that the materials applied will become increasingly sustainable compared to the traditional concrete still being used on some projects. On a positive trajectory, replacement alternatives are already being looked into for 3D printing housing.

THE 3D PRINTED COMMUNITY FIRST! VILLAGE IN AUSTIN, TEXAS PROVIDES SUPPORT PROGRAMS FOR RESIDENTS AND AIMS TO HOUSE 40% OF THE CITY'S HOMELESS POPULATION.[121]

We find another application of 3D-printed homes in disaster-affected areas where housing is needed quickly and at low cost. Often these printed homes are able to withstand severe storms and earthquakes, thus being disaster-resilient. Remaining sturdy in the face of a hurricane, flooding, or other disasters, 3D printed houses hold up to extreme weather brought on by climate change that we are witnessing more and more. The company We Print Homes constructs technologically advanced design-for-durability printed houses.[122] Their superior strength can withstand the forces of nature, while both materials as well as design aim for living in safety and comfort to improve the lives of residents.

Additive manufacturing derived single homes are indeed progress in societal development, but imagine printed neighborhoods. Charitable tech firm New Story and two Mexican construction companies are building just that - 3D-printed neighborhood of homes in Tabasco, Mexico.[123] The secure 500-square-foot houses each comprise a living room, kitchen, bathroom and two bedrooms. These will be available to 50 families, some of whom earn as little as $3 a day. Giant 3D printer Vulcan II builds these homes in pairs, taking around 24 hours of total print time per house.[124] This rapid construction is possible due to a specially mixed concrete that hardens quickly. While this is an impressive example where we see smart progress, we need to take one more step to replace traditional concrete with more sustainable source material that eliminates negative carbon footprint. The silver lining is that these homes too are built on reinforced foundations and have been designed to withstand earthquakes, which are common in the region.

CHARITABLE TECH FIRM NEW STORY HAS BUILT MORE THAN 2,500 HOMES IN HAITI, EL SALVADOR, BOLIVIA, AND MEXICO AND POSITIVELY IMPACTED OVER 14,00 LIVES.[125]

INNOVATING FOOD SYSTEMS

The 3D printing food industry is expected to have a massive impact on our economy. This new-age food market is predicted to reach $525.6 million by the end of 2023 globally, rising at an annual rate of about 46% through the year.[126] Specifically, it can bridge the gap between small and large-scale players within the food industry.[127] The additive manufacturing food market will give consumers access to more choice and accessibility to meals and nourishment and may feed the hungry in poor areas of the world. Furthermore, 3D printing meals will promote safer food production processes, healthier nutrient options, and more environmentally viable methods of food production for all sectors.

$1 TRILLION OF FOOD IS WASTED GLOBALLY EACH YEAR. 3D PRINTING WILL HELP ENSURE NO MATERIAL IS WASTED.

We have already talked about food wastage, which necessitates a discussion about related programs. Innovative startups, such as Genetics, are battling food waste by converting it into biodegradable plastics. Using the power of biotechnology, machine learning, and microbial engineering, the team at Genetics can manufacture a form of plastic from food waste that creates more sustainable toys, medical devices, and 3D printer filament. With a direct link to the circular economy, this tech solution fuels the possibility of bringing excess food to our homes and hospitals instead of wasting it. This is similar to what we have already talked about with Uprinting. Another very exciting possibility for 3D-printed food is its ability to be customized to individual needs. For example, additives can be formulated with extremely high precision to create foods with specific nutrient content. Even NASA is developing a 3D food printer that produces meals from powdered proteins, carbohydrates, macronutrients, and micronutrients.[128]

AT THE SINGAPORE UNIVERSITY OF TECHNOLOGY AND DESIGN (SUTD), RESEARCHERS ARE WORKING ON 3D PRINTING A NEW KIND OF FOOD INK WHICH CAN BE USED TO MAINTAIN FOOD STRUCTURE.[129]

The highly advanced printers can also modify textures for food, making it easier to swallow or chew. This has great value for elderly people. By printing the elderly's favorite dishes, everything from taste to texture to nutritional value can be recreated and subsequently enjoyed. Additionally, since food can be printed in every shape and form, some pleasure in consumption and visual value can be brought back to eating, just as in the original tasty nutritional product or meal. At Singapore

Polytechnic, for instance, researchers are exploring the idea of printing food for elderly that they crave. With several options, 3D printed meals can range from vegetables to meats to seafoods like crab. Lowering sugar and enriching foods with the vitamins and calcium elderly people need, ingredients added to 3D printers can be engineered to render healthier meals.

Nanyang Technological University is also collaborating with Anrich3D to create innovative 3D printed food products in the form of exciting edible treats like chocolates and pastries.[130] The company plans to bring 3D printed food to the market for both consumers and businesses in an effort to print out precise amounts of required ingredients for optimal nutrition – think mathematically optimized meals.[131] As a larger goal, Anrich3D will eventually mass-produce personalized meals such as burgers, pizzas, and sandwiches, leveraging apps and vending machines that allow customers to choose their own food ink ingredients.[132] Additionally, the Europe-based project PERFORMANCE uses the technology to recreate elderly's favorite dishes.[133] Beyond use for the elderly, this new type of food manufacturing could prove pivotal in relieving world hunger. This prospect can involve abundant and easily sourced food types rich in protein and antioxidants, such as algae.[134]

ADDRESSING RISKS AND CHALLENGES ON THE ROAD AHEAD

The 3D printing process eliminates many steps used in traditional manufacturing and facilitates the creation of complex structural components. The advancements made in this tech have led to significant success in the areas of rapid prototyping and product development. However, 3D printers are still potentially hazardous and wasteful. Moreover, their economic, political, societal, and environmental impacts have not been extensively studied because they have not yet been tested over the long term.

According to research, during the manufacturing process, 3D printers consume approximately 50 to 100 times more energy than injection molding – the process of melting plastic with heat or lasers.[135] For mass production, 3D printers consume a lot of energy and are therefore better suited for small batch production. 3D printers also use high-voltage power supplies, specialized equipment, and parts which make them difficult to use and manage; although improvements have been made in this regard and using this additive manufacturing tech is becoming a more viable solution.[136]

WITHOUT RISK THERE IS NO REWARD. BUT, WE NEED TO UNDERSTAND THE POTENTIALLY WASTEFUL NATURE OF 3D PRINTERS.

Equipment and materials are often costly, which make the technology expensive. Industrial grade 3D printers remain very expensive, costing hundreds of thousands of dollars, thus significantly raising the initial expenses of using the technology. For a single machine, capital investment starts in the tens of thousands of dollars and can increase to as high as hundreds of thousands of dollars or more.[137] Also, the materials used in commercial-grade 3D printers are often costly compared to product materials used in traditional manufacturing.

The potential for harmful emissions also poses a problem for the proliferation of the tech. 3D printers used in enclosed places such as homes can generate toxic emissions and carcinogenic particles. For instance, studies show that 3D desktop computers could emit large numbers of ultrafine particles and some hazardous volatile organic compounds during printing.[138] Also noteworthy is that popular and cheap 3D printers use a plastic filament. Although using raw plastic reduces waste generation, the machines still leave unused or excess plastic in the print beds. The plastic byproduct ends up in landfills, negatively affecting the environment.

IN BUSINESS

PERFORMANCE[139]

Initiative: Printing Nutritious Food for Elderly People
Headquarters: Bremerhaven, Germany

The European-based project PERFORMANCE (Personalized Food for the Nutrition of Elderly Consumers) was an initiative that leveraged the advantage of additive manufacturing technology to recreate meals for the elderly. The project involved many European countries, including Italy, Austria, Holland, and Denmark, and is run by the German-based food innovation company Biozoon Food Innovations. It was a multidisciplinary collaboration between SMEs in the field of food products and ingredients, a high-tech food equipment manufacturer, catering services, software developers, food and packaging technology providers, research institutes (food technology, process technology, packaging, and logistics) and nursing homes (SDG 17).[140] The partners developed an inkjet-based machine that 3D prints soft, appealing, and nutritious meals based on six components: pasta, potatoes, salmon, chicken, broccoli, and green peas (SDGs 3,9).

The initiative demonstrated success with 3D printed food in nursing homes, and now is innovating classical dishes in their original shape and form. By taking pureed ingredients and leveraging 3D printing technology, PERFORMANCE created healthy food for elderly persons living in nursing homes, ambient assisted living facilities, or at home (SDGs 10,11). For nursing homes and other patients, the initiative made use of the technology's ability for personalization, to fit necessary nutrients as well as portion size. Before the personalized food was printed, PERFORMANCE used an algorithm programmed by the German IT company Sanalogic to monitor the nutritional value of each patient on a weekly basis.

FOR ALL THE GOOD 3D PRINTING PROMISES, WE CANNOT DISMISS THE POTENTIAL OF THE TECH BEING USED TO DO HARM.

Perhaps the most dangerous aspect of 3D printers is the ease of creating weaponry. 3D knives, guns, explosives, and any other dangerous items are becoming more common among criminals and terrorists who are making such weapons without being detected.[141] Some criminal organizations have already used 3D printing technology to create card readers for bank machines.

Copyright infringements and counterfeiting are among the most significant disadvantages of 3D printing. This means that anyone with a design blueprint can forge products very quickly.[142] As time goes on, 3D printing technology will become more user-friendly and cost-effective. It is possible that the design and production of unlicensed weaponry and counterfeiting will then increase.

THE PRESENT SURGE IN POSITIVELY DISRUPTIVE TECH IS NOT PROGRESSING WITHOUT RISK. WE NEED TO BE AWARE OF THE POTENTIAL PITFALLS.

As with many of the other tech innovations in this book, human job losses and market shifts are inevitable. This additive manufacturing technology can make product designs and prototypes in a matter of hours, as it uses only one single step. It thus eliminates several stages that are used in subtractive manufacturing. Because of this, adopting 3D printing eliminates labor costs and may decrease manufacturing jobs. 3D printing, similar to other emerging positively disruptive techs, thus raises the prospect of technological unemployment. This is more threatening for countries that rely on a large number of low-skill jobs; the decline in manufacturing jobs due to 3D printing could dramatically affect the economy.[143]

WE HAVE

IMAGINED

The field of 3D printing is advancing rapidly. 3D tech innovation creates new values and transformative prospects in a diverse array of sectors. We have imagined the miraculous things 3D printing can achieve, such as 3D printing coral to preserve and restore our ocean's reefs by ,and 3D printing houses to provide shelter for homeless people and citizens of disaster-stricken regions. From healthcare to construction to food distribution, this 4IR additive manufacturing tech innovation benefits business, science, and society. Its contributions are impactful across the Global Goals, addressing several including no poverty, zero hunger, and responsible consumption and production.

As this chapter has depicted, next-gen manufacturing characterizes the blend of additive and traditional manufacturing with powerful results. In the world of 3D printed products, supply chains become shorter. We will be able to produce materials ourselves, on-site, on demand, at a lower price. While there are challenges and social anxieties associated with this tech in terms of socio-political to environmental impacts, we are constantly progressing toward resolving them. With its increasingly accessible and useful applications, 3D printing has unprecedented capabilities to propel our sustainable future

We have imagined 3D Printing for Good.

TECH FOR GOOD

THE FILM

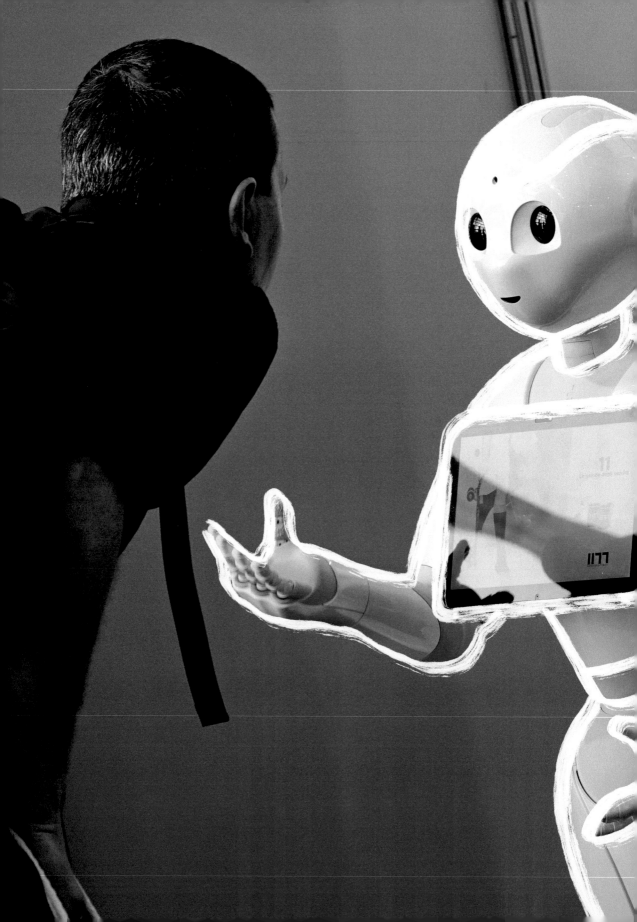

ROBOTICS 4

ROBOTIC ASSISTANCE IS ENHANCING OUR LIVES. ROBOTS HAVE THE POTENTIAL TO BECOME OUR ALLIES AND EVEN OUR FRIENDS.

WE ONLY NEED TO

IMAGINE

Imagine helping children with behavioral or mental disorders cope with daily life more easily. Imagine enabling them to learn in a way that is comfortable and reassuring for them. Envision facilitating interactions and communications in ways that match their needs. Imagine how kids suffering from disorders or struggling in the crucial developmental phase of their lives would benefit from learning valuable skills that will carry over into adulthood. More specifically, imagine a child with autism embracing a possibility that is beyond the current scope of treatments and services available to patients with disabilities, be it in hospitals or other facilities.

It is now estimated that one in 100 children is affected by Autism Spectrum Disorder, and this number has been steadily increasing since the turn of the millennium.[1] A particularly disheartening point is that 63% of parents do not believe their child on the spectrum has access to the educational resources that would best support them with social and emotional development. Autistic children frequently wrestle with themselves to understand social and emotional cues. Addressing these developmental aspects at a young age has dramatic, long-term positive benefits. In this context, progressive and engaging teaching resources for children with autism is vital.

Advanced technologies, specifically robotics, are powerful tools for kids with autism. There are already multiple friendly robots on the market to assist children in a variety of ways. Robots become companions, especially during times of isolation, which has unfortunately risen since the COVID-19 pandemic. Robots prove to make children feel safe. A robot does not care if you answer a question wrong, and it will never get bored, angry, or upset. Even the most compassionate human teachers cannot always control their tone of voice and facial expressions, but you can rely on a robot for consistency. Interactive robots helping with autism and other disorders are called "social robots." These social robots have exceptional skills in terms of really listening to what people are saying and even being able to read facial micro-expressions.

These comforting robots are developed to read all expression variations, including picking up on tiny verbal or physical cues and acting on them. Thus, even if autistic children are unable to articulate themselves, the robot is programmed to understand. Moxie, for instance, is a new social robot launched by tech startup Embodied, Inc. When creating Moxie, a social companion for children aged six to nine, Embodied designed the robot "to help promote social, emotional, and cognitive development through everyday play-based learning and captivating content."[2] Moxie is unique because it specializes in concentrating on one specific thing to keep its interactions focused, rather than trying to be a generalized robot friend.[3]

As a growing trend, there is now even more robot help on the way for kids. A Hong Kong-based initiative, Robot for Autism Behavioral Intervention (RABI), developed an educational program using role-playing robots to help children on the spectrum improve their social skills. Designed for people with autism between three and 18 years old, RABI aims to help them become more sociable and resolve issues such as conflicts and bullying.[4] We are witnessing robots acting as companions to children with special needs to bridge the gap between the world of technology and humanity's social universe. Through these initiatives, learning is more fun for children in addition to helping educators more effectively achieve learning goals.

Imagine educational robots providing stimulation and fun mental challenges to keep children engaged and entertained while educating them at the same time. Working with them results in improved creative problem-solving, communication, and interpersonal skills among students. While social robots for autistic children still have plenty to learn and require further development, the growing field of robotics is already showing promising signs. These tech friends will undoubtedly be made to play a greater role in supporting children.

Imagine helping children with developmental disabilities. This is Robotics for Good.

Marga Hoek

4 EXPLORING ROBOTICS

AI and mechanics tech has emerged as a pioneer in paving the way for robotics. This chapter explores the history as well as the business opportunities of the robotics industry. The journey touches upon global robotics innovations and the economics of enhancing the business models regarding how this tech is aimed at aiding humans. Then it progresses towards ways in which robotics help fight climate change, manage recycling, streamline healthcare, boost manufacturing, and much more. Revealing that robotics' maximum benefits for the SDGs are derived from the tech's accessibility and automation, the chapter presents exciting cases for these areas.

Remote and inaccessible areas are reached by bots and tasks deemed too dangerous are carried out by programmable machines. Farming operations become cost-effective with robot automation, causing productivity to rise while addressing world hunger as well. Specific industry cases are explored, indicating promising progress. Although the large-scale implementation of robotics poses some societal concerns and threats to humanity in terms of security risks, the tech has numerous benefits. Boasting the potential to bring dramatic enhancements to the world in many different sectors, the power of robotics to address global challenges is explored throughout the following chapter.

THE TECH

The new generation of robot designs is focused on making it easier and safer for humans to interact and work with them. There is ample opportunity for robotics to take over labor for humans working under adverse conditions in potentially complex, changing, and unpredictable environments. The variety and range of applications for next-generation robotics have increased significantly. We have new sensors (such as camera, distance, force, and proximity sensors) that enable robots to recognize and respond to their environment. The defining feature of robotics in operation is sensing and autonomy, which separates this field from other tech solutions such as drones. Yet, couldn't a drone that can take off and land on its own be considered a type of robot?

Indeed, it could be, which implicates a broader understanding of robotics as a distinct tech field. At its simplest, a robot is an intelligent, physically embodied machine that can perform tasks autonomously to some degree. A defining feature of the current advancements in robotics tech is that a robot can sense and manipulate its environment.[6] Today, advanced robots are everywhere due to three technologies in particular: sensors, actuators, and AI. Sensors are what keep robots from smashing into things by using light detection and ranging (Lidar). Lidar sends out lasers to build a 3D map of the world and is the pioneering technology behind autonomous techs like self-driving cars. Researchers at MIT have developed a system that watches the floor in one area of a room, for example, and picks up on subtle movements reflected from another area that the human eye fails to see.

AI technological advancements have also transformed what robots are capable of doing. From streamlining operations to protecting workers, AI-enabled robots have emerged as being immensely valuable. Innovators in this space recognize the value of robots in improving the quality of life and creating better, safer opportunities for workers and consumers. A company called SynTouch, for instance, has developed robotic fingertips that can detect a range of touch sensations, from temperature to coarseness.[7] The robots employ software and algorithms (including artificial intelligence) to interpret the data collected and further enhance processes, thereby helping reduce the number of human operators required.

These automated production systems are becoming increasingly flexible and intelligent, continuously adapting their behavior to maximize output and minimize cost per unit. Take, for example, new robotics used in beverage filling and packing production which can automatically adjust the speed of the entire packing line to streamline needs for any given batch. This ability to make minuscule adjustments improves the overall balance of individual production lines, conserves resources and maximizes the effectiveness of the whole manufacturing system. These advancements are shifting the efficiency capabilities of entire industries.[8] We have prime examples emerging of shipping businesses like Amazon and FedEx testing autonomous delivery robots.

IN THE "LAST-MILE" DELIVERY MARKET, SHIPMENT FROM A LOCAL DISTRIBUTION CENTER TO THE CUSTOMER, ROBOTS HAVE THE POTENTIAL TO REDUCE DELIVERY COSTS BY 10% TO 40% IN CITIES.[9]

Current and emerging production technologies combined with robotics, such as computerized-numerical-control (CNC) cutting and 3D printing, enable components to be adjusted without any need for human work. By taking over the monotony of repetitive tasks, in addition to removing people from any danger due to perilous labor, automation could free up humans to do more thought-provoking or mentally challenging work. While robots engage in the mundane, people would interface with customers, develop better products, and manage the robots themselves. We find precedent for this shift from other historical transformations, such as the mechanization of farming in the 1900s when people switched to more industry work.

Beyond the sphere of consumerism, robots interact with humans in a variety of more personal ways. For instance, vacuum-cleaning robots are growing in popularity. Evidence suggests that a surprisingly large number of people give these robots pet names. It is a technical challenge to build a robot that can satisfy the criteria for friendship. Some robots seem to be getting closer, though. While many would think of Alexa or Siri, the focus here is on Hanson Robotics' Sophia, a humanoid chatbot whose behavior is based on a library of pre-prepared responses.[11]

ROBOTICS SOFTWARE PLATFORMS

Robotics software platforms are a key component of the tech. Software packages, which simplify the programming of different kinds of robotics devices, provide various benefits such as unified service execution and programming environment as well as a package of common facilities such as navigation, computer vision, or robotic arm control. According to the robotic industry experts, about 80% of the project cost is spent on system integration which includes software development or customization.[10] Robotic software platforms are used to standardize and simplify system integration, thereby reducing overall project costs.

SOUND FOUNDATIONS

Some of the earliest robots as we know them were created in the early 1950s by George C. Devol, an inventor from Louisville, Kentucky.[12] He invented and patented a reprogrammable manipulator called "Unimate" from "Universal Automation." In the late 1960s, businessman and engineer Joseph Engelberger acquired Devol's robot patent and modified it into an industrial robot. For his efforts and successes, Engelberger is known in the industry as "the Father of Robotics." Far more advanced than the original Unimate was Shakey, designed by Charles Rosen in 1958. Shakey could wheel around the room, observe the scene with his television "eyes," move across unfamiliar surroundings, and respond to his environment on a very basic level.

Until the mid-1980s, robots remained mostly in factories and labs. This trend changed with Honda's humanoid robotics program. Honda developed P3, which was mobile and responsive. P3 then transitioned into Asimo, designed to help people in their daily lives.[13] These early robot pioneers were created before factory robots could be conceived. With technological advancements, these systems established the archetypes of most of the robots we see today, from factory and warehouse robots to autonomous package delivery drones and subsea maintenance vessels.

ICONIC ROBOTS THROUGHOUT HISTORY

Tortoises (1949): First developed in 1949 by William Grey Walter, Tortoises boasted a light sensor, marker light, touch sensor, propulsion motor, steering motor, and protective shell. Walter claimed that these robots first exhibited what "might be accepted as evidence of some degree of self-awareness."[14]

Unimate (1961): The world's first industrial robot, Unimate, was employed by General Motors for transporting castings from the assembly line.[15] It was an early illustration of a modern robot used to carry out jobs that have previously been the domain of humans.

Shakey (1972): Shakey was a much-hyped 1960s robot developed at Stanford Research Institute. What made Shakey particularly impressive was its ability to analyze commands and break them into separate components, bringing together logical reasoning and physical action. Life Magazine described it, somewhat prematurely, as the world's "first electronic person."[16]

Freddy II (1960s and 70s): Freddy II was a robot arm with adaptive grippers, a camera, and smart image recognition technology.[17] Moving over a table like an arcade claw, Freddy II could construct a model boat and car out of wooden blocks within 16 hours.

P3 (1980s): Honda developed P3, which could walk, wave, and shake hands.[18] This product culminated in a robotic biped called Asimo (2000).

Genghis (1989): MIT debuted its Genghis hexapod robot consisting of 4 microprocessors, 22 sensors, and 12 servo motors. Genghis' walking action was revolutionary for its time.[19]

General Atomics' Predator (1990s): Predator, a remotely piloted aircraft originally named Amber, was invented by the Israeli Air Force's former chief designer, Abraham Karem, and later the CIA took over development. Powered by a single, rear-mounted propeller engine, the robotic drone could fly up to 460 miles to a target, cruise overhead for up to 14 hours, and then return to base.

ABE (1996): The Autonomous Benthic Explorer was created by the Woods Hole Oceanographic Institution and could autonomously survey large subsea regions. Although it started with a preplanned dive path, ABE could avoid collisions and move in for a closer look before swimming back to recharge.

Pathfinder and Sojourner (1997): NASA's mission to Mars entailed the Pathfinder deploying the smaller Sojourner rover which explored the Martian terrain for 83 days. It sent back plenty of images and took and assorted various chemical, atmospheric, and other measurements in the process.[20]

Furby (1998): Furby was the first domestic robot to achieve significant sales worldwide.[21] This holiday season toy was an electronic owl-like device that supposedly learned English as you spoke to it. Though limited in its ability, Furby remains one of the few robots in history that many people reportedly formed an emotional bond with.

Roomba vacuum cleaner robot (2002): iRobot Corp's Roomba vacuum cleaner robot is an example of a top-selling domestic robot that many people brought into their homes.[22]

BigDog and Spot (2005): BigDog was a Defense Advanced Research Projects Agency (DARPA)-sponsored creation capable of moving rapidly and efficiently across a range of different terrains.[23] The project was shelved after being deemed too loud for real combat. It has now been replaced by its smaller sibling, Spot.

MARKET SIZE OF ROBOTICS

The robotics industry comprises of more than 500 companies making products that can be broken down into four categories: conventional industrial robots and cobots, stationary professional services (such as those with medical and agricultural applications), mobile professional services (such as professional cleaning, construction, and underwater activities), and automated guided vehicles (AGVs) for transporting large and small loads in logistics or assembly lines.[24] With robots beginning to adopt roles beyond industrial - personal assistants, surgical assistants, delivery vehicles, and autonomous vehicles, among many other uses - the market is experiencing an unprecedented transformation. As robotics production has increased, costs have gone down and are expected to continue to do so. Over the past 30 years, the average robot price has fallen by about 50%, and even further than that in comparison to labor costs.[25] The rising demand for industrial robots has been triggered by the workforce shortage, owing to the COVID-19-related lockdowns and an upgrade of traditional industries.[26]

The global Industrial Robotics Market is majorly driven by an increase in labor costs worldwide, leading manufacturers to replace human labor with machines. Asia and Europe are the key growth regions, with prominent robotics developers being ABB, Fanuc, KUKA, Kawasaki, and the Yaskawa Electric Corporation. The global robotics market size grew from $69.55 billion in 2021 to $87.6 billion in 2022 at a CAGR of 25.9%.[27] Looking out to 2026, this number will steadily expand to $187.46 billion at a CAGR of 20.9%. In terms of the global industrial robotics market size, it was valued at $32.32 billion in 2021 and is predicted to reach $88.55 billion by 2030 with a CAGR of 12.1% from 2022 to 2030.[28]

THE GLOBAL ROBOTICS MARKET SIZE GREW FROM $69.55 BILLION IN 2021 TO $87.6 BILLION IN 2022 AT A CAGR OF 25.9%.[29] LOOKING OUT TO 2026, THIS NUMBER WILL STEADILY EXPAND TO $187.46 BILLION AT A CAGR OF 20.9%.

Today, there are several significant well-funded automated robot investments. GeekPlus worth $389 million, GreyOrange worth $170 million, and HIK Vision worth $6 billion in revenue have emerged, achieving promisingly rapid growth.[30] Despite the large deployments already, the global peak point is expected to hit around 2024. More than 1 million autonomous mobile robots will be sold cumulatively between 2020 and 2030.[31] During the 12-month period up to March 2021, venture capital firms invested $6.3 billion into robotics companies, which is up nearly 50% from what they invested a year earlier.[32] Industrial robotics firms garnered $1.9 billion of that funding. This suggests that firms that serve factories and warehouses are recipients of nearly one-third of total venture and generate more interest from venture investors.

THE GLOBAL INDUSTRIAL ROBOTICS MARKET SIZE WAS VALUED AT $32.32 BILLION IN 2021 AND IS PREDICTED TO REACH $88.55 BILLION BY 2030 WITH A CAGR OF 12.1% FROM 2022 TO 2030.[33]

Among all sectors, robotics utilized for service purposes are expected to experience the fastest growth.[34] The trend of investment in mobile robotic companies seeking to automate the movement of goods within warehouses, fulfillment centers, and manufacturing facilities continues to rise.[35] More specifically, in e-commerce, the need for automated warehouses is increasing, spearheaded by Kiva and Mobile Industrial Robots (MiR). Service robot technology allowed Amazon, from 2012 onwards, to boost the productivity of the latest generation of its product fulfillment centers. The robot fleet is estimated to have increased at an approximate rate of about 15 thousand per year, recently reaching over a total of 100 thousand units.[36] The medical use service robot market is also expanding, where in 2020 it recorded over 12,000 units worldwide from 9,000 units the year prior.[37] The total global medical robotics market will reach $ 30.41 billion in 2027 from $9.69 billion in 2021, growing at a CAGR of 21%.[38]

THE TOTAL GLOBAL MEDICAL ROBOTICS MARKET WILL REACH $ 30.41 BILLION IN 2027 FROM $9.69 BILLION IN 2021, GROWING AT A CAGR OF 21%.[39]

In the longer term, robotics investments have soared more than five-fold over the last half-decade, to $5.4 billion in 2020 from $1 billion in 2015. The number of firms that attracted investment reached 269, up from 169.[40] Meanwhile, industrial robotics investments have gone up to $1.9 billion from just $300 million in the same period, with the number of startups getting funded hitting 68, up from 48.[41] Prominent firm names among these include Locus Robotics, Tiger Global, Bond, Outrider, Neocis, and AMP Robotics. The market for mobile robots, drones, and autonomous vehicles in delivery and warehousing is likely to reach a staggering $81 and $290 billion in 2030 and 2040, respectively.[42] Along these lines, the global market for agricultural robots – which can also be designed to perform tasks such as seeding, harvesting, and environmental monitoring – is predicted to increase from $5.4 billion in 2020 to more than $20 billion by 2026.[43]

THE MARKET FOR MOBILE ROBOTS, DRONES, AND AUTONOMOUS VEHICLES IN DELIVERY AND WAREHOUSING IS LIKELY TO REACH A STAGGERING $81 AND $290 BILLION IN 2030 AND 2040, RESPECTIVELY.[44]

In August 2020, Shanghai SK Automation Technology Co., which provides intelligent equipment for automotive manufacturers, raised RMB 733.14 million for their robotics tech.[45] Alibaba upgraded to robotic labor in one of its warehouses, drastically reducing the labor workforce by 70%.[46] Automation could result in a net increase of 58 million jobs and add 5%, or $1.2 trillion, to US GDP in the next five years.[47] The largest contributor to the Global Robotics Market is Asia-Pacific, with 35.27% value share in 2020. China is the largest contributing country in the region with 42.73% shares in 2020, followed by South Korea, Japan, and India.[48] In June 2020, China's industrial robot production increased by 29.2% year-on-year, reaching 20,761 units in the first half of 2020.

Over **$17** billion poured into VC-backed robotic startups in 2021, nearly triple the 2020 investment.[49]

$42.4 billion global robotics industry size in 2022.[50]

$168.6 billion expected service robotics market size by 2028.[51]

ROBOTICS FOR GOOD

There is an increasing trend of progressive companies adopting robotics to achieve both business growth and sustainable societal benefits. From scientific advancements and breakthroughs to solving complex problems, robots are generating millions of new skilled jobs and improving working conditions. They are creating a better world. Industries and companies are finding ways to utilize robots to improve their processes, thus allowing businesses to be more efficient and improve sustainability efforts across sectors. Robots in today's world are helping to fight climate change, manage recycling initiatives, streamline healthcare, enhance manufacturing, and more.[52]

We have examples of the robotics industry combating global warming and natural resource protection through business practices. SkyGrow, for instance, has developed the Growbot that plants trees at a rate ten times faster than the manual process and reduces tree-planting costs and labor by around half.[53] Another innovative company, Urban Rivers, developed an autonomous trash robot that floats along the Chicago River. This tech innovation keeps the water clean, while preserving the river's plant and animal life.[54] Similarly, Ocean One, a humanoid robot developed by the Stanford Robotics Lab, explores the ocean without disrupting it and collects samples as effectively as a diver.[55]

ROBOTS FIGHTING CLIMATE CHANGE

In climate-related applications for good, robotics is bringing effective solutions. Green robots help mitigate climate change and lead us into a better future. Combining robots with other advanced technologies maximizes sustainability efforts that help reduce global warming impacts. Businesses employing green robotics technology bring financial benefits while also helping conserve the planet:

Sustainable agriculture: Green robots can simplify agricultural practices by helping automate and carry out environment-friendly tasks with utmost efficiency. Fighting wildfires that destroy plant and animal species and adversely affect human health and infrastructure is a prime example. The US alone witnesses an average of 100,000 wildfires annually.[56] Robots armed with fire extinguishers and water propelling agents can be leveraged to swiftly contain wildfires and help avoid risking the lives of firefighters.

Waste management: GPS and AI-enabled garbage collection robots can carry out household and industrial waste removal. These robots collect data through attached sensors with AI algorithms that determine the optimal route and process to minimize environmental impact. This robotics-enabled garbage collection process results in minimum use of resources and reduces CO_2 emissions. Robots used for ocean cleanup work to contain the harmful effects of oil drilling and ocean spills. A robot has already been designed that ingests microbes in the ocean and converts it into energy.[57] It can operate continuously for months and can generate more energy than it consumes, reducing the impact of oil leakages and helping remove chemicals from rivers and seas.

Robotics has proven to be critical in the recycling of material waste from all sectors. Robots make a significant difference when programmed to sort recycled products into categories depending on the materials. Recycling robots can make approximately 2,000 correct material picks per hour compared to humans making about 800 picks per hour.[58] The sorting robot at the Recon Services recycling plant in Austin, Texas has two arms with "smart grippers." It has increased the recycling rate by up to 70%.[59] These impressive pneumatic[60] arms are programmed to separate and pick different kinds of materials, including plastics, based on polymer, color, shape, and size.

Apple also employs robots in its recycling process of discarded iPhones. Their robot, named Daisy, picks out reusable pieces from old iPhones and repurposes them for other products. Reducing waste and saving valuable resources, Daisy pulls apart over one million iPhones per year at a rate of about 200 per hour.[61]

"WE BELIEVE TECHNOLOGY UNLOCKS CONSTRAINTS IN THE WASTE INDUSTRY, AND USE IT—NAMELY, ARTIFICIAL INTELLIGENCE AND ROBOTICS—TO PURSUE OUR MISSION."[62] - AMP ROBOTICS

Robots are becoming significant in the manufacturing sector by enabling companies to become more sustainable through waste and energy reduction. Approximately 60% of manufacturers are using robotics to help them increase productivity, efficiency, and product quality.[63] Robots also aid businesses in their energy-saving processes because they do not require as much energy to operate as humans do. Where humans need facilities with sufficient lighting and heat, robots can work under cold and dark conditions. This drastically reduces the amount of energy used in the manufacturing production process. It is estimated that swapping robots for humans can result in 8% to 20% of energy savings.[64]

Robots see an increasing role in healthcare, where support robots used to deliver medical supplies around hospitals are becoming more commonplace. Surgical robots, such as da Vinci, are gaining prominence. Thousands of surgeons around the world have been trained in da Vinci systems and have completed more than seven million surgical procedures.[65] Going beyond medical procedures and services, robots made to benefit health and wellbeing are assisting patients recover and rehab. The Phoenix exoskeleton by SuitX, for example, has enabled people paralyzed from the waist down to walk again.[66]

IN 2020, THE MEDICAL USE SERVICE ROBOTS MARKET RECORDED OVER 12,000 UNITS WORLDWIDE.[67]

Playing a crucial role in the battle against COVID-19, robots are making a difference. Many hospitals worldwide are currently using robots to aid healthcare staff and patients. Not only do robots have the potential for disinfecting areas, administering medications, and measuring vital signs, but they are also assisting border controls and delivering food. Self-driving Danish disinfection robot UVD shipped to several hospitals in China to help fight the coronavirus.[68] Manufactured by Denmark's Blue Ocean Robotics, these robots played a key role in controlling the virus in Wuhan.

The tech can also be used for societal good in the form of emotional and educational support. With social isolation and other societal challenges pervading, robots are a safe way to fill in where human interaction is sometimes impossible or unsafe. Robots For Good is an example of a project for five to 12-year-old children to connect with their friends during the pandemic's social isolation. To solve this challenge, the Robots for Good group at Yale University developed an application, and later a robot named Vector, that allows children to play remotely using an inexpensive, commercial robot. This development enables a child in one home to use a phone or tablet to take control and become the robot in another child's home through the robot's camera.[69] There are several hundred thousand Vector robots in the US, and many are still available from online retailers. The software was released through the Apple AppStore and Google Play, making it instantly available to tens of thousands of existing robot owners.

IN BUSINESS
RETHINK ROBOTICS[70]

Initiative: Sawyer
Headquarters: Bochum, Germany

Rethink Robotics, part of the Hahn Group, has introduced the Sawyer robot designed to work on production lines alongside humans.[71] Human operators can reprogram Sawyer by moving its arms into desired configurations, simulating teaching a child. This collaborative robot (cobot) is easy to train and retrain, as well as quick to deploy. The newest iteration, Sawyer BLACK Edition, contributes to a quieter work environment, has a robot arm with seven degrees of freedom, and a range of 1,260 millimeters.[72] Sawyer can also be used where there is no space for human employees. Its use applications include tasks that are dangerous or monotonous for humans such as machine assembly, circuit board assembly, metal processing, injection molding, packaging, loading and unloading, as well as tests and inspections (SDGs 3,9).

This cobot solution is ready for use immediately after delivery and equipped with the powerful Intera software and two camera systems. Sawyer is ideal for machine tending, picking and placing, light packaging, and inspection. The robot works well both autonomously and around people (SDGs 10,12). Sawyer's solutions help reduce the repetitive, mundane, and less desirable tasks performed by humans, so they can up-skill and take on higher-value work within the company (SDGs 8, 11). This approach is truly for good as it leads to greater productivity, reduced turnover, and increased customer satisfaction.[73]

ROBOTICS PROGRESSING THE GLOBAL GOALS

Robotics and automation will disrupt all areas of society. Partnering with AI, over the next 50 years, robots will likely have as much impact on our world as the Internet and mainstream IT has had over the last five decades. Subsequently, future generations will grow up as the first in daily contact with these technologies – "Generation 'R'" or "Robotic Natives" – and will often rely on the development of digital technologies.[74] Robotics could also play a key role in the implementation of international strategies to help shape the recovery and rebuild society and the economy more sustainably.

ZERO HUNGER

Modern robotics technologies can revolutionize farming with applications of outdoor agriculture robotics including aerial imaging, spraying, weeding, and harvesting. In the management of farm animals, such as dairy cattle, pigs, and chickens, robotic intervention of data could help reduce waste and pollution while boosting animal welfare and farm productivity. Robots can also make agriculture more environmentally friendly. As an example, they can be used to detect chemical levels in the soil. Robots attached with sensors and computer vision determine the optimum time for picking up fruits and vegetables, therefore aiding with crop harvest. Livestock farming benefits from robots when used for milking cows or managing a herd of domesticated animals. By analyzing the data, the optimum levels of fertilizers can be determined for maximum productivity. Other robots will automate tasks such as planting, sowing, and watering rapidly, precisely, and efficiently.

GOOD HEALTH AND WELLBEING

Emerging assistive technologies, including cognitive robotics, have vast potential to enhance lives by enabling patients with disabilities to function more independently.[75] Surgical and medical robots can change the standard of care for many diseases.

The COVID-19 pandemic boosted the market for professional service robots with high demand for robotics disinfection solutions in medical applications. Humanoid robots donated by Silicon Valley company CloudMinds Technology measure temperatures, deliver food and medicine, and entertain medical staff and patients.[76] The increasing number of medical robot systems-assisted surgeries is further accelerating the product innovation rate. For instance, Danish tech company Life Science Robotics developed and launched a rehabilitation robot called Robert. It helps health professionals with bed-ridden patients, reducing the dependence on nurses for necessary actions such as heavy lifting.[77] Robert is installed in leading spinal cord centers, rehabilitation centers, and clinics in large municipalities in Denmark, Germany, Hong Kong, Malaysia, and the US.

QUALITY EDUCATION

Robots are highly interdisciplinary and provide an education platform for experiential and challenge-based learning. An educational robot is "a learning support tool that uses realistic educational simulations to facilitate skill acquisition in students of all age groups."[78] Robots used for educational purposes deliver content based on all major science and humanities subjects. Owing to this, these robots find extensive application across academic establishments such as special-education institutes, schools, and colleges offering higher education. Robots can also be a useful language-teaching medium. Softbank Robotics programmed a robot called Robin and succeeded in teaching young children vocabulary of a second language – English language to Dutch students – using social robots.

DECENT WORK AND ECONOMIC GROWTH

Through automation and productivity improvements, robotics will create more high-paying jobs by taking over traditionally lower-paying and less skill-intensive jobs. This paves the way for manual laborers to learn and apply for more advanced positions. Ordering warehouses like Amazon use robots for tasks such as sorting and packing, which leads to efficient and rapid results. Being lightweight, easily programmable, and easily integrable with existing software systems, these "order-picking bots" are increasingly becoming a necessity in warehouses. Industry group MHI uses robots for more dangerous work, as opposed to simpler tasks, so that their employees can engage in higher-level and safer tasks. [79] Because robots come in a wide range of models with reach distance and load capacity, they help save workers from harm. Improving commercial cleaning as a sustainability measure using robotics is also a task these machines can facilitate. Sealed Air and ThingLogix, along with D6 Labs, developed a robotic solution that collects usage data for monitoring handwashing. [80] Staff is notified when soap levels are low and when to replenish stock, resulting in a leaner and less wasteful inventory process which has saved over $50,000. [81]

INDUSTRY, INNOVATION AND INFRASTRUCTURE

Smart technologies and robotics will become a viable alternative to industrial manufacturing processes. Not only can robots increase productivity, efficiency, and profit margins, but they also pave the way for industries to transition to a more sustainable future. AI and other technological advances will enhance innovations in human-to-robot interactions. Rapidly developing technological breakthroughs involving machine intelligence, connectivity, and control will enable expanded robot capabilities and scope while simplifying human-to-robot interactions. Developing robots to handle unsupervised or unexpected situations will increase the flexibility of mobile robots to share and alter tasks on location for enhanced autonomous inspections, analysis, and movements in all industries.

RESPONSIBLE CONSUMPTION AND PRODUCTION

Robots assist in precision manufacturing and production on demand, increasing flexibility and reducing waste and energy consumption. Moreover, they monitor environments, remotely inspect and maintain renewable-energy plants and power lines, improve deforestation-tracking methods, and fight wildfires. An Israeli startup has developed a robotic beehive to minimize the risk of bee colonies collapsing since bees are endangered and crucial for the environment. The hive, called Beewise, is roughly the size of a cargo trailer and houses 24 colonies. It is equipped with a robotic arm that slides between honeycombs with computer vision and cameras. The machine inspects colonies for disease, monitoring for pesticides and reporting in real-time any hazards that threaten the colony. This robotic solution assists in mitigating damages to beehives that harm honey production. Beewise has already raised $40 million of funding from private investors, and over 100 of its systems are in use in Israel and the US. [82]

LIFE ON LAND

Robots can collect forest data and measure light reflected from plants, which enables scientists to sample the vegetation's functional diversity and evolutionary history. Various robots have been developed with the capability to dig, seed, water plants, and monitor the environment. To assist in land management, environmental and disaster monitoring, scientists have been working to create flying robotic vehicles the size of insects. An example is of "RoboBee X-wing" which, at half the weight of a paper clip, has achieved untethered flight using ultra-lightweight solar cells. [83] Further, SMP Robotics is focused on developing the concept of a rover series, which will be used to scout and mine on the surface of the Moon. [84] The project is economically feasible and will help lower the price of space travel to Mars and other planets in the solar system.

ENHANCING BUSINESS MODELS

The robotics industry has revolutionized business models and is on the precipice of enabling economic growth on a global scale. Just as AI assists humans in intellectual tasks, robotics tech innovations such as exoskeleton robots help people perform more physical tasks.[85] The immense impact of this technology will be felt in business on both mainstream corporate and small-scale startup operations. Robots will undoubtedly enable many disruptive business models. The robots as a service (RaaS) business model is thriving. A combination of cloud computing, AI, robotics, and shared services, RaaS is a unique model. The robotics industry includes several companies offering RaaS business models. From mobile telepresence robots used for security to mobile robots for healthcare, many robotics suppliers are expanding their business offerings. RaaS enables them all to lower the technical and financial barriers to implementation and deployment, presenting a compelling value proposition for users and a game-changing strategy for robotics companies.

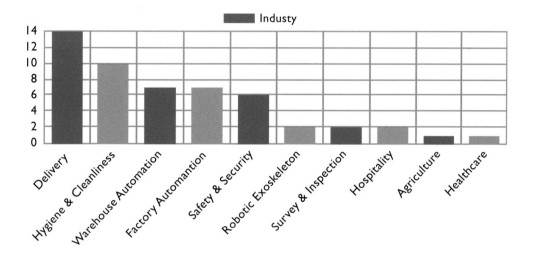

Figure 4

Number of RaaS companies in 2022 by industry, derived from Apera.[86]

This figure is sufficient to suggest the worldwide usage of the RaaS model is a growing tech business trend. Key market players include KUKA AG, Parrot SA, Lely International, DJI, Northrop Grumman, Intuitive Surgical, Inc., Aethon Inc., Kongberg Maritime AS, Honda Motor Co. Ltd., and iRobot Corporation. Dangerous, life-threatening, and labor-intensive tasks will be replaced by robots accelerating digitization. Profound implications will follow, radically transforming markets and at the same time changing the future of work. A market has hit its automation tipping point (ATP) when a RaaS solution is introduced with a unit cost less than or equal to the unit cost for humans to conduct the same task.[87] RaaS already affects industries all over the world, and their ATP as robots in crop-dusting ($70 billion), industrial cleaning ($78 billion), and warehouse management ($21 billion) cause total disruption.[88]

ZERO HUNGER

- Enable agriculture to be more cost-effective and sustainable by monitoring fields and managing weeds and herbicides.
- Improve farm productivity in areas where urbanization has affected rural populations.

GOOD HEALTH AND WELLBEING

- Allow medical care and access to doctors in remote or underprivileged areas.
- Help avoid injuries through automation for dangerous work.
- Improve quality of life for people with limited mobility, using exoskeletons.

QUALITY EDUCATION

- Provide accessible education to all.
- Implement high-level instruction for a wide range of students of all ages.

INDUSTRY, INNOVATION AND INFRASTRUCTURE

- Improve the efficiency of production in time, funds, and resources by implementing next-generation robotics.
- Support less developed countries to automate at lower market entry costs by creating comprehensive business structures.

ROBOTICS

DECENT WORK AND ECONOMIC GROWTH

- Augment the workforce by allotting simple and repetitive tasks to robots.
- Shift employment offerings and types of work, creating more thought-provoking work and fewer manual labor jobs.

RESPONSIBLE CONSUMPTION AND PRODUCTION

- Enhance monitoring of environmental impacts of farming operations and reduce the use of excess water, herbicide, and fertilizer.
- Augment manufacturing processes with automated design and precision robotics.

LIFE ON LAND

- Provide support for land management and biodiversity protection.
- Develop innovative natural processes for plant and animal life.

The enterprise building security market has already reached its ATP. Traditionally, humans have conducted office security, but robotics is enhancing this service. Cobalt Robotics hopes to change the security business with its platform, facilitating companies to replace guards with a 65% cheaper security robot.[89] For example, instead of manning a building with three to four people, businesses would employ one human to manage a few remote robots. Moreover, the data and insights collected via these robots will be beneficial. Not only does this enhance business models in terms of being cheaper for labor, but it is also better from logistical and safety standpoints. When companies drive increased efficiency and productivity, they make better products or provide better services. This value is passed along to consumers, employees, and shareholders.

THE RAAS INDUSTRY VALUE IS ESTIMATED TO SURPASS AROUND $44 BILLION BY 2028, EXPANDING AT A CAGR OF 16.5% BETWEEN 2022 AND 2028.[90]

Delivery services are becoming staffed mainly by autonomous robots. Crucial to enhancing this business model will be tech companies requiring practice data to draw on to improve their delivery and navigation algorithms. They can then operate increasingly larger robot fleets in complex environments with high-speed demands. Autonomous robots are also automating tedious work in retail stores. These robotic solutions are being offered as automated data acquisition tools, capturing data about items on the shelves with higher speed and accuracy than humans. Robots collecting data will have a beneficial impact on the retailer's bottom line, be it higher stock availability, better stock positioning on shelves, or leaner inventories. Thus, data-centric service-oriented robotic models are high-value business propositions.

ROBOTS COLLECTING DATA WILL HAVE A BENEFICIAL IMPACT ON THE RETAILER'S BOTTOM LINE, BE IT HIGHER STOCK AVAILABILITY, BETTER STOCK POSITIONING ON SHELVES, OR LEANER INVENTORIES.

Autonomous mobile robots are developed to perform various security-related tasks as well, for indoor, outdoor, and even rugged terrain operations. Some versions are equipped with more than 50 onboard sensors and deployed wherever security and monitoring are required. Companies like Ople.ai and SMP Robotics are at the forefront of this risk-reducing use of AI and robotics for good. SMP Robotics has become a leading provider of outdoor security robots and advanced monitoring solutions. Since its inception, the company has been instrumental in facilitating robots to improve the operational business processes of their clients.[91] SMP Robotics' security robot models cover restricted areas by patrolling a facility's perimeter and premises. These autonomous robots drive safety through intercommunication, resulting in cost-effective robotics solutions for large-scale and expansive facilities.

GLOBAL GOALS' GROWTH OPPORTUNITIES

Robots offer a wide range of tools to enable the Global Goals. Performing search and rescue missions in case of natural disasters or delivering food in dangerous zones, robots reduce the impact of such catastrophes. They can monitor environmental changes in air, land, and water, allowing for better understanding and preservation of ecosystems. Robots promise an increase in the overall productivity in industries as well as on farms. They also improve access to transportation and healthcare, as well as boost the quality of life for the differently-abled. Let us now study the social developmental impact of robots in the four large domains: healthcare and wellbeing; education and learning; biodiversity recovery, environmental protection, and precision agriculture; and manufacturing and shipping.

IMPROVING HEALTHCARE AND WELLBEING

From surgical applications to medication delivery, robotic healthcare solutions today provide several benefits. Robotic surgery improves surgical precision that contributes to safer procedures and quicker patient healing times. For instance, Swiss medical-device startup Distalmotion created its own surgical robot named Dexter. [92] As an open platform compatible with all laparoscopic technology and access to all instruments, Dexter allows operating teams to seamlessly switch between laparoscopic and robotic surgery at any time. Further, Dexter's open platform ensures rapid access to future technologies.[93] Google too has been working to create a surgical robot system with pharma giant Johnson&Johnson since 2015.[94]

THE TUG HAS BECOME COMMONPLACE IN HOSPITALS AND MAKES OVER 50,000 DELIVERIES EACH WEEK IN OVER 140 HOSPITALS IN THE US.[95]

As Aethon's version of a medical assistant, the TUG autonomous mobile delivery robot carries up to 453 kilograms in the form of medications, laboratory specimens, or other sensitive materials.[96] This means hospital staff can focus on other, more challenging assignments. The TUG has become commonplace in hospitals and makes over 50,000 deliveries each week in over 140 hospitals in the US.[97] Robotics are also playing a role in the protection of people from COVID-19. Since robots are immune to infection, they can efficiently replace humans for menial jobs. In China, robots from the catering industry have been placed in over 40 hospitals. [98] They clean the hospital to prevent the spread of the virus and save lives. Danish robotics company Odense UVD Robots also deployed hundreds of robots to Wuhan, Rome, and Veneto to help fight the COVID-19 infection.

IN BUSINESS
BLUE OCEAN ROBOTICS[99]

Initiative: UVD Robots disinfecting hospitals
Headquarters: Odense, Denmark

Healthcare associated infections are a significant and increasing problem in the global healthcare sector. Each year millions of patients are infected, and thousands of patients die due to infections acquired during hospitalization.[100] Furthermore, these infections generate massive financial implications. UVD Robots are working to address this challenge and they are already operational in more than 40 countries.

One example where they have been very beneficial is in China during the COVID-19 pandemic. More than 2,000 Chinese hospitals and medical facilities received and made use of UVD robots (SDG 3).[101] "The UVD Robot will kill the coronavirus, as it has a proven efficacy against MERS CoV and MHV-A59, showing over 6 log reductions in viral particles within 30 minutes ... the robot is much smarter and more cost-effective than what's available in the market today" explains UVD spokesperson Camilla Harkjær Frederiksen.[102]

Every UVD Robot is equipped with lidar. When first deploying the robot, a user guides it around via computer, entering information the robot stores in its system on which areas need disinfecting (SDGs 9,12). As the robot scans the rooms or area, it creates a digital map for itself to be autonomous. Once all information is stored, the robot uses simultaneous localization and mapping for navigation. It can self-navigate from the charging station, disinfect the rooms, and return to its resting place all on its own. The robot can detect using sensors if a human is present and will shut down the UV lights until the area is clear.

Some of UVD Robots' defining features include that they stand 5'6" tall (171 cm), 2'1" wide (66 cm), and 3 feet deep (93 cm); they move at speeds of 5.4 km/h or 3.3 mph; disinfect with a 360-degree radius, killing 99.99% of bacteria within 10 minutes; for each 90-minute charge, they can disinfect 9 or 10 rooms; robots are equipped with an emergency button and software and sensor-based safety features; and each robot costs $80,000 to $90,000 which eliminates the need for several human laborers' salaries (SDG 8).[103]

Robots have the potential to help keep people safe and secure, which is paramount to global wellbeing. Rescuing severely wounded soldiers under fire is an example of addressing a major cause of military death and traumatic injury. Reportedly, up to 86% of battlefield deaths occur within the first 30 minutes post-injury.[104] To counter this, life-saving training techniques and treatments, and more recently, robotic surgical systems (RSS), have been developed to provide battlefield casualty extraction. These robots are critical when performing life-saving interventions and aiding in physiological monitoring to reduce incidence. RSS ensures less blood loss during the procedure, less pain after the procedure, and a shorter hospital stay.[105] The level of dexterity is higher, and doctors can operate in tiny spaces inside the body that would otherwise require open surgery.

UP TO 86% OF BATTLEFIELD DEATHS OCCUR WITHIN THE FIRST 30 MINUTES POST-INJURY.[106] ROBOTIC SURGICAL SYSTEMS (RSS) HELP LOWER THIS NUMBER BY PROVIDING BATTLEFIELD CASUALTY EXTRACTION.

Robotic surgery results in smaller incisions, which reduce pain and scarring, leading to quicker recovery times.[107] Robotic procedures offer the surgeon an enhanced visual field with HD cameras that provide a magnified view. Employing arms that can rotate a full 360 degrees, surgeons can operate in a way that would be impossible without the robot. The emotional and psychological wellbeing of global populations of all ages is also essential. Companionship and communication for children can include social robots as pets. The robot dog Aibo offers a fun home companion who can learn from his environment and the child's habits to adapt to the home and family.[108] Kids can shake the smartphone to bring him running at the sound of treats, have him do tricks, or send him on "Puppy Patrol" to find someone on the platform's People of Interest registry.

THE UN PROJECTS THAT THE GLOBAL POPULATION AGED 65 AND OVER WILL GROW BY 181%, ACCOUNTING FOR 16% OF THE WORLD POPULATION, BY 2050. THIS ALLOWS FOR SIGNIFICANT GROWTH FOR ROBOTS IN DOMESTIC HEALTHCARE AND ASSISTANCE APPLICATIONS.[109]

In Japan, BOCCO is a communication robot that helps parents send text and voice messages to deliver to their kids. [110] As an additional bonus, BOCCO is continuously being developed for more features and is adorably cute! Social robots evidently reduce loneliness and feelings of isolation in the elderly and people with dementia. Dementia patients home alone or in residential care settings can use robots as support staff. In the coming decade, the amount of vulnerable older adults will rise. Reports from the Netherlands claim there will be a 25% increase in elderly who experience growing feelings of loneliness, rising more due to the COVID-19 pandemic, which will have a detrimental impact on physical and mental health. Therefore, innovations are taking place in the healthcare and wellness industry within robotics to mitigate these issues.

Stockholm-based Furhat Robotics is innovating a robot to combat social isolation with conversational intelligence.[111] It is a device that possesses human-like features and makes a great social companion through its ability to speak, listen, maintain eye contact, and express emotive facial gestures. An exciting feature of this tech solution is its animated yet realistic face. Benefits of using social robots include their constant availability and, unlike human caregivers, their calm and patient temperament. They neither judge nor have prejudice, which can greatly assist those who feel lonely, isolated, or are unable to talk about their true feelings with other people. Furhat can change its facial appearance to a character of varying ages and adapt to conversations to respond to the individual's needs. It can also alter the pitch and intonation of its voice along with vocabulary to customize the interaction. In addition to Furhat, a social robot named Alice is innovating to provide robotics tech solutions for social wellbeing.

IN BUSINESS
DELOITTE IMPACT FOUNDATION[112] AND VRIJE UNIVERSITEIT[113]
Initiative: Alice the social robot
Headquarters: Amsterdam, Netherlands

Alice, the social robot, plays many roles including an assistant for caretakers and a friend for the elderly (SDGs 3,10). The development of this robot, supported by collaboration between the Deloitte Impact Foundation and Vrije Universiteit, took two years (SDGs 9,17). Alice aims to relieve loneliness and improve the quality of life for the elderly.[114] The secluded and lonely older adults residing in care homes often miss social interaction and struggle with using new technologies. They can have a difficult time adjusting to tech and are dependent on an instruction manual or a caretaker helping them. Alice supports the elderly by engaging in tasks such as giving them reminders of their upcoming activities or dialing their relatives and friends (SDG 16). These are examples of functionalities that motivate the elderly to feel more settled and content. Alice can also support the user by serving as a listener, asking them personal questions. She also has the capability to be pro-grammed for personalization through the Alice App. She can play songs, narrate the weather forecast, and read the daily news.

INNOVATING EDUCATION AND LEARNING

Robotics used in education will continue to be in high demand internationally, driven in part by schools' continued emphasis on STEM and digital learning. The $1.3 billion international robotics education market is set to grow to $3.1 billion by 2025.[115] The field is not only expected to continue to grow in STEM and coding areas, but is also on track to provide applications in language learning and special education. We witnessed companies like Sphero merging with LittleBits and reaching combined sales amounting to $500 million in 2019; their products reached over six million students across 35,000 schools globally.[116] Moreover, robot tech companies that don't traditionally operate in the education sector are making moves in that direction as well. For example, Chinese drone manufacturer DJI and Texas Instruments recently moved into the educational space with robotics offerings.[117]

THE $1.3 BILLION INTERNATIONAL ROBOTICS EDUCATION MARKET IS SET TO GROW TO $3.1 BILLION BY 2025.[118]

In Greenville, Texas, VEX Robotics aims to interest students in STEM by teaching them to build and program robots. Its annual VEX Robotics Competition hosts primary school through college ages worldwide who compete in robotic construction, design, and programming.[119] To allow students to explore STEM education more thoroughly, Shape Robotics developed the Fable robot. Fable is a modular construction system that students can creatively use to make their own robot in just a few minutes. Being an open-ended system with advanced functionality, Fable is easily accessed across a range of subjects, allowing students to gain skills they will need in the 21st century.[120]

When remote learning became widespread during the 2020 coronavirus pandemic, robots stepped in to fill some of the gaps in education. Several innovative robots and tech companies came forth and helped the robotics generation. Important examples of robots in tech education include:

Miko 3: An adorable little robot that can hear, speak, and relate to children using a variety of speakers, algorithms, and cues from the child.[121] Miko 3 is also programmed to help kids learn, imparting knowledge and skills that are right for their age.

Owl: Owl is a smarter video conference camera that gives teachers the ability to better re-create a classroom experience even when their students are remote.[122] Owl can swivel and move to follow a teacher around a room.

Wigl: This tech solution combines music education with STEM training, spiking attraction towards STEM.[123] The little bug-looking robot dances based on the musical notes it hears. Children can learn the connection between their actions and the robot's movements by making it wiggle as they play a song or sing to it.

Perhaps one of the most innovative and globally recognized innovations for integrating child play and learning is Denmark's toy-maker LEGO. During the first half of 2020, LEGO's sales rose 14% compared to 2019, with its operating profit rising 11% to $622 million.[124] This growth was in large part due to the remote learning structure of the pandemic.

IN BUSINESS

LEGO[125]

Initiative: LEGO Education
Headquarters: Billund, Denmark

LEGO contributes with co-ed learning through play to build kids' socio-emotional needs in the world of virtual and hybrid learning (SDGs 4,5,10). LEGO Education SPIKE Prime App is a make-your-own robots coding, problem-solving, and creative design teaching platform.[126] Children as well as adults can play with these innovative toy bricks, simultaneously learning essential skills in science, technology, and innovation. These products use bricks, programming tools, and supporting lesson plans to help kids develop their communication, and critical thinking skills in a fun and exciting way. "We have worked hard to make LEGO Education solutions, like our newest product SPIKE Prime, approachable for anyone, no matter what their background is with coding and programming," expressed Siddharth Muthyala, Senior Concept Lead for LEGO Education.[127]

As part of this educational business endeavor, LEGO robot-building toys help kids learn to code while having fun (SDGs 9,12). No matter the hobby or interest of a child, these little bricks serve as relevant entry points to robotics and programming.[128] Whether they like kittens, music, or remote-controlled cars, all users will be inspired to create a robot that reflects their unique personality and interests by using speech, songs, sounds, lights, movements, and interactions. The company's annual revenues surpass $5 billion and in 2015 it was named the "most powerful" brand in the world.[129]

Higher education institutions are now heavily implementing robotics and tech learning into their curriculums. Resultantly, the field of Mechatronics Engineering has emerged to develop the best possible robotic design while seamlessly merging mechanical and electronics knowledge. We have university graduates shaping the future by building biomedical robotic devices, rehabilitation robots, service robots, smart vehicles, and autonomous farm equipment.[130] The Misty II robot by Misty Robotics is also partnering with universities for education and research purposes.[131] She offers opportunities to engage with cutting-edge technologies such as AI, Machine Learning, and Computer Vision. Misty is highly accessible, enabling students and faculty to learn coding and building skills through robot applications.

A prime example of robots in the realm of higher education has emerged thanks to the University of Southern Denmark. It combines education with robotics to study business models that solve some of the world's biggest challenges.

UNIVERSITY OF SOUTHERN DENMARK[132]

The University of Southern Denmark (SDU) has integrated the SDGs into the foundation of its structure. The focus at SDU Robotics is on:

SDG 3: Securing a healthy life for all and promoting the wellbeing of all.
In the medical area, an online learning platform is provided for grading medical images, access to training and development materials to medical workforces present in areas with poor access. SDU helps save lives in Denmark and globally by reducing the spread of infectious diseases with a robot that takes throat swabs. SDU also facilitates better hand sanitization in public spaces using socially interactive hand disinfection devices.

SDG 8: Promoting persistent, inclusive, and sustainable economic growth through employment for all. Collaborative robots will enable unskilled workers to be more comfortable in highly automated environments. SDU studies prove that robots create new jobs, and hence contribute to employment.

SDG 9: Building robust infrastructure, promoting inclusive and sustainable industrialization, and supporting innovation. By providing digitally supported robotic services, SDU offers new possibilities for innovation in general. The university also supports industrial development on a global scale.

REINFORCING BIODIVERSITY RECOVERY, ENVIRONMENTAL PROTECTION AND AGRICULTURE

The amount of land available for organisms on Earth to share is diminishing. Factors such as increased soil erosion and rising global sea levels are spurring a need to mitigate these large-scale environmental problems. Such loss of ecosystem services among terrains is a major driver of climate change and is estimated to cost up to $10 trillion annually.[133] Robots are aiding in these mitigation efforts. They are reducing the time- and cost-intensive use of heavy machinery to build massive environmental protection structures like dams and retaining walls. Harvard's Wyss Institute's Bioinspired Robotics Platform is experimenting with using a "swarm" of robots for environmental restoration. They can use sheet piles to form check dams along shore fronts, riverbeds, and other vulnerable ecosystems to prevent erosion, reduce flash flooding, and promote groundwater recharge.

LOSS OF ECOSYSTEM SERVICES AMONG TERRAINS IS A MAJOR DRIVER OF CLIMATE CHANGE AND IS ESTIMATED TO COST UP TO $10 TRILLION ANNUALLY.[134] ROBOTS ARE AIDING IN THESE MITIGATION EFFORTS.

The design is inspired by termites and ants that collectively build structures many times larger than themselves and has resulted in a sheet-pile-driving robot called Romu.[135] Other automation coming out of the Wyss Institute includes robots that help tackle ocean creatures considered "biofouling" species like barnacles, mussels, algae, and sponges. The US Navy alone spends approximately $1 billion per year on antifouling efforts.[136] Energy efficiency-based robots like the Row-Bot have also emerged. Invented at Bristol University in the U.K, Row-Bot walks on water and gets its energy by eating the microbes in dirty ponds and "digesting" them in its artificial stomach.[137] This helps it propel itself on the hunt for more bacteria to feed its nature-inspired engine.

The world of lizards, too, has also inspired active development and technological advances in robotics. A team of scientists from Ben-Gurion University in Beersheba, Israel, has developed AmphiSTAR, a high-speed robot whose motion comes from observing the actions of basilisk lizards.[138] The machine is capable of crawling rapidly across rough terrain, swimming, and even climbing over rippling pond waves. This little robot has four underbelly propellers that work as standard wheels over ground and as fins to help the robot both crawl and sprint over water. The creators envision that AmphiSTAR can be used for agricultural, search and rescue, and excavation applications that require both crawling and swimming.[139] Robotics is also being inspired by some of nature's most efficient processes to solve several of our pressing biodiversity challenges. For instance, bio-roboticists are building Envirobots, a sinuous robot that can venture into toxic waters for fieldwork, service, and search and rescue.

IN BUSINESS
ÉCOLE POLYTECHNIQUE FÉDÉRALE DE LAUSANNE ENVIROBOT[140]

Initiative: Amphibot
Headquarters: Lausanne, Switzerland

A team led by Swiss professors and roboticists at the École Polytechnique Fédérale de Lausanne created the Envirobots.[141] The team works in biorobotics, which draws inspiration from ecology to develop and use new robots to understand living organisms better. Researchers in the field are also building biologically influenced devices that assist humans, such as machines modeled after real animals capable of handling complex terrain (SDG 9,15). The team designed a robot called Amphibot that mimicked the undulating, wave-like movement of lampreys and eels (SDG 6,14). The key design decision was to build the robot out of detachable segments, so they could customize its length for different tasks. The autonomous Envirobot is roughly five feet long, controllable by researchers from the shore, and programmable to move on its own to pinpoint the source of pollution. The head module, which houses all the computing power, coordinates the movement of its components. The ultimate goal is to have a system where multiple rather than single robots could collectively create a map of pollution (SDG 12). [142]

As it swims, the sensors attached to the body take measurements and send real-time data to a computer, making collecting data a quicker process than traditional methods. This Envirobot can also collect up to three water samples at different points. Amphibot relies on biological sensors, or living organisms, to check the water. One sensor uses bacteria that researchers developed to emit light when exposed to mercury. Another sensor has two compartments that contain a tiny crustacean called daphnia: one is filled with clean water (the control group), and the other is filled with the water to be analyzed. By comparing the movement of the two groups exposed to the water, researchers can gauge water's toxicity. The Envirobot is portable, a feature that could make it useful in emergencies like chemical spills or natural disasters (SDGs 13,16).

Robots help undo some of the damage done to our environment. They are tracking endangered wildlife and assisting land conservation efforts by mapping ecosystems and monitoring protected areas. Robots are being developed that mimic the evolutionary traits of animals to interact with the world more efficiently. By mimicking how queen bees vibrate, for example, scientists have created robots that can integrate themselves as members of the beehive and give beekeepers new insight into population behavior. These little robots can artificially recreate several stimuli that can be both appealing and repelling for the living bees.

Sensors on the living bees allow the robotic bees to better interact with the insects as they feed information to an "evolutionary algorithm" that learns how to map their behavior.[143] This tech can help beekeepers look after their hives better, reducing the need to open them for inspection, which causes stress to the bees and even kills hundreds of them each time. Big corporations, like Walmart, are also interested in how bee robots can be used for business purposes.[144] This exciting innovation can lead to enabling robot bees to navigate and survey the crops using sensors and cameras. These tiny drones could potentially pollinate as effectively as real bees.

SENSORS ON LIVING BEES ALLOW ROBOTIC BEES TO BETTER INTERACT WITH THE INSECTS AS THEY FEED INFORMATION TO AN "EVOLUTIONARY ALGORITHM" THAT LEARNS HOW TO MAP THEIR BEHAVIOR.

There is a growing concern globally about the safety and quality of food. Thankfully, automation and robotics have aided a framework to make precision agriculture possible with minimal environmental impact, employing efficient instruments for food safety assurance. This tech solution can also be instrumental in boosting food production. Robots can improve agriculture, specifically in areas like assessing crop nutrient status. Optical reflectance sensors have emerged for such purposes. They successfully measure light reflectance from leafy crop canopies, which effectively estimate the nitrogen status of plants and ultimately how much additional nitrogen needs to be applied.[145] Tractor-mounted spectrophotometers can make use of multispectral sensors to derive chlorophyll content.[146] Analyzing such data from automation sensors can also aid in determining the optimum levels of fertilizers for maximum productivity.

ROBOTS WILL BE INSTRUMENTAL IN BOOSTING FOOD PRODUCTION.

Further, robots play a role in automated tasks such as planting, sowing, watering, and harvesting. Sensors and computer vision aid in the delivery of these tasks.[147] We find many examples of business value in precision agriculture robotic applications:

PRECISION FARMING: ROBOTS CREATING SOLUTIONS

California Bay Area-based **FarmWise and Bear Flag Robotics** are deploying physical robots on farms to carry out AI-guided precision agricultural production.[148] FarmWise's initial focus is on weeding, with a longer-term vision to use its robots across a broad spectrum of farming activities. Bear Flag Robotics has developed an autonomous tractor service.

Naio Technologies, based in southwestern France, has developed a robot to weed, hoe, and assist during harvesting.[149]

Robot Highways project is currently demonstrating multiple uses for autonomous robots made by Saga Robotics on a fruit farm in southeast England. Robots are treating plant diseases in fields and greenhouses, mapping terrain, picking, packing, and providing logistical support to workers throughout the project. This is achieved by attaching different tools to an autonomous "base robot." These autonomous farming robots have the potential to do some of the laborious agricultural work that helps keep costs down and food prices competitive.[150] Robots are available that can be charged from renewable sources that cut agricultural carbon emissions. Further, robots equipped with ultraviolet lights that can kill mildew on plants could reduce fungicide use by up to 90%.[151]

Energid Technologies in Cambridge has developed a citrus picking system by applying powerful computer algorithms that retrieves one piece of fruit every 2 to 3 seconds.[152] The development will leverage Energid's Actin and Selectin robotics software toolkits and advance RSS.

Blue River Technology has developed the LettuceBot2 that attaches itself to a tractor to thin out lettuce fields and prevent herbicide-resistant weeds. Due to its precision, the robot uses 90% less herbicide on crops.[153]

Small Robot Company has built machines that can navigate in tight spaces between objects like trees, so they could potentially perform weeding, disease treatment, and mapping in agroforestry systems.[154] They could reduce chemical use on farms by targeting individual plants rather than whole fields.

STRENGTHENING MANUFACTURING AND SHIPPING

Robots are taking vital steps to reduce pollution and emissions from manufacturing operations. They are also a crucial part of optimizing the manufacturing process to reduce energy consumption. In addition, they reduce our reliance on larger and more harmful vehicles and machines. The human-robot collaboration makes manufacturing processes faster, more efficient, and cost-effective, with idle time reduced by 85% with the involvement of a human-aware robot compared to manual labor.[155] By reshaping production processes and aiding sustainability, modern robotic automation can deliver significant benefits for companies that often see investment being recouped within just 18 months.[156] Within manufacturing, robotic handling operations (machine tending, palletizing, and molding) account for 38% of operations.[157] Also, robotic welding, robotic assembly (press-fitting, inserting, and disassembling), robotic dispensing (painting, gluing, and spraying), and robotic processing (laser and water jet cutting) account for 29%, 10%, 4%, and 2%, respectively.

THE HUMAN-ROBOT COLLABORATION MAKES MANUFACTURING PROCESSES FASTER, MORE EFFICIENT, AND COST-EFFECTIVE, WITH IDLE TIME REDUCED BY 85% WITH THE INVOLVEMENT OF A HUMAN-AWARE ROBOT COMPARED TO MANUAL LABOR.[158]

Electronics giant GE is at the forefront of robotics manufacturing technology. Its value proposition of robotics ties tightly to productivity in field service and manufacturing, bringing potential cost savings into operations.[159] The company works closely with GE business units, GE customers, and strategic partners across the globe to envision and build intelligent robotic technologies from idea to commercialization, delivering industrial-grade service robotic systems that enable automation, productivity, and safety for GE and its customers. Building and finishing tasks, such as sanding and polishing, are being increasingly performed by robotic automation, too. A robot can improve both product quality and work experience through efficient material removal, waste reduction, and more efficient energy use.[160]

The push for automation to increase efficiency and handle surging demand – and compete with big shipping companies like Amazon – has only increased during Covid-19. Robots that can help retailers keep up with Amazon are valuable, and investors are taking notice. Locus Robotics creates autonomous mobile robots that pick up items at warehouses. This is a prime example of robotics doing good while also creating business value. The company raised a sizable $150 million in early 2021 and, just seven months later, Tiger Global invested another $50 million in the Massachusetts firm.[161] The last round gave Locus unicorn status, with the company's total funding rising to around $300 million.

The work environment can benefit from robots, ultimately achieving improved productivity in labor-intensive industries through technology, a target of the SDGs. Robots in manufacturing improve productivity and reduce the stresses of the night shift for workers. They also help protect the health and safety of people by performing hazardous jobs. According to statistics by the International Federation of Robotics, the number of industrial robots in operation has and will continue increasing year by year.[162] In this regard, the case of the Japanese company FANUC is interesting. They develop robots that can help solve society's issues and improve the productivity of their customers' factories, addressing the issue of the decreased working population.

IN BUSINESS
LOCUS ROBOTICS[163]
Initiative: Logistical solutions
Headquarters: Wilmington, Massachusetts USA

Locus Robotics makes autonomous mobile robots called "LocusBots," which can pick up items at warehouses. The company is growing rapidly with some 4,000 robots in the field currently and more than 40 customers. These include shipping giant DHL and British health and beauty retailer Boots UK that focus on safety and women in robotics (SDGs 3,5).[164] These 4,000 robots have picked a total of more than 300 million units, including 70 million during the 2020 holiday season. "This is an industry that operated the same way for 50 years, and it sort of worked. Now they understand that to survive, they need to automate. The Amazon effect is really driving the industry," says Locus Robotics CEO Rick Faulk.[165]

During the last six months of 2020, online ordering increased from 11% of total business to 16%, putting pressure on operators to increase automation. Approximately 100,000 warehouse buildings worldwide still continue to operate manually. Locus believes that it can double, or even triple fulfillment productivity with near-100% accuracy (SDGs 9,12). With the new funding of more than $260 million, the company intends to expand its global operations, including Asia, and continue investing in research and development to add new features and functionality. Beyond real-time data visualization to track warehouse operations on an iPhone or wearable technology, the company plans to continue adding to those capabilities with AI and machine learning.[166]

IN BUSINESS

FANUC[167]

Initiative: Cobot innovation in manufacturing
Headquarters: Oshino-mura, Yamanashi Japan

FANUC exclusively targets industrial robots and concentrates on helping customers automate or robotize their factories for improved productivity. It is a leading supplier of automation for manufacturing including robotics, CNCs and motion control, and robomachining centers. The company's industrial robots, which include types for welding, material handling (transportation of articles), assembly, and painting are used in wide-ranging industry sectors. The market for "collaborative robots" (cobots) is growing. As cobots automatically and safely stop when touched by humans, they do not require safety fences. By assisting work alongside human workers, operators can avoid strenuous work. The CRX series, lightweight collaborative robots FANUC announced in December 2019, are a new type of cobot developed to achieve thorough ease of use for customers. The manual-guided teaching feature allows users to directly move the arm by hand, enabling intuitive robot operation. Users can design teaching programs in a smartphone-like operation with high reliability. Key features of FANUC that signify areas of contribution to environmental and social issues include the robot's measures to address skill building for the decreases in the working population and to train highly-skilled engineers (SDG 4), focus on improvement of factories' work environment and safety (SDGs 3,8), and industry productivity as well as waste reduction and energy savings (SDGs 7,9,12,13).[168]

ADDRESSING RISKS AND CHALLENGES ON THE ROAD AHEAD

The changes taking place in the robotics sector are expected to impact consumer markets and, ultimately, society at large. These changes will be profound and potentially life-altering across all fields and sectors. It is vital to note that next-generation robotics also poses some concerns. Although the proliferation of this tech will bring a range of new industries and job creations, the prospect of robots replacing human laborers means jobs will be lost. For example, a future where unrestricted use of autonomous agricultural robots prevails may prove detrimental to farmers. In parts of the world where there is no agricultural labor shortage, reducing the demand for human workers would entail people needing resources and opportunities to retrain in other sectors. In this instance, laborers may be forced to transition into dangerous and underpaid jobs in other industries such as mining.

A FUTURE WHEREIN THE UNRESTRICTED USE OF AUTONOMOUS AGRICULTURAL ROBOTS PREVAILS MAY PROVE DETRIMENTAL TO FARMERS.

Robots replacing human laborers in the present and future does not take into consideration that people may lack the motivation or opportunity to learn skills for higher-paying jobs. With the increasing automation of labor in several industries, there is a concern that business owners will be able to hire fewer workers for lower wages without fear of competition from other companies. This means that income inequality may continue to grow with this new form of robotics technological innovation. In industry roles, such as manufacturing plants, robots are becoming more common. One of the main issues with robots in this regard is that they require highly skilled operators, which excludes many people who lack access to the necessary education and training. There will be a shortage of qualified people for these jobs, signifying that companies will likely have to pay these individuals disproportionately high wages.[169]

ROBOTS REQUIRE HIGHLY SKILLED OPERATORS, WHICH EXCLUDES MANY PEOPLE WHO LACK ACCESS TO THE NECESSARY EDUCATION AND TRAINING.

Many ethical considerations also arise when introducing robots into environments where they can make decisions that affect human lives. Especially the use of autonomous robots in the military or robotic surgeons in hospitals. Businesses and governments alike will need to address these issues. One worldwide change required will be for education to improve public understanding and perception of robots and how they will interact in our digitally-enabled society. There will be an extensive need for policies to ensure the smooth adoption of robots in various public environments.[170] We will need to better understand and explain the capabilities and limitations of robot platforms. As with many of the other techs in this book, the threat of cyber security is another important consideration. Since more autonomous robots operate in safety-critical environments, someone could hack or manipulate a robot and impose significant harm. If left unregulated, hacking incidents and data breaches could undermine the public perception of robotics being a beneficial technology. Similarly, the ownership of data collected by robots operated by commercial companies could pose further challenges.[171] This is because those data could be used for the pure benefit of big companies at the cost of societal good.

WE HAVE
IMAGINED

We have imagined robots supporting us, entertaining us, and working alongside us. These tech companions aid in the psychological and physical health of vulnerable people, like autistic children and the elderly. They have the unique capacity to give emotional, social, and educational support whenever needed without getting tired. In times of isolation, robots emerge as a best friend and confidant. We have also imagined how the field of robotics is advancing to protect us. While keeping us healthy and safe, robots also work to limit strains and serious injuries for workers on industrial jobs.

The robotics industry weaves through countless business models, and this chapter has taken us on an imaginative journey of the possibilities for robotics innovations. Robotics' unique qualities in terms of accessibility and automation prove to be beneficial to all 17 Global Goals. In addition to aiding children, robots are helping fight climate change, manage recycling, streamline healthcare, and boost manufacturing. Remote areas that are too dangerous for humans are easily accessed by robots, thus no longer requiring companies to send workers down dangerous ditches or hazardous caves to extract minerals and gems. Agricultural operations are made more cost-effective through automation, which increases productivity and staves off world hunger as well.

Imagining a sustainable world full of possibilities includes robotics in all facets of global business. As our lifelike counterparts, with intelligent AI-enabled operating systems, robots instill an element of trust and safety into the human experience. Let's not fear a robot uprising, since the benefits outweigh the threats.

We have imagined Robotics for Good.

TECH FOR GOOD

THE FILM

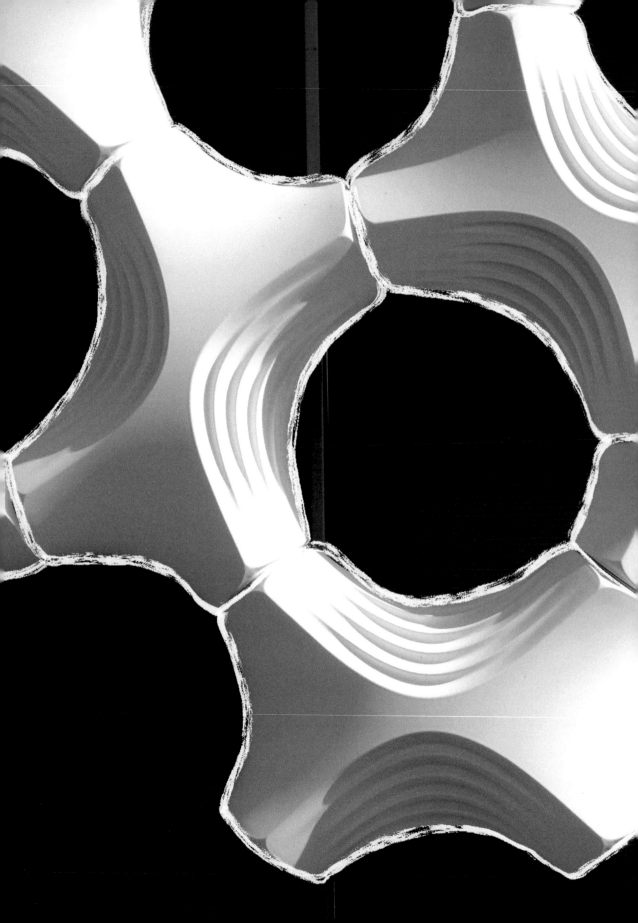

ADVANCED MATERIALS

5

TIMES ARE CHANGING AND MATERIALS ARE TRANSFORMING.

NEW SCIENTIFIC CONFIGURATIONS WILL REDESIGN AND REVOLUTIONIZE OUR WORLD.

WE ONLY NEED TO

IMAGINE

Imagine redesigning infrastructure in our cities and communities by incorporating environmentally responsible processes in construction. Imagine new, sustainable materials that could help us build next-gen urban landscapes. Visualize eco-friendly buildings made of materials that go beyond traditional bricks, concrete, and wood. Imagine how we could use these advanced materials to substantially increase the value and functionality in a forward-thinking market while saving on utility and maintenance costs.

Materials science tech innovations will propel us to a cleaner and healthier future. New and advanced materials are transforming the way we live in unprecedented ways. Breakthroughs in construction-materials development are creating sustainable business solutions for an economically and environmentally prosperous world. Materials are not only enhancing infrastructure capabilities to be energy efficient and carbon neutral, but they are also mitigating their own negative impacts. Recognizing this enormous potential for "net positive" gains, we experience advanced materials of the cityscape architecture reducing pollutants in the environment.

The notoriously smoggy Mexico City benefits greatly from this tech. In 1992, the UN declared it the most polluted city in the world and since then significant efforts have been made to improve air quality. In the southern corner stands a beautiful 100-meter tall, 2,500-meter wide, serene white façade of a hospital building called the Torre de Especialidades that was inspired by fractals in nature. A delight for the eye, this structure works to benefit our planet's sustainability efforts by cleaning up the pollution of thousands of vehicles passing by every day. The Torre de Especialidades hospital is enclosed with special tiles that have air-scrubbing capabilities.[1] The façade is made up of a new genre of tile called "proSolve370e," which neutralizes the chemicals produced by 8,750 cars daily.[2] The key to the smog-fighting powers of the hospital building's façade is in its paint. Concocted from a titanium dioxide-based pigment, proSolve's antimicrobial and de-polluting properties provide smog-eating benefits as well as visual complexity in a memorable form. When sunlight's ultraviolet rays touch the titanium dioxide on the tiles, it triggers a chemical reaction between the tiles and the smog in the air (mono-nitrogen oxides). While the pollutants are broken down into safer substances such as water, carbon dioxide, and calcium nitrate, the titanium dioxide remains unfettered and unchanged.

The innovative lattice-like design of the tile is another work of scientific art. The shape is specifically designed in a purposeful manner to slow wind speed and create turbulence for better distribution of pollutants across the active surfaces. Finally, the structure's outer layer produces shadows inside the building so that it catches light from all directions, helping keep it fresh and cool by natural means rather than costly or artificial air conditioning.

Materials science is focused on the understanding and application of the properties of matter. Specifically, it is the study of "connections between the underlying structure of a material, its properties, its processing methods, and its performance in applications."[3] The engineering possibilities of inventing novel solutions for materials to be utilized in various real-world applications is the playful meeting of science and technology. This tech merges the natural world with the art of generating exciting new materials for the benefit of the planet and its people. Imagine the infinite number of breakthroughs that remain hidden in the chemistry between the elements and materials all around us.

Imagine what awaits humankind if we find new chemical configurations and compositions to produce advanced materials that shape a desirable future of innovation and sustainability. In this regard, the possibilities are truly endless for the construction sector. It is no surprise that entrepreneurs and scientists are infusing their intellect and aesthetic creativity with the promise of chemical compounds to enhance buildings' capabilities to combat pollution and slow climate change. People and businesses all over the globe are invested in developing materials that will make a difference in urban infrastructure planning.

Imagine slowing global warming with smog-eating buildings. This is Advanced Materials for Good.

MargaHock

5 EXPLORING
ADVANCED MATERIALS

From paper to plastics, metamaterials to nanomaterials, materials innovation has been relying heavily on tech advancements. Novel chemical configurations develop new products, and the technological implementation looks toward using them for maximum market and scientific advancement. This chapter talks about some of the most notable advanced materials - graphene, glass, algae, solvents, membranes, nanomedicine, and nano crystals. But how do these and others drive the economic growth market while ensuring the tech is used for good?

Some of the ways this tech could revolutionize business include achieving a recycle-based and low-carbon society that new and advanced materials make possible. Industrial waste, which is severely hazardous to the environment, can be transformed into an advanced material with the potential to be utilized for the reduction of CO_2 emissions. Acid-enhanced fertilizers to improve agricultural yields are also coming forward, as are augmented plastics that can reduce transformation costs. With sustainable business growth improving thanks to advanced materials, the capabilities of tech for good are becoming more prominent.

Maximizing the value of advanced materials does, however, mean consideration of some of the challenges that may present themselves along the journey. There are, of course, risks tied into the use of these advanced materials, as is the case with every tech discussed in this book. Health implications are most important to research for innovations like these, since they can be significant in terms of both limiting business growth and stalling environmental goals. Although this novel field of materials science comes with some risk, its applications will advance our world and create new, sustainable business opportunities.

THE TECH

Advanced materials are a new class of materials with enhanced properties that are continuously being developed. They are intentionally designed for superior performance. The major scientific breakthroughs of the last century, along with a new understanding of atoms, laid the foundation for advanced materials to be a vital component of our high-tech economy.[4] It is amazing to see how rapidly material sciences introduce a wide variety of technological advancements. If these materials are developed while keeping their constructive purpose in mind, such as to produce positive benefits for both the planet and people, they can have a huge impact. In this exciting first phase of the 4IR, we see these new materials blend with digital technologies, underpinning the mere essence of this next industrial phase. Advanced materials can alter and enhance our way of life. There is a reason the world celebrates the Bronze Age and the Iron Age – these eras marked significant points in human and societal advancements. Concrete, stainless steel, and silicon are other notable materials that have made the modern era possible, but they are also soon to be history.

A NEW CLASS OF MATERIALS IS EMERGING, BOASTING POTENTIALS NOT YET ENTIRELY GRASPABLE BY THE HUMAN IMAGINATION.

Throughout history, advances in materials technology have influenced humankind. At this stage, the world is on the verge of the next shift, where materials tech innovations enable products and functions that were previously believed impossible. Modern industry requires materials to be lighter, tougher, thinner, denser, and more flexible or rigid, as well as to be heat- and wear-resistant. Simultaneously, researchers and organizations employ their imagination and push the boundaries. They seek to improve and enhance existing materials to contrive completely new iterations that, while years away from day-to-day use, can take us into entirely new technological realms of sustainability and progress. These exciting potentials are utterly promising and appealing to an almost futuristic type of novel application.

This chapter discloses a variety of these materials as we know them today. When applied for good, materials have an enormous beneficial impact throughout all business sectors. Metamaterials, which allow scientists to control light waves in new ways, could improve daily functions as prevalent as streamlining smartphone usage and changing how we use other tech applications.[5] Let's take a metamaterial example that has already come a long way: graphene. In the world of advanced materials, carbon-derived graphene outperforms even the most robust tiny creatures like insects in terms of proportional strength. Graphene is a single atom thick (one million times thinner than a human hair) but 200 times stronger than steel by weight, extremely flexible, super light, and almost transparent. It also boasts excellent heat and electricity conductivity.

WHEN APPLIED FOR GOOD, MATERIALS HAVE AN ENORMOUS POSITIVE IMPACT THROUGHOUT ALL BUSINESS SECTORS.

Graphene's density is only 5% that of steel, yet believe it or not, it is hundreds of times stronger! Researchers at Nankai University in Tianjin, China, recently found that a graphene sponge can turn light into energy, thus taking humankind one step closer to a fuel-free spacecraft that runs by the light of the sun.[6] A new class of materials is emerging, boasting potentials not yet entirely graspable by human imagination and leading us to a sustainable and innovative future. Graphene takes on numerous forms. At once a powder, then dispersed in a polymer matrix, the material is capable of being applied to several already new materials like composites, 3D printed materials, and batteries. Potential areas of application for graphene are wide-ranging, from water purification and energy storage to household goods, computers, and other electronics.

"MATERIALS HAVE ALWAYS BEEN ABOUT ENTHUSIASM. MATERIALS ARE A DREAM THAT WE HAVE REALIZED. EVERYTHING IS POSSIBLE; IT'S JUST THAT WE HAVE TO MAKE IT HAPPEN."[7] - MARK MIODOWNIK, AUTHOR OF "STUFF MATTERS"

New materials like graphene are advanced materials with engineered properties, created through specialized processing and synthesis technology. Hence, they are often used in high-technology applications. These materials are a cornerstone of the 4IR, which blends digital and physical technologies. Advanced materials can be either new materials with advanced characteristics – in which case these materials are really "created" – or existing materials with additionally engineered properties. A vast range of materials is appearing and evolving, including ceramics, high value-added metals, electronic materials, semiconductors, composites, polymers, biomaterials, carbon fiber, smart materials, and nanoengineered materials. Nowadays, much of the development for novel materials occurs in science labs and is far more experimental than in former revolutions.

MANY NEW MATERIALS OFFER THE PROMISE OF DECREASED ENERGY USAGE, BETTER PERFORMANCE AT LOWER COSTS, AND LESS DEPENDENCE ON VIRGIN MATERIALS.

Today, scientists are testing combinations of ingredients, heating, mixing, and other processes to continue unprecedented materials research and experimentation. During the last few decades, a scaled-up, highly organized and automated research system called "combinatorial chemistry," which involves the synthesis of compounds, has produced new materials.[8] These include automotive coatings, hydrogen storage materials, materials for solar cells, metal alloys, organic dyes, and many others. With so many chemical advancements on the horizon, there are promising developments in materials science for the future. As the world of materials science and development has become much more aware of resource scarcity and climate change, along with health and wellbeing challenges, we have evidence before us for meaningful and favorable progress. For instance, many advanced materials today in the development and research stage offer the promise of decreased energy usage, better performance at lower costs, and less dependence on diminishing natural resources.

In 1931, American scientist Samuel Stephens Kistler discovered silica aerogel, a material that can be described as "strange and ghostlike."[9] This material is solid in form despite being 99.98% air. Made by sucking the liquid out of gel using a supercritical dryer, aerogel consists of air pockets that make it ultralight and capable of trapping heat. Its applications are encouraging too, such as the possibility of being used on Mars. It can be used to build settlements (domes) near the planet's polar ice caps where these structures will trap heat, melt polar ice into usable water, and block harmful ultraviolet radiation while allowing visible light through. The material's light weight is an added benefit, making it easy to transport to Mars.

"MATERIALS THAT HEAL THEMSELVES ARE COMING."[10] - MARK MIODOWNIK, AUTHOR OF "STUFF MATTERS"

With all these new, advanced materials the sky's the limit. This concept is further exhibited in nanocomposite research which is opening the possibility of materials that fix themselves, much like the way the human body heals itself. These self-fixing or self-healing materials have the built-in ability to automatically repair damages without any external diagnosis or human intervention. Researchers in the Beckman Institute's Autonomous Materials Systems Group at the University of Illinois are working on fiber-composite materials with self-healing properties.[11] Self-healing materials are used in the autonomic repair of composites to restore functionalities and structural properties.

PHOSPHORENE NANORIBBONS

Phosphorene Nanoribbons, an accidental discovery in recent years, have altered the field of battery technology.[12] The structure of this technology means the charged ions in electric vehicles, aircraft, and solar batteries can now move up to 1,000 times faster.[13] As a result, we would see a decrease in charging time and a 50% increase in battery capacity. It could also mean a transition for innovative tech companies, such as Tesla, away from hard-to-source lithium ions to abundant sodium ions.[14] At merely one atom thick and 100 atoms across, they span up to 100,000 atoms in length.[15] They are uniform but manipulable, meaning their properties (such as electrical conductivity) can be fine-tuned. Their flexibility means they can be malleable and can perfectly follow the contours of surfaces. Moreover, this innovative new advanced material tech marks the emergence of altogether novel phenomena and unique constructions for utility and applications such as thermoelectric devices and integrated high-speed electronic circuits.

This self-fixing quality is one step closer to automatically improving the life of a material, as well as the life of the planet. The possibilities for this tech to fix anything on demand, from airplane wings, to bike frames, to car parts crucial to the safety of vehicles and passengers is becoming viable. Researchers are even working on new materials that will allow a roadway to repair itself instead of waiting for a maintenance crew to arrive.[16] Advanced materials are on the cusp of having a massive sustainable business impact on product development and lifecycle attributes across several sectors.

SOUND FOUNDATIONS

Materials incorporated into prominent technologies have a long history that dates back to the Stone Age prior to 3000 B.C.E. During prehistoric times, human technologies relied on found objects and substances harvested from the earth. Modifying these materials, early man formed them into different and useful forms. This was the beginning of technological materials advancements. Humans of the Bronze Age (3000-1200 B.C.E), the Iron Age (1200 B.C.E. – 300 C.E.), and the Middle Ages (300 - 1300 C.E.) introduced materials such as metals and clay along with tech advancements in furnaces developed for metal extraction and processing, which brought about profound changes in lifestyles. Additional metallurgical advances, such as the introduction of the Bessemer Process, established steel as the material that defined the industrial timespan.[17] New materials have been continuously developed throughout history that were advanced for their time. From achieving the capabilities necessary to produce iron to creating techniques required to make porcelain, the most cutting-edge examples of advanced materials technology are evident in every era.[18]

RECENT ADVANCES IN MATERIALS SCIENCE UNLOCK EMERGING TECHNOLOGIES THAT ARE A DEFINING FACTOR OF THE 4IR.

Since the 1950s, the information era in which we currently live has been defined by the ubiquity of computers. The material substrate that enables tech advancements in modern computing is the semiconductor, which is primarily silicon-based. There are numerous other new materials that make technologies possible, such as advanced composite materials for aerospace applications and the polymers for a variety of consumer goods. The surging field of nanoscience and nanotechnology is spurring design of materials as well. Materials defects, also called crystallographic defects, are now being used in the storage and retrieval of quantum information for quantum computing purposes.[19] When the novel effects demonstrated by these materials become commonplace, the technologies that define the next era will be based around custom-made matter with structures that span length scales, from the nanoscopic to the macroscopic, and that have superlative (or conventionally impossible) thermal, optical, tribomechanical, and computational capabilities.

ADVANCED MATERIALS MARKET SIZE

Innovative advanced material technologies are expected to impact economic growth directly and positively through improved products and processes.[20] While nations around the globe are developing low-carbon technology to tackle climate change by introducing low-carbon vehicles and low-energy buildings with strong material structures, businesses are competitive in this tech area as well. Emerging with advanced materials such as gorilla glass in smartphones or composites in the Boeing Dreamliner aircraft, companies across the healthcare, aerospace, packaging, and construction industries are financially benefiting from the use of new materials through improved productivity, performance, sustainability, and regulatory obligations. [21]

Companies and their competitors are launching new materials that unlock revenue potential and market share, help meet unmet customer needs, assist in achieving profitability goals, and provide a base for satisfying sustainability and regulatory requirements. Profitability can be achieved from the molecular level and up, as new materials utilize the research community's understanding of chemical compound structures and other properties to improve product performance, capability, and efficiency. The advanced materials market is classified into lightweight materials, ceramics, glass, polymers, composites, metals and alloys, nanomaterials, and others. Of these, ceramics holds a significant market share, which can be attributed to the increased usage in the electronics industry in recent years.[22] Moreover, the market for lightweight materials and nanomaterials is expected to witness considerable growth due to the increasing usage of nanomaterials in prominent industries like automotive and healthcare.

THE RAPIDLY GROWING ADVANCED MATERIALS TECH MARKET IS TRANSFORMING THE GLOBAL MANUFACTURING INDUSTRY, ESPECIALLY IN ITS REPLACEMENT OF PLASTICS AND METALS.

The advanced materials market is forecasted to reach $2.1 trillion by 2025,[23] recording a 10% CAGR globally from 2019 to 2025.[24] Asia Pacific is expected to account for a majority of the advanced materials industry market share at 58% by 2024.[25] China is leading the way from $3.9 billion in 2016 to an anticipated $5.31 billion by the end of 2024.[26] Germany is projected to amass a 21% market share in the global advanced materials market by the end of 2024, with expected growth at a CAGR of 6.5% over the forecast period of 2019 to 2024. [27] Europe is also expected to observe significant growth in the coming years.[28] Economies of the United Kingdom and Spain are likely to be the key contributors to the growth of the materials market in this region.[29] Furthermore, the rising demand for energy in the Middle East and Africa region is expected to fuel the growth of advanced materials globally.

THE ADVANCED MATERIALS MARKET IS FORECASTED TO REACH $2.1 TRILLION BY 2025,[30] RECORDING A 10% CAGR GLOBALLY FROM 2019 TO 2025.[31]

The next phase of this tech is in plant-based new materials development, such as algae, where the market was valued at $592 million in 2019 and is projected to reach $967.3 million by 2027, growing at a CAGR of 6.3% from 2020 to 2027.[32] The building and structural materials segment is also dominant and will likely reach $1.8 trillion by the end of 2024, from $1.1 trillion in 2016.[33] The global advanced building materials market was valued at $56.7 billion in 2021, and is projected to reach $111.7 billion by 2031, growing at a CAGR of 6.8% from 2022 to 2031.[34]

Venture capital firms are driving market growth as well, promoting financing in advanced materials startups. Top Venture capital investors by value includes 8VC, Bessemer Ventures Partners, Sutter Hill Ventures LLC, and Coatue Management LLC that are investing in startups to develop innovative battery storage materials and advanced manufacturing technologies.[35] In addition, Yida Capital, ZhongWei Capital, Forebright Capital Management Limited, and Huiyou Capital are financially backing startups working on integrated circuits, sensor chips, and advanced manufacturing for lightweight applications. Collaborations exist in the new materials markets between investors and science.

This rapidly expanding technology is transforming the global manufacturing industry, especially in its replacement of plastics and metals with ceramics and composites in high-performance applications.[36] Growing business interest in end product replacements will further propel the overall market demand for new materials. The expanding electrical and electronics sector and the growing development of the aerospace sector are expected to drive the growth of the new materials market as well and will be essential to manufacturing processes across industries. The ceramics segment holds the largest share in the advanced materials market. Advanced ceramics such as alumina, aluminum nitride, zirconia, silicon carbide, silicon nitride, and titania-based materials, each with their own specific characteristics, offer a high-performance, economical alternative to conventional materials such as glass, metals, and plastics.[37]

$35.62 billion 2022 global advanced materials market size.[38]	$2.1 trillion forecasted global advanced materials market by 2025.[39]	Building and structural materials expected to reach $1.8 trillion by the end of 2024.[40]

ADVANCED MATERIALS FOR GOOD

Materials science, including engineering, research, and financing mechanisms, is rapidly moving forward to help address the Global Goals. New and advanced materials could have major beneficial impacts that include countering global warming and augmenting energy efficiency. There are several examples of advanced materials creating solutions in solar power, electric-car batteries, portable electronic devices, implantable medical devices for personalized medicine, lifesaving pharmaceuticals, streamlined industrial manufacturing processes, and cleaner energy usage. The potential for research and the development of advanced materials to create a better world is limitless.

IN BUSINESS
EARLY CHARM VENTURES

Initiative: Materic LLC[41]
Headquarters: Baltimore, Maryland USA

Early Charm, a Baltimore-based venture, merged six of its advanced materials holdings into one operating company, Materic LLC (SDG 17).[42] "By coming together under Materic, we now have sales into the aerospace, healthcare, biotechnology, electronics, automotive, athletic, energy and military industries, giving us contacts into each of the key sectors for advanced materials"[43] states Ken Malone, CEO with Abri Science, a Materic subsidiary. Early Charm Ventures creates, owns, and operates venture capital entities that convert science into revenue. Specifically, the VC firm has achieved its goals of providing more value to customers and accelerating the commercialization of each company's intellectual property (SDG 8). Materic's mission is to develop market opportunities to custom design and manufacture advanced materials (SDG 12).[44] As a chemical and specialty materials company, Materic works with clients to design and produce custom solutions to fit unique applications. The Materic team of scientists, engineers, and designers assists in all phases, from ideation to prototyping, to helping turn concepts into manufacturable products.

Materic has expertise in designing specialty material for industries such as: electronics, oil and gas, filtration, energy, textiles, and health and personal care. Solving customers' new materials needs, the firm brings together multiple technologies and a team with diverse expertise. Materic's newly combined capabilities include nanofiber electrospinning, nanoparticle separation, textile treatments, 3D printing materials, specialty inks, and encapsulation (SDG 9).

Materic's six advanced materials subsidiaries include:
Abri Science – enabling enzymes and catalysts to work in harsh environments through microencapsulation; DiPole Materials – electrospinning nanofibers including piezoelectrics for smart garments, scaffolds for tissue engineering and a wide range of custom products for industrial uses; NanoDirect – high efficiency separation technologies for nanoparticles and the Direct Silver line of silver nanowires and specialty inks for the electronics and energy industries; Ortuvo – 3D printing technology for tissue engineering and custom bio-inks for the healthcare and biotech industries; Synteris – 3D printing technology for ceramics in the aerospace, healthcare and automotive industries; SciGenesis – specialty textile inks, microencapsulated insect repellant treatments for textiles and heat reflecting camo face paints for the military and athletic industries.

FROM BIOMEDICAL APPLICATIONS TO STRUCTURAL BUILDING COMPONENTS, NEW AND ADVANCED MATERIALS CAN IMPROVE LIVES.

From biomedical applications to structural building components, the superior or more functional qualities of new advanced materials can improve societies while leveraging millions of investment dollars in the long and short term. A wide range of categories of advanced materials are available, and they tie into both the need and the opportunity to be materials for good. Biomaterials, for instance, are materials interacting with or being derived from biological systems in combination with synthetic materials. Harnessing cellular and molecular processes to develop new products for a range of uses, scientists are developing technological advancements to produce stronger biomaterials.[45] The science of advanced materials sheds a new light on the interaction between biology and nature. The continuously growing understanding of biological systems and their interfaces with materials is opening new pathways for the use of biomaterials. These materials have a wide range of applications with diverse requirements.

BIOMIMICRY: MATERIALS MIMICKING NATURE

Biomimicry inspires many new materials by looking to nature to inform their advanced solutions. If we as humans harness materials in a manner that mimics the natural world, we could apply nature's intelligence to many 4IR needs and solutions. Nature is packed with inspiration for scientists designing new materials or enhancing existing materials. Scientists use substances like waterproof adhesives and self-cleaning surfaces, mineralized teeth, hairy insect feet, and spider silk as nature-based templates to develop bio-inspired materials. For instance, possible applications for humans could be electrodes made from the materials silicon, platinum, iridium, and tungsten implanted into the brain in patients with Parkinson's disease, which is required to be stiff during insertion but flexible once in place.[46] Another potential is for protective clothing, which needs to be comfortable to wear but protective when necessary. The pathway from science to practice and commercialization may not yet have fully come to fruition for this tech, but there is a vast opportunity to use nature as a model for advanced materials.[47]

CarbonTech is an exciting growth area in materials science for the benefit of the planet as well. Referring to the wide variety of commercial products made with the CO_2 captured from power plants, biomass, or direct air capture. CarbonTech is an estimated $6 trillion available market globally.[48] Advanced materials in CarbonTech encompass a diverse set of goods and services, including global commodities like fuel, plastics, and building materials as well as valuable niche applications like cosmetics, food, beverages, and emerging technologies including carbon nanotubes. In energy efficiency and carbon storage applications, CarbonTech presents a range of innovative solutions. A startup in Iceland named Carbfix is tackling climate change with a unique approach to materials science (Case 30). By turning carbon dioxide into rocks, the tech solution allows the greenhouse gas to be stored forever instead of escaping into the atmosphere and trapping heat.

IN BUSINESS

CARBFIX[49]

Initiative: Turn CO2 into stone
Headquarters: Reykjavik, Iceland

Carbfix is an academic-industrial tech partnership that is intent on reaching one billion tons of permanently stored CO2 in 2030.[50] Vast quantities of carbon are naturally stored in rocks. Carbfix imitates and accelerates the natural processes of carbon drawdown from the atmosphere, where carbon dioxide is dissolved in water and interacts with reactive rock formations, such as basalts, to form stable minerals providing a permanent and safe carbon sink (SDGs 9,12). The Carbfix process captures and permanently removes CO2 (SDG 13). For the Carbfix technology to work, three requirements must be met: favorable rocks, water, and a source of carbon dioxide. The timescale of this process initially surprised scientists' projections. In the Carbfix pilot project, it was determined that at least 95% of the injected CO2 mineralizes within two years, much faster than previously thought.[51]

About 5% of the continents are covered by favorable rocks for carbon mineralization, as well as most of the seafloor. The global storage potential is greater than the emissions of the burning of all fossil fuels on Earth (SDG 7). In fact, Iceland alone could store many years' worth of mankind's carbon emissions. Europe could theoretically store at least 4 trillion tons of CO2 in rocks, while the US could store at least 7.5 billion tons (SDG 12).[52] "This is a technology that can be scaled—it's cheap and economic and environmentally friendly," Carbfix CEO Edda Sif Pind Aradottir said.[53] "Basically we are just doing what nature has been doing for millions of years, so we are helping nature help itself."

Carbfix was derived from a research project and founded in 2006 by Reykjavik Energy, the University of Iceland, CNRS in France, and the Earth Institute at Columbia University (SDG 17). It's owned by Reykjavik Energy. The startup recently raised $117 million from The European Innovation Fund in a June 2022 funding round, as well as an undisclosed amount from the Musk Foundation and XPRIZE in April 2022.[54]

The advancement of materials in energy and environmental design is being implemented across the globe to perpetuate sustainable business. Polymers (such as plastics) and soft materials like foams, emulsions, and gels are being further developed for a range of consumer products and high-end technological applications that improve both business and environmental performance. Nanotech and nanomaterials offer enormous opportunities for sustainable technologies. From saving raw materials, energy, and water to decreasing greenhouse gasses and excess waste, nanotechnology utilized in various products, procedures, and applications could certainly support environmental and climate protection. In application, improved methods to separate CO_2 from waste gasses are being constructed from nanomaterials. Researchers in Germany fabricated an ultra-thin nanoscale polymer film that filters out CO_2 with promising results.[55] This material could be used to treat large gas streams under low pressure, such as CO_2 captured from gasses in coal-fired power plants.

ADVANCED MATERIALS PROGRESSING THE GLOBAL GOALS

Advanced materials will have positive impacts on several Global Goals. They are particularly important for the proper and effective implementation of the SDGs. The rising use of new materials in areas like manufacturing processes across healthcare, energy, environment, and many more underpins the dynamic and functional qualities of the tech being essential for achieving the Goals.

ZERO HUNGER

There are many ways in which new materials will help mitigate this grand-scale challenge. Advances in materials will lead to better crop protection, for example, to guard plants from infestations. Progress in this tech will also drive improvement in new and better equipment involved in the agriculture sector. The production of crops and food distribution channels will see drastic enhancement too. Overall, the nanotechnology applications for novel and advanced materials hold great potential to facilitate technological advances that can help improve food security, supply, and production. Copper is necessary for the proper development of plant tissues, in addition to a positive effect on the photosynthesis process and nitrogen transformation. However, plants do not easily absorb natural copper that is necessary for high yield-quality. This prompted Polish AgriTech startup Strigiformes to manufacture a nano copper-based biostimulant.[56] Biosterilvita Plus, the startup's proprietary product, combines garlic extract and horseradish together with a nanomolar concentration of nano copper. The product stimulates the growth and development of plants by increasing the uptake of water and nutrients.

GOOD HEALTH AND WELLBEING

Materials have abundant applications in global healthcare and help enormously in ensuring healthy lives for people worldwide. Advances in materials sciences are facilitating progress for medical devices. With the assistance of new materials that have improved properties, medical equipment and devices function at a higher level and provide more precise services. These materials have better and enhanced physical, electrical, and chemical properties that stimulate innovation. Medical equipment made using Solvay's Udel high-performance polysulfone (PSU) thermoplastic is recycled at the end of their useful lives in a new sustainability initiative that the company has embarked on with Mitsubishi Chemical Advanced Materials (MCAM).[57] This advanced material product will help customers reach sustainability goals for high-performance healthcare business targets. Both companies are currently investigating the implementation of logistics for recovery, recycling, and reprocessing of Udel PSU medical components, with the aim of recycled material being suitable for reuse in the original applications.[58]

AFFORDABLE AND CLEAN ENERGY

New materials are indispensable to address the energy crisis and fulfill the demand for renewable power. Materials science is facilitating the development of photovoltaic components and thin films to increase solar energy production and its efficiency. The turbines used in wind energy are also made of polymer matrix composite materials. In the sphere of geothermal power, new materials technologies have become crucial for the success of enhanced geothermal systems. With structural materials, advanced ceramics, and coatings for fuels, these advanced substances are bound to play an important role in efficient energy transportation, storage, and buildings that help shape a sustainable world. Arkema's advanced materials used in solar panels, wind turbine blades, and electric batteries support society's transition to renewable energy.[59] The France-based materials innovator is developing new solar panel materials, especially polymers, with the aim to increase sturdiness, lifetime, and performance of solar panels. In addition, Arkema is providing the industry with products and solutions to reduce production costs and to save on silicon, while also making it easier to recycle end of life panels.

SUSTAINABLE CITIES AND COMMUNITIES

Materials science has enabled the efficient use of energy-intensive materials and the retention of materials that are indispensable for modern technology in urban regions. Moreover, by making possible the mitigation of corrosion and enhancing the processes of the energy sector, new materials have made sustainability an achievable reality. With sub-areas like structural materials, construction materials, lightweight cementitious composites, and many more, materials science holds enormous potential to help mankind realize the dream of sustainable buildings and eventually cities. Substances like shape memory alloys, piezoelectric, and magnetostrictive smart materials are extremely important for developing smart cities.[60]

RESPONSIBLE PRODUCTION AND CONSUMPTION

New materials enhance efficient consumption of resources. With the advent of advanced rubber composites, the life of tires has increased. Tremendous strides have also been made in energy efficiency due to low-emitting windows and green insulation materials. New and advanced materials create low emission chemicals, steel, and aluminum and can replace many materials throughout the chemical industry, ensuring higher performance with lower or zero footprint and less pressure on scarce natural resources.

Houston, Texas-based DexMat Inc. manufacturers products derived from carbon nanotubes (CNT).[61] From tape to insulated yarn, DexMat's patented material "Galvorn CNT fibers" has demonstrated breakthrough advancements in materials science in manufacturing. The Galvorn CNT fibers can be used to create various conductive products. With continued success, DexMat has been improving the electrical and mechanical properties of its developments by about 20% to 25% a year for the last 20 years.[62] This steady cadence of material and product improvements allows the company to maintain growth and innovate new products.

CLIMATE ACTION

Climate action is highly relevant for new materials solutions, as climate change is perhaps the biggest challenge that mankind faces in the 21st century. Advanced materials along with nanotechnology are powerful tools that can help us tackle this impending global threat. Lightweight nanocomposite materials help reduce the weight of commercial vehicles, which results in reduced fuel consumption. The nano-coatings have proven to be one of the best tools to reduce emissions and increase clean energy production. Moreover, nanostructured materials, like aerogels, lead to a reduction in heat transfer through building elements and significantly reduce loads on heating systems. A variety of critical materials enable clean energy technologies such as photovoltaics, wind turbines, electric vehicles, and energy-efficient lighting. Not only will they help cut carbon emissions and curb global warming, but these materials will also be an important factor in business success for climate-minded companies. Advanced substances such as CO_2 gas separation membranes, hybrid thin-film photovoltaics, solid-oxide fuel cells, and higher voltage and flow batteries will need further advancements for market integration.

LIFE BELOW WATER

Aquatic and marine pollution is another huge problem the world faces where materials will be highly relevant. The seas are home to innumerable organisms and a source of protein for billions of people. New materials have made possible technological progress in mitigating marine pollution. With sustainable, "green" submarine cables the ocean floor can be monitored like never before. Also, designing and synthesis of carbon materials for ocean monitoring leads to the detection and removal of dyes, pharmaceuticals, and heavy metals from salt waters. Canadian startup A20 Advanced Materials is developing the next generation of underwater adhesive and bonding coatings for anti-fouling purposes.[63] Oceanic organisms such as barnacles, sponges, and seaweeds attach themselves to vessels, slowing their speed while increasing fossil fuel consumption and transporting potentially invasive species from port to port. Through a sustainable, green chemistry-inspired route, A20 has created a new class of bonding materials that respond to the environment to produce durable and long-lasting coatings and adhesives for boats or ships.[64]

ZERO HUNGER

- Reduce agricultural damage using microorganisms.
- Improve agricultural yields to help restore farmland with acid-enhanced fertilizer.
- Employ lighter and harder augmented plastics to reduce transportation costs.

GOOD HEALTH AND WELLBEING

- Utilize new allergy-resistant latex adopted for medical, surgical, inspection, and industrial gloves.
- Contribute to a hygienic lifestyle with chemical-resistant plastic that is resistant to detergents and disinfectants.

AFFORDABLE AND CLEAN ENERGY

- Control heat and vibrations in materials used for clean energy consumption and production.
- Install safer, more stable, and higher-purity conductive materials for the inner and outer semiconductive layers of cables.
- Improve conductivity by replacing adhesive material with an enhanced volatile organic solvent.

SUSTAINABLE CITIES AND COMMUNITIES

- Allow for stronger and sturdier building structures that pollute less by incorporating cement additives.
- Reduce environmental burdens and improve working environments using rubber-based hot-melt adhesive without organic solvent.

ADVANCED MATERIALS

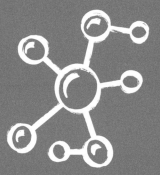

RESPONSIBLE PRODUCTION AND CONSUMPTION

- Develop new, recyclable products from diverse fields to create a recycle-based and low-carbon society.
- Enhance durability and functionality of products by developing additives and substances.

CLIMATE ACTION

- Utilize industrial byproducts of steelworks and thermal power generation plants as raw materials for the reduction of CO_2 emissions.
- Reduce the size and weight of commercial vehicles with nanocomposites, lowering fuel consumption and cutting CO_2 emissions.

LIFE BELOW WATER

- Reduce aquatic marine pollution with greener infrastructure derived from advanced materials.
- Eliminate toxic chemicals and harmful substances using carbon materials that can detect pollutants.

ENHANCING BUSINESS MODELS

Advanced materials offer opportunities to reduce costs and increase profitability due to their properties. Being stronger, lighter, and more durable, they last longer and save money on replacing parts. Additionally, they can compensate for operational and manufacturing challenges unsolved by less functional materials. Increased customer satisfaction and loyalty are also important for a business's bottom line. New and advanced materials help make final products that better fulfill customer requirements, thereby increasing competitiveness. These materials enable enterprises to create sophisticated products, design new business models, and achieve the Global Goals.

The drive towards sustainable business practices, large-scale manufacturing, and superior functionality is supported by advanced materials that prove fundamental to the 4IR economy. Advanced materials replace traditional materials to provide value for businesses and consumers. The contribution of new advanced materials in addressing the world's most urgent challenges is significant. Materials science companies are thus driving innovations in a number of business sectors with applications ranging from light-weighting materials in transportation, electrode materials in energy, biosensors in healthcare, and metal-organic frameworks (MOFs) to remove pollutants from the environment.[65]

NEW AND ADVANCED MATERIALS HELP MAKE FINAL PRODUCTS THAT FULFILL CUSTOMER REQUIREMENTS.

To improve the versatility of MOFs as sensors, semiconductor quantum dots have been introduced into the MOF pores to form composites. Quantum dots (QDs) are man-made nanoscale crystals that are capable of transporting electrons.[66] When UV light hits these semiconducting nanoparticles, they emit light of various colors. These artificial semiconductor nanoparticles have found applications in composites, solar cells, and fluorescent biological labels. Because certain biological molecules are capable of molecular recognition and self-assembly, nanocrystals could become an important material component of self-assembled functional nanodevices.

The atom-like energy states of QDs furthermore contribute to special optical properties, such as a particle-size dependent wavelength of fluorescence that is an important technology in applications like fabricating optical probes for biological and medical imaging. By leveraging the power of nanoparticles, modern companies secure their competitive edge, specifically in the electronics, energy, mobility, and manufacturing sectors. Singapore-based startup Nanolumi proliferates QD technology for electronic displays with its reliable and safe perovskite nanocrystals.

"THESE MATERIALS AND THIS ADVANCED EXISTENCE THAT WE NOW LIVE IS BROUGHT TO US NOT BY SMALL GROUPS OF PEOPLE OR EVEN TEN GROUPS OF TENS OF PEOPLE, BUT HUNDREDS OF PEOPLE IN THE LARGEST OF ORGANIZATIONS."[67] - ERICA NEMSER, CEO OF COMPACT MEMBRANE SYSTEMS

Advanced materials designed as sorbents, solvents, and membranes are also having a big impact, as they can absorb carbon and minimize emissions. Improving energy efficiency with new materials implementation in core business processes is a cost-effective way to lower CO_2 emissions by 15% to 20%, as well as increase the thermal inertia of building structures to reduce energy costs by 30% to 80%.[68] The European Commission considers hydrogen as an energy carrier with significant potential for clean, efficient power in stationary, portable, and transport applications. Advanced materials increase volumetric hydrogen capacities as well, which will have a net positive effect on the energy sector.[69] The use of lightweight composites and metals also help in a minimum of 10% reduction in a vehicle weight, which is estimated to result in a 6% to 8% improvement in fuel economy.[70]

IN BUSINESS

NANOLUMI[71]

Initiative: Quantum dot enabled production
Headquarters: Singapore

Nanolumi proliferates QD technology for electronic displays with its reliable and safe perovskite nanocrystals (SDGs 3,9). The company combines the advantages of cadmium-free origin, broad light spectrum coverage, purer color performance, and high-volume mass-production suitability.[72] Nanolumi's product also intends to supplant conventional perovskite nanocrystals for premium electronics with technology that brings colors and brightness to displays in addition to high performance advanced luminescent materials. The tech solution creates energy-efficient products that transform screen time into an enjoyable and immersive experience for work and leisure (SDGs 7,8).

Light emitted by perovskite nanocrystals are spectrally pure, offering highly saturated colors and a wider color spectrum. This is increasingly important as high dynamic range digital content becomes more readily available. Perovskite nanocrystals are the most efficient light-emitter – emitting a range of very narrow emission wavelengths even if the light absorbed (or being converted) is a broader spectrum – allowing more light to reach the viewer for a brighter display that consumes equal or less electrical power (SDG 12). The color performance of perovskite nanocrystals is determined by managing chemical composition and is not sensitive or dependent on individual particle size like conventional (metal chalcogenide) quantum dots, thus the company's core technology is designed for fast color tuning with scalability in mind. Achieving superior throughput synthesis and high yields of defect-tolerant perovskite nanocrystals, Nanolumi's proprietary continuous flow reactor system and Chameleon Film is produced through a cost competitive manufacturing process.[73]

The use and commercialization of advanced materials can indeed help us address some of the world's most pressing challenges. Boosting business growth, materials that are commercially applied for good will have a major beneficial impact. On a global scale, both public and private organizations are now more willing to invest in this tech area. They are dedicating resources to research and developing advanced materials that produce and commercialize higher quality finished products.[74] With newly developed advanced materials that are highly functional, smart businesses across industries are successfully improving their processes and manufacturing methods. This rising implementation of new materials in areas such as manufacturing processes in healthcare, energy, and environment have led them to be incredibly useful and essential for achieving the SDGs as well as for economic growth.

GLOBAL GOALS' GROWTH OPPORTUNITIES

Let us mention, first and foremost, that the potential of the advanced materials market may be bigger than nearly any other SDG growth lever. As evidenced throughout this chapter, the materials industry is pervasive and wide-ranging, with solutions addressed in a variety of sectors. From energy efficiency applications to structural building enhancements, medical healthcare initiatives to parts manufacturing, and agriculture to fashion, new materials can catapult products and services into unexplored realms. This immense potential points to two factors for materials in the market: 1) the tech is comprised of its own unique growth capabilities and 2) business opportunities for the tech abound in a vast sphere of possibilities. In exploring these concepts, we consider six overarching domains of impact: amping up the energy industry, revitalizing manufacturing processes, fostering health and wellbeing, augmenting food and agriculture, building better infrastructure, and enhancing textile and fashion production.

AMPING UP THE ENERGY INDUSTRY

Global energy consumption is rapidly increasing due to the rising middle class, saturation of new electrical devices, and global warming. These factors give rise to more intensive demands on worldwide power generation and services. Advanced materials play a fundamental role in achieving a more efficient energy supply based on renewable resources. By developing advanced materials usage that avoids rare, expensive, or toxic elements, the economy moves forward with the underlying foundation of recycling and reusing raw materials. Scientists and technicians are developing new materials to bolster renewable energy. One of the benefits it will bring is to help curb the accumulation of carbon dioxide in the atmosphere and associated global warming. We have already seen commercialization take place for photovoltaic cells that convert solar energy directly into electricity, as well as solar cells based on crystalline silicon.

ADVANCED MATERIALS PLAY A FUNDAMENTAL ROLE IN ACHIEVING A MORE EFFICIENT ENERGY SUPPLY BASED ON RENEWABLE RESOURCES.

Advanced materials play a vital role in the sustainable development of energy technologies spanning storage, conversion, generation, harvest, transport, and distribution. This application will leverage multi-disciplinary expertise to create new materials for clean energy production, storage, and conservation as well as for environmental remediation. Advanced materials for energy systems under development include dye-sensitized, bulk-heterojunction, and quantum-dot solar cells, which are made using low-temperature solution processing.[75] Notably, most of the focus is on halide perovskite materials that have exceeded a power conversion efficiency of 25%.[76] Furthermore, new energy storage approaches involving advanced materials include sunlight to produce solar fuels, where the energy is stored in the form of chemical bonds. These developments reveal there is a rising need for materials that are capable of capturing, converting, and ultimately storing energy. Several tech innovators are working on materials for energy efficiency initiatives in a range of market growth areas. British startup Opus Materials Technologies created forward-thinking anti-soiling and self-cleaning coatings for the aerospace, telecom, construction, mobility, marine, and renewable energy sectors.[77] The company aims to improve fuel consumption and airflow, diminishing corrosion and optimizing materials efficiency. Additionally, Opus allows for creating coating materials by design, and supports the establishment of the corresponding supply chain. Other tech businesses developing surface coatings for sustainable energy include Israel-based SolCold. Global warming and rising temperatures pose a major problem in surface-coating applications all over the world, and SolCold has come up with a solution that will lead us towards a more promising future. Materials science also plays a major role in batteries, which are a dominant technology for the direct storage of electrical energy. More than electrical storage, battery technology also supports the integration of renewable resources into the power grid. The global battery market is showing rising growth, as it was valued at $108.4 billion in 2019 and is expected to grow at a CAGR of 14.1% from 2020 to 2027.[78] We are aware that Lithium-ion batteries are used extensively in the increasingly popular electric vehicles. Yet, even with this progress, it remains that over two-thirds of global energy production is rejected as waste heat.[79] Within this reservoir of discarded energy lies an untapped opportunity. Scientists at MIT's Department of Nuclear Science and Engineering (NSE) are involved in exploring this potential. The goal of NSE's research is to find materials with conversion efficiencies high enough to make thermoelectric generation more practical. Thermoelectric generation technology offers a direct means of converting thermal energy, including waste heat, into electricity.[80] Realizing its full potential would mean opening a new chapter in the progress of sustainability.

REALIZING THE POTENTIAL OF LOSSLESS THERMOELECTRIC GENERATION WILL BE A NEW CHAPTER IN THE PROGRESS OF SUSTAINABILITY.

With forward-thinking movement, nanotechnology is being used in several applications to improve the environment. For this reason, carbon storage and management have become key instruments to mitigate climate change. It is worth noting that the carbon capture and storage market size is projected to be worth $10 billion by 2026 at a CAGR of 11.5%.[81] One objective of this includes making renewable energy sources more cost-effective, thus the use of new nanoporous membranes is a growing trend. This advanced material removes carbon dioxide from power plant smokestacks by allowing molecules to flow through the nanotubes to a storage tank. The rest of the exhaust stream, largely nitrogen, continues out the smokestack. Carbon nanotubes, unlike other nanopores, have a very smooth inside surface. Therefore, after molecules enter the openings of these nanotubes, they encounter less resistance and move through more efficiently.

REVITALIZING MANUFACTURING PROCESSES

The eclectic nature of advanced materials makes them an integral part of the manufacturing process across industries and all sectors of the economy. With the rapid digitization and the growing interconnectedness of the materials sector, the development of new materials comes in parallel with their industrial adaptation through the 4IR technologies. These newly developed and highly functional materials enhance businesses by improving their processes and manufacturing methods. This rising implementation of new materials in manufacturing processes across healthcare, energy, environment, and several other areas has led them to be incredibly useful and essential for achieving the Global Goals. Emerging additive manufacturing facilities continue striving to evolve beyond traditional thermoplastics and apply materials that offer greater flexibility, customization, and functionality while producing less waste. It is relevant to discuss thermosets here, which are polymeric materials that adopt a permanent shape upon curing. They boast a key role in the modern plastics and rubber industries. Comprising about 20% of polymeric materials manufactured today, with a worldwide annual production of about 65 million tons, thermosets include epoxies, polyurethanes, and rubber used for tires.[85] They are found in many products that have to be durable and heat-resistant, such as vehicles or electrical appliances.

IN BUSINESS

SOLCOLD[82]

Initiative: Anti-stokes fluorescence technology
Headquarters: Nes Ziona, Israel

Israeli startup SolCold has developed a surface modification innovation with a nano filter and the new material active cooling paint. Using anti-stokes fluorescence technology, SolCold transforms heat and radiation from the sun into a low-cost cooling system. The startup's technology achieves this by creating a reverse relationship between solar activity and heat transfer. SolCold's technology is based on the counterintuitive principle of laser cooling, in which hitting specially designed materials with a laser can cool them with up to 150° Celsius. The sun's rays trigger a reaction in SolCold's material. In turn, this converts the heat accumulated in the object it is applied to into radiation. This radiation is then emitted in a process called anti-stokes fluorescence, providing the cooling effect (SDG 13). SolCold's material basically functions as if it were a thin layer of ice that gets thicker and cooler as the sun gets stronger.

This tech solution has far-reaching applications, from transportation and construction to agriculture and textile industries (SDGs 8,9). In a $100 billion market, SolCold's innovation generates substantial savings in cooling costs, plus a major reduction in energy (SDGs 7,12). This breakthrough, patented coating material cools down objects when exposed to the sun and can be applied to anything that needs cooling: buildings, structures, vehicles, airplanes, storage containers, military apparatus, outdoor equipment, and more. It does not require electricity, fluids, or moving parts. SolCold's fully owned patented technology is registered in the EU, USA, Australia, and China.[83]

Among its negotiating partners are large paint and chemical companies, airplane manufacturers, and well-known global VCs (SDG 17). SolCold's target market is wide-ranging and sales of cool roof coating products for buildings alone are projected to reach a few billion dollars by 2025. Traditional reflective coating, which merely passively reflects the sun, is used in many other markets, thus providing SolCold with a total market potential of over $100 billion.[84]

Adesso Advanced Materials has developed the epoxy resin systems Recycloset, which are designed for applications in manufacturing the next generation of sustainable fiber reinforced epoxy composites. Recycloset reworkable epoxy resins have a fiber recovery rate of 95%, enabling manufacturers to virtually eliminate waste.[86] Adesso's recyclable composites have comparable thermal and mechanical properties to industry-standard non-recyclable thermoset composites. Further, the tech company has achieved a comparable cost structure of recyclable formulated resins, which allows the industry to manufacture green recyclable composites with comparable costs and profits. Water filtration and energy storage are the two major applications for nanomaterials; both address some of the world's greatest challenges and have enormous market potential.[87] Indian bio compound startup Mynusco creates sustainable solutions through biodegradable and recyclable compounds based on agricultural waste and renewable resources.

Although new materials have traditionally been difficult to dispose of and recycle, not to mention hard to integrate into existing systems, businesses are utilizing this tech in manufacturing innovations more than ever before. MIT chemists have now developed a way to modify thermoset plastics with a chemical linker that makes the materials much easier to break down yet still retain the mechanical strength that constitutes their useful qualities.[88] Top tech university researchers have produced a degradable version of a thermoset plastic called polydicyclopentadiene (pDCPD). This can be broken down into a powder, and then the powder is used to create more pDCPD. A true embodiment of upcycling, this recycled material has thermomechanical properties that exceed those of more traditional manufacturing substances.[89] There are several foreseeable opportunities for energy-efficient manufacturing of multifunctional pDCPD materials.

Also notable as an advanced material for sustainable manufacturing is the previously discussed graphene. Ionic Industries is another company bridging the gap between graphene research and its commercial applications. The Australian business incorporates the expertise of graphene and graphene oxide manufacturing. The company specializes in graphene additives for water treatment and nanofiltration, as well as for energy storage. Building on partnerships and technology innovations, Ionic has secured $3.4 million in R&D funding and is one of the first companies to demonstrate the large-scale, commercially viable application of graphene technologies in manufacturing.[90] Its collaborative model reduces technology validation risks and accelerates paths to market, thereby reducing uncertainty and business risks and expanding the market potential.

THE GLOBAL RECYCLABLE THERMOSETS MARKET WAS VALUED AT $1.2 BILLION IN 2020 AND WILL GROW WITH A CAGR OF OVER 2% FROM 2020 TO 2027.[91]

FOSTERING HEALTH AND WELLBEING

Advanced materials play a significant role in developing minimally invasive and personalized medical treatment. As medical technology companies increasingly outsource the design and development of new medical products, a variety of new materials are being introduced that offer additional opportunities for businesses to grow in this market.[92] Note that Biomaterials are in the same category as new materials since they have been engineered to be compatible with biological tissues and organs (muscle, bone, pancreas, or heart). The events of the past few years due to COVID-19 have accelerated digital transformation in the healthcare sector, and organizations at the forefront of technological advancements have seen significant returns on investments as a result.

One popular innovation driving this growth, which also improves outcomes and reduces costs, has been the effort to utilize new materials to make devices and implants smaller. For example, there is strong growth in minimally invasive implants and techniques, such as laparoscopic surgery

IN BUSINESS

MYNUSCO[93]

Initiative: BioDur and BioPur
Headquarters: Bangalore, Karnataka India

Mynusco, meaning "subtract the harm caused on our ecology" formerly known as Spectalite, is a Bangalore-based biomaterials company, established with the vision of assisting companies and consumers reduce their carbon footprint (SDG 13).[94] The Indian bio compound startup assists the automotive, logistics, packaging, hospitality, and consumer goods industries with their sustainability objectives.[95] Mynusco produces biodegradable and recyclable compounds based on agricultural waste and renewable resources. The startup's products contribute to conserving natural deposits and forests, while also ensuring scalability and adaptability for existing manufacturing processes (SDG 15). Mynusco Founder and CEO Mahadev Chikkanna says "Biocomposites made from crop waste, for example, eliminate a harmful industrial age agricultural practice of stubble burning, yielding a material that matches plastic in durability and versatility, while at the same time being climate-friendly and eco-friendly. It benefits farmers, industry, and the community (SDGs 2,11)."

Mynusco develops biomaterials platform for the circular bioeconomy, where they help companies choose from their wide range of biomaterials, develop new materials, design products with circular principles, convert materials into finished products, and assess lifecycle impact of the products (SDG 12). They are the world's first biomaterials company to use AI to choose the right biomaterial for diverse needs and to use blockchain to track the carbon footprint and resource stewardship across the product lifecycle (SDG 9). With more than 1000 biomaterials to choose from, Mynusco has helped companies across automotive, consumer goods, furniture, personal care, packaging and hospitality sectors to implement circular solutions with their biomaterials platform. Thus, materials are delivered as bio compounds suitable for manufacturing processes. Their BioDur and BioPur materials are 100% biodegradable with up to 100% bio-content.

BioDur:[96] Biocomposites made with fast renewable starch, bamboo, rice husk, coffee husk and olefin-based binders that are either bio-based or recycled. They are used for manufacturing sustainable durable products across automotive, houseware, furniture, toys, and more. Benefits of BioDur include reduced CO2 emissions, affordable sustainability, and light weight with better properties.

BioPur:[97] Biocomposites made with compostable binders and fast renewable resources. They are used for disposable and packaging products that need to biodegrade in home or industrial compost. Benefits of BioPur include reduced CO2 emissions, prevent pollution, and drop-in solution to replace plastics.

and robotic surgery. This approach leads to faster patient recovery times, less scarring (smaller devices mean the incision can be smaller), shorter hospitalization, and a lower total cost of care.[98] Miniaturized medical devices for the targeted delivery of drugs, or undergoing localized surgery, rely heavily on the ability to produce small-scale objects that can autonomously perform such tasks in living organisms.

UTILIZING NEW MATERIALS TO MAKE DEVICES AND IMPLANTS SMALLER IS AN INNOVATION DRIVING GROWTH IN MINIMALLY INVASIVE AND PERSONALIZED MEDICAL TREATMENT, IMPROVING QUALITY AND REDUCING COSTS.

Realization of this type of micro-device or nanorobots is primarily based on materials. In other words, these devices must be made of advanced materials that allow them to self-propel and move in a programmable way to navigate effectively in the human body. Medical devices must also be made of materials that can sense stimuli. One materials solution worth mentioning here is chemical gradients released by damaged tissue or temperature gradients generated by inflammation possessing the ability to react to the stimuli without external intervention. To develop smaller medical devices and minimally invasive techniques, medical device companies are searching for biomaterials that reduce size without compromising strength, durability, flexibility, and biocompatibility.[99] This has led to the increased use of ultra-high polyethylene fiber, a material that performs better than alternatives such as steel, polyester, and nylon fibers.

Nanomedicine is another application of nanotechnologies for healthcare. It uses the properties shown by materials at the nanometric scale (10-9 m), which often differ in terms of their physics, chemistry, or biology from the same material at a bigger scale. Nanomedicine has the potential to enable early detection and prevention and to drastically improve the diagnosis, treatment, and follow-up of many diseases, including cancer. Nanomedicine now has hundreds of products under clinical trials, covering all major cardiovascular, neurodegenerative, musculoskeletal, and inflammatory diseases. Enabling technologies in all healthcare areas, nanomedicine is already accounting for more than 80 marketed products, ranging from nano-delivery and pharmaceutical to medical imaging and diagnostics.[100]

THE GLOBAL NANOMEDICINE MARKET WAS $112 BILLION IN 2019 AND IS REACHING $261 BILLION IN 2023, AT AN ANNUAL GROWTH RATE OF 12%.[101]

One important application of nanotechnology in healthcare is that it considerably accelerates the growth of regenerative medicine. Regenerative nanomedicine is focused on developing and applying new treatments to heal tissues and organs and restore function lost due to aging, disease, damage, or defects. OPER Technology, a startup from Hong-Kong, develops technology in nanomaterial-based personalized and regenerative medicine.[102] This tech startup's innovations improve health and extend the life of patients with incurable diseases through real-time monitoring that enables specific cell harvests in complicated systems in the body, cell engineering, and drug delivery to specific cells in the body. Also in nanomedicine is business growth based on research and education. The joint Center of Excellence in Nanomedicine (CENM) at King Saud University in Saudi Arabia conducts research that applies the tools of polymer chemistry and nanotechnology to medical challenges.

IN BUSINESS

CENTER OF EXCELLENCE IN NANOMEDICINE (CENM)[103]

Initiative: King Saud University nanomedicine research partnership
Headquarters: Riyadh, Saudi Arabia

The joint CENM is a partnership between researchers at several Saudi research institutions, including King Saud University, King Abdulaziz City of Science and Technology, King Faisal Specialist Hospital and Research Center, and the University of California, San Diego (SDG 17).[104] CENM research applies the tools of polymer chemistry and nanotechnology to medical challenges such as disease drug delivery, disease detection, and stem cell-based therapies (SDGs 3,9). In the process, collaboration across continents strengthens the research infrastructure in Saudi Arabia by providing training opportunities for Saudi scientists and sharing technical expertise (SDG 4,10). Highlighting the importance of this materials tech research area, the global nanomedicine market was over $112 billion in 2019 and is reaching $261 billion in 2023, at an annual growth rate of 12%.[105]

There is a growing number of initiatives on nanotechnology research, education, and industry launched by several Arab countries. The region's leaders recognize the importance of harnessing nanomedicine and are investing heavily in materials for HealthTech.[106] The Saudi healthcare market generated approximately $464 million in 2022 and is expected to grow at a CAGR of 12.79% until 2025.[107]

Many large corporate entities have a stake in nanomaterials science. Multinational conglomerate Honeywell, with performance materials and technologies as one of its primary business areas, created an ultra-high molecular weight polyethylene (UHMWPE) fiber.[108] This material is often used in smaller medical devices or implants. It is strong enough to be used to suture bones, but also flexible for enabling surgeons to navigate sutures through narrow openings. In addition to greater strength and flexibility, the UHMWPE fiber is thinner and has lower friction and higher resistance to chemicals, fatigue, and abrasion than many alternative fibers. As an inert and hypoallergenic material, UHMWPE also avoids the health risks of alternative fibers, such as infection and pain caused by fibers disintegrating over time and entering a patient's bloodstream. Companies like Honeywell are manufacturing UHMWPE using a patented gel-spinning process. The global UHMWPE market is forecasted to reach $4.23 billion by 2026.[109]

AUGMENTING FOOD AND AGRICULTURE

Food shortages are addressed with materials science in a range of business applications. Roughly a third of all the food produced around the world goes to waste, which amounts to about 1.3 billion tons per year adding up to approximately $1 trillion.[110] The number of people affected by hunger globally rose to as many as 828 million in 2021, an increase of about 150 million since the outbreak of COVID-19 upended food supply chains.[111] This is enough to feed two billion people. With rising world hunger, this is truly a travesty. Even before the pandemic, over 50% of fruits and vegetables grown in the United States were wasted, which is a significant part of a $161 billion annual national food waste problem.[112] Approximately 54 million Americans have faced food insecurity during the pandemic, which is up by over 13 million people since 2018.[113]

MATERIALS SCIENCE ENABLES ENVIRONMENTAL SUSTAINABILITY AND HIGHER HARVEST YIELDS.

There are several entities implementing advanced materials tech to solve these global food and agricultural challenges. For instance, the Pangaea Ventures funded Calysta uses a FeedKind product, a substitute for fishmeal which will lead to feeding more people with less raw usage of resources, leveraging efficient gas fermentation.[114] If used as a substitute for fishmeal, 100,000 tons of FeedKind could replace between 420 and 450 thousand tons of wild-caught fish or the equivalent land area of Chicago.[115] StixFresh is another innovator developing a groundbreaking solution in the form of a sticker that acts in the same way as the natural protections used by plants themselves.[116] Simply sticking one to a piece of fruit can extend its shelf life by up to two weeks. Based in Hong Kong, the tech startup uses 100% natural ingredients which replicate the antimicrobial compounds that plants use to protect themselves against post-harvest diseases. The compounds making up this formulation work together to create a protective layer around the fruit, slowing down over-ripening and spoilage.[117]

ADVANCED MATERIALS TECH IS CREATING BUSINESS SOLUTIONS FOR THE FOOD PRODUCED AROUND THE WORLD THAT GOES TO WASTE, WHICH AMOUNTS TO ABOUT 1.3 BILLION TONS PER YEAR ADDING UP TO APPROXIMATELY $1 TRILLION.[118]

Companies with technologies that increase agricultural production use existing resources to provide more food to an increasing population, all the while helping to preserve vital ecosystems. The agricultural industry is being disrupted and is transforming into a high-tech industry. In this transformation to AgTech, there is expected to be major growth in venture capital and investment in advanced materials for agricultural applications. As the growing number of AgTech startups and investors shows, today's agricultural industry is on the verge of turning into a high-tech industry.[119] Of all the capital raised for AgTech in 2020, 61% was raised by just 28 companies that have each brought in over $100 million in investor capital.[120]

The AgTech materials science venture capital movement shows surging interest in agriculture deals. Even celebrities like Oprah Winfrey and Katy Perry are buying into the materials marketplace, investing in Apeel Sciences which is a company developing a plant-derived shelf-life extension product for produce.[121] The California-based AgTech startup announced a new round of funding in 2021 worth $250 million.[122] Most of the late-stage capital is still coming from seasoned agriculture venture capital investors like SoftBank, Temasek, the Bill & Melinda Gates Foundation, Data Collective, and S2G Ventures. Out of the top 25 publicly traded agriculture companies around the world by revenue, over 50% of these firms have some sort of corporate venture capital program, which is an important source of funding for AgTech materials startups.[123] New funding for these modes has helped drive the new materials research for food, with the future leaning towards indoor farming and plant-based meat.

OVER 50% OF THE TOP 25 PUBLICLY TRADED AGRICULTURE COMPANIES GLOBALLY HAVE A CORPORATE VENTURE CAPITAL PROGRAM, WHICH IS AN IMPORTANT SOURCE OF FUNDING FOR AGTECH MATERIALS STARTUPS.[124]

Novel materials are key to accelerating the evolution of farming and crop nutrient management. Mosaic, a producer and distributor of crop nutrient materials, provides feed ingredients, concentrated phosphates, potash, and related products to agricultural customers.[125] The earnings power resulting from materials tech advancements and strong global fertilizer markets increased Mosaic's profits. Delivering excellent earnings for the first quarter of 2021, their revenues were up by 28% year-over-year to $2.3 billion.[126] Solvay is also a company whose technologies bring benefits to many aspects of the agricultural sector. Solvay endeavors to address the sector's many challenges by promoting the advancement of sustainable new materials that boost production.

Another innovator in advanced materials for food, Hazel Technologies, developed biodegradable capsules that provide control of produce freshness, eliminating waste in the food supply chain and shrinkage for produce distributors.[127] The tech business raised $87 million in growth equity funding since its founding in 2015.[128] Its packaging insert for bulk boxes of produce after harvest emits methylcyclopropene gas to inhibit ethylene, which plants produce as they age. Hazel's products were used on over 6.3 billion pounds of fresh produce, preventing more than 500 million pounds of food from going to landfill.[129] Hazel aims to increase its commercial distribution to at least 15 countries by 2025 and invest in product development.[130]

BUILDING SMART INFRASTRUCTURE

Currently, trillions of dollars are being spent on smart cities. The most exciting part being the use of advanced materials, valued as a $400 billion opportunity.[131] This means new and advanced materials are urban regions' biggest enabler, with information and computer technology dropping to an important supporting role.[132] Multifunctional infrastructure, equipment, and materials are making independence possible in cities by providing citizens with energy, food, and water with zero emissions as well as greater security and empowerment of the disadvantaged. Analysts have identified more than fifty gaps in the market for smart city materials, many of which can create billion-dollar businesses, including photovoltaic paint that is non-toxic, solar roads, wave power, self-healing vehicle bodywork, making and storing electricity, solid-state LIDAR, and lithium-metal batteries.[133] New and advanced materials have the potential to be more sustainable and profitable.

ADVANCED MATERIALS INFRASTRUCTURE FOR SMART CITIES IS VALUED AS A $400 BILLION OPPORTUNITY.[134]

Replacing traditional concrete with green concrete is an important scope of the materials infrastructure market. With about 10 billion tons of concrete produced every year, it is one of the most consumed substances in the world - second only to water. Over 70% of the world's population lives in a concrete structure.[135] Green concrete is a form of eco-friendly concrete that requires less energy for production and is manufactured using waste from residual materials from different industries. Compared to traditional concrete, it produces less carbon dioxide, and is considered cheap and more durable. Further, green concrete uses fewer natural resources while increasing dependency on recyclable materials. Partial replacement of energy-consuming cement with reusable materials is among the best strategies used to achieve eco-friendly construction material.[136] Cement can be replaced with substances such as fly ash, silica fume, and wood ash.

Conventional materials augmented for enhanced performance are also integral to business growth in infrastructure. In this context, a $35 billion market is to be expected ahead for advanced materials providing ubiquitous photovoltaic power infrastructure that the usual silicon cannot serve.[137] This market includes advanced flexible organics, membranes, bioplastics, polymers, thermal insulation, 2D and 3D molecules, graphene, and materials for 5G, 6G, and THz electronics. Glass products for windows in buildings also assist in conserving and producing energy, as well as delivering many benefits to sustainable infrastructure design. Global materials company AGC solves infrastructure energy challenges with its cutting-edge glass technology.[138] AGC advanced materials applications for glass provide unique aesthetic, technical, and energy properties that inspire aspects of both sustainability and comfort.

Air pollution poses environmental and economic challenges in cities that technology can help overcome. According to the World Health Organization, 80% of the people living in the city are breathing polluted air, and these pollution levels are increasing faster than ever.[139] Special buildings constructed using new smog-eating concrete help neutralize the pollutants in the atmosphere, which we discussed in the beginning of this chapter.[140] Pollutants emitted by the vehicles and industries can be neutralized by this smog-consuming concrete. Another example of this features Mexico's Manuel Gea González Hospital. Mexico is a densely populated country and has high air pollution levels. The façade is spread over an area of 2,700 square feet and counteracts the pollutants emitted from at least 1,000 cars per day.[141] Apart from providing clean air to the patients inside the hospital, this advanced materials outer layer also acts as a natural light filter and solar blocker, thus keeping the hospital cool and reducing energy bills.

ENHANCING TEXTILE AND FASHION PRODUCTION

The global textile market was valued at approximately $1 trillion in 2021 and is anticipated to grow at a 4% CAGR from 2022 to 2030.[142] In recent years fashion has led the textile market, accounting for more than 73% of the global revenue share in 2021 due to increased consumer spending on clothing and apparel. As the global textile industry continues to grow, there is an increased demand for apparel from the fashion industry and eCommerce sales. This trend is generating greater demand for raw materials, novel applications, and new production processes.[143]

Advanced materials in the fashion industry are sustainable and replace non-sustainable ones, such as leather and other nanotechnology biofabrics. The major business-driven sustainability initiatives exhibited across the industry include circular fashion and closed-loop systems. Water use, for example, has been targeted as an area for improvement both economically and environmentally. It takes over 700 gallons of water to produce one cotton t-shirt.[144] It is not surprising then that addressing inefficiencies in textiles would play a major role in solving the world's water crisis. This excessive water consumption is just one aspect of the problem, though. Many textiles produced are not even used - an estimated $120 billion of unused fabric sits in warehouses annually.[145]

IN BUSINESS

SOLVAY[146]

Initiative: Biopesticide solutions
Headquarters: Brussels, Belgium

Solvay's powerful chemical formulations are geared toward sustainable solutions suited for crop protection (SDG 2). With green substances as building blocks for sustainable agriculture, Solvay offers a broad portfolio of advanced materials. AgRHO S-BoostTM, a biostimulant derived from natural guar beans, helps crops germinate faster and grow stronger. It favors water and nutrient uptake with its unique mode of action, and it can reduce synthetic fertilizer use by up to 13% while optimizing water usage (SDGs 6, 12).[147]

One of their novel products, exemplified in the development of Soprophor, is an industry-leading standard in crop dispersion, emulsification, and wetting (SDG 6).[148] It comes in wax form and is engineered using hydrophilic, multipurpose nonionic tristyrylphenol surfactant for emulsification and dispersion. As part of Solvay's Biopesticide Formulation Solutions, Soprophor is combined with the company's other material products that are specifically developed to address the challenges of formulating microorganisms (SDG 9). Related to their characteristics and mode of action, these specialty bioinsecticides and biofungicides require specific formulation types and functionality to ensure an optimized shelf-life and deliver biological viability.[149]

Using living microorganisms and natural substances, biopesticides prevent or reduce damage from pests, weeds, and pathogens, emerging as one of the most promising tools to empower a sustainable future of agriculture (SDGs 11, 15). Increased adoption of biopesticides is also a way for the agricultural market to respond to consumer demands for organic and residue-free food. This rise in environmentally aware consumers and increasingly stringent regulatory requirements continue to drive the agriculture market shift for Solvay from synthetic conventional pesticides to biological pest control. Solvay's chemical sales in 2021 reached $13.5 billion.[150]

THE GLOBAL TEXTILE ENZYMES MARKET WAS VALUED AT $178.3 MILLION IN 2019, AND IT IS EXPECTED TO REACH $209 MILLION BY THE END OF 2027, GROWING AT A CAGR OF 2.3% FROM 2021 TO 2027.[151]

What makes the sustainability projection even bleaker is that the production of textiles involves a long chain of resource-intensive, complex processes to convert raw materials such as fibers or petroleum into finished fabrics or fashion products. Enzymes are highly specific biocatalysts found within the cells of all living organisms. They offer the possibility of manufacturing textiles using simpler and less severe processing conditions with a non-toxic and eco-friendly component.[152] Enzymes have the capacity to reduce the consumption of chemicals, energy, and water, as well asreduce the generation of waste. Specifically, they are used extensively in textile processing, primarily for de-sizing and bio-polishing of various types of fabrics, including cotton-based ones. Changing fashion fads and rising disposable incomes of young adults worldwide are trends driving the expansion of the textile enzymes market. The global textile enzymes market was valued at $178.3 million in 2019, and it is expected to reach $209 million by the end of 2027, growing at a CAGR of 2.3% from 2021 to 2027.[153]

THE TEXTILE INDUSTRY IS RESPONSIBLE FOR 10% OF GREENHOUSE GAS EMISSIONS AND 20% OF WASTEWATER PRODUCTION GLOBALLY.[154]

The need for textile companies to alter their approach to manufacturing and production by implementing sustainable materials is on a drastic rise. This need becomes stark when we realize the textile industry is responsible for approximately 10% of greenhouse gas emissions and 20% of wastewater production globally.[155] Therefore, businesses are proactive in developing fibers and yarns as innovative solutions to address the growing demand for more sustainable systems.[156] Plant or fruit materials that replace more energy intensive fabrics, such as leather, are also starting to gain traction. Let's look at Piñatex "leather" made from pineapple leaves at the Hilton Bankside Hotel in London.

There has been a strong push to develop natural, environmentally sustainable fibers, as clothes made from artificial fibers release environmentally harmful particles into waterways via washing machines. One such natural advanced material is Lyocell, which is raw material cellulose from wood pulp.[157] Lyocell is sold under the trade name Tencel owned by Austrian company Lenzing.[158] The fibers of this product are biodegradable and compostable, and the production process has a low environmental footprint. Wastewater is recycled, and no toxic chemicals are used. Researchers have also used 3D printing to craft a tough, sustainable material from algae that could be used to make clothes and labels.[159] Because this material is contrived of living, breathing algae, clothing made from it would be photosynthetic, absorbing carbon dioxide from the air and breathing out oxygen just like plants. Engineers developing materials science continue to have an impact on the textile and fashion industry as we focus on sustainability, create new materials, and find ways to incorporate the latest technologies into the clothes we wear and products we use.

IN BUSINESS

ASAHI GLASS COMPANY[160]
Initiative: SunEwat solar panels for Hikari
Headquarters: Tokyo, Japan

Established in 1907 as the first flat glass producer in Japan. Asahi Glass Company (AGC) group has evolved into a world leading solutions company in materials industries - glass, chemicals, and ceramics.[161] SunEwat is part of the group's Active Glass for photovoltaics-embedded glass solutions, developed in partnership with solar providers (SDG 17).[162] SunEwat produces environmental performance and efficiency ratings consistent with zero-energy building standards (SDG 13).

AGC's vision of creating materials for the first positive-energy mixed-use building in Europe has been brought to life through Hikari. The Hikari project in Lyon, France remains the first positive energy infrastructure in the country, combining offices, shops, and housing spanning three city blocks (SDGs 9,11).[163] The 12,800 m² complex is designed by Japanese architect Kengo Kuma and is made up of three buildings. Photovoltaic panels are located on the southern façade to benefit from seasonal light energy, covering 400 m² with an electrical yield over 20 years of 26,560 kWh per year (SDG 7).[164]

Hikari means "light" in Japanese and everything in the project is designed to let natural daylight filter into the spaces to "improve the mood and lift the spirit."[165] Even more, the pioneering eco-friendly buildings generate more energy than they consume (SDG 12). By storing and pooling the energy produced, Hikari is able to provide its own energy. The innovative advanced materials-enhanced glass panes with embedded photovoltaic cells do the same job as the solar panels often seen on roofs, except they are part of the very fabric of the building.

ADDRESSING RISKS AND CHALLENGES ON THE ROAD AHEAD

New or advanced material market insertion has been known to be a time-consuming and costly endeavor, typically taking 15 to 20 years for successful entry.[166] Where materials are too difficult or expensive to produce, new methods or equivalent materials will be needed. At the same time, new or replacement materials will have to conform to increasingly stringent and broadening environmental impact restrictions. Advanced materials often drive device and system performance augmentation and reliability by reducing product weight and enhancing functional capabilities. However, these materials have historically been both sometimes financially burdensome and not readily available to manufacturers. New and advanced material development to increase device performance is becoming more prevalent, but this process has challenges we must navigate too.

Substantial technological and commercialization risks make it difficult for new materials to make the journey from the lab to industrial-scale production and the markets. Developing new materials is heavily science-based and requires much investment before a commercial stage is viable. Not many companies have that type of financial reach. Thus, science, governments, business, and foundations must collaborate to accelerate new materials coming into the marketplace and leverage their impact to achieve the SDGs.

This includes understanding material interface issues, adhesion, stress, and cross-contamination. Material handling challenges are a risk too.[167] Different chemicals that are required to clean or prepare advanced materials to reduce defects and improve their operational yield see increasing contamination that can be introduced in the product stream. For example, toxic chemicals are used at high temperatures to produce graphene, which often results in the material containing signs of some poisonous qualities.[168] Advanced materials undoubtedly have the potential to spur advances in a variety of sectors, from transport to medicine to electronics, but they are often resource-intensive and expensive to produce. In addition to the previously mentioned possibility of concerns over graphene toxicity, the costs of the material remain high.

TECHNOLOGICAL AND COMMERCIALIZATION RISKS MAKE IT DIFFICULT FOR NEW MATERIALS TO MAKE THE JOURNEY FROM THE LAB TO INDUSTRIAL-SCALE PRODUCTION AND MARKETS.

Nanomaterials are another new material to mention here as they are going to affect several aspects of human life, so it will be important to consider and mitigate detrimental effects. The downsides to these high-tech materials that currently exist are part of the reason the use of nanotechnology at a larger scale is not being encouraged more. Apart from lung damage, there are other notable side effects of nanoparticles. Persistent insoluble particles in the environment can have far bigger negative effects than those revealed by human health assessments.[169] There is still very little awareness about the side effects of nanotechnology, and there is a need for further research in this area. While nanomaterial technology holds immense potential, it requires a lot of caution, as its implications could be dangerous in the form of atomic bombs or weapons of biological warfare.

IN BUSINESS

ANANAS ANAM[170]
Initiative: Piñatex for Hilton London Bankside Hotel
Headquarters: London, United Kingdom

The world's first vegan hotel suite opened at the Hilton Bankside London, featuring Piñatex as its core material in 2019.[171] The suite features a large bedroom, sitting area, and bathroom. Piñatex is used throughout the suite, including the headboard in the bedroom and cushions in the sitting room which feature stylish embroidered pineapples (SDGs 9,11). Piñatex also covers armchairs, poufs, and even the hotel room key card is made from the sustainable leather. The suite was designed by Bompas and Parr, in consultation with The Vegan Society.[172] This novel approach to sustainable luxury upholstery is drawing new business and revenues, with suites selling for over $1200 per night.[173]

Piñatex is the pioneering plant-based textile made by Ananas Anam. It is a material made from the leaves of pineapples grown in the Philippines.[174] The leather substitute can be used as a sustainable and natural alternative to leather for the footwear, fashion, home accessories, and interior markets. Its production is much more sustainable than traditional leather and free of animal products. Piñatex is made of up to 95% renewable resources and uses no hazardous chemicals in its production, 100% vegan and cruelty free, and made from plant waste preventing equivalent to 12kg CO_2 from being released into the atmosphere per linear meter of vegan leather (SDGs 6,7,13).[175] The leather requires less water and contains no harmful chemicals ecologically toxic to wildlife. Any leftover leaf waste is recycled and used for fertilizer or biomass.

Following a range of fashion collaborations, including with Nike, Ananas Anam recently signed an agreement with Dole Sunshine Company – the world's largest producer of fruit and vegetables - to source raw material for its next-gen materials (SDGs 12,17). "At Ananas Anam, we aim at meeting the challenges of our times by developing innovative products in which commercial success is integrated with, and promotes, social, ecological and cultural development,"[176] said Dr, Carmen Hijosa, Founder and Chief Creative and Innovation Officer at Ananas Anam.

WE HAVE

IMAGINED

Beyond the traditional materials that have followed us into the 4IR, advanced materials surpass mere utility and focus on design, ergonomics, economics, and the ecology of a substance. We have imagined an era of advanced materials as a force for good in urban infrastructure. As evidenced by history time and again, breakthrough materials technologies have the power to set us on a new trajectory toward a more sustainable and productive architectural future. Not only do materials sciences offer unprecedented opportunities to reimagine buildings and their functionality, but the construction sector will expand in scope based on new and improved business models.

The field of materials science and engineering has many exciting applications on the horizon that are promising to improve the world as we know it. These changes are observed in the fields of healthcare, manufacturing, food and agriculture, cities and infrastructure, textiles and smart fashion, and many others. New and advanced materials provide businesses with unprecedented opportunities to manufacture products and incorporate services from the enormous largescale to the miniscule nanoscale. The sphere of not only animate but inanimate objects, too, is experiencing an upgrade like no other, owing to the amazing abilities of materials as a force for good.

Imagine the possibilities of improving our world by way of materials. Throughout history, some of the most impactful changes or breakthroughs have had to do with materials. Moving forward, advanced materials will become one of the most effective catalysts across numerous business sectors and industries as we move toward a collective sustainable future. This tech provides revolutionary innovations that steer the world toward a better future for all.

We have imagined Advanced Materials for Good.

EXTENDED REALITIES 6

LET US IMAGINE ANOTHER WORLD.

EXTENDED REALTITIES EXPAND OUR

PERCEPTION OF REALITY.

WE ONLY NEED TO

IMAGINE

Imagine taking a virtual trip around the globe and expanding our awareness to see things that were out of view before. Technology has the capability to move us into new worlds and transform our lives. Unlocking new spheres of awareness for our psyche and senses, technological advancements are revolutionizing how we experience our immediate surroundings and the universe at large. Imagine technology shifting and enhancing the reality we have always known, and extending it into unprecedented realms.

The ways we interact in our world are expanding. Imagine technologies in schools or professional settings that present learning opportunities and challenge our perception of what is possible. These educational possibilities of 4IR tech bend the confines of our human limits and bring into focus new immersive experiences. We then find our world transformed into an Extended Reality (XR). Although the concept of XR may have once seemed like science fiction - if not a merely fanciful, imaginative gaming experience - it is much more than that. It is indeed already here as our new reality.

XR transcends simply providing an escape from our routines and daily lives. This innovation is about moving into a universe beyond our seemingly solid foundation of current life, which could be just the answer to many of our large-scale societal challenges. It is a technology that can do amazing things. As we extend our scope of reality, the universe becomes vaster and more expansive than previously felt.

Let's imagine how this technology can improve lives from the education and learning perspective. XR creates a safe learning space in schools and universities, where students and educators are given the opportunity to explore experiential learning methods. While improving learning rates, XR is addressing the gap in conventional settings where learners tend to forget approximately 70% of the content they have been exposed to within 24 hours, and nearly 90% in a month.[1] Further, research shows that when the tech is employed in classrooms, students demonstrate improved comprehension and retention.[2] XR is also a valuable tool in engaging students who face cognitive challenges or those who respond better to alternative learning platforms.

Extended Realities are also highly effective for training and development purposes. Companies looking to help staff develop new skills in a safe environment are accessing the tech's many advantages, including knowledge retention, lower operational costs, and increased engagement. Currently, XR is providing benefits to business training for employees to practice high-risk activities such as machinery operation, handle fire emergencies, or deal with unhappy customers in an Augmented Reality (AR)/Virtual Reality (VR) simulated environment. For schools, universities, or workforce trainings, XR technology makes learning fun, interactive, and engaging. Whether it is learning a new language, practicing public speaking, or engaging in other soft skills, XR technology can help.

Psychologically and physically challenged people require extra educational support, and XR technologies are making up for the competencies they miss out on in life. The new field of VR therapy can help these people learn to manage everyday situations, allowing them to live a more conventionally normal life.[3] VR therapy is a computer-based simulation of the world around us, multi-sensory in nature, and provides both visual and auditory environments configurable to mimic any setting. By using an avatar to interact with others in a simulated environment, both children and adults are challenged and overcome their fears in a safe setting and in a way that gives them control. This rewires the regions of the brain that relate to social skills and amplifies those areas that relate to attention and information exchange.[4]

Supervised practice enabled by technology for people in situations difficult to replicate at home or office settings is no longer mere science fiction. A research team with the Institute of Neurosciences at the University of Barcelona has used immersive VR to observe the effects of talking to themselves as if they were another person or a therapist. Being their own therapist through the experience demonstrated an improvement in participants' moods, compared to just talking about one's problems in a virtual conversation with pre-scripted comments. The method will soon be used by clinicians to counsel and soothe people dealing with personal problems.[5]

From school children to adult professionals, this tech is key in educating people. It can also help both patients and doctors learn more about the symptoms of anxiety disorders and stress. Beyond these applications, XR is equally beneficial in tackling issues like health care limitations, climate change, and others. The endless possibilities of this whole new world will be explored throughout this chapter.

Imagine expanding our awareness into new worlds. This is XR for Good.

Marga Hoek

6 EXPLORING EXTENDED REALITIES

As we embark on our collective tech for good journey, we enter into a new realm of worlds upon worlds that enhances our reality beyond ways previously deemed possible. Expounding on a tech as revolutionary as XR means starting from the basics. This widely integrated tech involves computer-generated digital imaging superimposed onto our real world. More is expanded upon about the fundamentals of the tech before uncovering the market landscape. Business opportunities in various sectors follow the exploration of the Global Goals. Sections in this chapter show how those affected by mental health, as well as individuals who are developmentally deprived, largely benefit from AR/VR devices. The journey weaves the reader along a path showing how immersive VR experiences aid in diverse experiences, from surgical operations to infrastructure planning to gender equality promotion. Unprecedented design and development of products and services becomes possible through XR. The mainstreaming of XR over the next decade is an exciting prospect, but is it beneficial in all areas? While 5G is a seminal step in terms of its magnitude, the health risks it poses can be severe. Such critical considerations, and most importantly how to address and mitigate these risks, are discussed.

THE TECH

Computer-generated Extended Realities (XRs) fall into three categories: Augmented Reality (AR), Virtual Reality (VR), and Mixed Reality (MR). Although all three are similar and belong to the same group of technologies, in addition to occasionally being used in tandem, they are distinct. Each of these falls under the XR umbrella, yet they separately fulfill individual and specific goals. Augmented Reality (AR), currently the most widely integrated, is computer-generated digital imaging superimposed or overlaid onto the real world.[6] It does not require a large investment, and most of today's mobile phones are compatible with AR systems. The most notable mainstream AR tech applications are the popular smartphone apps Pokémon Go game and Snapchat lenses. Virtual Reality (VR) refers to a completely computer-generated, digital illusory reality.[7] VR devices such as HTC Vive and Oculus Rift transport users into new visual and imagined environments. As these techniques evolve, new varieties emerge, and we get Mixed Realities (MR).

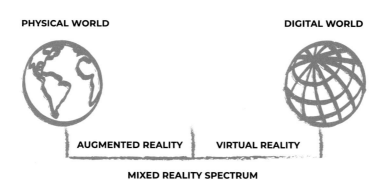

Figure 5
Mixed Reality Spectrum, based on Microsoft Learn graphic [8]

Real and virtual worlds interact in the MR experience, which combines elements of both AR and VR. One of the most notable early MR devices is Microsoft's HoloLens, used in business for precise, efficient, and hands-free work.[9] The term Mixed Reality was introduced in a 1994 paper by Paul Milgram and Fumio Kishino, "A Taxonomy of Mixed Reality Visual Displays." Their paper explored the concept of a "virtuality continuum" and the taxonomy of visual displays.[10] This leads to the concept that tech giants have called the metaverse. In early August 2021, Facebook announced it would become a metaverse company.[11] The intention is to build on top of the existing technological infrastructure of Facebook to create a system that enables users to move between AR, VR, and regular 2D devices.

Facebook founder Mark Zuckerberg has described the metaverse as an "internet that you're inside of, rather than just looking at."[12] Within the metaverse, users can socialize and interact with the world around them through digital avatars. XRs are the future of the global workforce and the next big computing platform.[13] The technology behind XRs is not new, though the computing power that renders them commercially viable has more recently developed.[14] It has allowed businesses to upgrade their computing capabilities and transform the way they operate. Facebook Reality Labs Research is already thinking ahead, building an interface for AR and developing intuitive ways to interact and connect with people all over the world using AR-computing-powered devices.

We find this technology becoming mainstream in the developed world in the same way the Internet and mobile devices did in the past. When we use an online platform to access social media through handheld devices, for example, we are often engaging with MR. The filters people use on Instagram are MR experiences. Yet, way beyond recreational use, AR and VR can influence the lives of societies all around the world. Advancements in computer vision, graphical processing, display technologies, input systems, and cloud computing comprise the MR tech space. Connecting people through AR, VR, and MR technologies could transform entire societal structures, from education and healthcare to mining and tourism.

EXPANSION OF THE 5G NETWORK IS WELL UNDERWAY AND INCREASINLY ACCESSIBLE.

In the coming years, AR and VR will be increasingly integrated into everyday life. Let's be mindful of the fact, though, that this implementation requires a combination of software and hardware integrating many other technologies – including 5G for connectivity, video standards for visualization, and AI for software algorithms.[15] In order to unlock the potential of XR for the good of the people and the planet, we would first need to build thorough and pervasive networks for everyone. Nearly 20 countries around the globe still lack 4G connectivity, let alone 5G, thus excluding these populations from the opportunities offered by digitalization. Because of this gap in infrastructure, the expansion of the 5G network is well underway and increasingly more accessible.

NETWORKS

The 5G network is no longer merely a concept for XR; it is already here. 5G has emerged for XR just as 3G did for mobile video and 4G for social media and apps.[16] Enabling richer visual content, 5G is bringing high-speed connection with greater reliability and lower latency. These improvements are advancing the entire tech ecosystem, opening up new business opportunities and industries, and enhancing experiences for end-users that are expected to enable major breakthroughs in XR applications. Creating the illusion of making people feel like they are in an entirely new digital world, hardware devices have started to trend towards wireless technologies for headsets. Multinational tech visionary Qualcomm invented underlying technologies that make 5G work. With its semiconductors, software, and services related to wireless technology, Qualcomm owns several patents critical to the network that enables the global expansion of 5G across industries.

QUALCOMM SNAPDRAGON XR2 5G PLATFORM

Qualcomm, headquartered in California with nearly $24 billion in revenue, is a leading wireless technology innovator and the driving force behind the global development, launch, and expansion of 5G.[17] Qualcomm Snapdragon XR technologies and platforms provide a robust computing power to deliver immersive AR and VR features that respond to the growing demand of the XR ecosystem. Being the world's first platform to unite 5G and AI, the Qualcomm Snapdragon XR2 5G Platform delivers immersive environments for sectors like healthcare, education, and entertainment, among others. This tech enables users to explore every angle of their virtual world in a 360° spherical view with rich 3D audio that captures the scene in vivid sensory detail.[18] In September 2020, Qualcomm Snapdragon XR2 Platform partnered with Facebook to launch Oculus Quest 2, its next generation all-in-one VR headset.[19] It is one of the most advanced and immersive gaming VR experiences for consumers running on the 5G network. The next generation Meta Quest Pro, also called Project Cambria, has now already been released as well.[20]

The burgeoning of rapid 5G mobile networks is expected to further boost the potential of XR to strengthen its presence in applications from work to entertainment. In combination with upgraded cloud and 5G technology, VR and AR tools will be unrestricted by a low bandwidth to deliver their experiences, resulting in cheaper headsets and viewing devices and more realistic VR simulations. New wearable products will also become increasingly popular with technological advancement. For instance, Apple launched its own set of MR glasses in 2022. As a stand-alone device, this tech hardware will be independent of computer or phone connectivity.[21] There is great promise for these tech glasses to assist XR in breaking into the mainstream market.[22] A product like Meta glasses, which overlays AR on top of the user's reality, is likely to become popular as a medium for game designers.[23] Based on holographic technology, Meta glasses can identify users' gestures to let them manipulate 3D projections of objects.

"THE FUTURE OF PRODUCTIVITY IS SPATIAL," SAID META WHEN INTRODUCING THEIR AR WORKSPACE.[24]

Improving 5G coverage is an important aspect of XR's development and widespread use. Los Angeles-based tech startup BadVR is working towards their business goal to have broad commercial impact, including the acceleration of 5G network planning and the ability to perform real-time monitoring of large infrastructures like utility grids. The company's product SeeSignal specifically offers recommendations to VR headset users for 5G network availability. This MR company's capacity to scan spatial data for network availability offers far reaching business benefits. Fusing VR technology with advanced visualization techniques, BadVR is developing a new method of analysis and shaping the way future generations will analyze data (Case 38). This is possible via a proprietary VR experience that enables users virtually to step inside their data.

IN BUSINESS

BADVR[25]

Initiative: SeeSignal
Headquarters: Los Angeles, California USA

BadVR is an innovative VR company that has developed technologies to help address 5G connectivity issues. By tapping into complex data spatialization, sampling algorithms, and machine learning, BadVR's SeeSignal Magic Leap VR headset enables users to look around any surrounding area and study the strength of cellular phone signals, WiFi, or Bluetooth networks.[26] A user's surrounding network data give real-time information about the environment and nearby devices that can be layered together to explore the complex interactions between the previously unseen digital worlds (SDG 17). This information, as displayed back to the user, is great for businesses. Beyond only showing network signals, SeeSignal also offers recommendations for ways to improve coverage (SDGs 10,11). There is potential for this tech innovator's 5G capabilities to revolutionize telecom planning with additional features for handling signal measurements at scale (SDG 9).

BadVR is a platform for immersive data visualization that enables users to "see the whole picture" and gain actionable insights into their surroundings. It also helps companies significantly increase the value of their data by giving users the tools they need to make faster and better decisions. "As a society, we have become aware of the power of data and the impact it has on our lives. It's important that we create tools that make it easy to work with this data," said CEO and founder Suzanne Borders.[27]

The startup's mission has broad commercial impact, including the acceleration of 5G network planning and the ability to perform real-time monitoring of large infrastructures like utility grids with minimal additional cost (SDG 12). By using MR tech and machine learning, BadVR unlocks the brain's processing potential, allowing users to get value from their data with minimal effort or special training. By making big data more accessible, people and companies can discover and identify hidden problems and opportunities, as well as make better decisions, faster. Founded in 2017, the startup has received over $3 million in funding.[28]

As of 2021, over 30% of the world's countries have access to 5G, with China, the U.S., and South Korea having the highest number of cities with 5G availability.[29] Some estimates forecast that by 2025, the global reach in total will be 3.6 billion 5G connections.[30] The XR market holds a promise in various countries of North America, Europe, Asia-Pacific and Japan, the Middle East, and Africa. North America has been a dominant player in developing XR, as the region has been attributed to the higher adoption of XR technologies in both consumer and enterprise application segments, and Europe is generating the second-highest revenues for the tech.[31]

"WHEN THE INTELLIGENT CLOUD AND INTELLIGENT EDGE ARE IMBUED WITH MR AND ARTIFICIAL INTELLIGENCE, WE HAVE A FRAMEWORK FOR ACHIEVING AMAZING THINGS AND EMPOWERING EVEN MORE PEOPLE."[32]
- SATYA NADELLA, CEO OF MICROSOFT

Every country has its own challenges related to infrastructure rollout, pricing, and access. The complete integration of 5G networks will need hundreds of thousands more cell antennae to carry the signals. This structure may be feasible for a metropolitan zone, but it is very costly for rural areas. In India, for example, data costs are low, helping affordability, yet geographic obstacles remain a major challenge with optical fiber connectivity needing to reach India's roughly 650,000 villages.[33] There is ample room for tech to expand across the world, and business can play a big role in accelerating this movement.

DIGITAL TWINS

Creating prototypes before the final product is critical in the manufacturing sector. Our physical world is increasingly being designed and simulated virtually through digitalized processes that produce a "digital twin" of a physical product before one is even created. This is done using the 3D visualization and digital mockup capabilities of AR and VR.[34] Smart manufacturing using digital mockup, VR, and AR tech applications in the 4IR are essential components of digitalization in industry, particularly in sustainable design and manufacturing.

87% OF BUSINESS EXECUTIVES AGREE THAT MASSIVE, INTELLIGENT DIGITAL TWINS—MODELING FACTORIES, SUPPLY CHAINS, PRODUCT LIFE CYCLES AND MORE—ARE BECOMING ESSENTIAL TO THEIR ORGANIZATIONS' ABILITIES TO COLLABORATE IN STRATEGIC PARTNERSHIPS.[35]

Digital mockup enables design teams to leverage advanced multi-CAD 3D visualization, large-scale product assembly analysis, and universal collaboration to reduce and, in some cases, eliminate expensive physical prototypes. Key enablers of the smart factory are VR and AR devices and techniques that give companies a competitive advantage. XR tech is being used to accelerate the product life cycle across concept, design, engineering, planning, assembly, marketing, and sales. Many of the VR use cases are geared towards upfront definition and inspection, whereas AR use cases are more predominantly found in assembly, manufacturing, and service areas to improve quality and efficiency on the manufacturing floor.

AZURE AND CLOUD COMPUTING

With the expanding implementation of XR comes the necessity of stable cloud computing. Cloud computing is the delivery of computing services over the Internet (the cloud).[36] The special thing about cloud services is they help businesses lower operating costs, run infrastructure more efficiently, and scale as businesses' need change. The Azure cloud platform comprises more than 200 products and cloud services designed to help users to solve today's computing challenges.[37] Azure is important to XR as it facilitates the tech to build, run, and manage applications across multiple clouds with the tools and frameworks of choice. The tech solution boasts over 90 compliance offerings, the largest in the industry; maintains 95% of Fortune 500 companies that trust their business on Azure; and $1 billion yearly investment in security to protect customers' data from cyberthreats.[38]

SOUND FOUNDATIONS

As early as the 1950s, examples of XR technology emerged. In 1956, cinematographer Morton Heilig created Sensorama, the first VR machine.[39] This movie booth combined 3D and color video using stereoscopic technology with audio, aromas, and a vibrating chair to immerse the viewer in the movie. Heilig then patented the first head-mounted display in 1960, which combined stereoscopic 3D images with stereo sound. Also in the 1960s, computer scientist Ivan Sutherland presented a paper outlining his concept of the "Ultimate Display," a virtual world so realistic that the user would not be able to differentiate it from reality.[40] This is widely considered the blueprint for modern VR, and in 1968 Sutherland created the first AR headset called "The Sword of Damocles," displaying computer-generated graphics that enhanced the user's perception of the world.[41]

EARLY CONCEPTS OF XR WERE IMAGINED AS CREATING A VIRTUAL WORLD SO REALISTIC THAT THE USER WOULD NOT BE ABLE TO DIFFERENTIATE IT FROM REALITY.

Moving into the 1970s, 1980s, and 1990s new technology emerged to enhance the VR experience. The first company to sell VR goggles and gloves, VPL Research Inc, was founded in 1985. Then along came VR arcade machines in the early 1990s, like the SEGA VR-1 motion simulator, as affordable VR headsets were becoming available for home use as well.[42] In 1998, Sportsvision broadcast the first live American football game with the yellow yard marker overlayed on top of the live camera feed via AR tech. This set the precedent for overlaying graphics onto the real-world view and quickly spread to other markets.

As we are accelerating to the fast-developing 4IR, XR technologies are creating applications to interact with smart objects and smart processes via cloud computing strategies enabled by AI and the IoT. Smart objects and devices have the capability to analyze and communicate with each other and their human co-workers, enabling the opportunity for smoother processes that free up employees for other tasks. Business is being driven by processes that can now be automated and by machines that are enabled with self-monitoring capabilities. This is possible thanks to the updated 5G network, through which 4IR-enabled smart objects possess the ability to be monitored, designed, tested, and controlled via their digital twins with processes and controls that are visualized in VR/AR.

MARKET SIZE OF XR

The COVID-19 pandemic undoubtedly forced a digitally integrated shift. With an increase in remote work and interaction, XR has become vital for business. This new need for technologies that enable virtual experiences has accelerated the adoption of XR, speeding up the market trajectory for the next wave of computing. XR tech enables shared experiences over long distances in real-time and allows for data to be accessed in a situation-based context. The investment opportunities are boundless. Given its vast potential, XR can be applied to a plethora of industries. With the increasing usage of smart glasses and headset displays, the market for XR has proliferated. The devices to emerge in the coming generation will likely be lighter and smaller, while offering an increased field of view and higher resolution displays and cameras.

As XR profits in economically prosperous regions soar due to market friendliness to immersive technologies, it is evident that consumers with financial means and tech knowledge are eager to invest in the product. The XR market was valued at $42.86 billion in 2021 and is expected to reach $465.26 billion in 2027, with a CAGR of 46.2% during 2022 to 2027.[43] Ambitious businesses eager to invest here can look forward to an improved design better suited for wearability and use in a work environment. Commercially, VR and AR technologies first became popular in gaming and entertainment, with over $7 billion expenditure in that sector alone back in 2018. This is now spreading rapidly to other sectors.[44] The estimated market size for VR and AR in 2022 is $37 billion and can reach up to $114.5 billion by 2027 at a market growth rate of 25.3%.[45]

The convergence of the real world and simulated content has allowed MR environments to emerge easily. The global MR market size is projected to reach $4.5 billion by 2026, from just $196 million in 2019.[46] Microsoft has been at the forefront of MR technology, using AI and the HoloLens to assist with viewing manuals and screens directly from the job site with image and object recognition and detection.[47] This tech allows employees to collaborate on issues and work more efficiently remotely. The development of enterprise XR solutions is overtaking that of consumer solutions. Industries such as automotive, education, healthcare, aerospace, and defense are significantly investing in virtual training and education solutions. For instance, in the automotive industry, the virtual training module offers workstation training for laborers to avoid accidents. Ford recently reported a reduction in employee injuries by 70% with the help of virtual training sessions.[48]

North America is a prominent region for the XR market, most notably because it has also been a pioneer in the adoption of innovations primarily within the United States. The adoption of AR in healthcare is forecasted to grow quickly as well, with the value of the market increasing by 38% annually until 2025.[49] Asia-Pacific and Japan currently hold a smaller role in global XR, as the market in this region is highly cost-sensitive, which has restricted early adoption.[50] Although other developing nations, such as India and the ASEAN countries, have a huge potential to become important markets for XR, they remain restricted in development due to cost and regulatory constraints.

These major market movements prove XR viewers can unlock a new generation of immersive experiences using 5G-enabled smartphones. Some organizations that promise this are Accenture, Qualcomm Technologies Inc., and other global operators such as Uplus, NTT DOCOMO, Verizon, and Vodafone. Important network solutions with elements such as 5G and the rise in mobile computing have seen significant growth in XR-based platforms in emerging regions. The Asia-Pacific region in particular will be a growth market to watch.

IN BUSINESS
JIO TESSERACT[51]
Initiative: Global Developer Program
Headquarters: New Mumbai, India

Jio Tesseract is India's largest MR company. The tech leader is working towards enhancing and developing products that disrupt the global MR market. Its Developer Program allows creators to build for the XR hardware and reach India's most extensive user base, including the 5G network launched by Jio (SDGs 9,10,17). With their built-in MR cloud for data computing that comes with the JioGlass Appstore, the company offers customers a comprehensive package. Businesses can publish and monetize their content on India's biggest MR marketplace through this Appstore. Jio's platform offers developers the opportunity to make tech companies' content accessible to India's largest user base, which includes 20 million households (SDG 11).[52] Engaging approximately 16 million enterprises, Jio supports businesses by helping them improve productivity through immersive learning and remote collaboration (SDGs 4,8).

SIEMENS[53]
Initiative: VRdirect EHS training
Headquarters: Munich, Germany

Siemens, one of the largest industrial manufacturers and most famous enterprises worldwide, has committed to environment, health, and safety (EHS) training that provides staff with valuable insights on underlying processes, and implements safety measures (SDGs 3,4). Because safety measures are a crucial component in industrial processes, companies are consistently looking for ways to make EHS training more efficient. Immersive technology such as VR elevates the learning effect for employees, helping them grasp the training content faster and apply it more confidently (SDGs 10,16). Siemens has successfully implemented VR to train its employees. By collaborating with VRdirect, Siemens created a virtual tour through one of their industrial facilities, digitally depicting the different work environments.[54]

This Siemens model that's tackling the challenge of training staff for plant security and occupational safety reveals the potential VR has for EHS workplace learning purposes. One major benefit of VR solutions is that they are available via many different devices (SDG 9). The immersive and interactive training environment enables active engagement with the necessary information. Overall, this tech solution is both accessible and adaptable. With no special development skills needed for implementation, Siemens' departments can create complete VR applications quickly and easily on their own (SDG 12). The platform allows for broad application in several business areas and the creation of immersive VR projects beyond virtual tours, too.

In India, the XR spending is expected to triple in size due to market penetration, from $2 billion in 2020 to surpassing an estimated $6.5 billion into 2023.[55] Jio Tesseract and Reliance Jio, India's largest telecom company, launched JioGlass in 2021 as part of their journey to disrupt the global MR market (Case 39). This is an example of a tech innovation that offers business solutions allowing users to create a 3D hologram of any object within view.

Global XR market expected to surpass **$1** **trillion** **by 2030.**[56]	**Increase of 38% annually AR in healthcare market forecast to 2025.**[57]	**Up to** **$114.5** **billion** **expected AR/ VR market size by 2027.**[58]

XR FOR GOOD

Extended realities are technological innovations that are poised to develop into the next computing platform. As we discussed, the 5G network will significantly influence millions of lives and benefit the whole world. Entrepreneurs and innovators in isolated or marginalized communities need access to XR technologies also. Economic and policy incentives as well as interventions can encourage individuals and businesses in disadvantaged locations to engage with the opportunities brought by XR. In many cases, these communities will have the most to gain, especially when considering the valuable skill-building, education, employment, and social benefits the tech offers. From the business perspective, XR enables creative problem-solving to improve efficiency and increase productivity while enhancing the customer experience.

Targeted incentives can empower people and communities to shape their own future and ensure the development of locally relevant products, services, and business models. Most importantly, XR presents an opportunity to create an enhanced experience to reach the Global Goals in almost all sectors and locations. This provides an unprecedented opportunity to design applications prompting broader societal impact. Some of the world's greatest challenges today can benefit immensely from the tech's broadscale reach.[59] Education is a key domain in which XR is used for good, especially in underserved areas. For example, a notable female-founded tech startup from Nigeria called Imisi 3D employs frontier technology solutions to create equitable opportunities for children.

Imisi 3D provides learning and educational experiences for children through VR tools, helping to address Nigeria's education challenge, as well as its economy at large. The new company's VR solution can provide better quality education in Nigeria and have a significant impact on educational problems such as out-of-school students with locally tailored educational VR content. Nigeria, with support from mobile operators like Huawei and Ericsson, ran spectrum tests for the 5G network in Abuja, Calabar, and Lagos in 2019.[60] This made Nigeria the first West African nation to initiate the 5G trial to deploy the technology towards achieving the best benefit for the nation and driving the 4th Industrial Revolution in Nigeria.

XR boasts an untapped potential to increase productivity and safety in several industries, which further makes it an attractive proposition for businesses. VR, for instance, can be used to simulate working in dangerous environments or with expensive, easily damaged tools and equipment, thereby eliminating the standard risks. AR communications, on the other hand, can be beneficial in reducing the time spent by engineers, technicians, or maintenance staff referring to manuals and looking up information online while on the job. Additionally, in AR, natural gestures could be the underlying driver of the experience. Google's Project Soli, a sensing radar technology, is a perfect example of promoting touchless interactions.[61] Operating with the tap of a finger or the movements of the body, it requires minimal personal interface with little to no visual overload.

XR BOASTS AN UNTAPPED POTENTIAL TO INCREASE PRODUCTIVITY AND SAFETY IN SEVERAL INDUSTRIES, WHICH FURTHER MAKES IT AN ATTRACTIVE PROPOSITION FOR BUSINESSES.

From the health perspective, there are several ways XR is adding value as well. VR and AR technologies are being used, along with other therapeutic techniques, to treat mental health conditions. Most applied in the context of anxiety disorders, XR programs offer treatments for those affected by mental illness. These technologies allow mobility, meaning treatment can take place where it is best for the patient and help minimize the impact of their chronic condition. One such project that addresses PTSD uses VR to send veterans back to Middle Eastern areas of conflict, where they are guided through a virtual war simulation.[62] This enables veterans to process their trauma, helping them overcome PTSD. The project has been considered successful due to its contributions to reduced panic attacks, facilitating greater concentration at work, and improving sleep in patients.

The sustainability context hugely benefits from XR as well. Nestlé is an example of a company leveraging sustainable packaging benefits, in addition to consumer engagement, that AR technology brings.[63] Connected packaging initiatives and AR are being used for spatial storytelling, while also for informing and instructing about a brand's purpose and sustainability. We also have organizations such as UNICEF that are investing in MR prototypes for identifying scalable solutions and providing the same technological advances to children from program countries as to their peers in other regions.[64]

FOR TOO LONG, THE TECHNOLOGY NARRATIVE OF NIGERIA HAS BEEN ONE OF CONSUMPTION AND NOT CREATION.

PwC in the Netherlands collaborated with a VR agency called Rooftop Immersive Studio to develop the SDG Dome experience. Its aim is to help people grasp the urgency of the SDGs while simultaneously showing them how new technology can offer solutions. This simulation uses VR goggles, taking visitors on a 360-degree journey to experience the consequences of current human activities on the planet, including the destruction of rainforests, the pollution of drinking water, or the production of cheap goods in sweatshops. The SDG Dome has seen over 3,700 visitors ranging from students and business leaders to politicians and policymakers since its launch in February 2019.[65] XR solutions also seek to address the climate change issue by exposing people to the conditions in different parts of the world with the most severe environmental impacts. In terms of facing global warming, MIT's Climate CoLab public space called Climaure has emerged as an initiative that endeavors to inform people and build global awareness about climate risks through personalized visualizations.

AR IMMERSION FOR PUBLIC GOOD: CLIMAURE – MIT CLIMATE COLAB[66]

As an AR public space installation setup, Climaure provides an immersive spatial view at a life-size scale of the environment around participants inside a cubicle booth. Physical movements from users inside the installation control the interactions, allowing the study of local residents' behaviors and analyzing their lifestyle habits. Such analysis can produce narratives that could be tailored to the specific audience to thus evoke the maximum sense of urgency to address the issue of climate change. What this AR application achieves is a personal level of connection to the climate change issue. Being able to see, feel, and hear a future environment, the participant is sensitized to climate change and resonates with a strong message. Climaure offers content and interactivity that exposes people to dire scenarios like rising sea levels, storms, acid rains, poisonous smog, floods, heat waves, and extreme weather scenarios. It is part of Climaure's plans to deploy AR installations at specific public spaces with high population densities for maximum impact, including in Bangladesh, Sri Lanka, the United Kingdom, the United States, and India.

Corporations are using XR in innovative ways often for twofold purposes: to enhance their market value and to manage employee satisfaction. VR technology allows users to interactively experience virtual surroundings, prompting technology to create virtual simulations for training and onboarding purposes, and for actual simulations of real circumstances. For this reason, Siemens, with more than 300 production and manufacturing facilities, and over 385,000 employees, is utilizing VR throughout their line of business to ensure the safety and health of their employees (Case 40).

XR PROGRESSING THE GLOBAL GOALS

Bringing together the right skills and knowledge in a diverse world has been made easier thanks to XR. In addition to promoting greater awareness in several sectors, and allowing access for expertise to be shared regardless of location, XR also has the potential for easing pain and addressing healthcare solutions through business service applications. Creating new business opportunities in various sectors that are not locationally determined, XR is altering how city infrastructure is designed and much more. Stepping into this parallel reality – an extended reality - we are experiencing a major market disruptor and a huge platform for business opportunities.

GOOD HEALTH AND WELLBEING

This benefits from extended realities, as the tech presents highly effective solutions in the medical and healthcare sectors. One of the ways in which AR is already being used is for disseminating educational materials for medical professionals and patients, such as simulations for surgeries and diseases to enhance patient treatments. We have the example of AccuVein, which uses projection-based AR, designed to scan a patient's body and show doctors the exact location and status of veins. This improves the injection of the vein on the first try by 3.5 times and reduces the need for further assistance or complications by 45%, saving hospitals an average of over $350,000 per year.[67]

In Brazil, doctors developed a project called VR Vaccine using VR to encourage children not to fear vaccinations. This involves children wearing a VR headset and watching an animated adventure story while a nurse synchronizes administering the injection with the story. Brazilian pharmacy chain Hermes Pardini has adopted this VR approach, which proved to be a very successful endeavor. The company has since installed VR headsets in all of its pharmacies to help with its vaccine campaigns. VR has also contributed to adult patients staying calm and relaxed during surgery. At St George's Hospital in London, patients were given the option of using a VR headset before and during their operation, resulting in 94% of VR-choosing patients to feel more relaxed and 80% to have less pain.[68]

QUALITY EDUCATION

XR technologies find applications in education for school age students (science, math, and languages) and workplace training (surgery, disaster response, and maintenance of power plants).[69] The COVID-19 pandemic especially illuminated the urgent need to recreate the education sector by moving to robust digital frameworks for remote teaching and learning. This is one of the reasons the International Telecommunication Union (ITU) and UNICEF launched the Giga project to expedite digital transformation in education, including connecting all schools to relevant AR/VR content by 2030.[70] XR solutions prove to be useful in communications education, too. These applications range from learning languages to practicing professional public speaking. VR educational software companies like Mondly provide immersive language-learning experiences without needing participants to travel to a foreign country. Mondly's VR worlds offer interactive conversations with real people, using cutting-edge technologies to teach 33 languages and improve business communication skills. MondlyWORKS, specifically, is a language solution for businesses with a global impact that increases productivity, fosters internal collaboration, and attracts and retains top talent.[71]

GENDER EQUALITY

XR technologies are useful for promoting this by reducing bias and enhancing empathy.[72] Through simulated environments that bring awareness to important issues like women's rights, XR may help users develop higher levels of empathy in terms of acceptance in real world applications.[73] REM5, a VR Lab, utilizes immersive technology to allow students, teachers, artists, and community groups to explore a range of subjects. These include racial and gender bias which can be simulated. For example, REM5 can show what it's like to be a woman in a meeting full of men.[74] This technology could also have very impactful and beneficial results in terms of mitigating human rights violations like rising cases of violence against females in underdeveloped regions.[75]

DECENT WORK AND ECONOMIC GROWTH

Promoting inclusive employment and sustained economic growth through XR tech has entered a new dimension over the past few years. This has become a focal goal due to employees and many organizations transitioning to remote work. AR is well-suited to help remote teams feel like they are virtually in the same space. Along with giving employees the feeling of being more connected in meetings, the tech has also provided a more natural environment to brainstorm and share ideas.

Workplace meeting and collaboration solutions will need an MR approach, including being accessible on desktop, mobile, and headset platforms through both AR and VR. In addressing this, Lenovo has created ThinkReality A3 smart glasses aimed at business travelers and remote workers. These glasses, connected to a 5G network, are useful for work-from-home employees who are unable to set up numerous computers or other necessary devices.[76] Since the glasses are capable of projecting up to five virtual screens for only the user's eyes, the tech allows for greater productivity overall.[77] Lenovo also allows VR images to be sent to others wearing the ThinkReality A3, thus creating a multi-user collaborative experience.

INDUSTRY, INNOVATION AND INFRASTRUCTURE

Industry, innovation and infrastructure, as well as investing in research and development, will be critical for businesses to sustain a competitive edge. Businesses with a vision will need to develop the right environment to support digital transformation. During the Covid pandemic, we have witnessed how a lack of digital networks caused widespread public service disruption, with entire economic sectors halted and millions left unemployed.[78] Without the widespread tech expansion involving 5G, the necessary conditions for an immersive XR experience will lag behind. Thus, the American multinational corporation Qualcomm invented the underlying technologies that are foundational for XR proliferation. These include immersive 3D graphics, computer vision, machine learning, intuitive security, and 5G technologies.[79] Qualcomm's research is geared toward solving industry-wide challenges and paving the way for XR breakthroughs by working with and investing in leading XR companies. With over 20% of revenue invested in research and development since 2006, Qualcomm's commitment to XR innovation is propelling the entire industry forward.[80]

REDUCED INEQUALITIES

XRs are being called on to equalize people across the globe to raise awareness of and foster understanding in diverse sectors. Data points processed with AR, VR, and MR solutions are reducing social conflicts and keeping people safe. Authentically Us, the first documentary VR series from Facebook and Oculus, has taken an emphatic step towards allowing viewers to enter into the lives of transgender activists who are working to make communities safer for LGBTQ+ people everywhere.[81] VR, in this case, enables viewers to confront the everyday challenges a transgender person faces and how they campaign to live free and equal via a 360-degree video depicting the viewpoints of three transgender identities: transmasculine, transfeminine, and gender non-binary.

SUSTAINABLE CITIES AND COMMUNITIES

Cities benefit from XR technologies that allow people to move through networks, search for locations, and navigate businesses. Sustainable cities are utilizing AR and VR, along with the location or spatial intelligence, to develop public spaces and services through provisions like environmental preservation, good governance, asset management, public safety and health, transportation, as well as preservation of an area's cultural heritage.[82] Singapore has planned the Virtual Singapore project, which would serve as a digital 3D city model. Investing $73 million in the project, the developers intend to use it as a test by government agencies, businesses, and researchers to build a more resilient city.[83] Business analytics, resource planning, management, and specialized services are some of the ways the project achieves its goals. Additionally, India became the first city to be designed with its digital twin using Cityzenith's Smart World Pro software. The program includes a digital twin user ID scheme for every citizen that will serve as a single portal for all government information, notifications, forms, and applications.[84]

GOOD HEALTH AND WELLBEING

- Support and compensate for developmental and mental health problems with AR/VR devices.
- Use VR headsets to relax patients during surgical operations.
- Locate patient veins through body scans with XR capabilities for medical professionals.

QUALITY EDUCATION

- Deploy training and information services with AR/VR experiences.
- Enable on-demand and remote learning through various MR tools.
- Offer VR for language learning and public speaking practice.

DECENT WORK AND ECONOMIC GROWTH

- Facilitate MR remote work from home.
- Build connectivity across teams, experiencing being together even when apart through XR.
- Innovate in the workplace by generating efficiencies enabled through AR/VR solutions.

INDUSTRY, INNOVATION AND INFRASTRUCTURE

- Improve effectiveness and speed of design and development through shared VR visualizations of products and services.
- Expand the widespread 5G network to allow for thorough XR market integration.
- Utilize AR/VR visualization for infrastructure planning and development.

EXTENDED REALITIES

GENDER EQUALITY

- Promote equality and build empathy through immersive VR experiences.
- Democratize XR experiences and provide ways to explore topics like racial or gender bias.
- Equalize learning by helping students better visualize complex subjects through MR platforms.

REDUCED INEQUALITIES

- Employ XR to help equalize populations in terms of raising awareness in diverse sectors.
- Promote empathy through VR experiences that enable users to confront the challenges of others.
- Give diverse populations equal access to MR services.

SUSTAINABLE CITIES AND COMMUNITIES

- Optimize city design and planning.
- Develop AR/VR solutions that reduce the need for traveling by providing digital experiences.
- Enable XR digital twins for prototyping for engineering and construction efficiency.

ENHANCING BUSINESS MODELS

Extended realities are on course to impact all areas of our lives. As it becomes mainstream over the coming decade, XR will enable several disruptive business models.[85] Global companies are already making the shift to incorporate this tech into their core operational practices. Economies are experimenting with how realities will shape the future of many sectors, including education, commerce, manufacturing, defense, retail, and entertainment. Fortunately, businesses are stepping up and laying the foundation for this tech to be disseminated more evenly throughout industries. The relatively low cost of XR technologies and their computing power allows startups to develop innovative applications, while bringing 5G network capabilities to the global market through internet-enabled distribution platforms.[86]

In these ways, XR emerges as an experiential solution to sustainable business in a changing world. XR technologies have wide-ranging impacts across sectors and value chains. In cases where remote collaboration is required, where people are far apart or unable to travel, this tech can make the difference between companies' abilities to adapt successfully and their failure to do so. Enhancing global collaboration in areas such as education, visualization, and simulation, XR brings people together in "real-life" settings to work together and see each other regardless of distances. Immersive learning for the future workforce is expected to be one of the most influential and immediately applicable markets for XR business breakthroughs.

Industries with high-risk working environments, such as energy, manufacturing, or construction, are already benefiting from XR's immersive training offerings. Other sectors are also now seeing the value and beginning to explore the space. XR unlocks new business value through an improved customer experience, optimized employee

BENEFITS OF XR IMMERSIVE LEARNING[87]

- **Medical training**: University School of Medicine in Atlanta uses VR for training surgeons who make 40% fewer mistakes than surgeons who are conventionally trained.
- **Retail training**: Walmart uses VR to prepare store managers for Black Friday, America's biggest shopping day, deploying the technology across 200 training centers for an 80% reduction in training time.
- **Outside sales rep training**: United Rentals uses immersive learning to bring construction sites into the classroom, attaining a 40% reduction in training time.

performance, and creation of new content and services. This tech gives rise to a more connected worker dynamic where access to data and digital systems enables them to be more efficient, accurate, and safe. AR, for example, can create an extra layer for business models that draws in audiences through fostering engagement, empathy, and action.[88] Luxury automotive brand Audi employs VR technologies to its digital twin approach, thereby giving consumers the ability to experience a new model of their car before even physically touching it.[89] The initiative, entitled "The Audi VR Experience", allows customers to look at every detail of the vehicle captured with a special 3D camera before market launch and purchase.

VR is a cost-effective method for developing products and services, and many businesses have embraced the tech specifically for this reason. Not only does it allow for more thorough product testing via prototypes, but using XR as initial models also gives businesses the product information they need without having to develop expensive physical versions. In addition, design problems can be detected at an early stage through VR prototyping, saving time and costs. Vuzix smart glasses are an example of a gadget that combines VR tech accuracy and human influence for the optimum working environment in warehouses.[90] For improved efficiency, Vuzix utilizes tailored information and video recording for errors to be spotted dimmediately. These smart glasses benefit workers greatly by bearing burdens for them, such as facilitating efficiencies that result in carrying less equipment and leaving both hands free.

Companies are positioning themselves to take advantage of these growing trends. AR is revolutionizing markets with AR mobile Apps being an easy way for businesses to visually communicate objectives to customers. Clients from several industries are currently employing AR mobile Apps in core business practices, including healthcare, education, manufacturing, construction, retail, education, and real estate. AR is currently worth $7.05 billion in the healthcare market, over 100 million consumers used AR to shop in 2020, and AR mobile users are expected to reach 1.73 billion by 2024.[91] SphereGen Technologies is an example of a company revolutionizing workplace training and employee engagement through XR innovations. Creating applications using an innovative approach to business solutions designed for multiple XR platform compatibility, SphereGen is providing leading-edge software to create XR collaboration and visualization experiences (Case 41).

By embracing new technologies to connect, XR experiences are popularizing and offering huge potential for a new way of learning and working. Industry leaders are investing heavily in this tech, and research suggests that businesses fully adopting XR technologies and innovations could grow five times faster than those who lag.[92] By experimenting with these realities and co-creating with partners, employees, organizations, and communities, businesses will reach the next level.

GLOBAL GOALS' GROWTH OPPORTUNITIES

XR is one of the leading tech business trends today and holds great promise to revolutionize the way we experience products and services across different sectors. Top brands and multinational tech giants around the world, from Microsoft and Facebook to Apple and Google, are creating immersive digital experiences. Their efforts to meet societal demands and solve sustainability challenges respond to target SDG growth markets by improving efficiency and streamlining business operations. We see an increasing number of companies harnessing VR, AR, and MR to keep up with current trends and improve consumers' perceptions of their brands and increase their market share. There are likely to be no industries that will remain untouched by the proliferation of XR across the commercial, governmental, and financial spectrums. The impactful SDG domains that the tech addresses in terms of business opportunities are interwoven. They include healthcare and medical services, education and training tools, cities and urban living, and creating awareness. Business opportunities for this tech are expansive and truly exciting, as they catapult us into new realities.

INNOVATING HEALTHCARE AND MEDICAL SERVICES

XR technologies present many benefits in the healthcare and medical domains. XR's use in healthcare is on the rise, from the operating room to medical classrooms, from pain management to mental health. Experts estimate the market for XR in healthcare could reach $7 billion by 2026.[93] One innovation in this regard is a calming VR experience for expectant

IN BUSINESS
SPHEREGEN TECHNOLOGIES[94]

Initiative: XR business solutions
Headquarters: New Haven, Connecticut USA

Responsible consumption and production SphereGen Technologies facilitates businesses custom solutions, allowing companies to harness XR across departments and industry fields. With a revenue of over $22 million, SphereGen provides services such as application modernization and XR development to help organizations in several industries (SDGs 10,12).[95] It specifically enables solutions using leading-edge software to create XR experiences. The company helps organizations improve employee engagement through innovative and compelling training applications (SDG 8). SphereGen largely caters to educating professionals by creating quality 3D models that can be viewed in VR headsets, HoloLens, and PCs and tablets. It also has clients across various industries such as manufacturing and engineering, education, healthcare, and finance (SDGs 3,4,8). SphereGen's Unity design team and Cloud specialists work together to develop holographic applications using an innovative approach to business solutions designed for multiple XR platform compatibility (SDG 9). This XR tech truly solves business process needs while analyzing data in real-time and developing the best tools to move businesses forward.

mothers, with the purpose of reducing pain levels during labor.[96] A study conducted shows that those who used VR headsets with the Labor Bliss visualization for up to 30 minutes during contractions reported an average pain reduction of 52%, whereas those who did not wear the headsets experienced a pain increase of 58%.[97] This tech paves the way for offering an alternative to other pain relievers during childbirth.

EXPERTS ESTIMATE THE MARKET FOR XR IN HEALTHCARE COULD REACH $7 BILLION BY 2026.[98]

Another beneficial application includes doctors and nurses in the emergency room. Working in a high-pressure, high-stress environment, medical professionals' roles sometimes involve making critical decisions for emergency procedures that require extra training. To tackle this issue, doctors from the Children's Hospital in Los Angeles teamed up with AiSolve and Bioflight VR, creating a virtual trauma room that more accurately represents how real-life emergencies may play out.[99] Utilizing this training tool enables trainee doctors to prepare for actual events without the fear of failure or dire consequences.

Dutch electronics multinational Philips focuses on health technology and has a presence across 100 countries in the world. In 2019, the company collaborated with Microsoft, combining Philips' Azurion image-guided therapy platform and Microsoft HoloLens 2 MR computing platform to develop an XR concept for future operating rooms.[100] This reality hybrid allows the tech initiative to create innovative applications for image-guided, minimally invasive therapies. Through multidisciplinary studies and examination of a 3D model of the patient case, collaboration with AR and VR imaging leads to more efficient planning and better time management.

Businesses are taking advantage of Microsoft's XR innovations. The tech giant's products are immensely powerful in the healthcare and medical sector, as the value creation can be fourfold: shorter procedure times, better clinical outcomes, enhanced prediction and execution of the procedure, and a more intuitive and comfortable experience for staff. One prime example is Medivis, a medical technology company harnessing augmented reality and artificial intelligence to advance medical imaging and surgical navigation (Case 42).

The tech has unprecedented potential to help with the visualization of medical data more effectively. Because it overlays digital images and information onto the real-world view, AR is ideally suited to visualizing medical information – such as overlaying anatomical data onto the patient in real life. This can help clinicians carry out procedures in a faster, more accurate way. A simple example comes from AccuVein, the global leader in vein visualization. Here, a map of veins is overlaid onto the surface of the patient's skin to help health professionals find veins more easily for applications like starting IVs and drawing blood. Evidence shows that vein visualization dramatically improves clinicians' ability to find them on the first attempt by as much as 98% in pediatric cases and 96% with adult patients.[101]

MEDICAL PATIENTS WEARING A VR HEADSET HAVE REPORTED AN IMPROVED OVERALL HOSPITAL EXPERIENCE, WITH 94% SAYING THEY FELT MORE RELAXED AND 80% REPORTING FEELING LESS PAIN.[102]

Further, VR has been proven to help patients stay calm and relaxed during surgery. At St George's Hospital in London, patients undergoing procedures with regional anesthetic were given the option of using a VR headset before and during their operation, which immersed them in calming virtual landscapes. This proved incredibly effective as an impressive 100% of participants expressed that wearing the headset improved their overall hospital experience, 94% said they felt more relaxed, and 80% reported feeling less pain.[103]

IN BUSINESS

MEDIVIS[104]

Initiative: Microsoft HoloLens 2[105]
Headquarters: New York, New York USA

Medivis is a leader in AR for surgery with powerful MR provided by Microsoft's HoloLens. Founded by surgeons, radiologists, and engineers, Medivis uses technological advancements in AR and computer vision to create a holographic future for surgery (SDG 3). It is enabling surgeons to perform routine procedures in a safer and more efficient manner. With $2.3 million in financing, the company launched the SurgicalAR platform, a visualization tool that guides surgical navigation while decreasing complications, improving patient outcomes, and lowering surgical costs (SDGs 9,12).[106] Medivis has successfully completed more than 200 surgeries with the HoloLens; decreased radiation exposure to patients of SurgicalAR, averaging 1 CT scan as compared to 10 CT scans with traditional 2D surgical solutions; and demonstrated the potential to place catheters with 1 mm accuracy (versus the 2.2 cm accuracy that is typical today).[107]

Medivis brings together doctors and engineers of all backgrounds from around the world, to ensure a comprehensive knowledge base backs up all projects (SDG 17). Using XR headsets and glasses, Microsoft HoloLens has developed a way for medical students and clinicians to learn about and study the human body using MR (SDGs 4,10). This initiative ensures medical objectives are realized through an understanding of the anatomical structure as well as how to treat different medical conditions. HoloLens 2 is able to perform vital imaging for medical staff, as it is operated using hand gestures and voice commands while enabling surgeons to view 3D holographic images of a patient's anatomy. Business benefits of HoloLens include reduced medical staff training by 30% at an average savings of $63 per hour; reduced average annual personal protective equipment costs by 75%, savings $954 per employee; and improved efficiency by 30% to complete ward rounds at an average savings of $41 per hour (SDG 8).[108]

UNLOCKING NEW EDUCATION AND TRAINING OPPORTUNITIES

In the educational setting, XR allows students to learn in new and innovative ways. The advancement of XR has benefitted the education secctor especially, with experiential learning, both in school and on the job. Learning takes many forms – from teaching children about the solar system and climate impacts to training the workforce both on the job and remotely. XR emerges as a sustainable solution because of its ability to mirror real-life situations, ultimately exceeding current teaching and learning limits. There is also evidence that students are more likely to remember learned information when using the tech. Stanford University and Technical University of Denmark discovered that incorporating XR technology improved memory retention rates by 76%, compared to traditional learning methods.[109]

From an educational and training perspective, participants can learn about abstract concepts and potentially intangible worlds via these new realities. With a basic VR simulation, for instance, students can start exploring the moon's surface within a matter of seconds. Teachers use the smartphone application called Human Anatomy Atlas to give students a virtual lab experience regarding the human body. This AR app is best suited for high school and higher education learners. Going beyond textbook-level definitions, it allows students to create, save, and share custom interactive 3D models. This multilingual AR solution has over 10,000 anatomical models, including a database of body organs, muscle compositions and actions, skeletal structure, and more.[110]

STANFORD UNIVERSITY AND TECHNICAL UNIVERSITY OF DENMARK DISCOVERED THAT INCORPORATING XR TECHNOLOGY IMPROVED MEMORY RETENTION RATES BY 76% COMPARED TO TRADITIONAL LEARNING METHODS.[111]

Throughout the past few years, educational experiences in XR continue to be increasingly common. We find exciting new realms being taught via this new reality, including subjects such as history and science. A VR experience named Rome Reborn was developed by digital archeologist Bernard Frischer of Indiana University. A team of 50 scientists collaborated for 20 years to complete what is the largest scale VR experience of a historical site.[112] Rome Reborn recreates an area of 5.5 square miles of the ancient city with 7,000 monuments and buildings. Another significant project is the NASA Space Launch System VR Experience, a virtual reality software program for learning about outer space.[113] Those using the software can even sit in the rocket's cockpit during pre-launch activities to experience what it's like to be an astronaut inside the Orion spacecraft.

XR opens the door for distance learning classrooms, where students can experience the benefits of learning in a collaborative environment while being remote.[114] What facilitates this structure are AR and VR training aids, ensuring that access to information is always available. With AR today, educational institutions can easily design courses using simulation, visualization, and interaction with both virtual objects and real environments. In schools across the US, semiconductor company Advanced Micro Devices (AMD) has emerged to develop VR-based learning to evaluate the potential for integrating VR effectively into the classroom while enhancing student learning.

There are several workplace training VR applications on the market, most commonly for safety, that businesses are finding beneficial. VR helps operators practice before an unfortunate event to respond quickly and reliably in an emergency. COMOS Walkinside as a 3D Asset Portal is a

VR solution that provides all project stakeholders and decision-makers with easy and fast access to all factory information, thereby ensuring a common understanding of its current state.[115] The integrated COMOS software solution lets operators create a virtual 3D representation of their facility, and this VR model of operations forms the basis for efficient maintenance and training, resulting in significant savings.[116] Using a VR software solution allows highly complex spatial 3D models for training purposes to be visualized immediately.

REDEFINING CITIES AND URBAN LIVING

Cities and urban areas are being redefined by transforming buildings and venues into intelligent, responsive, interactive, and sustainable architecture. Further, with the onset of climate change comes government planning to create sustainable cities that provide quality of life to citizens. Smart cities aim to incorporate climate-resilient infrastructure by installing technology add-ons that enhance convenience and aid in governance.[117] In this regard, AR and VR, along with location or spatial intelligence, can help develop public spaces to preserve environmental integrity, good governance, asset management, public safety and health, transportation, and preservation of an area's cultural heritage.[118] XR technology proves itself to be a crucial component to all future spatial planning projects, as it provides context for adaptation to improve models.

MIT's Media Lab worked with the City Science Lab of Hamburg on a project called Finding Places as part of its City Science initiative.[119] The researchers used optically-tagged LEGO bricks, simulation algorithms, and AR to model potential locations for refugee accommodations. Participants in this project identified 160 locations, and the government quickly authorized 44 and constructed 10 accommodations, thus compressing a process that could have taken years. In the commercial world, architects use this VR to provide consumers with virtual tours of buildings.

AR technology is also being used in the manufacturing sector for product training and field engineering services for the installation and maintenance of equipment. Companies can use XR in various professional trainings in urban environments. Police departments, for instance, are now using VR to train officers to deal with riots or arrest people in specific situations to make streets safer for citizens and officers alike.[120] In terms of urban design, Transmira and Kognition have collaborated as part of a consortium of XR companies to develop and implement the latest technology for the next generation of smart cities (Case 44).

Urban retail business is experiencing the shift to implementing AR in shopping and eCommerce. Online 3D environments that mimic city stores are providing shoppers with ways to connect without having to leave their homes. AR portals virtually transport the users into a desired retail environment to walk around and explore through an XR device. These shopping mini worlds have the potential to be integrated into existing virtual universes and apps, and could play an important role in shaping the city and urban life.

IN BUSINESS

ADVANCED MICRO DEVICES (AMD)[121]

Initiative: VR gadgets for school-based learning
Headquarters: Santa Clara, California USA

For more than 50 years, AMD has driven innovation in high-performance computing, graphics, and visualization technologies. It has recognized the potential of VR technology to better engage students and help them to retain key concepts (SDG 4). To test this theory, a collaboration emerged between Hunters Lane High School and AMD with a six-week experiment to determine student and teacher perceptions of, and attainments with, VR-based learning (SDG 17). The school set up a VR lab where the four classrooms, totaling about 150 students, could use the VR equipment.[122] Teachers learned about VR technology both to develop strategies for integrating it into their curriculum and to create computer programs and applications that troubleshoot various technology system issues (SDG 9). These educators also made use of Google Earth VR, as well as tested other apps and games to experience how the technology could be applied in different scenarios and subjects (SDG 16).

Given the reported shortage of tech talent in the workforce today, VR could help students learn tech skills quickly, increasing the number of graduates ready to enter into the tech job market (SDGs 8,10). "In my classroom, using VR helped the students retain knowledge more effectively," said Information Technology representatives at Hunters Lane High School.[123] "This could change the game for kids who are struggling because you immerse them in this world, and they can see it and feel it. It makes them more interested and engaged." In 2021, AMD had a reported record revenue of $16.4 billion, which was up 68% over 2020.[124] This was driven by higher revenue in the computing and graphics segment.

TRANSMIRA SMART CITIES[125]

Initiative: VR gadgets for school-based learning
Headquarters: Raleigh, North Carolina USA

Transmira is a North Carolina-based XR startup that has entered into a partnership with Kognition, the Philadelphia-based builder of AI technology for commercial property (SDG 17). Transmira and Kognition's collaboration is part of a consortium of XR companies that develop and implement the latest technology to create the next generation of smart cities and intelligent architecture (SDG 11). This infrastructure aims to include stadiums and arenas, office buildings, retail centers, university campuses, hotels, airports, and more (SDG 9). The consortium of XR companies plans to bring together AR, VR, digital twins, integrated IoT sensors and devices, blockchain technology, 5G, edge-computing and hybrid cloud, AI, and machine learning (SDGs 7,12).[126] "With our Omniscape technology and XR platform, we bring location to life using AR and VR technology, AI-driven holograms, data visualization, interactive content, as well as unique monetization capabilities" remarked Robert Rice, founder and CEO of Transmira.[127] This holistic approach gives a glimpse into the future of smart spaces, amplifying the power of building tech, resulting in enhanced customer experiences, streamlined operations, and safer spaces for people (SDGs 10,16).

INVESTMENT IN AR RETAIL PROJECTS

IT giants invest millions of dollars into various AR retail projects with new startups arising:[128]

- Google published Tango project and invested $1.4 billion into Magic Leap XR tech, which aids in remote training and collaboration.[129]
- Apple introduced the platform to develop AR for iOS devices, called ARKit, which provides a cutting-edge platform for developing AR Apps for iPhone and iPad.[130]
- Snapchat estimated $30 to $40 million to acquire Israeli AR startup Cimagine Media.[131]
- Facebook paid $2 billion for Oculus.[132]
- Commerce AR startups are heavily funded and have reached more than $650 million: Augment[133] ($1.8 million), VividWorks[134] ($1.7 million), and Sayduck[135] ($1 million).

From an efficiency and waste reduction standpoint, AR can allow customers to try products before they decide to spend money. Brands report over 60% of shoppers prefer to buy using AR, and 46% of shop owners express satisfaction about the transition to an AR/VR resolution.[136] Retail company ZARA has introduced a shopping App where customers can point their phones at the specific shop windows or sensors in the store to see models wearing selected outfits. This innovation allows customers to see how the outfit fits and moves without having to try it on. Other than ZARA, Art Labs has also recently introduced an AR platform where customers can try virtual footwear, decorations, or accessories to see how the item is suitable for them before their purchase.

Project Archer is an AR studio in Seattle dedicated to paving the way for AR applications in the sustainable retail space. With a focus on creating a productive and immersive real-world shopping experience, Project Archer combines diverse data streams with personalized information to make shopping experiences more productive and efficient.[137] Studies show impressive numbers for the future of AR in retail to enhance urban shopping experiences with a huge potential to boost sales. More than 50% of smartphone owners already use it when shopping.[138] These data reveal that XR for retail could be highly beneficial for business: 71% of shoppers believe they would shop more often if they used AR apps; 61% said they preferably choose stores with AR over those without it; 55% admitted that AR makes shopping more fun and exciting; and 40% of shoppers believe that they are ready to pay more for a product if they are allowed to test it through AR.

RAISING AWARENESS BY EXPERIENCE

Building awareness around important topics and providing people with the necessary information in critical sectors is necessary for various factors, such as health and safety, environmental protection, human rights, and economic growth and long-term prosperity. Expanding this tech into areas where knowledge is lacking, or where people are in emergency situations, is becoming a reality. In the hazardous mining industry, the need for improved safety measures and training is constant. Imagine how a rapidly growing fire could deplete oxygen inside a mine, subsequently harming the miners. Oculus Quest 2 all-in-one VR headsets can simulate disasters, preparing miners for these dire situations.[139]

We have the example of volunteer rescuers with Ontario Mine Rescue navigating emergency underground simulations, which hones their emergency-response skills in a safe but realistic environment. By creating awareness for miners about potential problems, mitigation tactics can be put in place to limit fatal accidents and ensure rapid responses to other dangerous events. Cultural virtual experiences are also driving the consumer market and breaking into a variety of sectors. Physically traveling is no longer a necessity, given that a new suite of virtual experiences is possible. These VR immersions range from online guided tours to film festivals, global wine-tasting to international exotic birdwatching.[140] The virtual experience can now allow people to learn about the world no matter where they are.

Creating a global awareness during the pandemic has been challenging, but several tourist businesses have relied on virtual remote experiential tours to maintain their standing. Some of Oculus' most popular experiences include National Geographic VR, which takes users to places such as Antarctica, making possible virtual trips navigating icebergs in a kayak, climbing an ice shelf, and surviving a blustery snowstorm as they search for a lost penguin colony.[141] Historic Portsmouth in the UK has a new project, The Mary Rose, that is garnering the attention of historians. The Mary Rose, a ship in Henry VIII's navy, was built when he came to the throne in 1509. It boasts a new interactive photosphere experiential tour that rotates 360 degrees along a walkway between the vessel's wooden structure and the artifacts that were found with the 16th-century wreck.[142] Historic Portsmouth provides the likeness of visiting the ship in person through rotating clickable icons.

Historic projects and social business endeavors are brought to our awareness through tech. Project Dastaan is an exciting initiative connecting generations and historians via XR advancements (Case 45). Founded in 2018 by a group of four students at the University of Oxford, the venture is advised by historians, filmmakers, and advocates. The Project is generously supported by the CatchLight Foundation, Digital Catapult and Arts Council England's CreativeXR Program, and a National Geographic Society Exploration Grant.[143]

Several other experiential XR initiatives in the sustainability realm are evolving as well. In 2021, centered around the theme of digital immersive content creation, Ithra Idea Lab in Saudi Arabia launched a VR program called Creative Solutions with an innovative event that provided opportunities to connect while showcasing the potential of immersive experiences. Creative Solutions is an annual thematic innovation program that covers the fields of art, science, and technology, aiming to develop viable solutions to identified opportunities and challenges.[144] Ithra was able to successfully maintain a sense of community while also providing an immersive experience that did not necessitate all the participants to have headsets, or be there in person.

IN BUSINESS
PROJECT DASTAAN[145]
Initiative: VR peace building initiative
Headquarters: India, Pakistan, and Bangladesh

Project Dastaan aims to act as a catalyst for fostering mutual understanding among India, Pakistan, and Bangladesh. Dastaan, which means "story" in several South Asian languages, works to bring awareness to the experiences of the 1947 Partition generation. While creating a lasting impact between generations, Project Dastaan seeks to reconnect displaced refugees with their childhood communities and villages through 360-degree XR digital experiences (SDGs 11,17).

The partition of secular India and Islamic Pakistan caused chaos, panic, and widespread violence (SDGs 1,16). Exactly how many people died is difficult to estimate, but visceral historical accounts of rivers of blood and trains reaching their destination full of bodies are built into cultural heritage. Figures range from 200,000 to 4 million dead and missing (SDG 3). An estimated 15 million people left for the other side of the new border, where Muslims went to Pakistan and Hindus and Sikhs to India.

Walking survivors and ancestors through the experience of VR can help them to remember and make peace with the historical event (SDG 10). "When Partition violence was at its height, Gandh had said that no peace would be possible until the refugees displaced were able to return to their homelands," declares Project Dastaan.[146] This return is made possible through VR. Project Dastaan endeavored to virtually reconnect 75 first-hand witnesses of the Partition to their ancestral homes by the end of 2022. The Project has several features including "Child of Empire," an interactive VR piece to be installed in museums, a feature film titled "The Lost Migration," and another film titled "Where the Birds Live."

ADDRESSING RISKS AND CHALLENGES ON THE ROAD AHEAD

The new and improved advancements of XR, made possible through the 5G network, are groundbreaking. With download speeds up to 20 to 30 times faster than its 4G predecessor, 5G promises a new world. It must be acknowledged, however, that there are still many people in the world that do not have access to the 5G network, and thus XR does not reach them directly. Further, while the tech is becoming a foundation for many modern services, it is also causing potential health risks and we still have very little concrete health data due to the nascent quality of the technology. Cancer and fertility damage are just some of the present and future possible concerns caused by 5G.[147] The difference between 4G and 5G in terms of gigahertz, the unit of alternating current or electromagnetic waves that affect the transmission speeds of devices, is significant. 5G technology has radio millimeter bands in the 30 to 300 GHz range, while 4G is down around 6 GHz.[148] This is a huge difference, and when applied to video latency, it translates to speeds up to 60 to 120 times faster.

As outlined in this chapter, XR investment is growing and will go toward a wide range of innovations, such as the ability to conduct remote surgery and training, as well as applications that will greatly increase productivity. But just like other transformative technologies, the rapid uptake of XR demands preemptive caution and monitoring. XR datasets could be profoundly personal, and these data concerns are becoming a growing impediment to the tech roll out. While XR tools make direct connections to our mental faculties and perceptions of reality, these capabilities are not yet fully understood and subsequently raise heightened privacy and security fears.[149] Mismanagement of XR technologies risks harm to individuals and society that may be extremely hard to reverse.

The urgency and necessity to get this right from the outset are paramount. XR is a relatively new concept coming into the mainstream, so very few companies have designed responsible measures to prevent, or at least mitigate, potential negative consequences of the technology. Accenture identified six risks that business leaders can begin to strategize around while they are still in the early stages of XR implementation.[150] These risks include misuse of personal data, creation of fake enterprises, addiction to technology, threats of cyber-attacks, antisocial behaviors, and digitally divided worlds. MIT and Harvard have also raised awareness recently about "adversarial attacks," where hackers expertly manipulate input to systems (like changing a VR image), altering the system to behave in unexpected or undesirable ways.[151]

WE HAVE

IMAGINED

At one time unimaginable, we now experience a combination of real-and-virtual environments helping humanity solve our Global Goals. We have imagined XR to be able to address complex challenges and enable us to see beyond the human eye. Complex challenges are being addressed through VR and AR technologies. XR enables us to travel the world in a blink of an eye, and gives people the opportunity to experience new realms of reality that were previously unavailable. Through this technology we are immersed in hybrid real-virtual environment that extend our scope of sustainable possibilities for all sectors, businesses, and settings.

Extended Realities technology has the capability and functionality to be used for more than entertainment purposes. Governments, NGOs, and companies alike all benefit from this tech. Whether it's for infrastructure and efficiency, rewiring the brain for learning purposes, treating ailments, or making leisure more interactive, XR enhances the way we live and experience reality, both literally and imaginatively.

We have imagined XR for Good.

TECH FOR GOOD

THE FILM

AUTONOMOUS VEHICLES AND DRONES

7

AUTONOMOUS VEHICLES AND DRONES ARE
INCREDIBLY IMPACTFUL.

THEY'RE AT THE FOREFRONT OF ADDRESSING
MAJOR GLOBAL CHALLENGES.

WE ONLY NEED TO

IMAGINE

Imagine if technologies could adequately and efficiently provide relief services that arrive swiftly, with precise navigation abilities, whereby both the people at risk and the rescue teams are safer. At the same time as natural disasters are becoming more prevalent around the globe due to climate change, technology is offering increasingly advanced emergency assistance solutions. Imagine drones or other autonomous vehicles swooping in to save countless lives in instances when urgent medical help is needed. Imagine a scenario wherein we would no longer require elaborate safety equipment, conventional vehicles, or manpower for search and rescue operations.

Advanced tech solutions are ramping up innovations in the emergency assistance sector. Designed resourcefully to integrate human genius into actionable products, autonomous vehicles (AVs) and drones have become a necessity in assisting us under pressure in high-stakes circumstances. There are many examples, but unmanned vehicles, especially aerial ones, have proven themselves beneficial in disaster relief. With the help of AVs and drones, remote places that were once considered inaccessible and unreachable due to limitations on infrastructure or inadequate resources, are now being accessed like never before. People are rescued quickly via life-saving technological innovations, rather than depending on slower-moving NGOs or governments.

Early instances of drones helping aid organizations emerged in 2013, at which time they assisted in identifying the precise areas of need in the Philippines after the destructive Typhoon Haiyan.1 Drones have since come a long way and greatly increased their potential capabilities. These tech champions have advanced beyond their original function of simply identifying where help is required, and have progressed to be the ones to deliver the help. Thriving in the face of such obstacles, drones are programmed to swerve past mountains, soar over roads, withstand extreme temperatures, and much more. Undeniably swifter and nimbler than many emergency vehicles, drones work their way through tough spots and emerge unscathed.

Although used throughout the world, Africa has been a crucial region in the proliferation of AVs. Drone use for assistance in African countries began in earnest around 2016. The most widely known drone programs in Africa have focused on the dire need for the delivery of blood, medical supplies, and vaccines.

German delivery company DHL provides a good example. Partnering with drone manufacturer and service provider Wingcopter in 2018, DHL ran a six-month pilot project in the Mwanza region of Tanzania. Medical care for the 400,000 residents in this region had been severely limited. As part of this program, drones delivered medical supplies to places in Mwanza deemed notoriously "hard to reach" via traditional transportation.2 On the return trip, drones transported laboratory samples back to the hospital's rooftop on the mainland, which allowed for faster analysis and significantly reduced waiting time for patients. The entire trip would have taken six hours with conventional means of transportation, spanning nearly 150 miles by truck or four hours by ferry. Drones, their autonomy and speed in high demand, could cover this area in 40 minutes while traveling a more direct route of only 37 miles.3

Beyond Africa, drones and unmanned vehicles have worked many wonders during the COVID-19 pandemic. Imagine the whole world plagued and isolated due to the rapid spread of the coronavirus, thereby catapulting the predominance of food and package delivery systems. Drones came to the rescue for many during the pandemic, flying with supplies into high-risk regions. With economic, environmental, and social benefits - safety on one hand, delivery time optimization on another - drones ended up being lifesavers, literally.

Autonomous vehicles and drones used for the benefit of sustainable business will be at the forefront of addressing many of the Global Goals. Scientists and researchers are hard at work to make progress on the viability of this tech for commercial use, which is proof that the effort is worthwhile from a societal perspective. Such endeavors are a testament to the fact that we continue to place trust in the technology beyond using autonomous vehicles or drones merely for recreational use.

By employing wisdom and decision-making skills, we bring forth AVs and drones as another technology for the benefit of both the planet and the people. Imagine when we persist in this choice, continuing along the development path and expanding our options, how millions more lives will be saved. With medicines transported by air, with ambulances that fly in, and with knowledge of exactly where to be and when, we can create efficient, intelligent systems that perpetuate economic gains while also meeting the needs of society.

Imagine flying in to tight areas and saving lives. This is AVs and drones for Good.

Marga Hoek

7 AUTONOMOUS VEHICLES AND DRONES

There is a broad range of autonomous vehicles – and not just driverless cars – referenced when the term AV is used. Here we discuss the range of AVs and drones, as well as dissect the developmental history and science in detail. Next comes the market perspective, which hails AV tech as one of the fastest, deepest, most consequential disruptions of transportation in history. Extensive research is drawn on throughout this chapter, connecting the tech's vast capabilities to current-day business use.

The beneficial way in which AVs and drones will accelerate the realization of the SDGs is not comparable to other technological advancement. This particularly relates to agricultural monitoring using drones and delivery bots aiding in underserved or disaster-affected areas. How underwater AVs and drones aid with managing and reducing ocean waste and marine threats is also explored. The tech has the potential to serve as a foundational innovation that lifts cities to sustainability status with gained control over traffic congestion and prevention of human-error-based dangers.

As business models are enhanced and Global Goals are promised to be met owing to contributions of AVs and drones, societal structures head towards an optimized sustainable future. But like all techs, the risks and downsides must be taken into consideration. Data security and surveillance privacy are valid concerns that need to be addressed.

THE TECH

Autonomous vehicles (AVs) are everywhere – the sky above, below ground, under water, on top of the water, in the future, and might even soon flow through our veins! The tech ranges from autonomous road vehicles including driverless cars, busses and trucks, to ships, to drones which refer to unmanned aerial vehicles (UAVs), to autonomous underwater vehicles (AUVs) or unmanned underwater vehicles (UUVs). This tech will revolutionize transportation, disaster relief, broadscale mapping functions, public safety monitoring, environmental conservation, and much more. AVs and drones offer huge advantages, from eliminating vehicle collisions and predicting deadly forest fires to optimizing vehicle movement and helping with transport during humanitarian initiatives.

The past half-decade has witnessed AVs making waves not only within the automotive sector, but also throughout society at large. This technology is impacting cars, trucks, buses and other public service vehicles. At the same time, we have often struggled with legislation, risks, responsibilities, and a host of other hurdles that foster skepticism about whether this development will truly become a viable option. Given there will be many hiccups, product versions, and development stages along the way, AV technologies may indeed take a long time to become viable solutions. However, the transition process itself ultimately promises beneficial societal and business model shifts in different shapes or forms on the way to full market saturation.

THE SHARE OF MILES DRIVEN BY NEARLY OR FULLY AUTONOMOUS VEHICLES IS EXPECTED TO BE 80% BY 2030.[4]

Tech giants realize the breadth of the applications of this innovation. They are aware, for instance, that the potential of AVs and drones range from road (cars, busses, and trucks), to water (boats and ships), to underwater (drones), and to air (drones) applications. Companies including Google and Apple are experimenting with AVs and drones. These players currently monopolize the market share, in addition to innovators such as Tesla producing electric vehicles. In the near future, innovations like micro drones could be developed that travel through our veins and are capable of transporting medicine.

The possibilities for breakthrough solutions with AVs and drones, which we will discuss later in the chapter, are truly endless. From the business perspective, this technology is enabling new models by transforming the efficiency and effectiveness of transport and logistics worldwide. By removing the need for human operators and developing new mobility service models, this tech will change the current car ownership model and vastly improve the utility of these vehicles. Autonomous vehicles and drones reduce costs and improve efficiency in terms of smarter routing on roads and improved accuracy in aerial monitoring. Not only will the tech transform business models for vehicle ownership, manufacturers and financial institutions will also be required to rethink their product and service offerings.

THE PUBLIC BENEFIT OF FULLY ADOPTING AUTONOMOUS VEHICLES IN THE US WOULD EXCEED $800 BILLION A YEAR IN 2030.[5]

Ahead of revolutionizing local and national transportation systems over the next decade, connected vehicle (CV) technologies are also poised to bring significant changes to the built environment and mobility. These include transforming how residents live, work, and move around their communities and in cities. Connected Vehicles offer communication with other vehicles, infrastructure, and devices via internet and radio frequencies. This CV tech has the potential to bring massive improvements to transportation safety and mobility through applications such as alerting drivers to nearby incidents, diversions, or heavy traffic.

One of the most familiar CV technologies supports short-range communications, providing wireless two-way communications used for traffic services like signal control, traffic monitoring, automatic toll collection, traffic congestion detection, and emergency vehicle signal preemption of traffic lights.[6]

It is equally important to explain the nuances across various levels of development in remotely operated and fully autonomous vehicles. Autonomous, automated, self-driving, and driverless are terms that are often used interchangeably, but there are subtle differences. Driverless, for instance, is more advanced than self-driving, as the former does not have the back-up of a person taking control, and the latter has the possibility of a human operator. In adherence to industry standards, driverless is classified as Level 5, while self-driving is Level 4 or below.[7]

Many companies such as Google, Uber, Lyft and Waymo are in the process of developing Level 4 vehicles. Waymo's Early Access program allows people to ride Level 4 cars in designated, low intensity locations and situations such as traffic jams. In Level 4 vehicles, the driver can retake control of the car at any time, but it is also equipped automatically to handle road construction sites and other challenging circumstances as long as they fit the operating parameters of the car's software. Honda plans to have a Level 4 car on the road by 2026, and Google has built Level 4 prototypes, such as its Firefly pod-car.[8]

Full automation is the ultimate goal of most self-driving tech initiatives. At Level 5, human intervention is never necessary, no matter the conditions. As an example, driverless taxis pick up passengers and have the possibility of being without a human operator. Regulators with the California Public Utilities Commission (CPUC) recently granted a permit to Cruise, the selfdriving vehicle subsidiary of General Motors (GM).[9] The first-of-its-kind permit allows Cruise to charge for rides in its autonomous taxi fleet, without a human driver in the car. Although very few Level 5 vehicles such as this are available on the roads at this time, tech leaders such as Tesla are working on making this inevitable future a reality.

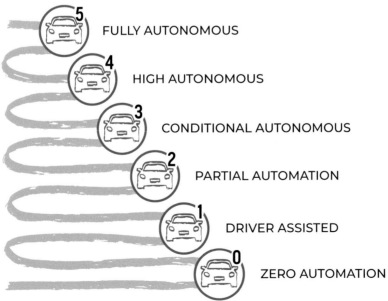

5 FULLY AUTONOMOUS

4 HIGH AUTONOMOUS

3 CONDITIONAL AUTONOMOUS

2 PARTIAL AUTOMATION

1 DRIVER ASSISTED

0 ZERO AUTOMATION

Figure 6
Categories of Autonomous Vehicles
Author © 2023

The standards mentioned above apply not only to the road, as there are UAVs that refer specifically to remotely piloted aircraft (RPA) that do not require a human onboard to fly. There are also completely autonomous drones that require no human intervention and are self-piloted via software. One RPA example is the Predator XP, equipped with cameras, sensors, and munitions. It was manufactured by General Atomics Aeronautical Systems and was designed for use by the United States Air Force and Central Intelligence Agency to complete aerial reconnaissance and surveillance missions.[10]

"I'M EXTREMELY CONFIDENT THAT LEVEL 5 [SELF-DRIVING CARS] OR ESSENTIALLY COMPLETE AUTONOMY WILL HAPPEN, AND I THINK IT WILL HAPPEN VERY QUICKLY."[11] - TESLA CEO ELON MUSK

On the other hand, we have fully autonomous drones that can take off, carry out missions, and land completely autonomously. In the case of autonomous drones, communications management software coordinates missions and pilots the aircraft instead of a human. The Sparrow I, manufactured by Percepto, is an example of an autonomous drone. It does not require an operator on the ground or in the air, thereby carrying out solo missions around the clock including pre-scheduled missions powered by PerceptoCore technology for aerial security, maintenance, and operations.[12]

Similar nuances and standards apply to unmanned surface vehicles (USVs) on and in the water. This tech is often used to monitor water quality in terms of contamination levels. Not only are USVs less expensive than human testing, but they offer more flexibility than traditional weather ships or research vessels. Fish farming is also being aided by the UAV market, given that the tech provides an affordable and reliable platform for aqua farmers to monitor water quality parameters and observe fish behavior during various processes in aquaculture.[13] Moving forward, we can confidently say that breakthroughs in CV and AV tech will enable manufacturers, software developers, auto companies, universities and many other industries to imagine and test methods to optimize global transportation and autonomous systems.

SOUND FOUNDATIONS

Although drones are often thought of as a modern invention, there is a long history of autonomous driving and flying objects. It may come as a surprise that the first UAV dates back to the 18th century in the form of hot-air balloons. Technically, these were the first aircraft not requiring a human pilot. The Montgolfier brothers were the first to famously host the public demonstration of an unmanned aircraft; it was a hot-air balloon in Annonay, France in 1783.[14]

Following that, advancements took off steadily over the years, ranging from military applications in the form of Austrian unmanned balloon bombs, to French aerial photographs taken from cameras mounted on UAVs in the 19th century. The year 1898 saw Nikola Tesla display a radio-controlled robot-boat in New York City's Madison Square Garden.[15] The progressive-beyond-its-years invention could respond to directional signals sent to it by Tesla from afar and could also flash its lights. This compelling demonstration was the beginning of what would evolve into radio-controlled aircraft and underwater vessels.

Throughout the 20th century, nations such as the United Kingdom, the United States, and Israel competed in developing UAVs for military and battle purposes. Radio-controlled target planes were deployed for bombing and surveillance, taking the monitoring and warfare capabilities to new heights worldwide. Some of these early applications were predominantly military-based operations. Since then, however, UAVs have evolved into being used for good.

It was after UAVs were allowed to fly in US civilian airspace and underwater for search and rescue, following Hurricane Katrina in 2006, that the consumer drone industry began to shift to what it has become today. Companies like Parrot, DJI, 3DR, and many others endeavored to take military UAV technology and repurpose it for good. This vast potential for industrial and consumer UAV markets ignited many businesses like FedEx, UPS, Amazon, Google, and Uber to invest in the technology. Since 2014, AVs and drones of all types have continued to expand in capabilities. The onset of the COVID-19 pandemic has further piqued industry interest in exploring how drones can enable safer and more cost-effective business operations. Rapid growth is expected in the coming years, and by 2030 the UAV market is forecasted to be worth $92 billion.[16]

MARKET SIZE OF AVS AND DRONES

From a market perspective, AVs could present one of the fastest, deepest, and most consequential disruptions of transportation in history. It is expected that by 2030, within ten years of regulatory approval of AVs, 95% of US passenger miles traveled will be served by ondemand autonomous electric vehicles owned by fleets, not individuals, in a new business model.[17] The disruption will have large-scale implications across the transportation and oil industries, shifting these industries' value chains and oil prices while also creating trillions of dollars in new business opportunities, consumer surplus, and GDP growth.

A change like this in the market of an automobile-centered society such as the US has the potential to save the average American family more than $5,600 per year in transportation costs, which is equivalent to an average wage raise of 10%.[18] These predictions signify an additional $1 trillion per year back into the American economy by 2030, potentially fueling wide-scale spending and economic growth. Simultaneously, savings on transportation costs could result in a permanent boost in annual disposable income for US households, totaling $1 trillion by 2030.

More autonomous vehicles will additionally mean fewer cars traveling farther, due to the potential of an increase in ride-sharing businesses.[19] The number of passenger vehicles on American roads will predictably drop from 247 million to 44 million, opening up vast tracts of land for other, more productive uses.[20] Market projections state that by the end of 2023, 7.3 million vehicles (7% of the total market) will have autonomous driving capabilities, requiring $1.5 billion of autonomous-driving-dedicated processors.[21] This is expected to grow to $14 billion in 2030.

Electric vehicles (EVs) with autonomy boast the capability as market accelerants to sustainable energy as well, which is a fundamental value of a company such as Tesla (Case 46). In terms of battery-powered electric and autonomous vehicles, Tesla has the potential to disrupt the automotive and power generation industries with its technology. Tesla will see higher profit margins as it achieves its plan to reduce battery costs by 56% over the next several years.[22] Through the combination of its industry-leading technology and unique supercharger network, Tesla has maintained its market leader status as EV adoption increases.

In the future, manufacturers will have options to produce more AVs, which will spur high levels of competition and new entrants from other industries. Projections suggest that the transportation value chain will deliver 6 trillion passenger miles in 2030. This is an increase of 50% over 2021 at a quarter of the cost, $393 billion versus $1.48 trillion.[23] Also significant from a market perspective, AVs are expected to generate at least $81 billion in new insurance revenues in the US between 2020 and 2025.[24]

IN BUSINESS

TESLA[25]

Initiative: Accelerating the Market
Headquarters: Austin, Texas USA

Tesla electric vehicles with autonomous driving systems are accelerants to sustainable energy, which is a fundamental value of the company. Spearheading the development of electric vehicles with autonomous driving systems, Tesla seized the opportunity to catapult itself into transforming the automotive and energy markets around the globe (SDGs 9,11). Tesla is the largest battery electric vehicle automaker in the world, also selling solar panels and batteries used for energy storage to consumers and utilities (SDGs 10,17). As the solar generation and battery storage market expands, Tesla is well-positioned to grow. "Tesla's fundamental value is to serve as an accelerant to sustainable energy," said Elon Musk.[26]

Tesla invests around 5% of its sales in research and development, focusing on improving its market-leading technology and reducing its manufacturing costs (SDG 12).[27] The tech company focuses on automation and efficiency in its manufacturing process, such as reducing the total number of parts that need to be assembled in a vehicle. Moving upstream into battery production as well, Tesla's goal is to reduce costs by over 50% (SDG 8). Tesla is focused on creating a complete energy and transportation ecosystem, from solar generation and energy storage to electric vehicles with autonomous driving that produces zero tailpipe emissions (SDGs 7,13). Musk explains that "You have to win on autonomy, you have to win on electrification, and you have to make a product so compelling that it is worth paying the premium relative to the incumbent competitors."[28]

Although Tesla did not invent electric cars, it was Tesla that became the real accelerant to developing AVs and sustainable energy. A small start-up that turned into a profitable company, Tesla's market capitalization now exceeds the combined market capitalization of the following seven automakers. As of October 2022, Tesla has a market cap of nearly $711 Billion.[29]

CONNECTED CARS

The market for tech advancements in connected cars is also on the rise. With the introduction of "vehicle-to-everything" (V2X) communication systems, where information travels from vehicle sensors through high-bandwidth links, cars can now communicate important road information about infrastructure such as parking spaces, traffic lights, and pedestrians.[30] In addition to improving road safety, many of the key features of 5G-enabled V2X technology could also help manage traffic congestion in major cities. This would be in the form of enabling direct communication channels between a vehicle and nearby road infrastructure, alerting drivers to an upcoming red light or traffic jam, or adjusting the vehicle's rate of travel to maximize fuel economy and reduce emissions. This bumps up a huge revenue opportunity for auto makers and surrounding tech components, with features such as remote diagnostics, predictive maintenance and online service scheduling, as the market for connected cars is predicted to jump to over $215 billion by 2027.[31]

Considering AVs in the air, the rise in the use of military drones by defense forces worldwide is one of the most significant factors projected to drive UAV market growth to reach $45.8 billion by 2025.[32] The increasing use of drones in various commercial applications, such as monitoring, surveying, and mapping, precision agriculture, aerial remote sensing, and product delivery is also contributing to the growth of the UAV market. Drone services will remain the biggest segment, with software growing rapidly. Asia is the biggest drone market today, driven by China and Japan, while India is expected to be the third-largest drone market in the world by 2025.[33] The global drone servicing and repair market is expected to grow from $8.61 billion in 2021 to reach $65.41 billion in 2026 at a CAGR of 49.5%.[34]

Underwater drones or UUVs are capable of functioning under the ocean without a human occupant. These vehicles are generally divided into two categories—remotely operated underwater vehicles (ROVs) that are controlled throughout their operations by a distant human operator, and AUVs which are capable of functioning autonomously without any real-time human inputs. The total global underwater drone market was valued at $3.59 billion in 2019, and is projected to reach $7.39 billion by 2027, thereby registering a CAGR of 11.7%.[35] Oceanographers using AUVs to check the water quality of the sea and maintain aquatic life is projected to create a business opportunity worth $46.8 million during the 2018 to 2027 forecast period.[36]

The unmanned surface vehicle (USV) market size was valued at $637 million in 2020 and is projected to reach $1.73 billion by 2028, growing at a CAGR of 13.35%.[37] At the same time, the global AUV market is projected to reach $596.7 million by the end of the forecast period of 2018 to 2027, registering a CAGR of 6.1%.[38] North America is the world's largest USV market, with revenues expected to reach nearly $2 billion by 2027.[39] The market's expansion in this region can be attributed to rapid technological advancements accelerating the industry's growth. Furthermore, due to the high demand for water quality monitoring and ocean data mapping, Europe is expected to have the highest CAGR during this forecast period. AUVs are generally used in aquaculture systems. Since aquaculture production has been increasing rapidly, making fish farming one of the fastest-growing industrial sectors across the world, this has been significantly contributing to the growth of the global AUV market. Industries such as shipping, shipbuilding, coastal aquaculture, fishing, offshore oil and gas, offshore wind, maritime tourism, and tidal and wave energy are all projected to boost the demand for AUVs in the foreseeable future.

The global AUV market is consolidated by 10 to 12 players with a significant presence. This includes Kongsberg Maritime AS that accounts for approximately 15% to 20% of the market.[40] The remaining share of the global AUV market is projected to be commanded by other leading players such as Saab AB, ECA Robotics SAS, and Fugro N.V., among others.

DRONE DELIVERY MARKET[41]

By year five of business rollout in a single US metropolitan area, drone delivery could:

- Serve up to 53.9% of the population.
- Recover nearly $582.5 million per year in total time savings for consumers.
- Support 3.6-6.6% of metropolitan residents without access to a vehicle (as many as 66,000 people in a single metropolitan area).
- Help 22,000 people with mobility challenges to obtain their prescription medication.
- Generate up to $284,000 per year in new annual sales for a participating local business (up to 250% additional sales compared to a scenario without drones).
- Refrain approximately 294 million miles per year in road use and around 580 car crashes per year.
- Reduce nearly 113,900 tons of CO_2 emissions per year.

All cities are different based on a range of variables, including size of the existing market, demographics, population density, and urban environment. Consumers in communities with greater distances between commercial centers and residences may benefit more from drone delivery through time saved – as much as 31 to 56 hours saved per person per year, averaged across all residents. In areas with more people and higher costs of living, consumers may benefit more from the value of time saved – as much as $323.5 to $582.5 million per year in total time savings.

Prominent corporations around the world are implementing these technologies for efficiency and business growth. For example, Chinese food delivery company Meituan has raised $10 billion in a stock and convertible bond sale to invest in autonomous delivery vehicles, delivery drones, and other cutting-edge technology.[42] AVs and drones also present growth potentials for the surrounding industries. The market for automotive software and electronics, for instance, is expected to grow by 7% each year for the coming years, becoming a $470 billion industry.[43] In 2030, 57% of this industry is predicted to have its foot in software development, sensors, and electronic control units.

Israel has spearheaded development of these technologies for the automotive world, primarily via start-ups. Since 2010, over 40 mobility-dedicated start-ups in Israel have received funding from investors, as have over 300 start-ups with possible applications in mobility.[44] Investment in auto tech in Israel has seen strong growth, totaling over $18 billion since 2010.

This total investment amount puts Israel fourth globally among countries investing in autotech, behind the United States, China, and United Kingdom, but ahead of traditional automotive leaders like Germany and Japan.

In 2018, Cruise, the autonomous-driving unit of General Motors, valued at $14.6 billion, was responsible for roughly a third of GM's overall valuation on the public market. Cruise and Honda collaborated on a new autonomous vehicle design, where Honda spent $2 billion in this creation over 12 years, making an additional $750 million equity investment in Cruise.[45] SoftBank Vision Fund made a $2.25 billion investment in Cruise to assist GM in deploying its autonomous cars for commercial use. Furthermore, SoftBank invested an additional $940 million in Nuro.ai, a driverless delivery option. These movements show significant collaboration among major businesses in this tech's market.

$30.6 billion 2022 estimated global drone market size.[46]

Global AV market size valued at $87.5 billion in 2021, predicted **$614.87** billion by 3030.[47]

Commercial & recreational drones estimated market $55.8 billion by 2030.[48]

AVS AND DRONES FOR GOOD

AVs and drones are enhancing our lives and the world at large in many ways. Prominent companies are actively investing in these innovations, including traditional car manufacturers and tech giants like Google. This tech's benefit to society is far-reaching.

SAVING LIVES

As we discussed at the beginning of the chapter, drone networks are beneficial for saving lives, and additionally for cutting costs and eliminating emissions. Avy's fully electric aerial network of drones offers rescue teams an affordable, reliable and integrated solution for their missions, without the environmental impact.[49] In case of dangerous fires, for example, Avy's drone can be deployed to fly over a target area to monitor heat while firefighters operate on the ground so they can act with speed and precision.

In rescue-related missions, drones became crucial tools during the December 2020 Gjerdum, Norway landslide.[50] Because first responders often bear the same life-threatening risks as the victims, DJI's first unmanned responders were called in to help increase the chances for success of the rescue operation and save lives. With seven DJI drones in action, rescue operations were able to successfully evacuate 1,000 people and save 13 lives in subzero temperatures.[51] These DJI drones were deployed on 570 firefighter missions over 230 hours of airtime to investigate 31 homes that had been buried in the disaster.[52]

In addition to saving lives through rescue operations, AVs and Drones bring a spike in safety too. Data suggest that self-driving cars will ultimately make roads safer.[53] The United States reports nearly 95% of serious automobile crashes are due to human error, caused by factors like miscalculations, poor judgment, speeding, drunk-driving, and phone use.[54] Fully autonomous vehicles would eliminate human error, thereby making our roads safer for drivers, passengers, cyclists, and pedestrians. Suppose 90% of the cars in the United States were to become fully autonomous. In that case, an estimated 25,000 lives could be saved every year, with economic savings estimated at over $200 billion a year.[55]

FULLY AUTONOMOUS VEHICLES WOULD ELIMINATE HUMAN ERROR AND MAKE ROADS SAFER.

Other societal benefits include easier parking and improved daily commuting. Reduced emissions are also a major plus. By employing electric and hybrid autonomous vehicles, societies could reduce greenhouse gas emissions by as much as 80% by 2050.[56] AVs would also offer major opportunities for public health if vehicles were used in a ridesharing format and integrated into a model that also prioritizes public transport, cycling, and walking. This type of model would promote physical activity, reduce air and noise pollution, provide more public space for a healthy urban design, and present new business opportunities.[57]

LAND MANAGEMENT

As drones become less expensive and more common today, they are a viable tool for countries with fewer resources to use for mapping projects. We take a look here at The Zanzibar mapping initiative that aims to create a high-resolution map of the Zanzibar and Pemba islands, covering an area of over 1,400 square miles. This is predicted to be done by using low-cost drones instead of more expensive satellite images or manned planes.[58] These maps are not purely informational. Zanzibar Commission for Lands will use the maps for better planning, land tenure, and environmental monitoring, which means that drones are and will be playing a vital role in helping to implement sustainable practices in Zanzibar.

Drones can also patrol forests to monitor environmental and ecological changes. Researchers at Imperial College London's Aerial Robotics Laboratory have developed drones that can shoot sensor-containing darts onto trees in tightly packed environments like forests.[59] The drones can also place sensors through contact or by landing precisely on tree branches. This saves time that human manpower would require as well as the cost of clearing a pathway for human entry. The end goal is to use these futuristic drones to create networks of sensors to boost data on forest ecosystems and to track biomes like the Amazon rainforest. Further, tech companies such as DroneSeed are planting millions of trees in reforestation efforts worldwide. (Case 47)

MARINE MANAGEMENT

USVs and AUVs are delivering safer and more sustainable approaches to constructing and maintaining marine assets as well. These play a valuable role in the maintenance and observance of oceans, seas, rivers, and lakes. To ensure safety to our most valuable natural resources, AUVs and USVs assist in performing important tasks on and within bodies of water. USVs and AUVs can cover and collect data in larger areas, at greater depths, and at quicker speeds than human divers and researchers. In addition, the deployment of a team of long-range and long-endurance AUVs and USVs are capable of collecting environmental measurements without adversely affecting marine life.

IN BUSINESS

DRONESEED[60]

Initiative: #Teamtrees
Headquarters: Seattle, Washington USA

DroneSeed is a tech company specializing in drone reforestation. They produce their own large UAVs specifically designed to plant trees over large areas efficiently, rapidly, and in ways that will maximize the survivability and success rate of the seeds. Incorporating a collaborative social component, a reforestation project was initiated when viral YouTuber Jimmy Donaldson was challenged by his followers to plant 20 million trees to celebrate reaching 20 million subscribers. He partnered with fellow YouTuber and former NASA engineer Mark Rober. Together, they worked with DroneSeed and the Arbor Day Foundation to create a campaign called #TeamTrees where every dollar donated would plant one tree (SDG 17).

Using drones to plant seeds has numerous advantages. For example, just three drones can plant an area six times faster than a man-powered planting crew (SDG 8).[61] In areas recently affected by forest fires, planting tree seeds quickly is crucial to preventing tall shrubs from taking over the area (SDG 15). Software analyzes the terrain data and determines the best locations to place seeds for the optimal survival rate (SDG 12). DroneSeed makes the tree-planting process easy by first sending out one drone to perform a 3D scan of the terrain. Software analyzes the terrain data and determines the best locations to place seeds for the optimal survival rate. Flight paths are created, and then another fleet of drones fly autonomously on the flight paths while dispensing DroneSeed's proprietary seed vessels. Each vessel contains a combination of seeds optimal for the location and the necessary fertilizer. By combining proven reforestation practices with new technology, the company regrows healthy, resilient, climate-adapted forests (SDGs 9,13).

SEA-KIT INTERNATIONAL[62]

Initiative: Furgo Marine Geo-Data
Headquarters: Essex, United Kingdom

Uncrewed surface vessel (USV) company Sea-Kit International partnered with geo-data specialist Furgo to offer hi-tech geospatial technologies (SDG 17). Providing data to maritime and research industries, Sea-Kit collaborates with Furgo to develop a new range of agile and compact uncrewed surface vessels capable of deploying USVs for marine asset inspections (SDG 14). These adaptable, uncrewed, and remotely-controlled vessels enable multiple use cases, including maritime logistics, environmental management, marine inspection, and efficient survey of the ocean floors (SDGs 9,12,13). Through extended mission capability and reduced downtime, the deployment of SEA-KIT USVs represents significant cost savings as well as reduced carbon emissions for companies operating in the commercial offshore sector (SDGs 7,8). Sea-Kit has accelerated the development and use of uncrewed vessels remotely operated from Fugro's remote operating centers; this will ultimately improve safety, efficiency, and reduce the environmental impact on marine activities (SDGs 3,16). This new range of maritime autonomous vehicles will consume up to 95% less fuel than traditional vessels, a prospect that supports international ambitions for zero global emissions in the marine industry.[63]

These innovative systems can increase the spatial and temporal scale of the monitoring while providing persistence and synopticity.[64] Sea-Kit International conducts important research to understand conditions of ongoing phenomena under the sea, such as oil spills or algal blooms, by deploying autonomous vessels to track activities (Case 48).

AVS AND DRONES FOR GOOD ACROSS SECTORS

Beyond human and environmental needs, AV and drone technology is now also widely used for commercial, professional, and industrial goods, as well as for private purposes. The tech is even being deployed for beauty and positivity, as visual artist Reuben Wu recently released a new series of photos called Light Storm featuring creative uses of drone lighting for surrealistic nighttime and dusk to dawn imaging.[65] Specifically, the artist creates mountain halo shots by leveraging long exposure times and pre-programmed flight paths to capture stunning images.

Different sectors of the economy, including agriculture, transport, infrastructure, entertainment, and telecommunications make use of UAVs, USVs, and AUVs applications. Drones of all types can prove to be a major force for good as they hold massive potential to meet the needs of the SDGs. Developing countries are facing famine, epidemic diseases, poverty, and other challenges. AV and drone technology can help address each of these problems. As an example, failing bridges are a severe economic and safety burden on cities and nations. Japanese drone company Skydio helps manage this infrastructure issue through inspection and monitoring (Case 49).

With the COVID-19 pandemic, the market for drones as delivery vehicles in agriculture, ecommerce, and healthcare has seen an exponential growth. As if these applications were not enough, drones also prove to be effective for monitoring and surveillance in international and domestic law enforcement, wildlife preservation, and scientific research.

"WE ARE BUILDING THE TECHNOLOGY PLATFORM FOR EXTREMELY FAST, POINT-TO-POINT, URBAN MEDICAL DELIVERY, ENABLING HOSPITAL SYSTEMS TO SHRINK PATIENT WAITING TIMES AND SAVE MILLIONS OF DOLLARS PER YEAR."[66] - ANDREAS RAPTOPOULOS, CEO OF MATTERNET

Markets across many sectors prepare for full autonomy and seek to increase profits from AV-critical technology capabilities. This will be important for AVs. These advanced driver tech systems expand from premium to mass offerings in developed markets, thereby leading to developing markets, including China, boosting the next growth curve.[67] It is natural that automobile accident prevention due to the technology will fuel more consumers willing to pay for enhanced features.

IN BUSINESS
SKYDIO [69]

Initiative: Japan's Bridge Inspections
Headquarters: Redwood City, California USA

Rehabilitating Japan's faltering national infrastructure is projected to cost the nation nearly $6 trillion.[70] By employing drones to help, it completely changes this equation for Japan Infrastructur Waymark (JIW) (SDGs 16,17). In just one year, drone technology has assisted JIW in decreasing the cost-per-bridge inspection by 75% and growing inspection volume by 7,000% (SDG 12).[71] To do this, JIW deployed Skydio drones, the largest US UAV manufacturer and a world leader in autonomous flight. JIW has been growing its business rapidly, providing bridge inspections to Japan's network of approximately 714,000 bridges (SDG 9).[72] Skydio enables JIW to inspect more complex bridges with greater precision.

Additionally, Skydio Autonomy division provides 75% cost advantages over pre-drone methods on jobs that manual drones cannot perform (SDG 8). JIW has on-boarded 68 new pilots in 12 months by lowering the training burden from 100 to 8 hours of flight time (SDG 4).[73] JIW's over 300 Skydio drones have enabled safe flights in complex environments, more precise data capture, and scalable systems (SDGs 3,14). Due to drone tech growth, JIW's inspection business grew an impressive 70 times in 12 months. In March 2021, the company became the first US drone manufacturer to exceed $1 billion in value.[74]

AVS AND DRONES PROGRESSING THE GLOBAL GOALS

AVs and drones at the peak of their application will have a significant impact on addressing all 17 SDGs. The United Nations states that by 2030, drone technologies could assist greatly in ending the epidemics in impoverished regions with high rates of AIDS, tuberculosis, malaria, and neglected tropical diseases.[68] They can combat hepatitis, water-borne diseases, and other infectious diseases through rapid and expanded delivery services. Drones also hugely benefit urban areas as they enable greener, more cost-effective inspections of aging and decaying infrastructure. Using UAVs for this necessary service cuts the carbon footprint of traditional inspection methods and ensures efficiency by completing more inspections in less time. As AV and drone tech is the future of transportation, these emerging technologies will provide safe travel by eliminating human driving errors and providing lucrative business opportunities in terms of sustainable development. Let's have a closer look at the targeted SDGs.

ZERO HUNGER

These technologies have great potential to curb global food shortages through enhanced delivery services and farming practices. Unmanned Aviation Systems provide data to increase farm productivity and enable sustainable farming. They can also be used to identify weeds and deliver herbicide only when needed, and eventually could replace herbicides altogether by locating and removing individual weeds.[75]

GOOD HEALTH AND WELLBEING

Global health benefits greatlt from AV and drone technology. One way is by providing patients in need with essential medical and nutritional supplies no matter how remote or inaccessible the area. In Ghana, Zipline drones are being used to collect COVID-19 test samples and deliver them to medical facilities for testing as well, resulting in quicker and more cost-effective deliveries.[76] UAVs can also reduce the delivery of blood samples for HIV tests and other time-sensitive supplies from 11 days to less than 30 minutes.

AFFORDABLE AND CLEAN ENERGY

AV and drone innovations are expected to enhance the energy sector. AV algorithms prioritize efficiency, which is predicted to reduce energy consumption by up to 20%.[77] In the US, drone delivery can reduce up to 113,900 tons per year of CO2 emissions, equivalent to 46,000 acres per year of new forest.[78] The renewable energy space has begun using UAVs where drones provide solar farm managers with accurate data via new technological developments, such as thermal sensors. This ensures that routine operations are conducted more efficiently. Energy providers are deploying drones to increase the efficiency of energy plant operations, with UAV monitoring systems playing a critical role in providing reliable and affordable energy to their customers.

REDUCED INEQUALITIES

Nearly one billion people worldwide have limited access to emergency services. Utilizing cargo AVs and UAVs to carry supplies to many of these isolated communities can save lives, and create jobs.[79] We have been discussing that due to the increased safety features of AVs, crashes are less likely to occur. The tech also allows for the reduction of vehicle weight and size, which decreases fuel consumption by 5% to 23% while also reducing costs for drivers.[80]

SUSTAINABLE CITIES AND COMMUNITIES

AVs have the potential to reduce traffic congestion and air pollution, while also saving lives and money on infrastructure projects in urban regions.[81] Connected car technologies, as well as vehicles that collectively travel close together, are expected to reduce energy consumption between 3% and 25%.[82] Electric, batterypowered drones are being hailed as a solution to necessary infrastructure inspections in cities around the world. Drones also make inspections quicker and cheaper, providing more thorough examinations that reduce the need for carbon-and labor-intensive inspections. Even if UAVs were to inspect only half of the bridges in the US, UK, Australia and Japan – just a fraction of the world's inspection agenda – it would be the carbon equivalent of removing tens of thousands of vehicles from the roads each year.[83]

RESPONSIBLE CONSUMPTION AND PRODUCTION

AVs are predicted to reduce the cost of driving because of decreased insurance prices and lowered time consumption. This is the result of improvements in productivity and driving comfort. Not only do AVs offer opportunities to reduce the cost of driving, they also create significant CO_2 emission reductions. Lowering CO_2 emissions by over 20 metric tons when the overall traffic speed rises from 34 to 53 miles per hour, AVs are poised to provide many benefits.[84] In 2019, nearly 4,500 drones in the Chinese province of Xinjiang accomplished agricultural productivity for 65% of the cotton fields in the region: raising Xinjiang's cotton output by 400,000 tons and increasing revenue by $430 million. Drones stimulate economic growth and support the rural working class in China by removing time and labor costs from the equation, helping farmers escape poverty.

LIFE BELOW WATER

Of Earth's 70% water surface, only about 20% has been mapped using modern, high-resolution technology.[85] An accurate seafloor map is vital for navigation, transportation, telecommunications, or physical oceanography. AVs and Drones generate numerous solutions for this.[86] Saildrone's fleet of sea-going AVs provide near-shore and open-ocean mapping solutions. Norway's Blueye underwater drone operates at waterworks and hydropower plants to inspect and document maintenance tasks in areas where humans have no access.[87] Additionally, research sites located along the Mekong River in South-East Asia, as well as along the Ganges River in India, use drones to observe plastic pollution in oceans and rivers.

TECH FOR GOOD

THE FILM

ZERO HUNGER

- Imaging crop health and causes of crop failure in famine-affected countries.
- Deliver food faster and more efficiently to underserved or disaster areas.
- Enable business opportunities through networks of innovative food production and transport.

GOOD HEALTH AND WELLBEING

- Allow for rapid delivery of medicine, vaccines, and pharmaceuticals.
- Reduce costs of transport.

AFFORDABLE AND CLEAN ENERGY

- Offer efficient energy output and a significant reduction in resource use.
- Conduct frequent aerial inspections of renewable energy systems across large areas.
- Provide comprehensive energy monitoring, leading to better data for consumer preferences.

REDUCED INEQUALITIES

- Ensure greater global access to healthcare products via drone deliveries.
- Improve human safety through AV technologies, allowing markets to emerge for new driverless products.
- Augment public safety initiatives via drone monitoring capabilities in terms of crime and disaster detection.

SUSTAINABLE CITIES AND COMMUNITIES

- Reduce traffic congestion in urban areas through CV and AV technologies.
- Inspect infrastructure in more efficient and cost-effective ways.
- Decrease the necessity for parking spaces in city centers.

AUTONOMOUS VEHICLES AND DRONES

RESPONSIBLE PRODUCTION AND CONSUMPTION

- Reduce CO_2 emissions significantly due to enhanced driving efficiency of AVs.
- Increase agricultural productivity through drone imaging and monitoring technologies.

LIFE BELOW WATER

- Engage in advanced underwater and deep-sea mapping capabilities.
- Observe the ocean to help reduce plastic pollution and mitigate environmental impacts.
- Monitor offshore energy with the efficient and streamlined processes of USVs and AUVs.

ENHANCING BUSINESS MODELS

The AV and drone sector's technological advancements offer a range of business benefits.[91] To name a few, mobility-on-demand services maximize efficiency and utilization of the vehicle network, including car sharing. Open-sourced driver assistance programs are being developed, including software to improve autonomous vehicles' functionality and energy efficiency. Not only do these techs stand on their own for business growth, but they also offer a host of other potential opportunities for associated companies that provide relevant services.

Data collection is becoming increasingly relevant for business forecasting. For many businesses, drones are quickly joining in on the inevitable digitalization strategies. Along with cloud services and big-data computing, the unprecedented data gathering capabilities of drones can radically alter the competitive dynamics of the information landscape.[89]

Drone data collections provide the precursor of a larger shift of imagery analysis and data science that goes beyond mapping to strengthen entire workflows within companies. Innovative industry leaders and business executives already see the benefits of integrating UAV tech solutions into their business practices by discovering ways to use drones to gather intelligence for market research. Of the many potential business models stemming from this tech, the most immediate intrigue that drones present is to enable us to go virtually anywhere.[90] It seems there will be no limit as more businesses discover how drones bring the world into highly advanced imaging.

Drones for renewable energy maintenance have made it easier to ensure that renewable installations are operational on a consistent basis, and drones for high-resolution real-time aerial data solutions can more efficiently manage land use, transport, and pollution. This tech allows businesses to serve their customers in new ways, enabling more effective and cheaper methods to monitor and collect data, maintain and service infrastructure and assets, and distribute supplies.[91]

STREAMLINING DELIVERY SERVICES

Over the last decade, the retail giant Amazon has spent billions of dollars working to streamline delivery. It has proposed the development of Amazon Prime Air, a drone delivery system that anticipates package deliveries in 30 minutes or less. More recently, an increasing percentage of that investment has been directed toward autonomous vehicle technology. In 2020, Amazon announced it would acquire Zoox, a startup developing autonomous driving tech geared toward ride-hailing customers. This $1.2 billion deal provided Amazon with access to software, AI, and a full-stack self-driving solution and put them a step ahead of its competitors. Zoox achieved a key milestone in the testing and rollout of its autonomous electric vehicle in June 2022 where it operated with no one inside, no chase vehicle, and no emergency stop, all on open, private roads.

App-based autonomous vehicle networks using the cloud and apps to optimize a network of autonomous vehicles have also seen significant growth. Middleware vendors, application players and cloud and telecommunications leaders are merging to form the connected car ecosystem. As technology continues to grow and play a larger role in consumers' lives, industries have transformed and adapted. With the onset of COVID and other factors, online services as a result of ubiquitous internet access have predominated. This movement in the market has shifted delivery methods and eliminated many human components.

GLOBAL GOALS GROWTH OPPORTUNITIES

Recent developments in AV and drone technologies promise an exciting future with a market growth potential of spread and breadth that has not yet been realized. With colossal funding allocated for these techs, the world will witness major business development and significant market opportunities. Along with early-stage startups, VCs and other investors, tech giants such as Tesla and Alphabet are pumping money into developing AVs. Many major automotive manufacturers, including General Motors, Ford, Mercedes Benz, Volkswagen, Audi, Nissan, Toyota, BMW, and Volvo are in the process of testing driverless car systems.[92]

INSURERS HAVE AN ESTIMATED OPPORTUNITY OF $81 BILLION BETWEEN 2020 AND 2025 FOR THE DEVELOPMENT OF COVERAGE OPTIONS FOR AUTONOMOUS VEHICLES.[93]

Drones can substitute traditional methods of operation in many business activities. The usage of drones has broadened in a variety of industries due to their ability to drive efficiency and data analytics. Data efficiency and data analytics allow companies to better comprehend and predict operating performance. In addition to these benefits, drones will enable new business models and opportunities across many industries.

PROVIDING HEALTH SERVICES

Drones and autonomous vehicles can invariably play a major role in the rapid delivery of vaccines, medications, and supplies directly to the source, thereby helping to manage outbreaks of life-threatening communicable diseases. With the capability for rapid delivery to areas where critical infrastructure damage would prevent humans operating typical ground or air transport, AVs and UAVs present several business opportunities in the healthcare sector.

AN ESTIMATED 23 MILLION FULLY AUTONOMOUS VEHICLES WILL BE DRIVING US ROADS AND HIGHWAYS BY 2035.[94]

Much of the global population lives without access to essential healthcare services. With over 40% of all people living in rural areas,[95] and only 30% of those living near an accessible road,[96] significant health challenges, poor infrastructure, and failing ground transport networks often result in a lack of supplies and care. The COVID-19 pandemic, along with numerous recent natural disasters, has highlighted the breakdown of supply chains in securing healthcare supplies worldwide. Drones have made it possible for healthcare workers to deliver blood, vaccines, birth control, snake bite serum, and other medical supplies to rural hard-to-reach areas.

These UAVs have the ability to reach victims requiring immediate medical attention within minutes. In some cases, this urgency could be the difference between life and death. Small indoor drones could deliver medicine to the bedside of a patient from the pharmacy, leading to more rapid and less erred medication dissemination.[97] The UPS Foundation, Zipline and the Vaccine Alliance Gavi recently formed a partnership to begin transporting blood and vaccines using drones to rural areas in Rwanda (Case 50).[98] With greater global adoption, we could thus see some human steps eliminated from the process.

In June 2020, CVS Pharmacy began a pilot program using a fleet of Nuro autonomous vehicles to bring prescriptions and other medical essentials free of charge to customers in the Houston, Texas metropolitan area.[99] Amsterdam-based drone developer Avy partnered with the European Drones for Health project to accelerate reduction of preventable maternal deaths by delivering health supplies, blood, and laboratory specimens promptly to those in need.[100]

We also have the example of Coldchain, a healthcare supply chain management company that recently announced plans to spend $750,000 on Draganfly's drone equipment to ship medical supplies and COVID-19 vaccines on an experimental basis.[101] Draganfly's drones use 12-inch, cube-shaped, thermal containers developed by Coldchain that can hold roughly 600 to 15,000 vials of vaccines. Similarly, US based tech companies Matternet[102] and Zipline[103] have used an innovative business model during the pandemic to make greater community access to goods more feasible.

Another company employing efficient medical courier solutions is Matternet. Based in North Carolina, the tech startup has been a support to the COVID-19 response in the United States. With their quadcopter (with four rotors) design, Matternet's drones offer reliable transportation of diagnostic samples and medical items between facilities. They also automate other steps in the delivery process including removing packages from the drone, storing them, controlling who can pick them up, and even giving the drone a new battery if needed.[104] Through an existing partnership between Matternet and UPS, drones have performed medical deliveries in North Carolina and have also supported a retirement community in Florida with more than 135,000 residents by dropping in prescriptions without human contact from a local pharmacy.[105] In the era of the coronavirus, contactless deliveries via drone have reduced the risk of infection for medical professionals working high-risk jobs, and also for the patients they are treating. This tech solution truly is lifesaving.

OPTIMIZING FOOD AND AGRICULTURE WITH DATA AND ANALYTICS

It is crucial to develop credible alternatives to the status quo of intensive agriculture as the world faces food shortages. By helping analyze crop yields and providing key data on soil quality and other crucial factors, the drone industry brings hope to the food and agricultural sectors. Drone startups present the possibility of helping farmers become more sustainable and increase their yield. The benefits to using drones in the agricultural sector are countless; farmers can not only optimize spraying of pesticides in areas that need treatment which significantly reduces the amount used, but they can also reduce water use, control crop quality, and access difficult-to-reach areas.

"WORLDWIDE, ABOUT A THIRD OF ALL CROPS ARE LOST. IT'S EASY TO BLAME BUGS, BUT REALLY, A LACK OF INFORMATION IS DESTROYING THESE PLANTS."[106] - NIKHIL VADHAVKA, CEO OF RAPTORMAPS

Agricultural drones are often programmed to take pictures of the crops and fields. These devices communicate with software to create high-resolution maps, ultimately informing farmers about irrigation, soil, and infestation problems. European startups such as Switzerland-based Gamava[107] and France-based Delair[108] provide visual intelligence solutions that allow farmers to capture, manage, and analyze their crops, thereby turning data into valuable insights. There is a large business opportunity for drones in several areas, which include helping protect food crops and making them more sustainable by reducing spraying. Further, UAVs could assist farmers in switching to organically certified products to spray over their plots of land.[109]

IN BUSINESS

ZIPLINE[110]

Initiative: Medical Delivery Drone Service
Headquarters: San Francisco, California USA

Zipline launched a medical-product-delivery-by-autonomous-drone service in 2016. The company was delivering life-saving blood and medical supplies to remote and underserved clinics and hospitals in Rwanda (SDGs1,3). Three years later, the tech company expanded operations to Ghana, and by 2021, they had made about 200,000 life-saving deliveries.[111] In response to the pandemic, in April 2020, Zipline added COVID-19 test samples to its medical delivery services (SDG 9). They used their drones to collect tests from 1,000 rural health facilities in Ghana and delivered them to the company's distribution center in Omenako before traveling again to health centers for analysis (SGs 8,10).[112] This marked the first time that autonomous drones made regular long-range deliveries into densely populated urban areas (SDG 11).

South Africa's recent founding of the Drone Council facilitates the expansion of the drone industry, with one of its objectives being to promote a more balanced involvement of women (SDG 5). The blood sent by drone is often used for postpartum blood loss and to treat malaria-induced anemia. "Basically, it's very doable to save a woman's life if they have blood, and it's very hard to save that woman's life if they don't," said Keenan Wyrobek, co-founder and head of product and engineering at Zipline.[113] "In terms of value to society, there's not only the loss of a life, but also a child growing up without a mother, so I think we've made a big impact on communities."

Zipline's delivery service allows the government to monitor and respond more closely to the disease spread in remote areas of the country, also reducing test wait times and the hazard of damaged samples (SDG 16). As of 2022, Zipline has amassed approximately 30.5 million miles flown, over 4 million products delivered, 450,000 commercial deliveries, and 25 million serviceable customers.

IN BUSINESS

XAG[114]

Initiative: P100 Agricultural Drone
Headquarters: Guangzhou, China

XAG is an agriculture technology company with pioneering expertise in precision agriculture and remote sensing drones, founded in 2007. XAG P100 Agricultural Drone is crafted so that it can integrate efficient spreading and precision spraying modules (SDG 9). It is a powerful and reliable drone with the intention to open a new era of smart agriculture (SDGs 15). XAG's latestgeneration agricultural drone is versatile with many applications for precision farming.[115] It can autonomously undertake spraying, fertilizing, and sowing functions for multiple crops. This agricultural drone is already assisting farmers across China, Vietnam, and Australia to reduce seeds, pesticides, and fertilizers without affecting crop yields (SDGs 2,12). These drones can finish the fieldwork much faster and with more precision than 20 to 25 laborers who would spray pesticides manually (SDGs 1,10).[116] Thus, XAG is also looking to address the ongoing labor shortage in the agricultural sector with this drone featuring several improvements over previous-generation models (SDG 8).

Agriculture technology companies across the world are increasingly relying on autonomous vehicles. Autonomous vehicles are helping yield more crops amidst growing populations. XAG is a Chinese drone tech firm helping make precision planting, spraying, and harvesting more streamlined and efficient processes, directly affecting crop output and profits (Case 51).

DRONES FOR AGRICULTURE – CHINA

New and unconventional technologies are combating poverty in rural China, providing solutions to low agricultural yields and unsustainable farming practices. These are three drone projects that are addressing business solutions in impoverished Chinese communities:

Satellite imagery: Drones continuously monitor crop health from the sky and assist in spraying herbicides and other supplements. In addition, UAVs can produce imaging of crop fields that farmers can then view for crop management purposes. These drone-enabled photos can determine the exact conditions and resources needed for agriculture to thrive, which is termed "precision agriculture." More than 55,000 agricultural drones are currently in use in China, spraying necessary crop-enhancing pesticides over an estimated 30 million hectares of land.[117]

Yields and incomes: In 2019, about 4,500 drones in the Chinese province of Xinjiang monitored for agricultural productivity for 65% of the cotton fields in the region.[118] This introduction of UAVs raised Xinjiang's cotton output by 400,000 tons, which subsequently caused a $430 million increase in revenue. As an added benefit, one drone can do the work of 60 farmers in one hour and can spray pesticides 50 to 80 times faster than traditional farming.[119] With efficient agricultural practices and harvesting, drones stimulate economic growth and reduce poverty by supporting the rural working class in China in terms of time and labor costs.

New networks: Drones are beneficial in rugged terrain, as they can travel through the air. Some drones can be controlled through cell phones, which is especially useful for farmers who cannot manage to survey certain problematic areas. Some drones have also allowed farmers to access weather and disaster warnings, saving both unnecessary labor and a loss in revenues.[120] This is hugely beneficial for dealing with poverty.

In addition, AVs can help supplement labor shortages on farms. Blue River Technology, a creator of autonomous planting and spraying solutions, records a savings of 90% on herbicides overall. Fighting weeds costs farmers an average of $11 billion each year.[121] We see a future ahead where autonomous, artificial intelligence-powered technology helps farms to better distinguish between crops and weeds, and kill only the weeds with exactly the right amount of herbicide.

ACCOMMODATING THE FUTURE OF CITIES

The global population is expected to rise to 9.7 billion in 2050.[122] Much of this population growth will occur in cities, putting stress on infrastructure and services. AVs and UAVs present several solution-based business opportunities within cities. The vision of the future of city infrastructure includes self-driving cars and shared mobility. These are futuristic ways of revolutionizing how we navigate through cities that fundamentally change their infrastructure. These autonomous solutions will not just change the way we travel, but they will also bring to cities more efficient and predictable traffic control and public transportation.

For example, AVs and UAVs can provide us with much safer roads. According to the US National Highway Traffic Administration, 94% of serious car crashes are caused by human error.[123] Autonomous vehicles and drones can replace traditional driving practices and potentially introduce and create new opportunities that were previously not possible. AVs can also be highly beneficial in cities to free up parking spaces and make room for business opportunities by redesigning roadways to accommodate fewer drivers. AVs and UAVs could bring all these benefits, improving millions of people's quality of life while also creating new business opportunities. Research suggests that the automotive software and electronics market will grow by 7% year over year in the coming years, becoming a $470 billion industry.[124]

ACCORDING TO THE U.S. NATIONAL HIGHWAY TRAFFIC ADMINISTRATION, 94% OF SERIOUS CAR CRASHES ARE CAUSED BY HUMAN ERROR.[125]

Predictions state that in 2030, 57% of this industry, including software development, sensors, and electronic control units, will aid in implementing autonomous infrastructure in cities. The appeal for more automation in cities translates to new revenue for businesses, especially if AV/UAV delivery can deliver orders more quickly or reach customers they would not otherwise have been able to. As we have been expositing, shifting deliveries from gas-powered vehicles on the road to electric ones in the air could relieve traffic congestion and reduce emissions. Similarly, startup Hoversurf developed a human-carrying drone serving as a taxi.

A recent study by Virginia Tech modeled how a simulated drone-delivery service might affect three U.S. cities: Christiansburg, Columbus, and Austin. Findings stated that the hours saved, revenue earned, and tons of carbon dioxide diverted would be worth the shift. Over a five-year period, retail stores could see an increase in sales between 50 and 165%; restaurants would benefit with sales growth between 121 and 250%; swapping car trips for drone deliveries could cut out up to 294 million miles of road travel and 114,000 tons of carbon dioxide in a single metro area annually.[126]

AMPING UP NEW ENERGY SERVICES

AVs and UAVs play an important and ever-increasing role in the energy sector. One of the several applications for drones in the energy industry is often related to wind turbines operating onshore or offshore. The flying monitoring of photovoltaic systems is also a prominent application. UAVs can help save potentially billions of dollars each year globally by increasing efficiency, reducing cost and time to complete audits and energy surveys, and improving worker safety.[127]

Drones provide safe and efficient inspections for applications across the energy industry, including traditional power generation, transmission, and distribution. Traditional groundbased data collection in the energy sector typically lacks the detail and flexibility that a drone can provide. Further, UAV technology can drastically reduce inspection time, save labor costs, and reduce hazardous labor.

Scientists claim drones are 97% more efficient compared to manual inspections for solar farms. Instead of human workers walking across many acres of solar panels or climbing onto roofs, drones complete a detailed inspection of 100% solar panels in a fraction of the time at about 10 minutes per megawatt.[128] UAVs can also conduct a complete thermal inspection using an infrared camera, identifying hotspots that manual inspections might miss. This data is often directly uploaded into interactive online web maps. Israeli tech company Nando is an example of

IN BUSINESS

HOVERSURF[129]

Initiative: Hover Flying Car
Headquarters: San Francisco, California USA

The Hover flying car is a fully automatic taxi drone operating system that specializes in Air Transport as a Service (ATaaS), allowing passengers to call an air taxi and travel via an approved route to their destination (SDG 9). Putting safety first, Hoversurf's patented software endeavors to consider all aspects of air travel. The unique drone layout with additional propulsion motors allows Hover to fly twice as fast as conventional drones (SDG 12). Hover has achieved the dimensions of a regular car with a range of 100 km, speed of 200 km/h, and altitude of 150 meters. In addition, this innovative tech company plans to secure 10% of the Smart City urban air mobility (UAM) market in 2040 (SDG 11).[130] Research predicts we could foresee a $2 billion market with 1,000 aircraft operating soon in several cities, growing to $18 billion and 12,000 units in 25 cities by 2025, and eventually reaching $58 billion and 43,000 units in 64 cities by 2030 (SDGs 10,17).[131] The company plans on smooth integration into the real urban infrastructure where drivers can park easily by landing in a standard parking space, maneuvering in the parking lot, and driving into the garage.

IN BUSINESS

NANDO[132]

Initiative: Drone Security For Solar Farms
Headquarters: Bnei Atarot, Israel

Nando drones help maintain safe, efficient operations at large industrial facilities such as solar farms (SDGs 7,16). Replacing human operators, who must constantly be aware of and manage on-site activity, equipment, technology, and ongoing processes, Nando autonomous drone-based platform turns the archaic model of site security upside down (SDG 8). Instead of guards making the rounds and patrolling a perimeter to detect intrusions into the secured site, with a response team on call, autonomous drones in the sky hover above a site for up to 70 minutes at a time. These technologically advanced UAVs are capable of detecting both movement and the human form at a range of up to 250 meters. Given the superior field of vision of drones, together with exceptional flight time, these "eyes in the sky" are capable of replacing perimeter patrol for a fraction of the cost (SDGs 10,12). Nando drones are coupled with another unique Israeli innovation – the camera. Utilizing advanced AI technology, an ANN (artificial neural network) algorithm enables the camera to perform deep learning (SDG 9). The camera has both night and daytime capabilities, which enables real-time onboard image processing and identification while the drone is in flight. When real-time identification of an object occurs, the control system transmits a warning to the management system which is capable of tracking the identified object.

Nando's platform is designed not only for the security needs of high-end industrial solar farms, cannabis fields, car lots, gas drilling sites, and factories but also for other non-security applications, such as monitoring capabilities for various parameters in mines and agricultural fields (SDG 11). Israel is one of the world's largest exporters of unmanned aircrafts, in terms of the number of systems sold. Over the last decade, Israel has exported $4.6 billion worth of UAVs to countries ranging from Great Britain to India to Uganda.[133]

drone providing innovative solutions for solar energy operations (Case 53). Repair personnel in the field can use uploaded maps on a smartphone app for maintenance.

ISS Aerospace, a UAV systems leader in the defense and energy sectors, increases efficiency for its customers and completes energy inspection and audit tasks much quicker.[134] Specifically, it eliminates the need for planes, helicopters, and climbers to undertake these tasks, thereby dramatically reducing energy survey costs and danger.

Key factors driving the market growth for AVs in the energy sector include the rising need for road safety, environmental impact of traditional vehicles, and increased energy savings by autonomous vehicles.[135] When energy savings are factored into the equation, the net result is a reduction in lifetime energy use and associated greenhouse gas emissions of approximately 10% compared to conventional vehicles.[136] Considering all of the potential uses of autonomous electric vehicles – including taxis and service vehicles in major cities, or the transport of goods on highways – it is increasingly evident how this technology has a significant positive impact on the environment through energy efficiency and savings.[137]

UAV INSPECTIONS OF RENEWABLE ENERGY ASSETS – LIDAR SENSORS – USA:[138]

Drones can improve the quality of information they supply to many energy stakeholders and partners. LiDAR sensors mounted onto drones have improved surveying efficiency and accuracy. Photogrammetry by UAVs provides valuable data of site monitoring to superintendents, power plants, solar farms, and dam managers. Power companies also invest in software to turn data collected by drones (photographic, GIS, thermal, and infrared) into actionable intelligence. Drones present ideal business opportunities for renewable energy assets through gains that reduce cost, improve critical energy and water infrastructure reliability, and enhance safety and decrease business risk.

Solar Energy – Drones can detect malfunctioning panels far quicker on more than 6,000 utility-scale solar facilities in the US that require regular inspections. For commissioning, warranty, or regular maintenance, drone inspections are 95% more efficient and can identify defects that manual inspections might miss. In addition, drone inspections save 10 minutes per megawatt and, on average, $1,200 per megawatt in costs, with larger sites saving more.

Wind Power – Drones eliminate much of the climbing hazards associated with inspecting more than 52,000 utility-scale US wind turbines. With a demonstrated inspection time of 15 to 30 minutes per turbine, drones reduce man-hours and turbine downtime for maintenance checks by over 75%. Drones equipped with a high-resolution camera also perform preventive maintenance inspections on wind turbines, whereby crews can locate and photograph problem areas on blades or the tower itself.

Hydroelectric Energy – Hydroelectric power stations produced 38% of the total renewable electricity in the country in 2019 and 6.6% of total electricity, the highest in the US for a renewable source.[139] For the safety and integrity of the dams located in at least 34 US states, regular inspection is necessary. Drones can largely undertake these tasks, along with fish ladder monitoring, aerial photography, construction monitoring, and dam monitoring during flood inspections.

SECURING WATER MONITORING

Unmanned underwater vehicles (UUVs) are the type of vehicles capable of functioning under the water in the ocean and rivers without a human occupant. These can be remotely operated vehicles (ROVs) controlled by a distant human operator, and autonomous underwater vehicles (AUVs) capable of functioning on their own. Some of the business opportunities with this tech include conducting marine research, environmental surveys, aquaculture, and inspections of tanks, propellers, and boat hulls.[140] Ocean floor mapping is also a growing business, as today, only 21% of the ocean is considered mapped to modern standards.[141]

The technological advancements in UUVs include high-resolution cameras and highly sensitive sonar that reduces the time required to inspect underwater equipment. These tech innovations have opened new avenues of opportunities in the underwater drone market. Companies operating in this market globally include The Boeing Company, Lockheed Martin Corporation, Bluefin Robotics, Saab Seaeye Ltd, Teledyne Marine Group, Kongsberg Maritime, Oceaneering International Inc., TechnipFMC plc, ECA Group, and Deep Ocean Engineering Inc.[142]

SUBMERSIBLE DRONES ARE ESTIMATED TO BE A NEARLY $5 BILLION MARKET AS OF THE END OF 2022.[143]

UUVs have a strong market presence among oceanographers, filmmakers, and the military. Although these submersible devices have traditionally been expensive, starting at about $20,000, there is currently a $2,000 version for consumers that represent the biggest future for these devices. They have many of the same features and capabilities as the more expensive professional drones. There are various technical demands of making high-performance underwater drones, including attention to how the ocean affects hardware in terms of currents, buoyancy, navigation, and other elements. Underwater drones are becoming increasingly popular with small startups and companies that are on a mission to address underwater sustainability challenges. Submersible drones are estimated to be a nearly $5 billion market as of the end of 2022.[144]

Unmanned surface vehicles (USVs) for mapping the ocean floor have a strong presence in international waters. Seabed 2030 is a joint project of The Nippon Foundation and General Bathymetric Chart of the Oceans (GEBCO), with a mission to map 100% of the ocean floor by 2030.[145] In addition to providing a much-needed force multiplier for surveying, USV systems lower environmental impacts by using harvestable energy, eliminating personnel at sea, and reducing ship-generated noise, overboard discharge, and potential for pollution. Compared to 350 ship years and a cost of over $3 billion using traditional methods, the Saildrone Surveyor USV offers a solution to successfully achieve the goal of Seabed by 2030, especially on the high seas (Case 54).[146]

In January 2020, Blueye launched a new product called Blueye Pro, which has proven an asset for all maritime businesses. It is a flexible, completely autonomous and easy-to-use tool to perform underwater inspections.[147] The installation of new features such as the camera-tilt functions can measure a depth rating of 305 meters, performing more use cases for underwater inspections. Autonomous high-resolution ocean mapping data for navigation and charting offshore energy, at a fraction of the cost of traditional survey methods, is also becoming more viable.

IN BUSINESS

SAILDRONE[148]

Initiative: Mapping the High Seas
Headquarters: Alameda, California USA

Saildrone Surveyor, a 22 meter USV, recently completed a mapping mission that traversed approximately 4,200 kilometers and mapped nearly 22,000 square kilometers of previously unmapped seafloor (SDG 14).[149] Primarily powered by solar and hydro energy, and propelled by wind, Saildrone Surveyor is at the forefront of long endurance and low impact for ocean mapping (SDG 7). The tech solution boasts autonomous high-resolution mapping data to 7,000 meter depth for navigation and charting, telecommunications, offshore energy, exploration, characterization, and physical oceanography (SDG 9). This is all at a fraction of the cost of traditional survey methods (SDG 12).[150] USVs emit very little or zero CO2 compared to a survey ship, which makes the overall carbon footprint of Surveyor extremely small and low impact (SDG 13). In addition, the Surveyor is incredibly quiet during operations, which is good for the environment and marine life, and even better for collecting sonar data. Saildrone vehicles have sailed over 800,000 nautical miles and spent more than 18,000 days at sea collecting data that provides unprecedented intelligence for climate, mapping, and maritime security applications.

ADDRESSING RISKS AND CHALLENGES ON THE ROAD AHEAD

Autonomous Vehicles will revolutionize mobility. In societies that have a driving culture, such as the United States, AVs could offer a positive outcome with a lot more public transportation. Yet, it is critical to consider the negative outcomes, which could be significant if we do not alter our behavior. Suppose people start traveling via AVs to work. They could then tell the car to go home, and then pick them up at the end of the day. This extra travel would double the number of miles, fuel costs, and environmental impacts. Autonomous vehicles are similar to computers on wheels, and there are times when computers malfunction. With the widespread implementation and millions of people driving AVs, difficulties would arise when drivers have to call somebody to service the car's misfiring operating system. These computerized cars are also at risk of being hacked any number of times. Thus, there are systematic challenges to both the safety and optimization that could occur in the event of widespread tampering with AVs at scale.[151]

Further downsides include the possibilities for potential economic losses as a result of markets shifting and jobs disappearing. Swathes of transit jobs will likely be lost, such as taxi and Uber drivers. As AVs would create ease of transport and parking within cities as well as driving across countries, they will disrupt the way we live and the service jobs associated with those changing travel dynamics. Turbulence in the parking sector could also occur due to the increase in AVs. This disruptive tech advancement has already been felt at airports around the world, as AV transport services that do not require parking will eliminate the need for customers to park at the airport. This could pose a big problem. Airports generally rely on parking for collecting money and several of them are already reporting a decrease in the number of people parking. By default, this lowers their revenue for parking, along with services like Uber and Lyft.[152] Parking lots could be eliminated altogether, with the space being reappropriated, causing financial losses and infrastructure shifts. Many of these areas, if not managed properly, could become fallow real estate or bankrupt properties.

From an environmental standpoint, AV production highlights intensive resource depletion. Many rare Earth elements are critical to the manufacture and production of electronic devices in AVs. There is 100% reliance on imports for these materials among a considerable number of countries and manufacturers.[153] Rare Earth elements are often located in regions that lack the economic or technological resources to harvest them. This is often due to mismanagement or local militia groups who control their mining and sale. The very process of obtaining rare earth elements is potentially harmful to the environment. Contamination from radionuclides is one example, as dust and metal are released into the atmosphere. Human rights violations are also common in this heavy metal mining process.[154]

Drones and unmanned aerial vehicles present associated security risks as well. Hacking into them could lead to main control systems being invaded, replacing the original users with new drivers or controllers of the devices. The network and control systems of drones often contain confidential information that hackers could obtain without the knowledge of the original user. In addition, drones have been known to be employed for criminal behaviors and unauthorized surveillance.[155] Aerial drones are sometimes equipped with heat and night sensors to detect any signs of life. They can easily target an individual of interest for a corrupt institution or group. Historically, instances of drones mistakenly firing at civilians have caused fatalities, injuries, and damage to properties.[159] Drones also have some detrimental ecological impacts. They have been attacked by animals, even in mid-flight, which poses a risk to the wildlife.

WE HAVE

IMAGINED

We have imagined a sustainable future that will begin to take shape as we collectively take on mass adoption of AVs and drones. These technologies provide a high level view of an aerial future where swift deliveries save time and money, while also benefiting the environment in terms of carbon emissions. Whether there be a need for search and rescue missions or a demand for medical supplies, remote autonomous vehicles are there to save lives. Thanks to AVs and drones, transport pathways are simultaneously less crowded and more safe. Roads are more open and the underwater world is more thoroughly monitored, thereby reducing fossil fuel consumption and ensuring regular inspection of ships.

We have imagined all that AVs and drones will do for the good of society and business. As we take a comprehensive look at the options available to make the right choices regarding this tech, there remains a long way to go and much is still required for achieving a sound regulatory framework. Considering current conditions, international and public/private collaborations, as well as hardware and software tech developments, will all be necessary to truly unlock the potential for good of these autonomous vehicles and drones.

We have imagined AVs and Drones for Good.

BLOCKCHAIN 8

BLOCKCHAIN IS THE ULTIMATE DATA MANAGER.
IT IS A TRUSTWORTHY VERIFIER OF
WHAT HAPPENS WHEN, WHERE, AND HOW.

WE ONLY NEED TO

IMAGINE

Imagine we could verify the origin and ownership or movement history of any item from the farmer to the consumer to maximize sustainable commerce. Imagine how, no matter what products or where consumers are around the world, everyone could have basic access to knowledge about the provenance of goods they purchase and use. A clear understanding of supply chains would allow us all the ability to know where our products come from and how they are produced. Imagine the benefits of technology allowing consumers access to the global market through information about pricing transparency between farmers and the marketplace.

Consider tracking and tracing cotton fabric down to the fundamental level of raw materials or crop, and ensuring transparency of the final product. Technology enables us to do just that. It provides the opportunity for people to gain access to verifiable origin and supply chain information about the cotton fabric they wear daily. Blockchain makes it possible to identify production aspects such as where the cotton came from or if it was grown organically. This innovative tech supports both vendors and consumers in gaining a clear picture of product origin and movement.

As the most widely used fabric in the world, cotton accounts for over 40% of the total global fiber market.[1] To meet this high demand, farmers are increasingly using high-yield genetically modified plants with excessive pesticides and fertilizers. Organic cotton initiatives being marketed by brands and retailers have enhanced the fiber's popularity to a point where demand far exceeds supply. For this reason, industry forecasts anticipate double-digit growth in the coming years.[2]

Today's apparel and fashion industries are confronted with the big challenge of ensuring product validity through transparency and tracing. Tracking products to their source and along the supply chain is often fragmented and complex. It involves many players, as it is difficult to trace finished products and raw materials to their origin. This is where blockchain can play a significant role.[3] Through blockchain and IoT technologies, the origin of organic cotton is verifiable across the entire supply chain; it is now possible to acquire data and metrics throughout the production process, even when operations are located in remote regions.

This development is significant, as it is a verifiable way to answer consumer concerns and questions: "Has my organic cotton shirt or dress actually been made from genuine organic cotton?" After all, there have been instances of fraud in sourcing organic cotton.[4] Many textile companies at the forefront of sustainable business solutions are now engaging in more rigorous supply chain tracking. Cross Textiles, a Turkish innovator in the sustainable fashion market, participates in the Jeans ReDesign project with the Ellen MacArthur Foundation.[5] Setting an example as a sustainable business, Cross Textiles monitors the supply chain and shares it transparently with customers when requested. This exemplary and progressive company invests in technology to lower the use of resources in its jeans production process, deriving a competitive edge through engagement in the circular economy.

Blockchain takes tracking sustainability across the supply chain a step further than its tech predecessors by providing a verifiable and secure method for transparent assessment. Businesses like Denim Deal, a Dutch-based multi-stakeholder initiative, are implementing blockchain to navigate the challenges of textiles in the circular economy. The denim industry's use of textile waste in garments and overcoming traceability supply chain challenges is the initiative's primary goal. By partnering with Aware - a tracer particle and blockchain technology by Dutch company The Movement - businesses can distinguish false material from authentically sustainable fabric with a simple scan.[6] Aware's tracer particles, which are added to the fiber before production, make it possible to prove that the original recycled feedstock was used in the final product. This capability allows companies to accurately measure their environmental impact targets and prevent fraud.

Denim Deal partners, such as Dutch brand Kings of Indigo and Turkish denim mill Calik Denim, use blockchain to track products. Calik collaborates with Denim Deal to trace its recycled cotton and polyester fabrics.[7] More specifically, the technology creates a digital twin version that is registered into a secure blockchain to be completely absent of fraud. By adding tracers, every garment receives a unique fingerprint, and this can be read with an easy-to-use scanner for authentication. As the first company in the world to make recycled cotton traceable, Aware's use of blockchain tech is a crucial tool applicable to many brands as they begin to switch from the current linear sourcing model. The Movement, the company behind the sustainable solutions Polylana Fiber and Aware validation technology, successfully raised €1 million in pre-seed funding in early 2022. This early-stage capital will allow the startup to grow its team, invest in technology, and create more sustainable alternatives for the textile industry.[8]

Improving transparency and traceability has become a priority for the garment industry to increase its ability to manage supply chains more effectively, while still embracing sustainable production and consumption patterns. This, in turn, ensures business success. Imagine the benefits blockchain brings to suppliers and consumers who can get the full report behind their cotton products. This reliable, decentralized technological solution unlocks markets and services across industries that were once unimaginable.

Imagine tracing product materials back to their origin. This is Blockchain for Good.

8 EXPLORING
BLOCKCHAIN

Blockchain's popularity rose with the emergence of Bitcoin in 2008, but there is more to the history of this innovative digital roster tech that goes further back. This groundbreaking technology is significant for both the present and future of business, particularly due to its disruptive possibilities. Beginning with the concept of blockchain, as well as its foundations, the chapter explores tech and its transformative qualities at length. Critical questions regarding the tech's efficacy and sustainable nature emerge: To what extent does blockchain add value to a sustainable economy? How does it enhance business profits? Answers to these questions are revealed in detailing investments and a market-based future structured around blockchain and its unique product tracing capabilities. Subsequently, the respective implications for the business sector are discussed.

Blockchain's contributions to poverty management are considerable, too, especially for farmers who are exploited for their crops' low market prices due to the obscure pricing mechanisms structured to benefit big business. As a core element in its application as a Tech for Good, blockchain uncovers new horizons for economic and social systems. This chapter recognizes blockchain as an essential tool for building a fair, inclusive, secure, and democratic digital economy. The optimistic assessments of the tech's potential that follow are enhanced with exciting new business ventures highlighted in case studies from around the globe. Although barriers to blockchain utility exist, which include its substantial energy consumption, the chapter reveals how breakthrough solutions are addressing this concern and how the tech brings forth a plethora of evolving sustainable business models that promise to outweigh associated downsides.

THE TECH

Among innovative technologies, blockchain has the unique potential to establish new foundations for global economic and social systems. Blockchain shows great promise to become a truly disruptive technology that enables the sustainable development of new business models. As defined by the European Commission, Blockchain is "a technology that allows people and organizations to reach agreement on and permanently record transactions and information in a transparent way without a central authority."[9] More specifically, it can be described as a public ledger consisting of all transactions across a peer-to-peer network.

Blockchain serves as a distributed ledger or database shared across a public or private computing network. Each computer node in the network holds a copy of the entire ledger, so there can be no single point of failure. Because every piece of information is algorithmically encrypted within this immutable ledger, the process of recording transactions and tracking assets in a business network is deemed secure. These encrypted data are added as a new "block" to the chain of historical records that forms the database or "blockchain."[10] Blockchain requires no central authority, which means various consensus protocols are used to validate new blocks. This, in turn, prevents fraud. The possibilities for blockchain to have a significant impact on business are unprecedented. It is the first native digital medium for value, just as the Internet was the first native digital medium for information.

BLOCKCHAIN TECHNOLOGY IS "A DATA STRUCTURE CONSISTING OF LINKED BLOCKS OF DATA, E.G., CONFIRMED FINANCIAL TRANSACTIONS WITH EACH BLOCK POINTING/REFERRING TO THE PREVIOUS ONE FORMING A CHAIN IN LINEAR AND CHRONOLOGICAL ORDER."[11]

This revolutionary tech started with the creation of Bitcoin, the world's first digital and decentralized currency, also known as cryptocurrency. As an important element of the 4IR, blockchain's defining features enable the transfer of a range of assets. This transfer occurs among parties in a secure and inexpensive manner, without third-party intermediaries.[12] By design, the tech paves the way for a form of financial democratization. As a decentralized and global computational infrastructure, blockchain can transform many existing processes in business, governance, and society, thereby allowing for greater freedom and autonomy among underserved communities. The benefits of blockchain allowing new players to enter the market are vast, creating distributed value and growing participation in the economy.

A decentralized open-source network enables businesses to independently take action in response to unsatisfied market needs. This flexibility boosts the tech's market potential, especially in sectors that are dedicated to driving social impact and generating profits. But blockchain's applications extend far beyond commercial use and are being spread across many different sectors. Various social innovation organizations – philanthropies, NGOs, non-profits, social enterprises, government agencies, and even for-profit organizations promoting social benefits – adopt blockchain in a variety of humanitarian cases. These include a range of projects, from monitoring the extent of human trafficking to restoring pertinent land records.[13] Prominent agencies such as the UN have also recognized the potential of blockchain, noting that effectively delivering mandates in the digital age requires embracing technologies like blockchain that will help accelerate the achievement of SDGs.

MADE POSSIBLE WITH THE WFP INNOVATION ACCELERATOR, THE BUILDING BLOCKS BLOCKCHAIN PROGRAM BOASTS APPROXIMATELY $2.5 MILLION IN SAVED BANK FEES.[14]

The tech allows the development of a participatory business model. In other words, it eliminates the presence of a middleman who retains profits. In the blockchain system, the overall process is organized through smart contracts, allowing automated transactions and reducing processing fees. These benefits are particularly relevant in many areas of the developing world. For example, UN Aid programs have implemented blockchain technologies for the purpose of guarding against fraud, hefty administrative fees, and mismanagement of funds. To provide the maximum amount of aid to those who need it the most, the World Food Program (WFP) implemented a blockchain pilot project in 2017 called Building Blocks, which served vulnerable families in Pakistan, Bangladesh, and Jordan. The project was made possible with the WFP Innovation Accelerator, boasting approximately $2.5 million in saved bank fees.[15] Building Blocks has been scaled to provide $325 million worth of cash transfers to one million refugees, making it the world's largest implementation of blockchain technology for humanitarian assistance.

SOUND FOUNDATIONS

The incorporation of IoT has been instrumental in the proliferation and dissemination of blockchain tech. By bringing the objects around us to life and making them "smart" and capable of communicating with each other, IoT can amass significant data through constantly capturing and optimizing the physical world. A critical component of current IoT solutions is the centralized party (like a cloud server) for connecting and communicating via the Internet. In contrast to current trends, the original architecture design did not have a decentralized system.[16] But that gap posed a great threat to the privacy and security of data being generated. Blockchain arbitrates this concern by providing a secure and trustworthy approach to sharing information using a distributed peer-to-peer model. Featured parts of this distributed ledger technology include increased transparency, security, privacy, auditability, resilience, access authentication, and data immutability.

Blockchain technology first emerged in 1991, when W. Scott Stornetta and Stuart Haber created a cryptographically secured blockchain featuring unalterable timestamps of records.[17] Yet it was not until 2008 that the term "blockchain" began to acquire the significance it has today. Satoshi Nakamoto (this name could be a single person or a group of people) molded Bitcoin into the blockchain structure as a primary application of this digital roster technology.[18] Nakamoto improved the blockchain structure by utilizing a decentralized strategy, keeping records of the time and date of added "blocks." In 2009, the blockchain structure was recognized as a central part of the hyped cryptocurrency Bitcoin, acting as the public record for all exchanges on the network.

In August of 2014, the size of stored records of all exchanges recorded on the Bitcoin blockchain network was up to 20 GB. By January 2015, this amount reached nearly 30 GB. Signifying blockchain's notable impact and influence, the size expanded from 50 GB to 100 GB between January 2016 to 2017.[19] It doubled again and exceeded 200 GB before 2020. In the latter half of 2022, all exchanges recorded on the Bitcoin blockchain network are approximately 425 GB.[20]

The breadth of blockchain applications and platforms has expanded in recent years and continues to do so, thereby becoming more widely utilized. This was observed when Ethereum followed Bitcoin. Ethereum, the community-run technology powering the cryptocurrency ether (ETH), emerged as a platform for building decentralized applications through smart contracts.[21] It inspired a whole new realm of possibilities for a "token economy" through the creation and exchange of non-fungible tokens (NFTs), which are non-interchangeable tokens connected to merchandise and sold as unique digital property.[22]

DISTRIBUTED LEDGERS

Blockchain - The "block" refers to digital data; a "chain" is characterized as a common information base. Therefore, 'blockchain' describes digital data kept in a public dataset.[23] Blockchain is a disseminated network comprising computer systems and the Internet that keeps an account of transactions. Specifically, it is a digital ledger of transactions that is distributed across the entire network of computers (or nodes) on the blockchain. Within a blockchain, one record is dispersed and protected across the system while every computer involved individually approves the exchanges. By incorporating a sequence of blocks, blockchain comprises information units used to store value-based data. Since it is a decentralized system, no single entity has authority over the network. Each exchange is compiled in a block validated by a group of computer networks, and each block has its own separate data and is given a hash to identify it from different blocks.

Cryptocurrency - Cryptocurrency is a digital currency that allows parties to transfer money without involving a central authority, such as a bank. It is secured by cryptography, which renders it nearly impossible to counterfeit. The price of the most well-known cryptocurrency, Bitcoin, which was valued at less than $100 in 2013, sold for a high of $68,000 per coin in November 2021.[24]

Cryptocurrency Mining - Cryptocurrency mining is a transactional process that involves using computers and cryptographic processes to solve complex functions and record the data to a blockchain.[25]

The most widely used application of blockchain technology is online payment systems management with fast, inexpensive, and secure transactions that do not require intermediary agencies. There are hundreds of cryptocurrencies and projects within the blockchain sphere, including some of the more well-known such as Bitcoin, Ethereum, Litecoin, Solana, and Cardano. These also encompass protocol tokens like Ether, utility tokens, securities tokens (e.g., crypto equities and crypto bonds), natural asset tokens, crypto-fiat currencies, and stablecoins.[26] There is no doubt that blockchain has global transformational potential. If harnessed and disseminated properly, this distributed ledger tech will be instrumental in enabling the shift toward sustainable decentralized solutions in several sectors.

Blockchain applications have now expanded far beyond cryptocurrency. With its ability to create more transparency and fairness while also saving businesses time and money, the technology is positively impacting a variety of sectors. Ranging from enforcing fair contracts to making governments work more efficiently, blockchain's benefit to a sustainable future for all continues to be realized.

BLOCKCHAIN MARKET SIZE

Blockchain is projected to alter markets and shift commerce structures in the coming years. The tech has huge market potential with a wide range of applications, such as banking, cybersecurity, energy, and IoT. Companies both big and small are implementing blockchain to gain competitive advantages. Statistics show that blockchain implementation could generate $700 million in increased productivity.[27] Large multinationals such as Walmart have partnered with Nestle, Dole, Unilever, and Tyson Foods to implement blockchain in the food industry. In one project example, blockchain made it possible to trace individual mangoes back to the farm in only 2.2 seconds.[28] Walmart says that without blockchain it would take more than six days to identify the original farm. European retailer Carrefour is the first company on the continent to introduce blockchain for food products. The company believes that the technology is revolutionizing its supply chains by helping to raise $5 billion in organic food sales in 2022.[29]

As a result of blockchain's proliferation, the payments industry is growing with fintech startups and smaller banks providing consumers with more choices for their financial wellbeing. Silicon Valley technology conglomerate Cisco reported that as much as 10% of global GDP will be stored on blockchain by 2027, which could be a predominant factor in distributed ledger tech seeing large investments in recent years.[30] The global blockchain market was valued at $4.67 billion in 2021 and is projected to grow from $7.18 billion in 2022 to $163.83 billion by 2029, at a CAGR of 56.3%.[31]

It is also expected that Blockchain as a Service (BaaS) will grow in demand in the coming years. Tech giants like Amazon, Microsoft, and Google have already invested heavily in the development of this service. Several other well-known brands that constitute big portions of the market have also invested and are developing their own solutions at a rapid pace.[32] These brands include IBM, Oracle, Alibaba, and French energy company EDF. The additional value potential of BaaS is huge, expectantly rising to an estimated size of $360 billion by 2026 and reaching $3.1 trillion by the end of 2030.[33]

Over the past decade Blockchain has revolutionized access to capital for new ventures as well as shifted markets. Investment funds flowing to tech startups in this space have grown significantly. In 2017, blockchain-based startups raised approximately $4 billion in total through a process known as an ICO (initial coin offering).[34] Fast forward to 2021 and in Q2 alone blockchain startups raised nearly $4.4 billion in funding, which was 30% more than in Q1 that same year.[35] Also, in 2017, venture capital funding for blockchain startups consistently grew and reached $1 billion.[36] Compare that with venture capital funding for crypto startups that surged in 2021, rising more than in any other year with over $27 billion invested globally as of late November. This figure is more than the previous 10 years combined.[37] The global blockchain AI market size is also projected to grow more than threefold from $228 million in 2020 to $703 million by 2025, at a CAGR of 25.3% during this period.[38]

Blockchain's ability to create and transfer digital assets through smart contracts enhances existing commodities trading processes, which characterize inefficiencies that lead to a loss of income and opportunities for businesses. Blockchain technology's growth with an expected rise in the rate

CERTAIN BLOCKCHAIN SECTORS SEE GREATER FOR-PROFIT ACTIVITY[39]

Overall, 61% of the blockchain initiatives are for-profit. Those with the greatest commercial opportunity include energy (94%), health (87%), and financial inclusion (78%). Conversely, those sectors traditionally rooted in non-profit or government activity include philanthropy, aid, and donors (76%) and democracy and governance (33%).

of adoption will thus help firms, investors, and the other parties involved in commodities trading realize greater gains and increased profitability.

Implementing blockchain technology can overcome the various issues that occur throughout the regulatory compliance process. The historical record and transparent ledger provided by blockchain networks allow near real-time monitoring of transactions for multiple parties involved.[40] Out of the $4.4 trillion commodities markets, banks, financial institutions, institutional investors or funds, those entities claim approximately 30% of the benefit from blockchain-enabled trade financing.[41] Global trade finance markets can prosper by identifying how blockchain can address the more than $3.4 trillion gap between supply and demand for trade finance, particularly for trade flows to and from emerging markets addressing the SDGs.[42]

By the end of 2024, it is expected that businesses around the globe will spend $20 billion per year on blockchain technical services.[43] As many as 74% of tech-savvy executive teams say they believe there is huge business potential in blockchain technology.[44] Financial institutions alone have spent about $552 million on blockchain-powered projects, and 25% of companies invested between $5 million and $10 million in blockchain during 2021.

$10.02 billion 2022 global blockchain market size.[45]	$67.4 billion 2026 expected blockchain market value.[46]	Nearly $1 trillion cryptocurrency market capacity at the beginning of 2023.[47]

BLOCKCHAIN FOR GOOD

Blockchain has uniquely triggered innovative activity across the globe with an explicit moral, ethical, and responsible intent. Because the technology eliminates the role of intermediaries, central authorities, or third-party assurance providers to validate transactions and processes, it presents a new level of organizational transparency and trust.[48] This means that a business entity's full potential can be brought to bear when making more informed decisions without the common financial risk. There are thus expectations for the tech to unlock financing mechanisms to deliver on core business missions. The impact and potential of Blockchain today is recognized across regions and industries, spanning from the financial and business sectors with cryptocurrency transactions to the retail and agricultural spaces with product traceability.

The UN Innovation Network set up five blockchain projects to integrate this technology for inter-agency cooperation. One of many examples includes a partnership between the UN International Telecommunications Union and the Food and Agriculture Organization to track pig supply chains in Papua New Guinea.[49] Additionally, to use blockchain as a force for good while profiting from the cryptocurrency investing market, UNICEF developed The UNICEF Crypto Fund. The Fund is a prototype that lets the agency accept Bitcoin and Ether donations and invest them directly into blockchain startups. Upon its commencement in October 2018, there was immediate uptake from the cryptocurrency community as a donation of one Bitcoin and 10,000 Ether came from the Switzerland-based Ethereum Foundation.[50]

Although blockchain and cryptocurrency have been identified as high energy use industries, research from the University of Cambridge shows that the renewable share of energy mining pools is as high as 78%.[51] The majority of identified mining facilities use some share of renewable energy sources as part of their energy mix. Further, Ethereum 2.0 and the move from a proof of

IN BUSINESS
ENERGY BLOCKCHAIN LABS INC.[52]
Initiative: Green Energy Marketplace
Headquarters: Beijing, China

Energy Blockchain Labs Inc. is focused on mitigating climate change (SDG 13). It works to create a more efficient way for organizations to meet government-mandated carbon emissions reduction quotas. Using IBM blockchain technology, Energy Blockchain Labs created an efficient, transparent platform that allows high-emission businesses to meet quotas by buying carbon credits from low emitters (SDGs 7,8). Energy Blockchain Labs bases its business model on the assumption that blockchain technology could bring a higher level of efficiency to carbon asset trading in China, thereby helping expand market integration and environmental benefits. "Creating a blockchain platform for carbon trading will help facilitate more seamless collaboration among all participants and parties," says Cao Yin, Founding Partner and Chief Architect at Energy Blockchain Labs.[53]

China taking on this initiative is an important step, given that the country is responsible for approximately 25% of the world's CO_2 emissions. Businesses electing to go green in the country often experience high renewable energy costs, especially when compared with fossil fuel prices. Further, traditional market mechanisms in China have not been historically aligned with the proliferation of green energy production and consumption (SDG 12). By addressing emissions challenges with blockchain technology, businesses in China anticipate a reduction in emissions of 20% to 50% within the average 10-month carbon asset development cycle; efficiency improvements within the green economy by increasing adaptability to new energy market dynamics; and the ability to increase promotion of green technology by channeling more funds to low-emission organizations.

work (PoW) consensus to a proof of stake (PoS) model has led to reduced energy use.[54] In this endeavor, Ethereum is joined by other next-generation blockchains like Cardano, Polkadot, EOS, and Cosmos, each implementing their own PoS versions.[55] Since a PoS model demands significantly lower hardware requirements than a PoW consensus, the energy needed to facilitate secure transactions will only continue to fall in the future.

Blockchain also contributes to climate change management. AI and IoT services can enable blockchain to reduce administrative reporting requirements and support the green bond market, thereby helping access capital to meet the annual funding deficit of the SDGs.[56] Blockchain applications for climate change also include the new carbon emission trading schemes. These employ blockchain to improve the carbon asset transactions' systems. The Chinese government has come forth and established Carbon Emission Reduction (CER) quotas to reduce emissions and green energy costs, which allocate carbon emissions limits to enterprises.[57]

The CER quotas have spurred the growing trade in carbon assets – also known as "carbon offsets" – to serve as accounting mechanisms by which high-carbon emitting enterprises can buy the equivalent of their reduction quotas from low-emission enterprises and use those funds to invest in more green technology. With IBM technology behind it, Energy Blockchain Labs created a blockchain platform to trade carbon assets in China. Bringing a new level of efficiency to carbon asset trading, the tech solution helps expand the market and its environmental benefits.

BLOCKCHAIN AS A KEY TO SUSTAINABLE TRANSPARENCY

With blockchain providing a verifiable record, it is now possible to assess companies' claims of being resource-positive and energy efficient. These metrics for business success can now all be fact-checked and verified, thanks to the tech. Crucial to sustainability in the tech sector is the concept of the circular economy which focuses on reducing waste, reusing products, and recycling materials. Blockchain technology enhances the circular business model by providing adequate information to stakeholders about truly sustainable products. With the fact-checking capabilities blockchain provides, consumers have more information about how to choose the items they purchase, and businesses have more control over the products they sell. The outcome is streamlined supply chains, like those of Walmart, Amazon, and IBM. This tech solution can help companies optimize processes, create innovations, and increase productivity.[58] Ultimately, businesses can yield simultaneous beneficial results such as reduced operating costs and reductions in waste.

Healthcare in the US also benefits from the circular economic nature of this tech, which fosters trust and transparency. An astounding $100 billion in medication is discarded or destroyed annually.[59] This is coupled with the reality that there are nearly 32 million Americans who cannot afford the medication they need. RemediChain has come forth as a blockchain platform that gives vulnerable patients access to medication while at the same time ensuring any surplus medication is redistributed properly.[60] It provides a tech solution and elevated trust through the redistribution of unused medicine to patients who need it.

APPROXIMATELY 60% OF CONSUMERS ARE MORE INCLINED TO BUY PRODUCTS WITH CLEARLY DEFINED SUSTAINABILITY POLICIES.[61]

Another innovative sustainability-focused business, Provenance, promotes product transparency through a software service. Using blockchain, mobile, and other open data, their software gathers product information in a trustworthy and accessible manner. Provenance labels this information "Proof Points," which are made public for consumers to evaluate for themselves to make informed decisions about their purchases.

IN BUSINESS
PROVENANCE[62]

Initiative: Proof Points
Headquarters: London, United Kingdom

Provenance's innovation, "Proof Points," responds to the UN SDGs by enabling consumer goods brands to be publicly transparent in their social and environmental business practices (SDG 12). The platform and its services provide all the tools for digitization of supply chain impact transparency – essential to the needs of conscious shoppers today. Founder and CEO Jessi Baker explains: "We created Proof Points during the Blockchain for Social Good prize period to enable commitments, impact progress, and process claims to be digitally authenticated in a straightforward way we can all understand and trust. This will enable the brands of the future to win."[63]

Provenance uses blockchain technology to enable the secure traceability of certifications and other important information in supply chains. The digital 'passport' structure the platform introduced creates a type of auditable record of the journey behind all physical products that relates to aspects such as environmental impacts and labor practices (SDGs 8,13). It prevents the selling of fake goods, as well as the problem of 'double spending' on certifications present in current systems (SDGs 9,10).[64] In the company's effort to secure a competitive business advantage in the blockchain marketplace, Provenance facilitates transactions at a reduced cost compared to some legacy blockchain platforms. Provenance is also offering grants to developers to accelerate growth in the blockchain ecosystem. Hash, the digital token native to Provenance, is both the means of payment for transactions as well as a method of governance of the blockchain.[65]

It is precisely blockchain's decentralized foundational structure that promises to eliminate the threat of fraud in all areas of banking and trading platforms. With a defining feature being the ability to be made transparent and immutable, the tech addresses burdens such as operational risk and administrative costs. If widely adopted, these interoperable digital financial solutions could provide more of the population with access to important financial tools while adding $3.7 trillion to emerging countries' GDPs by 2025.[66] The open-source payment platform Mojaloop, developed by the Gates Foundation, is a prominent example of this application.[67]

Mojaloop aims to level the economic playing field by building inclusive payment models that benefit the world's poor.[68] The initiative uses distributed ledger technology to enable interoperability between financial institutions, which can speed up transaction times. The increase in efficiency can lower costs and expand access to financial services to the 1.7 billion people who do not use banks. Mojaloop's Ripple provides open-source code and developer tools for furthering innovation across global payments and beyond. The founding vision for Ripple is "to make it possible for the people in the world from all corners to be able to move value like they are moving information."[69] The tech startup calls this concept IoV (Internet of Vision).

BLOCKCHAIN AS A DISRUPTOR FOR GLOBAL PROGRESS

The decentralized model of blockchain technology has the potential to alter entire business segments, challenging traditional market and financial structures. Technology platforms are promoting and deploying blockchain solutions specifically designed for the SDGs. According to the Center for Global Development, remittances are the largest single source of international development finance, as they play an important role in propelling developing countries forward economically. For some countries, remittances are the primary driver of economic activity – they make up over 20% of the GDP in Nepal, El Salvador, and Haiti.[70] With approximately one billion people in the world using remittances, the impact on poverty reduction is significant. The average cost of sending remittances through traditional channels is roughly 7% globally, which accounts for approximately $35 billion worth of payments remitted lost each year to fees.[71]

In countries like Venezuela, where unfavorable market conditions have caused traditional financial institutions to pull back, blockchain businesses - including Ripple mentioned above - are working with banks and traditional money transfer organizations to help modernize the processes. Other business initiatives such as Stellar are taking a more consumer-focused approach and transforming the world of finance. They are giving even small businesses the disruptive power and reach of international banks.[72]

EACH YEAR, WORKERS ABROAD SEND OVER $500 BILLION IN REMITTANCES TO FAMILY AND FRIENDS BACK IN THEIR NATIVE COUNTRIES, WHICH AMOUNTS TO OVER THREE TIMES GLOBAL FOREIGN AID.[73]

Ethereum's "Next Billion" and Cardano's "Project Catalyst" are two large initiatives in the blockchain space disrupting industries and services while promoting Tech for Good. Cardano's Project Catalyst is a series of experiments seeking to generate the highest levels of community innovation as a force for good.[74]

IN BUSINESS

CARDANO[75]

Initiative: Project Catalyst
Headquarters: Zug, Switzerland

Cardano is proactive in funding crypto and blockchain solutions to tackle critical development challenges, especially in Africa. Project Catalyst is a blockchain-led initiative that disrupts static and outdated systems by aiming to increase Cardano's business and create solutions to community challenges. The Ethiopian government, for instance, is exploring the technology to provide personal digital identification (ID) for 5 million students across 3,500 schools (SDG 10).[76] Cardano's project also targets locations and causes of educational under-achievement across Africa (SDG 4). It further supports the efficient allocation of resources while reducing fraudulent university and job applications (SDGs 8,16).

Dor Garbash, Cordano Head of Product Governance, says: "I think a nice aspect of Catalyst, if you really think about it, is it's almost like a machine that converts these raw tokens that sit in a treasury into a resource in the hands of the people who are building the network. And that's what it does — it just transfers the wealth to the doers and to the reviewers, and the maintainers of the system."[77] The decentralized nature of this innovation enables the distribution of funds to proposed projects, which helps position smaller local initiatives at the same level as large international projects. Project Catalyst's grant funding rounds have increased from $250,000 to $2 million in less than a year, thanks to the IdeaScale platform.[78]

BLOCKCHAIN PROGRESSING THE GLOBAL GOALS

Blockchain can move the world forward across multiple platforms and sectors by laying the foundation for long-term and inclusive progress. From retail-level investment in green infrastructure projects to enabling blended finance for developing countries, blockchain can be a potent force for facilitating a systematic shift and expanding traditional financial capital, while also capturing social and environmental capital. As illustrated below, harnessing blockchain technologies to drive sustainable and resilient growth and a new wave of value creation will require global action through business targeting the SDGs.

NO POVERTY

This employs cryptocurrencies and other blockchain-based tokens to allow the world's two billion unbanked people to trade and transact in a trusting and transparent way.[79] Initiatives such as BitPesa, BitSpark, and CariCoin are beginning to gain traction by using blockchain technology to ease the difficulty and high costs of sending money across borders.[80] By using crypto for transactions, blockchain platforms are sharply reducing fees and transferring money. It is important to note that cutting prices to transfer money by just 5% can save $16 billion a year. This tech solution of peer-to-peer transactions from migrant workers to family or friends living in their home country is transforming the vast global remittances market and easing the burden of migration.

GOOD HEALTH AND WELLBEING

Blockchain can prove the authenticity of medical products, thereby helping reduce risk and potentially minimize costly or fatal incidences. The tech improves data security, makes medical records more accurate, and cuts the operational costs for information management and storage. The World Health Organization reports that an estimated 1 million people die every year as a result of taking counterfeit medications.[81] The incorruptible medical blockchain technology is a solution to reducing such risks caused by fake medications and, consequently, saves lives.

Blockchain applications make it practically impossible to change information stored in its sections. It can additionally help pharmacists identify at which stage the violation was made in the case of detecting a low-quality product. Blockchain software AsliMedicine aims to trace medication through the entire healthcare chain, ensure its integrity, and identify fakes.[82]

QUALITY EDUCATION

The market for EdTech is growing rapidly, with blockchain as a major component to keeping student information and records secure and safe.[83] Security and verification are becoming a major concern, as data breaches often target student records and steal information that can be used to create fake identities or be sold by hackers. Blockchain could make these attacks ineffective by protecting student identities and school records. As more schools from kindergarten to university go digital, this could be key in ensuring student privacy. The Social Alpha Foundation, an entity that accepts material assistance in cryptocurrency, raises funds to award grants to projects that are engaged in social support and training for blockchain technology.[84] One grant of $30,000 was awarded to the Social Impact Hackathon winners at the Impact Summit.[85] Attended by 350 students from IT departments, the event demonstrated how technical knowledge learned in schools can help in solving global social problems.

AFFORDABLE AND CLEAN ENERGY

Platforms that collate distributed data on resources, such as household-level water and energy data from smart sensors that can help mitigate current gaps in information between stakeholders. This would enable more informed and decentralized decision-making regarding power system design and management of resources. It would also allow for innovative financing and payment structures that are beneficial to businesses. A platform built on the Ethereum blockchain, The Sun Exchange is a peer-to-peer marketplace that allows anyone, anywhere, to invest in solar panel projects using Bitcoin.[86] The South African startup enables Bitcoin users to purchase solar panels and lease them to schools, factories, and communities to earn rental income. It is designed to make solar asset ownership more affordable with incentivized token features that include access to discounts and lease bonuses when using The Sun Exchange and priority access to new solar projects on the platform.

Supply chains are an important component of sustainable development worldwide across all sectors. Blockchain for supply chain management has reflected a wide variety of improved industry uses. We have examples of multinational development banks investigating the use of blockchain for trade projects in regions such as South Asia and Latin America. Energy utilities are increasingly considering blockchain's potential to improve the efficiency of electricity markets. Russia's national grid operator is testing the technology to improve the efficiency of electricity metering, billing, and payments by end-users.[87] This solution will enable consumers to monitor their real-time energy consumption via a mobile app and automate payments within the network.

RESPONSIBLE PRODUCTION AND CONSUMPTION

This gives rise to technological change actions taken by conscientious consumers. Consideration of overall levels of consumption could be important areas for business growth. Blockchain has enormous potential to help organizations verify the sources of their goods and track their movement, strengthening transparency in any supply chain. Fraud, contaminations or counterfeits can be pinpointed immediately, in turn ensuring customer safety and enhancing business efforts to be socially and ethically responsible. Launched in December 2017, WaBi is an Ethereum-based crypto-token for safe consumer products. As a blockchain-based service, WaBi aims to provide solutions for the global circulation of fake goods. The network connects consumers and brands by linking the physical and digital assets through RFID (Radio Frequency Identification) labels equipped with anti-copy functionality.[88] By incentivizing users with WaBi token rewards, this business innovation allows brands to generate new types of data for market research, testing, and strategic decision-making.

PEACE, JUSTICE AND STRONG INSTITUTIONS

These are critical, as more than a billion people globally do not have recognized personhood, which is the most basic of human rights.[89] Lack of officially recognized identity impacts every aspect of life since. Without valid proof of identity, many basic services and rights are out of reach. The blockchain-based platform offers methods for securing identity data. By making an immutable record of the actual or attempted illegal transfer across borders, it helps prevent severe human rights violations such as human trafficking. Public procurement is one of the largest sources of government spending and one of the greatest sources of official corruption worldwide. The World Bank estimates that public procurement represents, on average, 13% to 20% of global GDP.[90] Each phase of the small and large public procurement process comes with its own challenges and opportunities for corruption, bribery, undue influence on government assessments, and more. In this regard, blockchain is evidenced to increase external oversight. The Colombian government undertook a proof-of-concept for a blockchain-based procurement system, as approximately $6 billion were compromised by procurement corruption between 2016 and 2018.[91] By removing the barriers to adoption, Modex, an early player in the blockchain procurement field, makes blockchain implementation straightforward and affordable for many businesses and industries, including governmental processes.[92]

NO POVERTY

- Provides blockchain identification and payment services for the most vulnerable population segments.
- Facilitates transparency in pricing around locally sourced crops for which farmers have been historically underpaid.

GOOD HEALTH AND WELLBEING

- Facilitates responsible and effective use of personal health data.
- Proves the authenticity of medical products, helping reduce risk and potentially minimize the amount of costly or fatal incidences.

QUALITY EDUCATION

- Eliminates data breaches in education records, including test scores and transcripts.
- Improves the quality of education by sharing exam scores and research data across multiple institutions.

AFFORDABLE AND CLEAN ENERGY

- Makes renewable energy available at a lower rate and in an optimized manner by eliminating intermediaries and significantly reducing transaction costs.
- Records, verifies, and makes transparently available to all network participants data for each transaction.

INDUSTRY, INNOVATION AND INFRASTRUCTURE

- Enables creation of incorruptible databases for records.
- Allows records to be synchronized, keeping information up to date and authentic.

BLOCKCHAIN

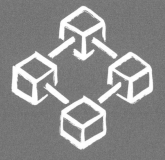

RESPONSIBLE CONSUMPTION AND PRODUCTION

- Provides solutions for the global circulation of fake goods through safer consumer products.
- Verifies the sources of goods and tracks movement, strengthening transparency in any supply chain.

PEACE, JUSTICE AND STRONG INSTITUTIONS

- Secures identity data and makes an immutable record of the actual or attempted illegal transfer across a border.
- Increased transparency and reduced fraud are beneficial byproducts of the tech that has a disruptive quality.

ENHANCING BUSINESS MODELS

Companies and processes across industries can employ blockchain to enhance their business models. It can serve as a tool to execute and record transactions and track ownership for assets that change hands several times before settlement. Business executives report that not only is blockchain a necessity for solving some of a company's most pressing problems, but it also has the potential to stimulate improvement over other methods.[93] The tech can enormously reduce paper consumption by securely and permanently recording continuously retrievable data on a base level.[94] Monitoring the supply chain through blockchain technology makes it possible to identify inferior products earlier in the process. Product recalls and new products can thus be reduced. The entire business world can benefit from more trusting, transparent, and direct relationships catalyzed by sustainable blockchain solutions.

Digital technologies and ubiquitous data are increasing visibility, transparency, coordination, and information sharing across companies. This trend enables smarter, more informed decisions and greatly improves operating efficiency. Blockchain will likely serve as the underlying structure for several industries' transactional infrastructures. The energy industry network is particularly suited for blockchain technology applications. Further rise in technological advancements is expected to transform operations within the energy and resources industry into a vast global network of connected devices that gather digital data on a blockchain platform.[95]

"ANYTHING THAT YOU CAN CONCEIVE OF AS A SUPPLY CHAIN, BLOCKCHAIN CAN VASTLY IMPROVE ITS EFFICIENCY – IT DOESN'T MATTER IF IT'S PEOPLE, NUMBERS, DATA, OR MONEY."[96] - GINNI ROMETTY, FORMER CEO OF IBM

By incentivizing circular economies, blockchain could fundamentally change how materials and natural resources are valued and traded. This can be done by incentivizing individuals, companies, and governments to unlock financial value from things currently wasted, discarded, or treated as economically invaluable. An example of this shift is seen in the way consumer demand is driving fashion brands to use more organic cotton.[97] Despite growth in production, companies struggle to meet that demand. The fragmented nature of supply chains makes it difficult for manufacturers to know if the cotton they are buying is truly organic. To tackle this, Bext360, an agricultural blockchain startup, has emerged and will be explained in the next section. As businesses endeavor to reach sustainability goals to enhance profit and brand value, carbon footprint reporting becomes increasingly important.

Given that 40 countries have already either applied or are in the process of implementing a carbon pricing system, enterprises need ways to manage this tracking through an avenue that is transparent and organized.[98] Blockchain provides a solution to this challenge. It offers validation from external parties, covering the supply chain, value chain, and footprint of all products, and also enables participation of other stakeholders. Next-gen sustainability monitoring and verification in blockchain have the potential to transform both sustainability reporting and assurance, thereby helping companies manage, demonstrate, and improve their performance. Meanwhile, consumers and investors are able to make better-informed decisions through verifiable blockchain data. This drives a new wave of accountability and action, providing business executives and managers with a complete picture of managing risk and reward profiles.

Blockchain platforms are further being harnessed to use cryptographic tokens with a tradable value to optimize existing market platforms for carbon. This creates new opportunities for carbon credit transactions. The Carbon Utility Token (CUT) is an example of a growing class of green assets designed to help corporations manage their carbon allowances.[99] The sale of each CUT token goes towards investments in carbon capture and carbon offsetting programs. As more and more corporations begin to add cryptocurrencies to their core business practices, CUT provides an avenue to completely offset the carbon footprint behind each coin.

GLOBAL GOALS' GROWTH OPPORTUNITIES

Blockchain was initially developed to move Bitcoin from one point to another. It has now evolved far beyond and is being used by a number of companies in diverse sectors to move assets and monitor business progress in various areas. Enterprises all over the world are now using the tech to speed up business processes, increase transparency, and potentially save billions of dollars. Blockchain use-case solutions are particularly relevant across sustainability applications. These tend to fall into the following cross-cutting themes that address new financing models for environmental and social outcomes: streamlining supply chain transparency and management, realizing the value and natural capital for food and agriculture, enabling the green economy and decentralized energy systems, and reducing fraud and organizational management in healthcare.

BOOSTING SUPPLY CHAIN TRANSPARENCY AND MANAGEMENT

Today's supply chains are more globalized than ever, and economic opportunities are emerging for businesses utilizing blockchain and cryptocurrency. The traditional model of supply chains being opaque with inaccessible or unverifiable data points is slowly changing with shifting demand and regulations. Consumers are requesting more transparency about the origin of their products, while companies realize the need for sustainable and responsible procurement practices. Monitoring the supply chain makes it possible to identify problematic products earlier in the process, thereby reducing recalls. This leads to reduced production, which positively affects the greenhouse gas balance and other resources. In this context, technology emerges to support supply chain management, especially in terms of transparency and traceability.

SUPPLY CHAINS TODAY ARE MORE GLOBALIZED THAN EVER AND ECONOMIC OPPORTUNITIES ARE EMERGING FOR BUSINESSES TO UTILIZE BLOCKCHAIN.

Blockchain provides many solutions specific to the traceability of goods such as food, minerals, raw materials, textiles, or pharmaceuticals. It can significantly improve supply chains by enabling faster and more cost-efficient delivery of products, enhancing product traceability, improving coordination between partners, and aiding access to financing. This technology can enable supply chain management's transition to a sharing economy where people and companies reduce waste and decouple growth from the consumption of finite resources.[100] The end result is increased sustainability and profitability at the same time. Due to their international, complex, and multi-stakeholder characteristics, global supply chains generate sizable environmental and social impacts. This is especially true in the agricultural sector, which employs 28% of the world's population.[101] Bext360, a Denver-based startup, is utilizing blockchain technology to better track and verify the authentication of the organic cotton supply chain (Case 58). With sustainable green trade valued at more than $1 trillion per year, companies are adopting better ways to assure their goods' origins, identity, and traceability. The estimated annual cost of Indonesia's illegal, unreported, and unregulated fishing is approximately $5 billion.[102] By adopting a blockchain traceability solution, tuna industry actors are increasing their supply chain speed by overcoming operational and market gaps. They are delivering sustainably caught fish to consumers with fewer health and safety risks and less product spoilage.

IN BUSINESS

BEXT360[103]

Initiative: Organic Cotton Traceability Pilot
Headquarters: Denver, Colorado USA

Focused on transparency and greater insight into the agricultural market, Bext360 is partnered with the C&A Foundation, Fashion For Good, and the Organic Cotton Accelerator to form an initiative called Organic Cotton Traceability Pilot (SDG 17).[104] The primary purpose of Bext360 is to trace organic cotton from farms to the gin, where it is processed for textile use. The second phase of the pilot ensures cotton can be traced from the gin to the consumer. Finally, the initiative is aimed at scale so it can be used for organic cotton farmers, textile producers, and fashion companies around the world. Blockchain allows textile producers and fashion companies to identify authentic organic cotton traders. Coming as close as possible to full traceability of the cotton's origin, purity, and distribution, this method seeks to give the complete picture of the product's life cycle within the current landscape.

At the consumer level, the solution can be used to communicate which suppliers and manufacturers worked together to create the final product. "The success of the Organic Cotton Traceability Pilot provides a positive impulse towards traceability and transparency in the value chain," says Katrin Ley, Managing Director of Fashion for Good.[105] "In addition, the process shows enormous potential for further expansion to include other fibers in the fashion supply chain." Bext360, with its vast network, is able to decrease the cost of people to manage its supply chain and increase the ability to prove authenticity, sustainability, and origin (SDGs 8, 12). Beyond enterprises, the use of Bext360's software is also highly beneficial to farmers. Cotton is traced to the level of the individual farm and the payment process is digitized, ensuring that producers are given their fair share of the cotton proceeds (SDG 10). Additionally, the blockchain tokens are designed to provide incentive payments to producers at various steps of the process.

NOURISHING VALUE AND NATURAL CAPITAL FOR FOOD AND AGRICULTURE

The rising demand for food in the present era creates new issues, such as counterfeit products that threaten farming supply chains at different stages. Blockchain technology tackles this by enabling the traceability of information in the food supply chain and thus helping improve food safety and security. The secure data management and storage facilitates the development and use of data-driven innovations for smart farming and smart agriculture insurance. To allow food production and transport to operate with more confidence, AgriDigital has developed the ability to eliminate counterparty risk by running commodity transactions on a blockchain (Case 59).

The World Food Programme's (WFP) Building Blocks project has notably emerged recently, which uses blockchain for authenticating and registering transactions that expand refugees' choices in how they access and spend their cash assistance.

Weather conditions affect global nourishment sources, such as crops and livestock. Climate change is expected to further exacerbate weather conditions in the future. Thus, agricultural insurance schemes are an increasingly important aspect of food production as a risk management tool for farmers. Blockchain can contribute to improving index insurance in two dimensions. First, it makes automated payments in a timely manner based on weather data that triggers the payout as defined in a smart contract. Second, it automatically integrates weather information and other data points based on risk reduction analyses, such as plant growth information and smart improvements, thus making the payout process more efficient.[106]

Etherisc, a Swiss company, provides decentralized crop insurance using blockchain technology that administers payouts based on weather data in Decentralized Insurance Protocol tokens as the native currency.[107] Alibaba spin-off Ant has more than 50 blockchain applications in development on its blockchain platform, AntChain. AntChain Traceability-as-a-Service (TaaS) is a blockchain-based food traceability solution combined with IoT technologies to enable trust, increase efficiency, and provide end-to-end transparency on food and agricultural information along the supply chain. Leading Chinese restaurant group Oversea Enterprise Berhad is the first local business adopting AntChain TaaS in Southeast Asia to trace its mooncake products.[108] In 2019, Ant Group processed $17 trillion in transactions on mainland China and a further $90 billion overseas.[109]

STRENGTHENING GREEN ECONOMIES AND DECENTRALIZED ENERGY SYSTEMS

The energy sector is already one of the most rapid adopters of blockchain technology. Due to its distributed nature, Blockchain can make energy networks much more secure if implemented correctly. In coordination with burgeoning technologies such as AI and IoT, blockchain can help secure networks and grids because it is managed by a distributed group of peers rather than by a central server or authority.[110] Blockchain manages energy demand and supply, enables peer-to-peer trading, and facilitates distributed energy generation by allowing consumers to buy and sell their own energy. Historically, national energy systems relied on large, centralized power plants to produce electricity and transmit it over networks to households or industrial and commercial customers.

However, new sustainable energy technologies such as wind and solar, energy storage and smart grids, and digital tools like IoT, AI, and machine learning are allowing more small producers to generate and transmit electricity. In this regard, blockchain contributes through "smart contracts," which allow real-time pricing and make the grid more flexible.[111] Blockchain also enables consumers to sell excess power to the grid at wholesale rates rather than retail prices and to buyers in their local communities. It also helps boost efficiency, thereby reducing waste. The unique characteristics of the peer-to-peer trading platform that blockchain enables can also be used to link carbon-trading schemes from different countries.

IN BUSINESS

AGRIDIGITAL[112]

Initiative: Blockchain-Based Agricultural Solutions
Headquarters: Sydney, Australia

AgriDigital is an Australian company with a cloud-based commodity management platform that connects farmers and value chain actors through a blockchain-enabled system (SDGs 9,17). It is aimed at helping farmers suffering from counterparty risk when selling their crops. The blockchain component allows each transaction to be immutably tracked on the platform. Their payments occur in real-time through smart contracts, creating a better life for low-wage farmers (SDGs 8,10). "In a trading environment where margins are so thin, AgriDigital enables us to be running as lean as possible, and this system is far ahead of everything else in allowing us to do this," says Jackson Morris, Commodity Trader at OTOCHU Australia for AgriDigital.[113] Currently, AgriDigital generates a transaction value of over $3.5 billion, a product volume of nearly 25 million metric tons, and has approximately 7,000 active users.

WORLD FOOD PROGRAMME[114]

Initiative: Building Blocks
Headquarters: Rome, Italy

The World Food Programme (WFP) has been using Blockchain to deliver food assistance to 106,000 Syrian refugees in Jordan (SDGs 2,3). Specifically, it facilitates cash transfers while protecting beneficiary data, controlling financial risks, and allowing for greater collaboration (SDG 9). Globally, WFP is the largest agency delivering humanitarian cash and in 2019 distributed a record of $2.1 billion, reaching over 28 million people in 64 countries. WFP also initiated a proof-of-concept project in Sindh province, Pakistan to test the capabilities of using blockchain for authenticating and registering beneficiary transactions. The blockchain technology behind the project allowed direct, secure, and fast transactions between participants and WFP – without requiring a financial intermediary like a bank to connect the two parties (SDG 10).

After refining the project's approach, the next phase of Building Blocks was implemented in two refugee camps in Jordan. Now, over 100,000 people living in the camps can purchase groceries by scanning the iris of their eye at checkout (SDG 11). Cash value from WFP or other partners is stored in a beneficiary account maintained on the blockchain. The cash that beneficiaries receive or spend on goods and services is paid to the beneficiaries or to the retailers through a commercial financial service provider built on a private, permissioned blockchain and integrated with existing biometric authentication technology. Building Blocks save on financial transaction fees in the camp setting and ensure greater security and privacy for Syrian refugees (SDGs 1,16).

Facilitated clean energy trading through this tech could also allow for the development of peer-to-peer platforms on which renewable energy would be traded. Consumers would be able to buy, sell, or exchange renewable energy assets with each other by using tokens or digital assets that represent a certain quantity of energy production.

Smart contracts can also empower environmentally-conscious businesses to drive the green economy. This could be through a reforestation or carbon restoration smart contract. Enterprises could be paid in the form of tokenized carbon credits which would, in turn, be sold to charitable organizations, crowdfunding campaigns, or even companies seeking to show they have made a green impact.[115] Further, smart contracts can also give environmentally-conscious consumers more options in terms of their energy consumption. Decentralized energy grids, like the Brooklyn Microgrid Project, use smart contracts to give consumers the ability to produce and trade solar electricity with their neighbors through an exchange that uses a blockchain as a coordination mechanism (Case 61).[116]

Incorporating smart contracts and blockchain technology creates a secure and automated process that cuts costs for users and removes the need for energy suppliers or transmission companies. Decentralized grids are more resilient in emergencies like natural disasters because the energy is generated, stored, and consumed within a small geographical area. By tracking and reporting emissions reductions, blockchain technology can ensure more transparency around greenhouse gas emissions and make it easier to track and report emissions reductions. It could serve as a tool to monitor the progress made in implementing the Nationally Determined Contributions under the Paris Agreement.[117] Traditionally high-polluting industries are employing blockchain to clean up their operations, which can lead to significantly reduced emissions from Bitcoin mining. Take for example, Genesis Mining, an Icelandic company which enables crypto mining in the cloud and uses 100% renewable energy to power its computers.[118]

BLOCKCHAIN HAS THE GREAT POTENTIAL TO EMPLOY TECH IN SOLVING ENERGY RISKS AMONG SOME OF THE WORLD'S MOST VULNERABLE POPULATIONS.

There are numerous blockchain energy initiatives across the globe, including several tech startups, guided by the promise of greater transparency and accuracy. They not only address consumer needs but also create business opportunities. Several blockchain initiatives and startups focus on energy sharing, virtual power plants, and decentralized energy resources, as demonstrated in the case of Brooklyn Microgrid. New systems are emerging where power flows from microgrids to smart meters connected to the blockchain network. Modern energy services are vital to the wellbeing of humans and a country's economic development. Yet, 800 million people globally lack access to electricity. Around 95% of these people are in either sub-Saharan Africa or developing Asia, with 80% in rural areas.[119] Innovative initiatives address consumer concerns around the world in vulnerable areas, such as Haiti, where locals can interact with their smart meters and purchase power directly from their mobile devices.

Distributed, renewable energy blockchain solutions empower underserved communities to reduce the use of fossil fuels and mitigate the effects of climate change. ImpactPPA identifies the fundamental issue restricting access to critical resources, solutions, and capital as the existing legacy financial institutions that govern how and to whom access to capital is deployed.[120] The US-based startup solves this problem by using blockchain for new sources and methods of effectuating change, while also enabling communities through self-determination to rise out of poverty and move forward in the global economy.

IN BUSINESS
BROOKLYN MICROGRID[121]

Initiative: Exergy
Headquarters: Brooklyn, New York, USA

Through blockchain technology and the company's own innovative solutions, Brooklyn Microgrid developed Exergy. Exergy facilitates peer-to-peer transactions between its microgrid participants using blockchain technology and smart contracts (SDG 10). It is a permissioned data platform that creates a localized marketplace for transacting energy across existing grid infrastructure (SDGs 7, 9, 11). The full potential of the Exergy platform has yet to be realized, but it is designed to influence the energy model of the future. Participants access the local energy marketplace through the Brooklyn Microgrid mobile app. In the app, people can choose to buy local solar energy credits. Prosumers sell their excess solar energy to the marketplace where consumers purchase the available solar via auction (SDG 12).

According to Lawrence Orsini, CEO of LO3 Energy (the organization behind the Brooklyn Microgrid), "Exergy is about enabling the market shift to an economy that looks towards useful work more than it does to the production of energy. The platform itself is, at its core, about releasing grid edge data, so that devices can start to respond in real time to actual grid edge telemetry, enabling devices to respond to a burn out, or a congestion, or over-voltage. Getting that data and localizing, at the granular level, is really the function of the platform."[122] Purchasing local solar energy through Brooklyn Microgrid supports the local economy and reduces greenhouse gas emissions and air pollution (SDG 13). Additionally, Brooklyn Microgrid provides users with control over where their energy is sourced.

BLOCKCHAIN IN THE ENERGY SECTOR

Innovative companies around the world using blockchain tech in the energy sector include:

- The Energy Web Foundation, which is building an open-source, blockchain-based digital infrastructure for the energy sector in **Germany** with a growing portfolio of cutting-edge pilots.[123]
- **British** startup Rowan Energy that develops a blockchain-based reward system for solar power producers.[124]
- Startups like GTIME Blockchain in **Chile** provide energy traceability platforms that directly connect to renewable energy plants and provide real-time information about the energy source.[125]
- **Estonian** startup Powerchain, which provides decentralized energy storage and trading systems for electricity manufacturers.[126]
- EPC Blockchain, a **Malaysian** startup that offers a Platform-as-a-Service (PaaS) solution by using decentralized storage to enable energy project owners to keep track of their energy savings and renewable energy generation.[127]

REINFORCING SUSTAINABLE BUSINESS SERVICES IN HEALTHCARE

Blockchain technology can transform healthcare by enhancing data security, privacy, and interoperability. In 2018, healthcare institutions were subjected to cyberattacks, resulting in the violation of more than 15 million patient records.[128] In 2019, the number of breaches increased by 60%.[129] Blockchain can tackle such attacks by providing a new model for health information exchanges where electronic medical records become more efficient, disintermediated, and secure. Improving the interoperability and security of today's electronic health record management system and drug supply chain requires blockchain-based solutions. Every year, the healthcare industry carries out high-cost transactions, although 63% of physicians still do not receive the data on time or adequately.[130] As a result of inefficient supply chains, patients' deaths and the inclusion and sale of counterfeit pharmaceutical products is quite common in the medical industry.

These challenges result in the loss of over $200 billion per year for the healthcare industry in the U.S. alone.[131] Blockchain can solve these problems efficiently and minimize loss while making data interoperable and providing doctors with real-time access. Blockchains will enable the storage of all data in a single place that the patients themselves could control and monitor. Interoperability of the blockchain system will allow doctors easy access to a patient's accurate medical history. Medical professionals can thus better identify health conditions and formulate a more effective care process. Blockchain also ensures unparalleled security for patients' data, giving them control of the parties they share their records with.

BY 2025, 55% OF ALL HEALTHCARE APPLICATIONS WILL HAVE DEPLOYED BLOCKCHAIN FOR COMMERCIAL PURPOSES. BY THE SAME YEAR, THE VALUATION OF BLOCKCHAIN IN HEALTHCARE IS EXPECTED TO JUMP TO $5.61 BILLION FROM THE PRESENT $170 MILLION.

Vancouver's Coral Health emerges as an example that employs the tech to accelerate the care process, automate administrative procedures, and improve health outcomes.[132] By inserting patient information into a blockchain platform, the company efficiently connects doctors, scientists, lab technicians, and public health authorities. Coral Health also implements smart contracts between patients and healthcare professionals to ensure that data and treatments are accurate. COVID-19 has highlighted the challenges and vulnerabilities in global supply chains, alerting the need for better transparency and traceability.

IN BUSINESS

KOIBANX[133]

Initiative: VitalPass
Headquarters: Buenos Aires, Argentina

The digital passport VitalPass was developed with the technological support of Koibanx, a Latin American company with experience implementing blockchain-based asset tokenization and transactional solutions for the financial and government sectors.[134] Koibanx is a private software company focused on smart contracts solutions and blockchain services. As part of a collaborative effort between Koibanx and blockchain ecosystem Algorand, the world's first blockchain based COVID-19 passport was launched by the Colombian government in 2021 (SDGs 3,17). The system uses the blockchain technology to generate records of patients' experiences from paper to digital certificates (SDG 10). This tech solution provides security, traceability and openness throughout Latin America (SDG 16).

When a person visits a participating location for vaccination, an email address is used to assign a username. The certificate is then issued at the healthcare location and registered on the Algorand blockchain through a user interface designed by Koibanx. This system provides the person with a passport-like document linked to a vaccine verification on the blockchain. The details are subsequently accessed through a simple QR code. Talking about the collaboration, W. Sean Ford, COO of Algorand said: "We are excited about the innovation coming out of Latin America, particularly when it comes to the ability to harness the power of efficient and advanced blockchain to quickly bring innovative solutions to life."[135] This digital vaccination passport is free and cannot be falsified, since it creates a permanent and inalterable record on Algorand blockchain, which is a public, decentralized network that was purposefully built for global applications that can scale to mass adoption (SDG 9).

As of its latest funding round in August 2022, Koibanx raised a $22 million.[136] The investment round was led by Algorand and included the participation of Borderless Capital, Kalonia Venture Partners, G2 and Innogen Capital, among others. Koibanx also plans to allow developers to create financial products on the blockchain, with the aim of reaching 10,000 developers by the end of 2023.

Blockchain is being used to track vaccine delivery, thereby addressing large global inefficiencies that cost lives and money, especially in rural areas where supply chain inefficiencies slow the vaccine delivery rate. One in five infants fail to obtain basic routine immunizations, resulting in 1.5 million annual deaths of children from preventable diseases.[137] It has also been critically important for global healthcare to track COVID-19 vaccinations on blockchain. The digital passport known as VitalPass has been developed by Koibanx, a Latin American asset tokenization company, to monitor immunizations utilizing the powerful Algorand blockchain technology.

ADDRESSING RISKS AND CHALLENGES ON THE ROAD AHEAD

Although blockchain presents many exciting solutions, advanced ledger tech has some possible downsides and risks to consider. Blockchain is a relatively untested technology in widespread application and presents some sustainability challenges in a rapidly changing world. Beyond its potential beneficial impact across public and private sectors, blockchain has also garnered skepticism related to its scalability and the high-energy use of early platforms. Companies employing this tech as a model for sustainable business must simultaneously be critical of the controversial aspects and how to address them. While crypto-mining processes have traditionally used large amounts of energy and blockchain governance and user protections remain an area of concern, there are numerous benefits to this decentralized transactional structure with proven Tech for Good power.

Crypto-mining processes engage powerful computers that run complex calculations to solve equations. Naturally, the more high-powered the computer, the more electricity used. Some miners even connect entire warehouses full of computers to the network to increase their computational power. The increasing need for advanced systems is generating complexity in algorithms, a trend that requires more energy. Recent studies have revealed that Bitcoin consumes around 121.36 TWh per year, more electricity than the entire country of Argentina.[138] While this is still a fraction of the energy the Internet uses in total, it is something to be cautious about as blockchain use grows.

BEYOND ITS POTENTIAL BENEFICIAL IMPACT, BLOCKCHAIN HAS GARNERED SKEPTICISM RELATED TO ITS SCALABILITY AND THE HIGH-ENERGY USE OF EARLY PLATFORMS.

Also important to note, despite the enhancement blockchain brings to security, accountability, and transparency for people worldwide, this innovation needs sufficient monitoring for governance and user protection. Guarding against undesirable outcomes will be necessary for individuals, companies, organizations, and societies at large. With this in mind, there has been encouraging momentum towards defining and self-regulating user blockchain protection, such as the Global Digital Finance Code and the WEF Global Blockchain Council's Presidio Principles.[139]

Blockchain is still a nascent technology despite its vast, exciting potential and the promising cases presented throughout this chapter. Regulatory uncertainty, immature infrastructure, technological limitations, and risks constrain the tech. Governments and policymakers may be cautious about supporting the maturation of blockchain while they create coherent regulatory frameworks. Several countries worldwide, like the US, Malta, and Belarus, have stated the need for instituted blockchain regulations.[140] All these potential risks, downsides, and challenges are important considerations when addressing the complexities of blockchain's consumer protection, infrastructure capabilities, and its influence on politics and cultural norms. Resolving these ensures that the technology will be able to meaningfully contribute to sustainable development aims.

WE HAVE

IMAGINED

We have imagined how blockchain simplifies all stages of agriculture supply chain. Supply chain management in agriculture is often more complex than in other sectors, as food production depends on factors like weather, pests, and labor structures that are sometimes hard to predict and control. Blockchain tech enables transparency, trust, and a high degree of efficiency throughout the agriculture network. With verifiable data for sustainable business across the entire product movement, the technology solution seeks to ensure transparent transactions and eliminate fraud. Moreover, distributed ledger applications can be extended to help mitigate taxing and inhumane labor practices and promote safe and verifiable access to medicines and vaccines. Hence, blockchain simplifies all stages of the agriculture supply chain.

The cotton farmers can now track fair pricing with greater ease and consumers are able to verify the provenance of organic goods. As blockchain increasingly expands for business management practices, society will also experience improved energy efficiency through supply chain movement. Just imagine the ease with which we can gain access to information about the agricultural practices and labor markets behind the products we buy. The data are now at our fingertips, providing the knowledge we need to make more informed choices that will move markets toward a sustainable world.

We have imagined Blockchain for Good.

TECH FOR GOOD

THE FILM

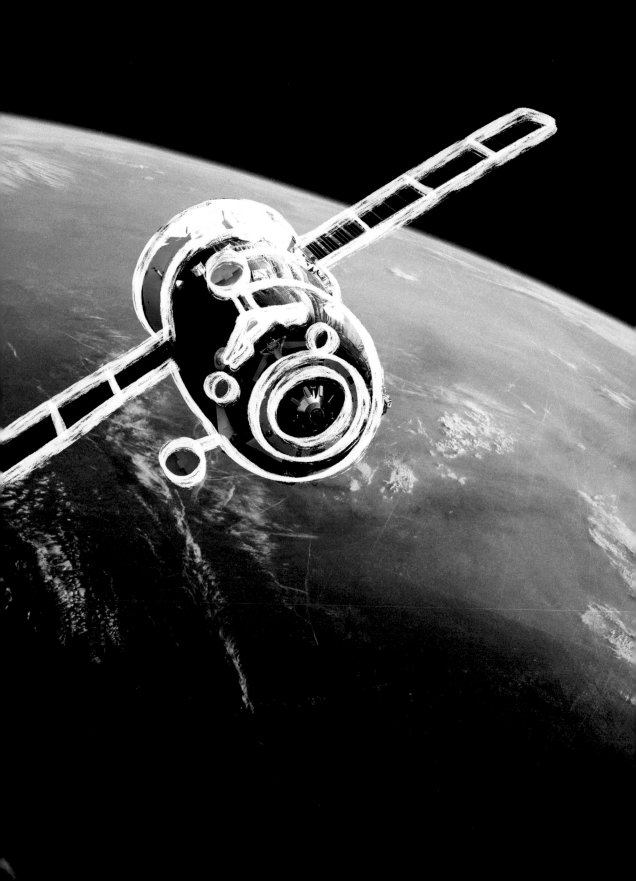

SPACETECH 9

OUTER SPACE IS A VAST FRONTIER YET TO BE FULLY EXPLORED.

IT UNLOCKS UNPRECEDENTED OPPORTUNITIES TO ADDRESS OUR GREATEST CHALLENGES.

WE ONLY NEED TO
IMAGINE

Imagine peering across the stars from our celestial vantage point of the International Space Station, or peeking out the window of a seat on the SpaceX Starship and seeing the Earth from afar. When viewing Earth from outer space, we see the entirety of the planet's beauty. The view from space shows us the deep blue of water surrounding the greenish-brown patches of land. From space, our habitable planet appears beautiful, and this distant perspective gives us a new appreciation for the place we call home. Imagine if we could witness this view with our own eyes and not merely through images.

This far-off view has an appearance of ample water supply, yet we soon find our eyes are misleading us. The majestic cobalt oceans, lakes, and rivers we look at on the map do not give the full picture of the water supply on Earth. Despite the abundance of water sources we may see, the optical illusion is that many regions fall short when it comes to access to potable water. On Africa, which is the second-largest continent, although groundwater sources are vast, countries and populations in arid regions lack the necessary infrastructure and technology to access water. Urgent action is paramount to overcome the global water crisis, and advanced technologies are an essential tool for monitoring and managing water resources on Earth.

Outer space has always fascinated humankind. Now, the intrigue is focused in a completely new way in which space technologies are being employed to protect people and the planet. Albert Einstein once said, "look deep into nature, and then you will understand everything better." Equally important is to look at nature from a great distance. Space tech solutions come to mind, such as satellite imaging within hydrological and hydro-geological systems that are integrated with other geospatial data sources.

The integrated approach of the Geographic Information System (GIS) and remote sensing has been recognized universally as a unique, effective, and highly versatile technology for evaluating, managing, and monitoring water resources. Similarly, earth observation satellite data can help address water shortage problems in different ways. The archives of space agencies contain a valuable and extensive mountain of data awaiting exploitation. By utilizing space tech to zoom in on Earth and see beneath the surface, we can get a better picture of what needs to be solved and where to help address the SDGs.

NASA's Gravity Recovery and Climate Experiment (GRACE) provided excellent opportunities to enhance groundwater data as well.[1] The mission involved twin satellites that took detailed measurements of Earth's gravity field anomalies from its launch in March 2002 to October 2017. Among its innovations, GRACE monitored the loss of ice mass from Earth's ice sheets and improved understanding of the processes responsible for sea-level rise and ocean circulation. It also provided insights into where global groundwater resources may be shrinking or growing, and where dry soils are contributing to drought.

Water is indeed crucial for economic survival and poverty alleviation. Hence, water conservation and protection are essential aspects of managing Africa's water resources. According to a United Nations Environment Program (UNEP) assessment, two-thirds of the Earth's population will live in water-stressed conditions by 2025 if current consumption patterns continue; in this category are 25 African states.[2] Furthermore, in the African Water Vision for 2025, the World Commission of Water for the 21st Century emphasized several obstructions that affect water resource management.[3] These issues include the abundance of transboundary water basins, the fluctuation of climate and rainfall patterns, the scarcity of water and groundwater resources, increased demand and water pollution, and environmental degradation.

To this end, the Commission Internationale du Bassin Congo-Oubangui-Sangha (CICOS), based in the Democratic Republic of Congo, leads a consortium that deals with water resource management by providing user-customized GIS information on navigation, meteorological, hydrological, hydropower and drinking water production, agro-pastoral services, forest management, and protected areas, among others.[4] These satellite technologies used for water supply management are vitally important to the African people.

Imagine how leveraging space tech to transform how we manage water resources and deliver water and sanitation services for humankind could transform our lives. The vast realm of outer space provides ample inspiration to design technological breakthroughs and reimagine our relationship to the vacuum beyond Earth's atmosphere. As we journey into outer space to unlock solutions that address the Global Goals, the view from this extended vantage point will include seeing how space technologies can help us preserve our beautiful planet Earth.

Imagine solving our water resource challenges on Earth from outer space. This is SpaceTech for Good.

Marga Hoek

9 EXPLORING SPACETECH

Throughout the book thus far, we have predominantly explored technologies on, just above, and beneath the surface of planet Earth. In this chapter, however, the narrative navigates a journey to discover the possibilities for technologies in outer space and the ways in which they benefit the Earth and surrounding solar systems. Advanced space tech solutions span across technologies and come together to form a comprehensive network, many of which are already mentioned in previous chapters, such as robotics, AI, and drones. The infrastructure supporting these techs in space goes beyond our earthly applications into exciting new genres as well. Satellites in outer space, for instance, play a prominent role in improving the world today and have beneficially disrupted human endeavors, particularly in reference to science and technology.

Yet important questions arise: Why seek to explore space when numerous challenges remain unaddressed here on Earth? Why travel into outer space when our home planet's resources have yet to be fully managed and utilized? Why build satellites for space when there are so many opportunities to focus on and resources to manage here on Earth? The answer is that the world needs to explore opportunities and solutions that go beyond this stressed planet to help resolve threats here on Earth.

This chapter takes on a metaphorical concept of viewing Earth from space. It will describe the different technologies applied in space and how space tech has huge economic impact by itself. Most importantly, the following pages present space tech as an impressive force for Good throughout many business sectors. Businesses are now identifying new opportunities in space tech. This shift of paradigms, sometimes called Space 4.0, is a period that has seen changes in motivations, actors, and technologies.[5] Space 4.0 is similar to the concept of Industry 4.0 - accentuating the impact of the 4IR on manufacturing and services. Organizations that employ a combination of digital technologies, such as cloud, machine learning, and blockchain, are developing a strong competitive advantage in addition to impacting both upstream and downstream parts of the space value chain. Innovations go hand in hand with related risks and challenges. How these can be effectively addressed is considered at the end of the chapter.

THE TECH

Space technology is the application of engineering principles in the design, development, manufacturing, and operation of devices and systems for space travel and exploration. Space tech is currently used to explore other planets, study the universe, and provide communication and navigation services to support human activities.[6] This tech solution encompasses a wide range of concepts, including instruments such as satellites and human aspects of space travel including astronautics, physics, chemistry, and biology. Space tech also covers research and development of new technologies, new applications for existing technologies, and improvement of technologies for existing space systems.

THE TERM "SPACETECH" REFERS TO ANY TECHNOLOGY THAT SUPPORTS OR ENABLES TRAVEL TO SPACE OR ACTIVITIES CONDUCTED IN SPACE.[7]

With the launch of Sputnik in 1957 and the subsequent beginning of the space age, the progression of space technologies has spurred the development of numerous applications that use satellite data. Space tech also underpins scientific progress in earth and atmospheric sciences, as well as in astronomy and astrophysics. Some of the most notable contributions from the field include satellite measurements that showed the extent of the ozone layer depletion in the atmosphere.[8]

Over 2021 and 2022, many innovative companies made substantial progress in the space tech sector. Beyond the groundbreaking space tourism voyages sending wealthy billionaires into space, there are significant beneficial advances in a number of areas throughout the sector: these include rockets and launch systems; Earth observation, which has a wide variety of applications for businesses and society; small satellites for next-generation communications and sustainability efforts; and systems to defend against asteroids and clean up space debris. Rocket Lab, Relativity Space, and ABL Space Systems are companies at the forefront of the industry, finding their own novel angles in the new space tech realm. The most well-known and prolific is SpaceX, a private aerospace manufacturer founded by Elon Musk (Case 63). SpaceX continues to lead the pack of launch vehicle manufacturers, with a record number of launches last year and deliverance on its promise to get NASA and its corporate customers into orbit at a lower cost than ever before.

The historical contexts of the variety of space technologies are important to discuss, including the description of what they are, both in relation to space and other technological categories. Categories in space tech are distinguished here by infrastructure that utilizes a variety of previously mentioned technologies that create outer space-specific applications and installations. Here, there is a clear categorization of five space technology groups: spacecraft and gear for astronauts; satellites; space stations and deep-space communication; orbital launch vehicles including in-space propulsion; and a wide variety of auxiliary technologies including support infrastructure, equipment, and procedures.

SPACE VEHICLES, SUCH AS SPACECRAFT, AND GEAR FOR ASTRONAUTS

Robotic spacecrafts are specially designed and constructed systems that function in the hostile environment of outer space. With complexities and capabilities that vary greatly, their purposes are diverse and unique. NASA categorizes these space vehicles in eight broad classes of robotic spacecraft, according to the missions they are intended to perform: Flyby Spacecraft, Orbiter Spacecraft, Atmospheric Spacecraft, Lander Spacecraft, Penetrator Spacecraft, Rover Spacecraft, Observatory Spacecraft, and Communications and Navigation Spacecraft.[9]

OVER THE YEARS, MORE THAN 1,300 NASA TECH DEVELOPMENTS HAVE GONE INTO COMMERCIAL PRODUCTS.[10]

Since space can be very cold or very hot, specific gear for humans in that environment needed to be devised. Solar radiation is intense, but objects in the dark lose heat quickly. The temperature can vary by 135 degrees Celsius from one side of an object to the other. As a result, scientists at NASA have developed ways to warm, cool, and insulate people and equipment. Over the years, more than 1,300 NASA tech developments have gone into commercial products.[11] The space blanket, for example, is probably the best-known NASA product for keeping warm, and it was originally designed to protect against temperature extremes in space and used on almost all manned and unmanned NASA missions.

SATELLITES

Satellites are objects in orbits around the Earth. The idea of communications satellites came from Sir Arthur C. Clark in 1945. The first communications satellite (a simple reflector) was the U.S. Echo 1 in 1960, and the first "geosynchronous" satellite (having a period of rotation synchronous with that of the Earth's rotation), Syncom, went up in 1962. As of the December 2021 Satellite Database, experts at the Union of Concerned Scientists (UCS) list more than 4,852 operational satellites currently in orbit around Earth.[12] Satellites have become essential for modern life. Among the important applications of satellite technology are video, voice, mobile, IP data, radio, Earth and space observation, global resource monitoring, military, positioning (GPS), microgravity science, and many others. Satellites are classified by the distance of their orbits above the Earth. In 2020, 1,283 satellites were launched.[13]

AS PER DECEMBER 2021 SATELLITE DATABASE, EXPERTS AT UCS LIST MORE THAN 4,852 OPERATIONAL SATELLITES CURRENTLY IN ORBIT AROUND EARTH.[14]

Low Earth Orbiting (LEO) satellites are located at an altitude of from 100 to 1,200 miles, and Medium Earth Orbits (MEO) are located at an altitude of from 4,000 to 12,000 miles. Geo-stationary orbits are located exactly 23.4 miles high. LEO and MEO (sub-geosynchronous) orbiting satellites can communicate with the Earth by "passing off" to a fleet of like satellites, thereby providing full Earth coverage. They can also pass off to a geosynchronous relay satellite, or they can deliver data to the ground as they pass over a ground station. The top ten countries dominating the satellite industry are the United States, China, Russia, the United Kingdom, Japan, India, Luxembourg, Canada, Germany, and European Space Agency (a multinational alliance of 22 European nations). The growth in the number of satellites over the last decade was mainly driven by the development of the smaller CubeSat, which allows a large number of small-sized satellites to launch at the same time.[15]

SPACE STATIONS AND DEEP-SPACE COMMUNICATION

A space station is a large man-made spacecraft that floats and orbits in Earth's space. While small space stations can be sent to orbit fully assembled, larger space stations are sent to space in modules and assembled there. They store supplies, energy, and environmental systems that can support human habitation. Scientists and astronauts who inhabit the space stations engage in activities such as scientific experiments, maintenance, spacewalks, and social media updates. The essential task of all ground tracking stations is to communicate with spacecraft, transmitting commands and receiving scientific data and spacecraft status information. Since 1971, 12 space stations that were launched into a low orbit around Earth have been occupied for varying lengths of time. An example is the European Space Agency's tracking station network – Estrack – which is a global system of ground stations providing links between satellites in orbit and ESOC, the European Space Operations Centre, in Darmstadt, Germany.[16] The core Estrack network comprises seven stations in seven countries. In a typical year, the Estrack network provides over 15,000 hours of tracking support to 20 or more missions, with an enviable service availability rate above 99%.[17] These technically advanced stations can track spacecraft almost anywhere – circling Earth, watching the Sun, orbiting at the scientifically crucial Sun-Earth Lagrange points, or voyaging deep into our Solar System.

PER YEAR, THE ESTRACK NETWORK PROVIDES OVER 15,000 HOURS OF TRACKING SUPPORT TO 20 OR MORE MISSIONS, WITH AN ENVIABLE SERVICE AVAILABILITY RATE ABOVE 99%.[18]

Good communication is vital not only for collecting science and status data but also for navigating spacecraft through the Solar System. To navigate spacecraft, it is necessary to know their position, which is no easy feat when they are so far away. However, by measuring three parameters – distance, velocity, and the angle at which a spacecraft is located in the sky – it is possible to calculate a satellite's position down to a small box-shaped region of space. The Deep Space Network (DSN) is NASA's international array of radio antennas that support interplanetary spacecraft missions, plus a few that orbit Earth, with communication ground segment facilities. The DSN also provides radar and radio astronomy observations that improve human understanding of the solar system and the larger universe.[19] The antennas of the Deep Space Network are essential to space travel. They provide the crucial connection for commanding spacecraft and receiving their images and scientific information on Earth, all necessary for propelling human understanding of the universe, the solar system, and our place within it.

ORBITAL LAUNCH VEHICLES, INCLUDING IN-SPACE PROPULSION

Orbital launch vehicles are internally propelled vehicles used to carry payloads from Earth's surface to Earth's orbit or beyond. The payloads vary, but they can be satellites, spacecraft, or interplanetary probes. Today, orbital launch vehicles are powered by rocket engines that generate large amounts of thrust even in a vacuum by means of expelling hot gas through a nozzle. The primary function of rocket engines is to convert chemical energy to kinetic energy. There are several different styles of rocket engines that are used. However, they perform those functions in slightly different ways with slightly different architectures primarily determined by their fuel type and their fuel consumption method. Spacecraft propulsion is any method used to accelerate spacecraft and artificial satellites.

There are several different methods, but most current spacecraft are propelled by forcing gas through the rear of the vehicle at high speed through a supersonic nozzle of a rocket engine. All spacecraft use chemical rockets to launch, although some (such as Pegasus missiles and Space Ship One) use air-jet engines in the first step. Most satellites have simple chemical thrusters or missiles that resist jets to maintain orbit.[20]

IN BUSINESS

SPACEX[21]

Initiative: Starship
Headquarters: Hawthorne, California USA

SpaceX is an innovative tech company that has attained some significant milestones in the global sustainability agenda, both on Earth and in orbit. The tech company developed fully reusable spacecraft sending civilians beyond the Earth's atmosphere. Their reusable rockets, for example, allow them to simply refuel the rocket in question, aim it back at the sky, and send it right back into space (SDGs 9,12). SpaceX rockets use liquid kerosene, which is not hazardous or toxic like hypergolic propellants.[22] In the future, the company aims to use the natural gas methane as a greener alternative to rocket fuel (SDGs 7,13).

NASA chose SpaceX's Starship rocket to send humans to the moon, investing $2.9 billion in the vehicle that Elon Musk's team is developing with the goal of sending a man to Mars (SDGs 10,16).[23] Starship is built to be fully reusable and the world's most powerful launch vehicle, capable of carrying more than 100 metric tons of passengers and cargo. The rocket and satellite company became the most valuable private startup in the world in August 2022 when its valuation rose to $127 billion.[24]

MAXAR[25]

Initiative: A New Era of Space Operations
Headquarters: Westminster, Colorado USA

Maxar is a tech solutions company that partners with innovative businesses and more than 50 governments to monitor global change, deliver broadband communications, and advance space operations with capabilities in space infrastructure and Earth Intelligence (SDG 17).

In space - With more than 60 years of experience, Maxar designs and manufactures satellites and spacecraft components for communications, Earth observation, exploration, and on-orbit servicing and assembly (SDGs 9,12).

On Earth - Maxar capabilities in Earth intelligence help customers map, detect, and predict change across the globe. Fueled largely by Maxar's own constellation of high-resolution imaging satellites, the company provides high-resolution satellite imagery and data layers, machine learning, and domain knowledge so organizations can make decisions with confidence (SDGs 4,10).

Maxar's initiatives include 1300 Class, the world's most popular spacecraft platform to accommodate evolutionary advances in technology. Also relevant in the company's portfolio are satellite imagery, robotics, power and propulsion elements, and SAMPLR, the first robotic arm to return to the moon in over 50 years.

Soviet bloc satellites have used electric propulsion for decades, and the new Western geo-orbital spacecraft are also using electric propulsion for orbit maintenance of north-south. Advanced in-space propulsion technologies will enable much more effective exploration of our solar system, near and far, and will permit mission designers to plan missions to "fly anytime, anywhere, and complete a host of science objectives at the destinations" with greater reliability and safety.[26]

AUXILIARY TECHNOLOGIES

Increasing demands for global connectivity, enhanced national security, and advanced space exploration is driving commercial innovation in the space industry. There are a variety of other technologies, including support infrastructure, equipment, and procedures taking place. Businesses are providing solutions for space infrastructure, and NASA is spearheading the charge to develop new technologies for a variety of space tech solutions. NASA has selected nine space technologies under the agency's 2021 TechFlights solicitation for testing aboard parabolic aircraft, high-altitude balloons, and suborbital rocket-powered systems.[27] This $5.5 million investment in technology demonstration activities will support the advancement of a wide range of technologies that address mission needs for both NASA and the commercial space industry. These supporting technologies are selected under the Flight Opportunities program within NASA's Space Technology Mission Directorate (STMD), which develops transformative space technologies to enable future missions.[28]

INCREASING DEMANDS FOR GLOBAL CONNECTIVITY, ENHANCED NATIONAL SECURITY, AND ADVANCED SPACE EXPLORATION IS DRIVING COMMERCIAL INNOVATION.

By supporting suborbital flight testing, the Flight Opportunities program aims to help ensure that space innovations are well-positioned to address NASA's space exploration and scientific discovery goals while also supporting commercial space infrastructure. These three focus areas are: Supporting National Efforts at the Moon and in Cislunar Space, Inclusive of Human and Robotic Exploration and Scientific Discovery; Earth-Observing Capabilities to Support Breakthrough Science and National Efforts to Address Climate Change; Technologies that Ensure National Leadership in Space and Help the Commercial Space Industry Grow.

Beyond NASA's ongoing efforts, startups of varying degrees of funding are emerging to provide things like life support systems, crew habitats, device connectivity, satellite traffic management, and food solutions. These types of technologies are crucial to space commercialization efforts. There are a number of business applications supporting the space tech industry. Maxar, a space infrastructure company, is leveraging its capabilities to continue redefining what's possible in space with innovations both on earth and in outer space. Maxar supports commercial and government missions with Space Infrastructure capabilities (Case 25).

SPACETECH MARKET SIZE

The space tech industry encompasses a wide variety of spheres. From companies that study propulsion and manufacture engines to entities that develop medicine for astronauts, the industry is made up of businesses that both only produce specific materials and those that design software and hardware for the launch vehicles. Space tech is a broad industry, and there are many companies that work with space-related technologies, yet not all of these reach the scale of space exploration. However, there is a significant number of companies of many different genres that are important in the space frontier and have large market capitalizations and investments. Together, telecom, internet, finance, and all other industries leveraging satellites are worth $10 trillion.[29] The range of companies across the spectrum goes from fully manufacturing unmanned and/or manned launch vehicles that carry the payload to different levels of Earth's orbit to leading companies that manufacture the crucial parts of the launch vehicles.

TOGETHER, TELECOM, INTERNET, FINANCE, AND ALL OTHER INDUSTRIES LEVERAGING SATELLITES ARE WORTH $10 TRILLION.[30]

In 2021, the global space market was valued at $388.5 billion and is expected to reach $540.75 billion by 2026.[31] The sector expanded by an impressive 70% between 2010 and 2020. The space economy is expected to grow at a CAGR of 6.84% between 2022 and 2026. The fastest growth is predicted to stem from new space applications and industries. Innovation in space continues to soar as investment pours into the sector. In the decade leading into 2021, $178 billion in investment flowed into the space economy.[32] And in 2021, investment reached $14.5 billion for space infrastructure companies.[33] This amount includes a record-setting fourth quarter for the year, which brought in $4.3 billion due to $250 million by Sierra Space, SpaceX, and Planet Labs.[34] Space-related companies received $17.1 billion in venture capital in 2021, which was up 3% of total global venture capital investment for the year.

THE GLOBAL SPACE SYSTEMS, SATELLITES, AND LAUNCHERS MARKET SIZE IS ESTIMATED TO GROW FROM $32.9 BILLION IN 2020 AND TO $64.72 BILLION IN 2026.[35]

Space as an investment theme is also likely to impact a number of industries beyond aerospace and defense, such as the IT hardware and telecom sectors. It is estimated that the global space industry could generate revenue of more than $1 trillion in 2040, up from $350 billion in 2020.[36] Estimates predict that satellite broadband will represent 50% of the projected growth of the global space economy by 2040, and this could be as much as 70% in the most optimistic scenario. Further, Partnerships with investment companies have allowed space sector players to accelerate the development of their corporate venture arms, while also improving their ability to move quickly on promising investment opportunities. For example, the aerospace private-investment company AE Industrial Partners partnered with Boeing to manage HorizonX, Boeing's venture capital fund, in July 2022 with the goal of raising $250 million to invest in promising start-ups in digital enterprise applications, future mobility, networks, security, space, and sustainability.[37]

The space tech financial services sector is the largest in the space tech Industry, valued at $4.75 billion.[38] In-orbit satellite services (IoS) have cumulative revenues of $6.2 billion by 2030.[39] The IoS Market will see more commercial players using the various services over the next decade generating 63% of global cumulative demand. Growth in satellite constellations greatly increases the addressable market in Non-GEO, where services will focus mostly on de-orbiting and space situational awareness (SSA). NSR's latest report forecasts both ground and space-based SSA revenues to represent a cumulative revenue opportunity of over $1B through the next decade.[40]

THE GLOBAL SPACE PROPULSION MARKET IS PROJECTED TO GROW FROM $6.7 BILLION IN 2020 TO $14.2 BILLION BY 2025, AT A CAGR OF 16.2% DURING THAT TIME PERIOD.[41]

The space economy is seeing the growth of jobs in various areas. Today, the number of jobs in the space sector is estimated to be around 400,000, but that number is forecast to skyrocket to 1.5 million jobs in the future.[42] Workers are needed in accounting, marketing, design, IT, manufacturing, and STEM. Launch services in the United States alone rely on advanced manufacturing, which is the source of 40% of all commercial launches, more than any other country in the world. That brings more than $2 billion per year in revenues to US manufacturing industries.

Space-related technologies are being developed at a rapid rate. The launch vehicle, satellite, propulsion, manufacturing, and other technologies are behind some of the most prominent companies in space tech innovation. Several countries are planning their Mars colonization projects, and others have a clear vision of lunar scientific stations. Space tourism has also become a viable possibility and is increasingly more accessible. Tech support for market investments is gaining traction as well. SpaceTech Analytics (STA) is a leading strategic and analytical agency focused on emerging markets in Satellite Technology, Advanced Startups, Space Law, Economics, and other industries of space tech (Case 65).

$68 billion total early-stage space tech investments in 2021.[43]	**$6.2** billion 2030 estimate of in-orbit satellite services cumulative revenues.[44]	Market expansion will drive total value of space tech sector to **$10** trillion by 2030.[45]

IN BUSINESS

SPACETECH ANALYTICS[46]

Initiative: Strategic analytics agency focused on markets in space tech
Headquarters: London, United Kingdom

SpaceTech Analytics is a strategic analytics agency focused on markets in the space exploration, spaceflight, space medicine, and satellite tech industries. The range of activities includes research and analysis on major areas of high potential in the space tech industry, maintaining profiling of companies and government agencies based on their innovation potential and business activity, and providing consulting and analytical services to advance the space technology industry (SDGs 8,9). The think tank's reports deliver information about major industry trends and sector insights on over 350 space tech publicly traded companies and 700 investors.[47] It estimates the space industry will grow by $10 trillion in the next decade.

SpaceTech Analytics is a strategic partner to the leading space tech organizations, investment institutions (VC funds and investment banks), and governments across the globe — in matters related to investments, strategic positioning, and policy development in the areas of space tech research (SDGs 12,17). SpaceTech Analytics regularly produces open industry reports covering high-growth sectors in the industry, including spaceflights, satellite technologies, space exploration, and new space discoveries (SDGs 10,16).

SPACETECH FOR GOOD

As the new space economy develops, it increasingly overlaps with sustainability in areas such as Earth observation, energy, and communications. These developing technologies from both public and private companies may soon become a new avenue for investors interested in pursuing both sustainability and investor returns. Many sustainability-oriented projects across industries employ space-based technologies and services to contribute to sustainability efforts and the Global Goals. Among others, satellite-based Earth observation, positioning, navigation, and communication services are used in an array of sectors ranging from monitoring environmental conditions and changes to supporting search and rescue missions.

MANY SUSTAINABILITY-ORIENTED PROJECTS ACROSS INDUSTRIES EMPLOY SPACE-BASED TECHNOLOGIES AND SERVICES, TO CONTRIBUTE TO THE GLOBAL GOALS.

The United Nations recognizes the role of Earth observation and geolocation provided by Global Navigation Satellite Systems (GNSS) in supporting the achievement of the SDGs.[48] Orbiting in space, Earth observation satellites equipped with specialized sensors provide data on vast and remote areas of the Earth, thereby improving our knowledge of the atmosphere, land, oceans, ice extent, and ecosystems. Geolocation and, in particular, GNSS, is used to incorporate position information into data and provide location-based services to both humans and machines (e.g., drones or self-driving cars). In addition to Earth observation and GNSS that are mentioned specifically in the 2030 Agenda for Sustainable Development, an array of equally important space-based technologies, such as satellite telecommunications (SatCom), already contribute to several SDGs and associated Targets.[49]

Space tech applications, such as satellite technology and space exploration, offer exciting potentials and new opportunities to assess and address climate change and sustainability on a global scale. In the coming years, these technologies could enable humankind to have a more powerful global view of climate data. Those insights, in turn, can help enable the deeper integration of sustainability considerations into investment decisions. Current research from Morgan Stanley shows that sustainability may be one of the most prosperous and underappreciated subdomains of the emerging space economy.[50] Space and sustainability efforts are increasingly predicted to align by way of innovative applications of satellite technology and the many data that space infrastructure will produce over time.

SATELLITES SUPPORT NUMEROUS VITAL SERVICES ON EARTH (E.G., WEATHER FORECASTING, NAVIGATION, COMMUNICATION, ETC.) THAT CAN ONLY BE MAINTAINED BY ENSURING ORBITAL SUSTAINABILITY.[51]

From a data perspective, satellite technology and remote sensing introduces real-time, high-frequency tracking of relevant environmental degradation. Remote sensing via satellites, particularly on a daily basis, could reduce delays in the collection and analysis of key sustainability data points that financial markets increasingly rely on. The plethora of data collected from space, and the associated geospatial analytics, could be the key to reorienting market perspectives on how to approach sustainable finance in the coming years.

Satellite communications, in particular, are increasingly relevant to global challenges. Benefits of this tech solution are widespread and span across development sectors. A few examples include improving people's lives by helping relief agencies and first responders get information in and out of disaster zones; reducing illegal fishing and improving safety and livelihood security; and increasing connectivity to provide better access to health care providers for patients in remote and rural areas. Tech company Inmarsat, the leading provider of global mobile satellite communications services, delivers solutions for maritime safety and distress.[52] Inmarsat aims to help the world by focusing its business services on the SDGs and addressing the role satellite technology plays in global progress. As part of the UK Space Agency's International Partnership Programme, which co-funds UK-based operators tackling environmental and social challenges in developing countries, Inmarsat is deploying satellite communications equipment in pilot regions to help maintain communication in the case of an earthquake or other natural disasters.

Predicting climate patterns is an imported application in space technology for Good. Earth-imaging technology as a business proposition is gaining traction, and several space tech companies are employing the tech to capture data for effective strategies to combat imminent environmental threats. Pixxel, an Indian earth-imaging space technology startup, uses hyperspectral imaging satellites designed to beam down data in hundreds of wavelengths to detect problems that are invisible to today's more traditional satellites (Case 50). This space tech solution is on a mission to build a health monitor for the planet.

SPACETECH PROGRESSING THE GLOBAL GOALS

The United Nations acknowledges the importance of space-based technologies to be crucial in understanding climate change and during the full disaster management cycle.[53] Not only does space tech help to address these environmental and social impacts, but it also creates business value and offers unprecedented opportunities for businesses to do good while also building a competitive advantage. Space technologies have positive impacts on every single SDG.

The space tech sector adds immense value to life on Earth. Satellites that circle the globe provide the most accurate weather reports and warn us of impending storms. They monitor our climate every day by tracking increasing temperature and the effects, such as rising seas and changing moisture levels, wildfires, and atmospheric conditions. They also connect millions of people and have the ability to connect billions more who currently lack access in rural areas, help us see and stop illegal fishing and deforestation, and ensure transparency and security of states by monitoring and verifying actors' behaviors. Scientific research that takes place in orbit is helping to push the frontiers of human understanding of health and material science, robotics, and other technologies.

ZERO HUNGER

Space technologies can be vital in agricultural innovation, modern agriculture, and precision agriculture. The lower costs of geospatial information technology facilities have stimulated the adoption of space technologies worldwide, particularly in developing countries, through initiatives such as Open Data Cube.[54] Space-based technologies offer tools to help in a wide spectrum of agricultural activities, ranging from monitoring crops, livestock, and forestry to fisheries and aquaculture.[55] They are essential for supporting farmers, fisheries, foresters, and policymakers in the decision-making process by enabling a timely and effective response to adverse weather conditions, land degradation, vegetation fires, and disasters triggered by natural phenomena.

Satellite imagery plays a very pertinent role in agriculture and is a vital component of "smart farming," which integrates a precision agricultural system using spectral bands that develop a vegetative index representing crop vigor. WEO, a Luxembourg-based startup, enables environment management by analyzing earth observation data. The startup utilizes AI-powered radar along with optical and thermal imaging sensors aboard satellites to build an accurate map of vital soil characteristics across a broad area at a low cost.[56] WEO assists farmers and the agricultural sector by providing insights into industrial and governmental concerns such as sustainable agriculture, climate change, water resource management, and soil health.

IN BUSINESS
PIXXEL[57]

Initiative: Hyperspectral imagery for targeted monitoring
Headquarters: Bengaluru, Karnataka, India

Pixxel is a space data company building a constellation of hyperspectral earth imaging satellites and the analytical tools to mine insights from that data (SDG 9). The constellation is designed to provide global coverage every 24 hours. It detects, monitors, and predicts global phenomena. Hyperspectral imaging (HSI) is a technique that analyzes a wide spectrum of light instead of just assigning primary colors (red, green, blue) to each pixel. The collected spectra are used to form an image in a way that each image pixel includes a complete spectrum. Pixxel's hyperspectral imaging satellites are uniquely designed to beam down 50 times more data than existing multispectral satellites. Through this technology, the satellites enable the detection and monitoring of ground-level phenomena that had previously remained unseen.[58]

The company's impactful solutions include:

Agriculture – The tech covers large areas daily with up-to-date data across the entire season to monitor crop health, detect variations, and improve yields (SDGs 1,3).

Environment – Pixxel's HSI maps and monitors forest cover and deforestation (SDG 15). Regarding the environment, the satellites measure climate risks such as flooding and wildfires (SDG 13). By tracking natural capital utilization, Pixxel assesses water resources and gives insights based on data for sustainability management (SDG 6).

Energy – This unique technology is simple, affordable, and precise for energy surveying and extracting (SDG 7). Pixxel's energy solutions monitor the state of vegetation stress near oil and gas pipelines, as well as quantify pollution stress levels due to pipeline leakages. In 2022, Pixxel raised $25 million to launch this constellation of satellites to monitor a wider view of the electromagnetic spectrum that can reveal all kinds of details not visible to ordinary cameras. "The quality of our data is the best — and a bonus is we're doing it in a much more inexpensive way," said Founder and CEO Awais Ahmed.

GOOD HEALTH AND WELLBEING

In recent years, space-based technologies have played a growing role in furthering global health objectives. Information from remote-sensing technologies is used to monitor disease patterns, understand environmental triggers for the spread of diseases, predict risk areas, and define regions that require disease-control planning. For example, a malaria early warning system based on geospatial data is responsible for 500,000 fewer new cases in 28 countries.[59] In addition, the World Health Organization uses digital elevation models provided by the Japan Aerospace Exploration Agency to map difficult-to-access areas to implement efficient measures for infectious diseases, such as polio in Niger.[60]

Some startups are exploring the potential of space to develop the "factories of the future" for pharmaceutical products and medicines. There are already two startups focusing on this aspect - Varda Space and Space Forge. Varda Space is building what it claims to be "the world's first commercial zero-gravity industrial park at scale" to produce pharmaceuticals, among other things.[61] Space Forge is planning to launch a pioneering autonomous manufacturing facility that could produce medicines in orbit.[62] They have both raised significant amounts of money despite being in their early stages of growth ($11 million for Space Forge and $51 million for Varda Space).[63]

GENDER EQUALITY

The growth of the space sector encourages women to pursue STEM education and develop the required skills to access the meaningful employment and the leadership opportunities it provides. The UN's Space4Women project helps empower women in space and STEM by creating an online mentoring platform to network with experienced "Space4Women Champions."[64] Space4Women provides policy-relevant advice, knowledge management, and evidence-based awareness raising, research, and data to institutions and governments to implement programs supporting "space for women" and "women for space." The African Astronomical Society established the African Network of Women in Astronomy (AfNWA) to guarantee female participation at all levels of the new and important developments within the space industry.[65]

Anza Capital is a female-led investment firm that is addressing the funding gap for early-stage businesses with a focus on gender-inclusive tech businesses in Southern Africa.[66] The firm aims to unlock the immense potential of African tech entrepreneurs to create impact and prosperity on the continent. It is a very inclusive startup fund that targets diverse industry sectors, including space tech, with a 50% female founder focus.[67]

CLEAN WATER AND SANITATION

Space tech is leveraged to improve investigations into the global water cycles, map watercourses, and build early warning systems to mitigate the effects of floods, landslides, storms, and droughts. The UN partnered with the Prince Sultan bin Abdul Aziz International Prize for Water (PSIPW) in 2018 to promote the use of space-based technology for increased access to water.[68] This collaboration led to the establishment of a Space4Water Project, which is a unique online platform that brings together space and water experts to share knowledge and resources. The project has helped to create an enabling environment for leveraging space technologies and space-based solutions to improve water management, monitor SDGs and indicators directly or indirectly linked to water, facilitate improved water use and water resource sharing globally, and assist in related disaster management.

Satellite-based sensors are able to effectively measure nearly all the direct and indirect components of the hydrological cycle. These advancements range from spatial resolution to enhanced opportunities in the data collection of both water quality and availability.[69] Not only does the tech manage water resources on earth, but it also enables sustainable use of water in space. Japanese startup Pale Blue provides sustainability in fuel usage by adopting water as the propellant for space mobility.[70] The startup uses patented electron cyclotron resonance technology to generate water plasma, which is the power source for its satellite thrusters. Pale Blue's thrusters provide satellites of many types and sizes with non-toxic, sustainable, and affordable space mobility solutions to satellite manufacturers.

AFFORDABLE AND CLEAN ENERGY

Satellites can be used to collect solar energy so that it can be distributed for use all over the world. Solar power satellites, otherwise known as powersats, orbit the earth and are designed to capture solar energy and transmit that energy to receiving stations that are situated thousands of miles from each other on the surface of the Earth.[71] These satellites are made up of a number of modules outfitted with lightweight photovoltaic solar panels. Additionally, technologies such as solar panels for spacecraft where solar radiation is enough to power the on-board instruments have applications on Earth where they have been used to power unmanned facilities. Moreover, the quality of solar energy forecasts can be improved by 30% using space technology.[72] Norwegian startup Solstorm enables hybrid propulsion.[73] Its propulsion system, Magbreak, does not use external engines, propellants, or internal supply for propulsion.[74] It converts energy from solar wind to propel satellites, rockets, and other space transport. Magbreak deploys and generates a magnetic field by harnessing power from the ionosphere. The field induces electromagnetic drag that de-orbits and disposes of dead satellites after their mission is complete. This minimizes space debris and enables a sustained presence in space.

INDUSTRY, INNOVATION AND INFRASTRUCTURE

Global navigation satellite systems (GNSS) contribute to the construction of buildings and city infrastructure. The use of GNSS for machine control, for example, automates construction activities by controlling the blades and buckets of construction equipment based on information provided by 3D design. It increases the speed by more than 50% relative to non-automated machines and reduces resource consumption by 9%.[75] Other applications include topographic surveys of construction sites and subsequent infrastructure monitoring. Satellite technologies are well placed for the delivery of broadband services in hard-to-reach areas either on their own or in combination with other technologies and existing infrastructure. Satellite communications can help connect the 49% of the world's currently unconnected population and extend the reach of terrestrial networks enabling 5G on a global scale.[76] For example, Bangladesh has recently launched a telecommunications satellite that is also broadcasting television and radio programs and will soon provide Internet, telemedicine, and distance-learning facilities for people in remote areas.

There has been a 15-fold growth over a decade in the number of space start-ups, thereby driving innovative products and services.[77] US-based startup Leviathan Space Industries is developing a space station network.[78] The network consists of 14 space stations and uses artificial gravity to advance space travel, trade, and tourism. In addition, Leviathan leverages a spaceport on the equatorial line to maximize launch vehicle fuel savings and payload maximization. Its infrastructure thus enables a sustainable ecosystem for safe and democratic space exploration.

SUSTAINABLE CITIES AND COMMUNITIES

Earth Observation and GNSS data support urban mapping and infrastructure monitoring to help plan and manage city services and structures. Space tech satellite create smarter, more sustainable cities by optimizing traffic management, reducing energy consumption, improving urban mobility, and monitoring air pollution. Over 5 billion mobile phones now have satellite chips for mapping, traffic routing, tracking, and logistics.[79] The role of space science in urban planning and housing is important. Satellite imagery has provided a great platform for town planners to analyze and draft plans for appropriate housing.

A pioneering United Kingdom start-up is using satellite technology to transform 3D urban models for towns and cities, thereby making the urban planning process more accessible, efficient, and collaborative. Start-up company Digital Urban is elevating 3D digital modeling capabilities with the help of satellite technology.[80] It uses data and optical imagery generated by an Earth observation satellite to develop a cloud-based platform that provides a more accessible way of developing and managing interactive 3D urban models. Digital Urban is part of the recently launched northwest space cluster funded by the UK Space Agency and led by the Science and Technology Facilities Council's Daresbury Laboratory.[81] This major multi-partner project was set up to enable northwest businesses to play a more significant role in the rapidly expanding multi-billion-pound United Kingdom space sector.[82]

RESPONSIBLE CONSUMPTION AND PRODUCTION

Earth observation is an essential tool for managing natural resources and the environment. It is highly relevant for both achieving the Goals and monitoring progress.[83] This space tech solution provides information to support agricultural production, fisheries, freshwater, and forestry management and can also help monitor activities harmful to the environment such as fires, illegal logging, mining, and poaching. In space, there are several applications that address responsible consumption and production. For example, 93% of the water onboard the International Space Station is reclaimed.[84] Also, currently 40% of the oxygen in the International Space Station is recycled, but NASA is researching technologies to increase that rate to 75%. Asteroid mining to extract minerals such as platinum, gold, iron, or even water by private individuals and companies is also on the rise through advancements in space cameras and satellites that assist in identifying the precise location of asteroids. The economic incentive for space mining is vast and it is predicted to potentially translate into a billion-dollar industry. There has already been an 80% reduction in the manufacturing cost of satellites since 2013.[85]

Australian mining startup High Earth Orbit Robotics combines intelligent control with space-based cameras to acquire high-quality imagery of satellites, space debris, and resource-rich asteroids.[86] This imagery is then useful for locating and observing asteroids for sustainable mining. The startup builds small satellites that operate in high-earth orbit to observe celestial bodies. Totum Labs, the satellite connectivity startup, developed a novel Doppler Multichannel Spread Spectrum. This space tech solution introduced a global tracking chip that can monitor anything anywhere in the world, both indoors and outdoors. With a combination of worldwide satellite reach and indoor coverage, Totum offers a unique connectivity option for supply-chain monitoring, transportation, agriculture, and other markets.[87]

CLIMATE ACTION

Climate action is addressed by companies and governments that use satellites and spectroscopy for greenhouse-gas monitoring. They monitor emissions data, thereby helping to detect CO_2 emissions and natural-gas leaks from a range of sources including oil wells, landfills, industrial operations, and farms. In response to climate change challenges, the UN is working with key partners from the space, earth observation, civil protection communities, and regional and international organizations to launch the Global Partnership using space-based technology applications for disaster risk reduction.[88] This partnership, entitled GP-STAR, aims to promote the adoption of space-based technology applications including Earth observation, global navigation satellite systems, and satellite telecommunications for Disaster Risk Reduction in accordance with the Sendai Framework for Disaster Risk Reduction. By strengthening existing mechanisms and expanding the use of Earth Observation and relevant space-based technologies at all levels, GP-STAR will contribute to a better integrated and wider use of such technologies in disaster risk reduction worldwide. Over 99% of accurate weather forecasts come from space technologies in outer space, and over 50% of essential climate variables can only be measured from space.[89]

Canadian company GHGSat states that it operates the world's only fleet of satellites that can detect greenhouse gas emissions from space and determine the exact facility from which the emissions have leaked.[90] In 2021, GHGSat detected large methane leaks from landfills in Dhaka, Bangladesh, and Madrid and eight natural gas pipelines in Turkmenistan. Subsequently, the Canadian government announced that it would be contributing the first high-resolution satellite dataset to the International Methane Emissions Observatory based on GHGSat's findings. The climate-focused company currently has three satellites in orbit and plans to have a fleet of ten commercial satellites in space by the end of 2022.[91] Over 99% of accurate weather forecasts come from space technologies in outer space, and over 50% of essential climate variables can only be measured from space.[92]

LIFE BELOW WATER

Advanced GNSS is used to monitor compliance with fishery regulations and the effect of protection policies (such as fishery or navigation limitations) on the marine environment. Focusing on improved productivity, Earth observation satellites collect data on different parameters to help identify the most productive areas, thereby allowing for more effective catches. Regarding the detection of illegal fishing, Earth observation satellites can be used to identify illegal fishing activities with high accuracy through radar imagery.[93] These data provide critical information to the fishing authorities about the location, speed, and course of fishing vessels operating, therefore allowing authorities to detect and track movement and activity in restricted fishing grounds. Satellites help stop illegal logging, fishing, and wildlife trade that accounts for over $73 billion per year.[94]

New Zealand-based space technology start-up Xerra Earth Observation Institute launched its Starboard Maritime Intelligence in mid-2021 and has recently secured its first international contract with the Australian Fisheries Management Authority.[95] Starboard's space tech solution targets fishing in regions of Australian intelligence interest. Specifically, the initiative uses satellite data and advanced analytics models to track vessel behaviors, including identifying when vessels are fishing or when vessels meet at sea to transport fish, fuel, crew, or supplies. The tech is reducing the time users spend on data collection and enabling them to share their expertise more readily, thereby making compliance and inspection activity more effective. Starboard supports governments, border security teams, NGOs, and fishery organizations to navigate the vast amounts of maritime data available from satellite sensors – including around 35 million ship positions every day – and to focus on the vessels that matter to them.[96]

ZERO HUNGER

- Optimize crop productivity through an informed management process and increase efficiency in the use of existing resources.
- Improve livestock management through enhanced monitoring and identification of suitable grazing.

GOOD HEALTH AND WELLBEING

- Study disease epidemiology by enabling increased use of spatial analysis to identify ecological, environmental, and other factors that contribute to the spread of diseases.
- Monitor factors that affect human health and wellbeing like air quality and traffic.

GENDER EQUALITY

- Allow access to quality education even in remote and isolated communities.
- Support female entrepreneurship through access to training, information, and safety in the work environment.
- Offer career development opportunities, specifically within STEM.

CLEAN WATER AND SANITATION

- Integrate GIS and remote sensing for evaluating, managing, and monitoring water resources.
- Address water infrastructure challenges using Earth observation satellite data.
- Utilize water as fuel for spacecraft and other space tech innovations.

AFFORDABLE AND CLEAN ENERGY

- Provide infrastructure monitoring, particularly with regards to energy networks.
- Facilitate power grid synchronization, seismic surveying, and other space monitoring for energy production purposes.
- Identify optimal sites to produce renewable energy; solar and wind energy production forecasting to estimate the energy needed from other sources.

INDUSTRY, INNOVATION AND INFRASTRUCTURE

- Augment satellite-based infrastructure mapping and monitoring, including maintenance of road infrastructure in rural environments.
- Enhance construction surveying on Earth through machine automation; build advanced telecommunications networks with space tech-enabled systems.

SUSTAINABLE CITIES AND COMMUNITIES

- Pinpoint structures and reference points for urban planning purposes via space tech applications.
- Apply GNSS, Earth observation, and satellite telecommunications for smart cities.
- Improve city services such as smart waste management systems, quality monitoring, disaster management, infrastructure monitoring, and search and rescue operations.

SPACETECH

RESPONSIBLE CONSUMPTION AND PRODUCTION

- Manage natural resources, food, and dangerous goods traceability through satellite imaging.
- Monitor smart agriculture by combining Earth observation, satellite telecommunications, and GNSS.

LIFE BELOW WATER

- Map and monitor natural and protected aquatic areas, including fishing vessel tracking and navigation.
- Trace fishery products (endangered species, exploitation of fishery resources); assess and monitor marine and coastal resources through satellite imaging.
- Monitor climate change impacts via remote sensing, particularly water temperature.

CLIMATE ACTION

- Monitor climate change through space tech-enabled weather forecasting.
- Manage disasters and global warming effects by detecting greenhouse gas emissions from space.

ENHANCING BUSINESS MODELS

Beyond exploration, space tech enables commercial and governmental endeavors conducted in space, from communications to scientific experiments. This technology, and its numerous systems, have far-reaching business applications with a profound impact on our daily lives. Examples include meteorological satellites that allow scientists to predict and track global weather patterns and geolocation technologies that are embedded in almost all our electronics. The democratization of space is a growing phenomenon involving the introduction of new actors and business opportunities. Today, space is the ecosystem providing a background for countless enterprising ideas and business startups. Companies of all sizes are using outer space to do business on Earth, as it enables them to offer new services or generate key data for processing and commercialization purposes.

Space tech activities have undoubtedly enlarged our economic sphere, which now extends into space, including the low Earth orbit up to geostationary distances. Recently private initiatives have been launched to extend the economic sphere even further, reaching to the Moon, asteroids, and all the way to Mars. This relies on space exploration which drives the development of new technologies and capabilities (e.g., heavy-lift launchers, human and robotic servicing, and autonomous space operations).[97] By developing reliable space exploration systems that incorporate human decision making, troubleshooting, and flexibility, possibilities are created for enhancing the economic development of space driven by private sector investments (e.g., new means to service in space infrastructure for applications and science purposes).

"INVESTMENT IN SPACE BASED ENDEAVORS IS BECOMING SUFFICIENTLY ATTRACTIVE TO PRIVATE ENTREPRENEURS."[98]

Space tech includes a broad range of activities in low orbit, high orbit, and outer space and is seen as essential to unlocking new growth in wireless telecommunications, autonomous mobility, commercial space exploration, and national defense.[99] The space economy is highly diverse, and the number of companies developing technology in support of space exploration, commercialization, habitation, and defense is growing. Businesses whose specialization is space technology are receiving more late-stage venture capital and increasingly going public, while those existing and established entities in the aerospace and defense industry are simultaneously making significant investments in space tech.[100]

Long-term strategists look to space for population expansion and risk mitigation. A human presence in space, on the moon and then on Mars, is built into NASA's current priorities. Private sector businesses are working to enable humans to live in space. SpaceX CEO Elon Musk stated in 2020 that he is "highly confident" that humans will land on Mars by 2026.[101] While permanent human habitation in space may seem a distant future, the pace of space tech advancement is a rapidly accelerating business. Companies such as SpaceX are developing reusable launch vehicles to further reduce the cost of launching rockets into space. Not only is this expanding the commercial space tech sector by making space travel more accessible, but it is also creating new business models across industries.

The space industry is utilizing several advanced and emerging technologies - including 5G, satellite systems, 3D printing, AI and big data, blockchain, robotics, and quantum computing - to advance and scale operations in space. Many services, such as weather forecasting, remote sensing, GPS navigation, satellite television, and long-distance communication, rely on space infrastructure. As we look farther away from planet Earth, space tech trends such as smart propulsion, space robotics, and space traffic management are also gaining traction in the space industry. Together with increasing government and private investment in the industry, businesses and startups are developing technologies to ease movement, operations, and communications between earth and space.

IN BUSINESS

SPEQTRAL[102]

Initiative: Quantum Key Distribution (QKD) SpeQtral-1 satellite mission in space
Headquarters: Singapore
Case applied in: Singapore, Space

SpeQtral is an emerging leader in quantum-secure communication systems. The company's mission is to deliver tamper-proof and computationally uncrackable encryption keys within and across global communications networks, thereby securing data against present and future threats brought on by advances in computing (SDGs 10,12,16). Specifically, SpeQtral is reinventing cryptography for the quantum age by using satellites in low earth orbit to secure data networks across the globe. SpeQtral's QKD technology solution is an important element in building global quantum-secure communication networks. QKD uses quantum physics, as opposed to current mathematically based encryption technologies, to distribute symmetric encryption keys that can be used to secure communication networks. The SpeQtral-1 satellite is expected to be launched in 2024 and is projected to be one of the first few QKD satellite missions to be launched by a commercial entity. It will demonstrate the technological feasibility of intercontinental communications delivery with a focus on addressing the practical commercial requirements of end-users (SDGs 9,11).[103] SpeQtral will work with local and international partners in executing the vision to realize global QKD (SDG 17). These partnerships include the Centre for Quantum Technologies at the National University of Singapore and the European Space Agency, with the participation of a consortium of European entities in establishing a Singapore-Europe QKD link.

Startups and scaleups are quickly emerging onto the space tech business scene with new ideas and applications. These tech innovators are building small satellites like CubeSats and NanoSats to reduce launching costs.[104] Fast and secure communications using satellites incorporate advancements in hardware like antennae, transmitters, and receivers. With an expected growth in space traffic, startups are creating feasible solutions for space travel and traffic management, as well as junk and debris removal. Space tech business models generally focus on the future of space business and digital transformation for space business.[105]

SPACEX CEO ELON MUSK STATED IN 2020 THAT HE IS "HIGHLY CONFIDENT" THAT HUMANS WILL LAND ON MARS BY 2026.[106]

Quantum space data science is one aspect of the tech that holds the promise of disrupting digital communications markets by operating computing functions millions of times faster than conventional computers. Distributed quantum sensors, those that are capable of obtaining highly sensitive and accurate gravity measurements, may lead to new understandings of Earth and our place in the universe by measuring minute changes in gravity.[107] In order for quantum computers or quantum sensors to communicate, however, they will require a dedicated communications network. Advances in quantum technologies are giving rise to a revolution in future disruptive technological applications of quantum physics. The space-based environment may open many new avenues for exploring and employing quantum physics and technologies.[108]

Recently, space tech players of all sizes are participating in the realm of quantum communications as a business model. As NASA launches more frequent and complex missions into space, managing communications with the growing number of spacecrafts is becoming increasingly challenging. Microsoft's Azure Quantum team has partnered with NASA's Jet Propulsion Laboratory to develop a system to communicate more efficiently with spacecrafts.[109] SpeQtral, a Singapore-based company in quantum-secure communication systems, is an innovative space tech company that is designing and manufacturing satellite-based quantum communication systems (Case 67).

Also emerging in business is the connection between space tech and blockchain. The ways these industries could connect and integrate with each other are numerous, starting with the tokenizing of space assets, supply chain applications, and many others like security, data, financing, and sustainability issues.[110] As blockchain moves into outer space, its ability to tokenize spacecraft and payloads could help in large upcoming space projects such as the international, collaborative Gateway space station NASA wants to build in lunar orbit.[111] The application of blockchain in space is a growing trend and the leaders in the industry are represented by a fairly limited number of companies. Blockchain offers possibilities for space tech innovations to further optimize and improve the industry, with several cases of space tech companies applying blockchain technology as a sustainability measure.

Blockchain can be used effectively along with geospatial technologies in IoT applications. As technologies and data collection and processing become more complicated, blockchain provides a secure way to collect and process geospatial and satellite data. XYO Network is the world's first blockchain geospatial network backed with cryptography that anonymously collects and validates data with a geographic component. XYO calls itself the Reality Oracle, a technology protocol designed to improve the validity, certainty, and value of data. It is seeking to build a data marketplace that gives users more control and understanding of any apps, websites, and blockchain technologies that rely on trusted data.

IN BUSINESS

XYO[112]

Initiative: World's first Reality Oracle
Headquarters: San Diego, California USA
Case applied in: California, USA

XYO calls itself the world's first Reality Oracle, which empowers people to participate in the global data economy through the validation of anonymous and secure geospatial data. XYO harnesses the power of data to address real-world challenges in various scenarios that help businesses gain competitive advantage and consumers make smart spending choices (SDGs 10,12). XYO's parent company XY Labs provides a connection between the real and digital worlds through blockchain, IoT, and data-focused products that the business leverages to "make human lives easier" (SDG 3,11).[113] For example, the company's COIN App empowers its over three million users to be rewarded for validating geospatial location and other data.[114]

XYO, the link between hyper location and blockchain, is a decentralized network of devices anonymously collecting and validating data associated with geography, temperature, humidity, and even speed, among other components. While the nature of geospatial data has been historically complex and cumbersome to leverage, XYO's advancements in the area, along with industry collaborations, are allowing commercial enterprises to tap into and harness this information in new and innovative ways (SDGs 8,9). Markus Levin, the Co-Founder of XYO Network, articulates, "We believe most people don't fully understand the power and value of the data they generate every single day. XYO educates users about that power by encouraging them to harness it."[115]

XYO is partnering with HERE Technologies, a location solutions company.[116] As leaders in location technology, the collaboration represents an opportunity to expand the availability of secure, verified geospatial data and to bridge real-world location data with blockchain-based smart contracts (SDG 17).

GLOBAL GOALS' GROWTH OPPORTUNITIES

Space tech businesses focused on sustainable growth, those both more established and in the startup phase, seek to provide value to the environment and humanity. Today, as commercialization for space tech grows with players like Blue Origin and SpaceX sending people beyond Earth's atmosphere, this next frontier is part of a new generation of entrepreneurs who see space sustainability as a necessity of existence. Meanwhile, legacy space and satellite enterprises have recommitted their business models to sustainability through both investments and innovations in the areas of space debris removal, space situational awareness, and space traffic management. These range from the development of Northrop Grumman's Mission Extension Vehicles (MEV),[117] which have provided refueling services for Intelsat GEO satellites, to the endeavors of communications leaders like OneWeb,[118] which installed Astroscale's next-generation ferromagnetic docking plate to its satellites to enable more efficient servicing.

Meanwhile, space tech applications here on Earth are presenting exciting growth opportunities as well. There are many aspects behind the anticipated geospatial industry growth. Governments use GIS for city planning and public health initiatives, while companies utilize spatial tools to evaluate demographics and markets. Further, the evolution of geospatial technology is fueling GIS business opportunities and making new careers possible. Fresh approaches to spatial problem-solving have emerged out of innovations such as LiDAR and cloud storage. Space tech startups and innovative companies are employing sustainable business models, while at the same time addressing multiple sectors and aspects of the industry. Alén Space is a tech startup developing space infrastructure in a small-scale size (Case 69). Not only does the company manage data through nanosatellite technology, but it also expands its business proposition and provides value in the forms of connectivity, asset tracking, and educational services.

Space tech is a growing market with expanding business applications. Below are five areas for industry growth opportunities being explored including climate monitoring and energy, space connectivity and data, sustainable infrastructure and transportation, collision avoidance and debris management, and agriculture, education, and equality.

CLIMATE MONITORING AND ENERGY

While space-related technologies cover activities related to space exploration, that is, looking beyond the Earth to understand other planets and systems, a large part of space operations is dedicated to the study, monitoring, and understanding of our own planet for the benefit of its citizens. Satellites, as well as ground-based, airborne, and seaborne sensors provide real-time measurements and information to service providers, public authorities, and organizations to improve people's quality of life. One of the main applications of this information is climate change.[119] Information from Earth observation satellites in space can help manage climate impacts in several ways, from improving agricultural yields to mitigating environmental disasters. There are currently more than 160 satellites measuring different global warming indicators, with more than half of essential climate variables only measurable from space.[120]

Deep reductions in carbon dioxide emissions remain critical over the long term. But methane emissions from fossil fuel operations, livestock production, and other industries are responsible for more than 30% of the current temperature rise.[121] Cutting these emissions will significantly help curb climate change. Therefore, tracking these invisible emissions is imperative. MethaneSAT, a compact new satellite being built by the Environmental Defense Fund (EDF), is specifically designed to locate, measure, and track reductions in methane emissions anywhere on Earth with greater

IN BUSINESS

ALÉN SPACE[122]

Initiative: Small satellites for the new space
Headquarters: Galicia, Spain

Alén Space specializes in sustainable solutions for space business. The company capitalizes on the new opportunities that arise every day in the space tech business. Alén Space, with experience in the design, manufacture, and operation of small satellites, assists enterprises in putting their projects in orbit (SDG 17). Core business services include IoT communication with sensors located in remote areas and real-time data delivery machine-to-machine; asset tracking and geolocation of any kind of asset (ship, plane, vehicle) out of terrestrial systems range; earth observation capturing of images for mining, agriculture, industry, as well as for the environment, security, and climate purposes; and spectrum monitoring the location of emissions from the Earth and space by third parties and electromagnetic spectrum analysis (SDGs 9,11,12).

In 2021, two space tech products were developed for sustainable business, including:[123] 1) Sateliot – the launch of a constellation of nanosatellites to democratize IoT with 5G coverage. Its future constellation of up to 100 nanosatellites is scheduled to start offering commercial service in 2023 (SDG 10). 2) Alfa Crux - a team of students from the University of Brasilia participated in a complete CubeSat-type mission that will allow experiments to be carried out in the communications field and study the effects of the space weather on satellite communications in equatorial latitudes (SDGs 4,13).

DAWN AEROSPACE[124]

Initiative: Orbit Fab space refueling stations
Headquarters: Canterbury, New Zealand

Dawn Aerospace builds same-day reusable launch vehicles and high-performance, non-toxic propulsion systems for satellites of all sizes (SDGs 7,13). The startup's SmallSat Propulsion Thruster replaces poisonous gases with safer nitrous oxide and propane (SDGs 9,12). For CubeSats, it significantly improves performance compared to electric-based propulsion systems with the same propellants. Orbit Fab, a Californian company offering a refueling service in space, and Dawn Aerospace collaborated to make on-orbit refueling stations available to satellites utilizing nitrous oxide and propylene (SDG 17). These gas stations in space offered by Orbit Fab help extend the life of spacecraft by equipping them with on-orbit refueling. Spacecraft can now make frequent orbit and altitude changes with cleaner fuel and without a problem.

precision than any other satellite.[125] The oil and gas industry is a leading source of methane emissions. From remote wellheads to gas utility lines, companies release at least 75 million metric tons a year — enough gas to produce electricity for all of Africa twice over.[126]

METHANE EMISSIONS FROM FOSSIL FUEL OPERATIONS, LIVESTOCK PRODUCTION, AND OTHER INDUSTRIES ARE RESPONSIBLE FOR MORE THAN 30% OF THE CURRENT TEMPERATURE RISE.[127]

Copernicus is the European Union's Earth observation program providing indicators and services related to atmospheric quality, land, and marine monitoring, climate change, and emergency service (including natural disasters).[128] The climate data gathered by the program's satellites and sensors can be used across many end-user sectors such as urban planning, agriculture, forestry, and marine. Space4Good is another progressive entity monitoring climate impacts through air pollution and, in particular, nitrogen dioxide (NO2).[129] In a joint effort with the World Bank Group, the initiative uses NO2 emissions data to assess socioeconomic developments. The NO2 monitoring platform is a new satellite mission that provides economists and decision-makers with an alternative big data source to observe changes in socio-economic activities as a result of the COVID-19 pandemic. Sentinel-5P can detect tropospheric NO2 using its TROPOspheric Monitoring Instrument.[130] The high resolution enables analysis on a regional, national, and sub-national scale with monitoring in Indonesia, Vietnam, and selected MENA cities.

SPACE CONNECTIVITY AND DATA

Satellite data can help monitor the global supply chain including mining, ground transport, shipping, and port activity, as well as activities that create demand such as building demolitions and construction. Providing Internet access for billions of people is also part of Earth's connectivity that happens in space. The deployment of satellite constellations could bring web access via orbital Internet to billions more people who live in regions where installing traditional internet access infrastructure is uneconomical or unfeasible.[131] A UN study found that 52% of the world's population still lacks access to the Internet, and 90% of those people are from developing countries.[132] Research has shown that access to Internet use could mean up to a 2.5% difference in a country's GDP.[133]

A UN STUDY FOUND THAT 52% OF THE WORLD'S POPULATION STILL LACKS ACCESS TO THE INTERNET, AND 90% OF THOSE ARE FROM DEVELOPING COUNTRIES.[134]

Collecting and managing data is also a major component of space connectivity. LEO satellites and multi-satellite constellations are increasingly in use for communication, spying, earth monitoring, and other imaging applications. With large volumes of data from these satellites, there is a need to process, treat, analyze, and manage the information. Startups connect with space tech data using AI, blockchain, and big data to offer secure data solutions for the space industry. Luxembourg-based startup Kleos Space delivers its data products via application programming interfaces that adhere to customers' requirements.[135] The first Kleos Space satellite system, known as Kleos Scouting Mission, launched in 2020 and currently delivers commercially available data. The Scouting Mission targets daily geolocation services with a full constellation, giving nearly real-time global observation.[136]

SUSTAINABLE INFRASTRUCTURE AND TRANSPORTATION

In terms of sustainable transportation use in the orbital realm, space tech companies are creating green and sustainable business services. In the case of typical air transportation, the growth expectations are around 4% annually over the next two decades. But in the design of aerospace vehicles, including developing new structures, energy conversion materials, or fuel types, growth potential is estimated at 10 or 20% per annum.[137] These sub-sectors are mainly driven by the environmental aspects of aviation - the need to reduce carbon footprint and make air transportation much more efficient while keeping the costs in check.

In-space propulsion is another important transport subsystem for satellite constellations. Given the costs and environmental impacts that come with space missions, companies seek ways to ensure the sustainability of these missions. Hence, global startups and scaleups develop several solutions ranging from electric, green, and water-based propulsion to iodine-based propulsion systems in order to enable the next generation of clean rockets in space. Spacecraft propulsion is any device that is used to propel and accelerate spacecraft and satellites. In-space propulsion directly refers to transport systems used in the vacuum of space. Space traffic management is highly relevant to businesses and often an overlooked capability required for successful space tech commercialization. Although space gives the perception of being infinitely vast, the orbital space around the Earth is becoming increasingly crowded.

Orbital congestion is particularly concerning given the thousands of satellite companies and governments are looking to deploy, which could more than triple within the decade.[138] There are already nearly 2,000 active satellites in orbit and thousands more that are inactive.[139] Companies like Houston-based startup Cognitive Space are working to solve this space congestion problem.[140] Similar to what many companies are aiming to do for road vehicle traffic here on Earth, Cognitive Space is developing an AI-driven control system that will automate satellite operations, alleviating the need for people to monitor and manage each individual satellite. By increasing the intelligence of each satellite, the company hopes to eliminate the largely manual processes satellite operators rely on today while making space a safer, more efficient, and more manageable place for the people and technology in orbit.

THE USE OF INFLATABLE HABITATS HAS THE POTENTIAL TO GREATLY ACCELERATE THE COMMERCIALIZATION OF SPACE BY ENABLING LARGER STRUCTURES TO BE DEPLOYED MORE RAPIDLY.[141]

Another company developing infrastructure systems for space is Bigelow Aerospace.[142] Founded by billionaire hotel developer Robert Bigelow in 1999, the company attracted widespread attention in 2016 when it launched its expandable activity module, an inflatable habitat that's significantly easier and more cost-effective to transport than traditional fixed modules.[143] In 2018, Bigelow announced the creation of Bigelow Space Operations to develop a private space station built around its expandable module technology.[144] The use of inflatable habitats has the potential to greatly accelerate the commercialization of space by enabling larger structures to be deployed more rapidly.[145] This has several benefits to the business model, ultimately making living in space more accessible and more affordable for all: lower costs, quicker deployment, and more flexibility.

COLLISION AVOIDANCE AND DEBRIS MANAGEMENT

Of all the man-made LEO satellites, a vast majority of them are now space debris. This includes rocket thrusters, unused satellites, and most of all, tiny fragments of debris from collisions and explosions. In total, there are around 800,000 pieces of space debris traveling around at speeds of thousands of kilometers per hour.[146] All of this debris can be dangerous for orbital movement, threatening the future of space exploration and travel. Large quantities of space junk end up staying in various orbits around Earth and pose a danger to satellites, the International Space Station, and for future missions beyond Earth's vicinity – to asteroids, the Moon, and Mars. Debris can be parts of old satellites, from paint chips to bolts to larger sections and entire defunct satellites; it can also include old rocket bodies, the sections of rockets that do not fall back to Earth after a rocket's launch. The total known number of debris pieces larger than a marble counts more than half a million, and the unknown are likely in the millions. After around 60 years of space activity, the total mass of debris is more than 7,500 tons.[147]

THERE ARE AROUND 800,000 PIECES OF SPACE DEBRIS TRAVELING AROUND AT SPEEDS OF THOUSANDS OF KILOMETERS PER HOUR.[148]

The serious danger occurs when objects in orbit are moving at fast speeds of 28,000 km/h – the speed required by the laws of physics for objects to stay in orbit and not fall back to the ground. At that speed, even a small bolt could destroy an entire satellite or even endanger the entire Space Station.[149] The most polluted orbits, in general, are considered to be those between 200 to 2000 kilometers above Earth (LEO) and the 36,000-kilometer orbit (Geosynchronous). Out-of-control space junk in LEO orbit – known as the Kessler Syndrome – is a serious and ever-growing threat. To tackle this situation, startups are developing feasible solutions for debris retrieval and space traffic management. The Japanese startup Astroscale is the industry leader in orbital sustainability work (Case 71).

Space debris monitoring and removal is a nearly $1 billion market with characteristics that present several unique challenges. Elements of this space tech business sector include the development of particularly robust solutions for rendezvous, proximity operations, and robotic capture that form a solid foundation for addressing a wide variety of services in the future for both government and commercial customers. OrbitGuardians is a US-based commercial provider of active debris removal services.[150] The startup aims to protect space workers, tourists, and operating satellites by actively removing dangerous space debris smaller than twenty centimeters. By utilizing computer vision, AI, and IoT, OrbitGuardians enables low-cost debris removal by acquiring all the available debris parameters like location, size, and the number of debris chunks.

SPACE DEBRIS MONITORING AND REMOVAL IS A NEARLY $1 BILLION MARKET.[151]

For a sustainable space environment, collision avoidance with space debris is a priority for the World Economic Forum.[152] It is therefore, German startup OKAPI:Orbits is enabling space loose particle and junk management through its AI solution. The startup's risk monitoring and automated collision avoidance software equip satellites with neural networks that learn from a catalog of space objects.[153] This cloud-based service optimizes risk reduction maneuvers and fuel consumption. The startup also meets the mission-specific needs of small and large satellite operators through its flexible modules and standardized interfaces. These include environmental visualization, maneuver designing, orbit propagation, and determination as well as predicting ground station pass and orbital re-entry.

AGRICULTURE, EDUCATION, AND EQUALITY

There are many potential benefits emerging from space tech. Food security, for instance, could be proliferated through observation from satellites to help monitor illegal fishing, improve the traceability of products, and support predictive models for food supply around the globe. Combining imagery with weather, temperature, or air pressure could optimize agricultural yields and help farmers improve efficiency. Space technologies can continue to ensure access to safe, nutritious, and sufficient food year-round through precision agriculture and crop monitoring for food security.[154]

IN BUSINESS
ASTROSCALE[155]
Initiative: Cleaning up space
Headquarters: Tokyo, Japan

Astroscale is a Japanese startup specializing in cleaning up space. The company showcased a new universal docking device in November 2021. It was built to attach to satellites to help them be captured at the end of their missions, so they do not remain in space as debris (SDGs 9,12). The device, designed with the goal of being used by all satellites in LEO, includes a standardized interface that can operate with both magnetic and robotic capture mechanisms (SDGs 10,16). Astroscale's new technology is an expansion of its innovative End-of-Life Services for satellites, which completed a successful demonstration of satellite-capture technology in August 2021.

The UK Space Agency (UKSA) has shortlisted satellite groups led by Astroscale for a mission to remove two spacecraft from LEO in 2026 (SDG 17).[156] The new docking device is currently undergoing testing in LEO. Astroscale has raised more than $300 million, including $109 million in a round of funding in November 2021.[157]

Hummingbird Technologies is a global leader in remote sensing, artificial intelligence, machine learning, and data analytics for agriculture.[158] The company is headquartered in London, with satellite offices in São Paulo, Sydney, Lviv, and Moscow.[159] Hummingbird's mission is to improve the sustainability of global food production. As well as using precision agronomy tools to facilitate sustainable management decisions, Hummingbird's remote sensing monitoring capabilities allow users to monitor, verify, and report on-farm sustainability practices and outcomes. Satellite-enabled remote sensing offers a scalable and reliable approach to detecting key metrics, including regenerative agriculture principles such as no-till, cover crops, and crop rotations.

Education and equality are becoming increasingly important in space tech. Giving communities and people access to knowledge and business opportunities in the space sector is vital for sustainable global economic growth. Space Technology Education Popularization (STEP), a startup of the Institute of Space Technology in Islamabad, is a space science and technology awareness firm providing services for the popularization of space science and technology through events, workshops, training, activities, seminars, webinars, conferences, e-learning, online courses, publications, knowledge-based contests and themed vocational schools.[160]

Along the space tech education value chain is the Space and Earth observation program EIT Climate-KIC, which is working on upskilling and reskilling students, young graduates, and professionals.[161] The agency partners with specialists from the Earth observation and geographic information field, renowned universities, successful businesses, and far-reaching associations and networks to bridge the gap between the supply and demand of Earth Observation and geoinformation skills in the EO4GEO project.[162]

ADDRESSING RISKS AND CHALLENGES ON THE ROAD AHEAD

The space industry is dynamic and ever-changing. It has many challenges, which are both technical and regulatory. Space exploration has been a topic of interest for many countries in recent years. However, the technologies used in these missions are often costly and difficult to maintain. Moreover, space technology is highly complex and has proven to be a challenge in terms of maintenance and usage. Not only does it involve considerable financial costs, but it also involves the risk of life if something goes wrong.

The high failure rate of space tech missions is another challenge facing the space industry. For example, satellites used to provide communication services are very complex and are susceptible to faults and breakdowns due to natural and human related causes. Although governments regulate many aspects of space activities, including the launch of satellites, the use of space technologies, and access to outer space, different space-related agencies also enforce these regulations. This causes increased confusion, project delays, and failures in systems. Besides this, there are also regulations relating to the use of space resources, spaceflight safety, and space debris.

SPACE EXPLORATION AND ITS IMPACT ON THE ENVIRONMENT MUST BE CONSIDERED.

Another significant challenge of space exploration is its impact on the environment. For example, the use of high-powered rockets to launch satellites creates significant amounts of dust which pollutes the Earth's atmosphere. Space activities are also responsible for the creation of space debris which can cause severe damage to the Earth's orbit. Many risk factors make space exploration difficult including space-related risks such as orbital decay, space weather, radiation, and debris.[163] Other risks include technical risks, such as failure and malfunctions, as well as political risks, such as conflict or environmental factors.

LET'S
IMAGINE

We have imagined traveling back to Earth from space. From our seat on the SpaceX Starship, the blue patches of water we left behind grow near again. Africa's water crisis looks less bleak upon our return. While on our journey to space, we came into contact with satellite-based sensors that effectively measured nearly all the direct and indirect components of the hydrological cycle. The data we extracted from the CubeSats provided valuable information on how to manage the water shortage. Looking out from the International Space Station, we could see the satellites that manage the Earth's communications sprinkled throughout the expanse of outer space.

We have imagined how other advanced technologies, such as blockchain and 3D printing, can be applied to space-specific innovations. Space technologies have far-reaching Tech for Good applications. We have only just begun to imagine all the possibilities space has to offer.

We have imagined SpaceTech for Good.

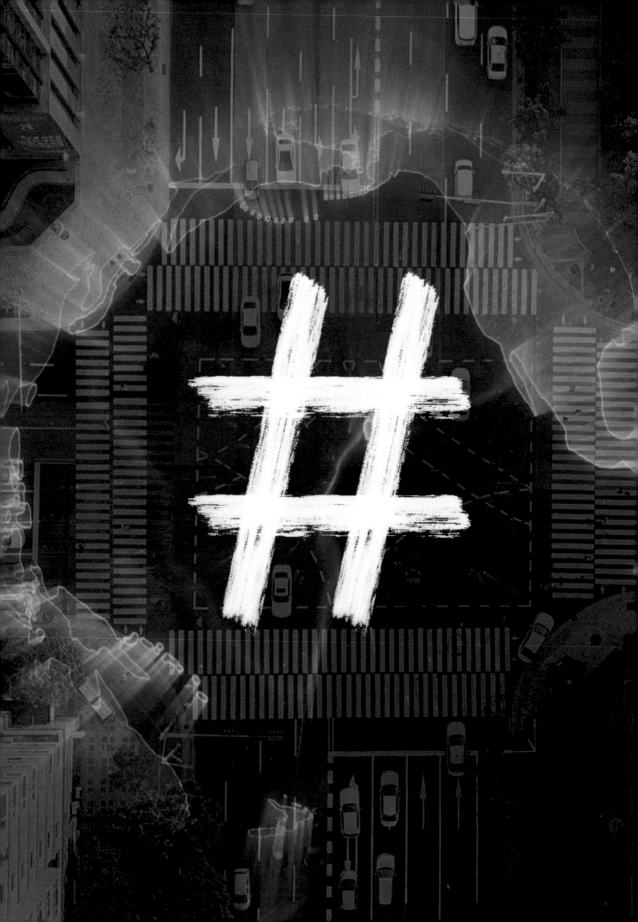

SCALING TECH FOR GOOD 10

#TECHFORGOOD IS MUCH MORE THAN A HASHTAG.

IT IS A GLOBAL MOVEMENT.

IMAGINE

Imagine a journey through the technological landscape. Once a mere imaginal concept associated with far-off notions of large inaccessible machines, technology now constantly surrounds us and is no longer out of reach. Although our tech world takes on many shapes and forms, Tech for Good serves as a pathway forward. Engaging with the #TechforGood movement and driving the conversation is the solution we need to solve our global challenges. When we dare to imagine our collective objective, technology will surely address it.

Envision a world in which technology helps restore our biodiversity. Let's imagine tech solutions protecting the environment, such as the Spatial Planning for Area Conservation in Response to Climate Change (SPARC) SpaceTech tool. This tool uses supercomputers and GIS-based mapping to build a global picture of the migration of all known plants, birds, and mammals in response to climate change.[1] Imagine homes where people with progressive memory loss caused by dementia would benefit greatly from effcient, cost-effective, tech-based strategies like 6G communications and AI-empowered health solutions to help bridge cognitive gaps.[2]

Imagine if the billions of people who rely on a healthy marine ecosystem for their food and livelihoods could farm fresh fish sustainably. With micro-bubble aeration technology that boosts oxygen levels in water and increases the productivity of seafood, this tech innovation is brought to life.[3] Imagine a healthcare system that prescribes medicines tailored specifically to you and your genome, thereby transforming how we diagnose, prevent, and treat disease.[4]

These ideas are no longer simply fantasies, but are technological possibilities well within our grasp. Just as we see these first signs of our imagination becoming reality, this is when we need to dream even bigger.

Envisioning a new reality, and bringing what we imagine to life, requires leveraging tech innovations at scale. We must take it upon ourselves to apply Tech for Good, thereby embarking on the journey together, with decisive action, so that #TechforGood grows into an impactful global movement.

Tech for Good aims to inspire and inform sustainably minded businesses. With a purpose-driven approach to the way we deploy technologies, business will undoubtedly play a crucial role in realizing the 4IR's enormous potential to help address our Global Goals. Currently, we tap into only a fraction of this unprecedented era of technological potential. Businesses that leverage 4IR innovations in the transition toward positive social, economic, and environmental solutions will create market value and accelerate growth.

We should scale the #TechforGood movement now, and carry it out into the future, effectively keeping pace with the much-needed transformative change. Let's revisit the overarching themes covered throughout the preceding chapters and assess what is needed to propel Tech for Good innovations that are vital to forward progress.

Tech for Good is already here.

Marga Hoek

10

SCALING TECH FOR GOOD

EVER-CHANGING HORIZONS

The 4IR is the blurring of boundaries among the physical, digital, and biological worlds. It is a combination of advances in tech innovations such as IoT, AI and data, 3D printing, robotics, advanced materials, extended realities, autonomous vehicles and drones, blockchain, and space tech. 4IR technologies are already the collective force behind many products and services of modern life, and this tech presence will only increase into the future.

WE ARE IN AN ERA OF UNPRECEDENTED TECHNOLOGICAL POTENTIAL. TECH FOR GOOD CAN INSPIRE SUSTAINABLY-MINDED BUSINESSES.

With the ever-changing developments and rapid acceleration of the 4IR, the information here sheds light on the immediate tech scenario and looks ahead to what appears on the horizon. Exciting business cases throughout the chapters give an overview of the most relevant tech advancements. Market mechanisms and product developments are not absolute, however, since in no time we will witness new variants and combinations of technologies that were at the conceptual or experimental stage just a moment ago.

Advanced technologies rapidly evolve and grow, some more easily or quickly than others depending on complexities, existing foundational tech infrastructures, regulatory frameworks, and investment flows. Simply put, we distinguish among emerging technologies in three ways: those just appearing on the horizon (emerging), techs currently being developed (improving), and others that have already succeeded in their applications (mature). We have seen many of the most prominent 4IR tech solutions implemented in practice today for each of the 17 Global Goals.

MATURITY STAGES OF 4IR TECHNOLOGIES

The World Economic Forum has categorized 4IR tech solutions into varying levels of maturity which have been classified into low (emerging), medium (improving), and high (mature).[5]

High (mature) stage techs
- AI
- Satellites
- Drone-enabled disaster risk insurance products and microfinance
- Virtual Reality training, information, and remote learning experiences
- AI-enabled identity tax fraud identification
  (using browsing data, retail data, and payments history)

Medium (improving) stage techs
- AI sensors to eliminate spoilage/loss in food value chain, including smart food storage
- Blockchain-enabled circularity and sharing business model incentives
  (like tokeniztion to encourage collection and recycling of waste)
- Autonomous vessels and connected sensors for automated ocean health mapping

Low (emerging) stage techs
- Advanced construction materials
  (e.g., low/zero emissions steel and aluminum, zero/negatjve emissions concrete)
- Advanced waste heat capture and conversion
- 4IR improved living conditions for disability groups
  (e.g., AI sensory augmentation, robotic exoskeletons)

We have encountered these three stages, and examples of their associated technologies, throughout this book. For instance, the case of Farmbeats in the AI and Data chapter is a high-tech stage example. This agri-business product brings in cloud-based AI models, low-cost sensors, drones, satellites, and image-based machine learning algorithms to increase the productivity and profitability of farmers.[6] Similarly, we discussed a medium-tech stage example in the Blockchain chapter with US-based startup ImpactPPA. This system provides a blockchain-based prepaid mobile application for energy consumers to buy renewable energy where power flows from microgrids to smart meters connected to the blockchain network. Lastly, we referenced an emerging stage innovation in the Advanced Materials chapter when discussing how the automotive sector is aiming to improve fuel economy and emission control. The industry is currently finding ways to use materials such as advanced high-strength steels, non-ferrous alloys (aluminum and titanium), and a variety of composites (carbon fiber and metal matrix) to produce lightweight vehicles.

Within a few years, we will move through the referenced technologies and implementation of many business solutions to address the world's large-scale obstacles. Some futuristic tech ideas we expect to come to fruition during the 4IR include: brain hacking through monitoring of thought patterns associated with sensitive information;[7] the highly-trending Metaverse, which is a virtual universe for people to play, study, work, meet, and shop; self-fertilizing crops, with plants like soybeans that can be stimulated to produce their own nitrogen or grains like corn to self-fertilize;[8] super-effcient cobots specially designed to interact physically with humans in collaborative environments; and prototypes developed quickly, accurately, and economically with 3D and 4D printing.

The 4IR enables business as well as society at large to employ smart products and services that are beneficial for a multitude of stakeholders. Thanks to the combinatorial power of technologies like AI and blockchain, and their fusion with exponential innovations such as genomics and quantum computing, there are unprecedented opportunities to help solve our biggest problems. While enabling radical solutions at scale, these advanced technologies are effectively assisting us on the journey toward a more sustainable present and future.

A JOINT, MULTI-STAKEHOLDER APPROACH AS A PREREQUISITE FOR SCALING TECH FOR GOOD

Harnessing the power of technology for good will require a multi-stakeholder approach, as we need active engagement from many actors across the business spectrum to achieve this transition. In realizing the multi-stakeholder economic model, we are all aware and responsible for capturing the positive force of tech as a collective unit. No single agent, whether a business, government, civil society, academic, or anyone else, can do it alone. Collaborations and coalitions are key to success.

HARNESSING THE POWER OF TECHNOLOGY FOR GOOD WILL REQUIRE A MULTI-STAKEHOLDER APPROACH.

As previously mentioned, technology has no overall purpose on its own. Its impact is driven by human choices and actions. In this context, although Tech for Good is about technological and scientific innovation, true scaling and advancement is determined even more by social innovation. From businesses to governments, NGOs to entrepreneurs, we all hold a collective responsibility together. Throughout the last five years we have seen unprecedented innovations, such as AVs revolutionizing the automotive sector. But we have also seen some AV tech applications struggle when they do not have the necessary government backing to realize this development as a truly viable option. Such setbacks indicate how private-public collaboration will be at the forefront of the 4IR.

TECH FOR GOOD IS ABOUT TECHNOLOGICAL AND SCIENTIFIC INNOVATION, BUT TRUE SCALING AND ADVANCEMENT IS DETERMINED EVEN MORE BY SOCIAL INNOVATION.

Tech for Good demands collective action. We currently face huge gaps in the necessary conditions for Tech for Good to evolve to its full potential. The movement should align with a strong foundation of ethics that are reflected in legislation, regulatory frameworks, and laws. We all have a critical role to play in how technologies will shape our common future. As discussed in the opening chapter, we have a long way to go to restore and build trust in technology. Jim Snabe and Lars Thinggaard stated in their book Tech for Life that we need to "put trust back in technology."[9] While working together to engineer the necessary conditons, diverse sectors including businesses and governments will be called to cultivate talent, skills, education, as well as investments.

The pace of technological change must be accompanied by ever-faster and smarter regulatory changes. We thus need policies and regulations that address new challenges, risks and threats, including privacy and security. Businesses, along with other ecosystem partners, have an essential role to play in helping governments develop effective regulations that can steer the impact of advanced technologies in a positive direction. Ethics are a crucial base on which our actions, systems, regulations, and policies must rest. Not self-interest, but collective interests, will engage everyone in this forward movement. Further, this will undoubtedly take shape as a global action, not just as a few projects in the developed world.

THE PACE OF TECHNOLOGICAL CHANGE MUST BE ACCOMPANIED BY EVER-FASTER AND SMARTER REGULATORY CHANGES.

The emergence of technology governance from both industry and the public sector is a positive signal. Recent examples include industry-led efforts such as Global Digital Finance's cryptocurrency code of conduct, or the Cybersecurity Tech Accord, government-led multilateral efforts such as the EU's General Data Protection Regulation (GDPR), the G20 AI Principles, and the creation of the public-private Global Partnership on AI. Entrepreneurs and innovators may be weary of codes and regulations, perceiving that such stopgaps could potentially hold them back.[10] The intent, however, is not to slow down innovation. Rather, these boundaries and protections are put in place to prevent fraud or misuse that could further damage trust in technology and subsequently stall progress. Building momentum backed by bold commitments and ethical intents directs tech toward addressing global challenges that are centered around a strong moral compass.

IT IS CRUCIAL THAT WE MOVE AWAY FROM THE INCREMENTAL AND DEFENSIVE "DO NO HARM" MENTALITY TO THE PROGRESSIVE AND FORWARD-THINKING "DO GOOD" MENTALITY.

Business leaders must demonstrate courageous leadership. More specifically, they must demonstrate the willingness to develop and strengthen ethical foundations based on long-term goals. This positive momentum prevents downsides that could damage trust in technology, which would throw us off our course or worse, force us to stop. While developing these 4IR solutions, it is crucial that we move away from the incremental and defensive "do no harm" mentality to the progressive and forward-thinking "do good" mentality. If we agree technology should add value for all stakeholders, we steer ourselves in the right direction. The Tech for Good movement has a responsibility to utilize technology for collective benefit.

Encouraging examples of collaborative action in business exist throughout initiatives that address the Global Goals. For instance, movements aiming to address SDG 13 on Climate Action include the Step Up Coalition of 25 firms with leadership commitments, Net Zero and RE100 climate-related pledges made by multiple technology firms, or the Breakthrough Energy Coalition of private investors, tech firms, industry, and financial institutions collaborating to invest in decarbonization.[11] Emerging focus on tech and the Global Goals more broadly is resulting in projects such as 2030Vision, which brings together over 18 companies and organizations to look at how technology can help advance a sustainable future.[12]

Further, the Global Partnership for Sustainable Development Data includes hundreds of organizations such as governments, companies, and civil society groups. The Cybersecurity Tech Accord, with more than 120 companies that have committed to protecting customers and users, is helping people defend against malicious threats.[13] Other initiatives like the Partnership on AI, with more than 90 multi-stakeholder partners committed to advancing positive AI uptake, are vital to tech proliferation and safety.[14]

Currently, however, these efforts are far from the scale of collaboration that society needs. Public, private, and multi-stakeholder partnerships, with active leadership from the tech industry, are urgently required to tackle the most systemic challenges and facilitate business to be able to create profitable opportunities. This applies to industry codes of conduct and frameworks on responsible technology, in addition to R&D deploying technology to tackle the challenges underpinning the Global Goals. To meet societal demands, tech advancement must be geared toward digital infrastructure and upskilling in underserved regions. Along with a change in economic allocations, public policies will also evolve as government support aimed at shaping new standards and regulations for tech becomes increasingly important.

THE NEW WAY OF THINKING FOR BUSINESS

To successfully develop, deploy, and scale Tech for Good, businesses need to think and act differently. This progressive course of action will help create markets for tech solutions where none exist today, or address cracks in the current business platforms that prevent profitable growth. It is the combination of renewed market forces, new digital technologies, and updated ecosystems that will solve complex social issues and drive impact at scale. Businesses will excel by responding quickly, as well as by addressing new challenges head on and taking advantage of opportunities presented as exponential technological growth.

ALONG WITH A CHANGE IN ECONOMIC ALLOCATIONS, PUBLIC POLICIES WILL ALSO EVOLVE AS GOVERNMENT SUPPORT AIMED AT SHAPING NEW STANDARDS AND REGULATIONS FOR TECH BECOMES INCREASINGLY IMPORTANT.

We discussed in earlier chapters the need for moonshot thinking as a catalyst for radical change. Requiring a major mindset ship, new business approaches must start with the sustainable end goal and then reason back to the fundamentals. If the goal is transformational change, it is critical to start with the intended societal outcome in mind and then work back to the business and technology solutions that can be applied to address challenges. Progress will not be realized without a clear direction from the start. There is no doubt that this is easier said than done. John F. Kennedy famously remarked in 1962, "We choose to go to the moon and to do other things, not because they are easy, but because they are hard."[15]

"WE CHOOSE TO GO TO THE MOON AND TO DO OTHER THINGS, NOT BECAUSE THEY ARE EASY, BUT BECAUSE THEY ARE HARD." - JOHN F. KENNEDY

Truly transformational, moonshot thinking and acting could be challenging at first as we unlearn old habits and enter a completely unknown realm. As humans, navigating amidst the unknown is often scary and laden with obstacles that make us want to turn back. Still, we must persevere. Moonshot thinking comes with the core competence of being adaptive, which is based on gaining skills and capabilities that are precisely what the future needs from us. With potential benefits ranging from the creation of technologies essential for harnessing big data, to furthering the development of the metaverse, the moonshot concept is increasingly used to describe a giant leap of innovative tech advancements with ambiguous goals.[16] If realized, these technological moonshots could be hugely beneficial for us all.

To transform the world, we must transform ourselves. This transformation requires radical moonshot innovation. Yet, the value of incremental innovation should not be discounted as an equally important step along our journey. In fact, when implemented deliberately and at scale, incremental movement often generates major, short-term results such as cutting costs significantly and bringing our carbon footprint back to a more manageable level. Sometimes taking the smaller methodical steps, those that realize incremental progress, are the very action that must be taken as a precursor or supplement to the moonshot.

TO TRANSFORM THE WORLD, WE MUST TRANSFORM OURSELVES.

This slower, incremental pace, however, comes with a limit. The business-as-usual model will not suffice over the long term, and we are running out of time. Thus, to solve the world's largest challenges, radical solutions are paramount and they come by way of radically expansive thinking. In transforming ourselves while making progress, we must look at our role in accelerating forward movement. We will need to imagine a new future, reset our agenda, and be open to a mindset that is inherently radical. Moonshot innovations that leverage advanced technologies will be the radical 4IR solution necessary to catapult us forward.

Figure 6
Moonshot Blueprint, based on model developed by X - The Moonshot Factory.[17]

Technology unlocks possibilities beyond what was previously thought possible. By embracing moonshot innovations to achieve our global challenges, businesses boldly embark on this journey. As explained at the beginning of the book, combining sustainability and technology is key to business success. Equipped with that new mindset, businesses will redefine their roles in the marketplace and among consumers. In this multi-stakeholder era, business has the capacity to be the instigator of the Tech for Good movement and convene all parties. The new way of thinking should be one based on the awareness that collective intelligence and action matter more than ever. We all need to act together while distributing and sharing knowledge and experience throughout social and economic systems within and beyond business.

There are several exciting examples of tech businesses reaching for moonshot innovations to curb climate change. These leaders are reshaping how we think about and use carbon. Prominent players Microsoft[18] and Google[19] are gaining a lot of attention for their investments to boost carbon removal. However, there are also strong signals suggesting that lesser-known companies are entering the arena with big ideas that have the potential to create massive, positive change and disrupt markets. Stripe, the online payments company, is a prime example of a tech innovator successfully inspiring investment in moonshot carbon-removal technologies (Case 72).

NEXT GENERATIONS SPUR GROWTH

Seizing and scaling opportunities is characteristic of emerging generations who will soon make up the majority of the workforce, marketplace, and wider stakeholder landscape. The next generations, millennials, also referred to as Generation Y and the following Generation Z, are known to be purpose-driven and action-orientated. Young Swedish environmental activist Greta Thunberg, along with her millions of followers, highlights these generational priorities. Capitalizing on the benefits afforded them by their parents and ancestors, next generations are taking full advantage of their power and utilizing it as a force for good.

Gen Y and Gen Z are increasingly sustainability-minded and often "vote with their wallets" to drive their agenda. According to a recent study, the vast majority of Gen Z shoppers prefer to buy sustainable brands and they are more willing to spend an increase of 10% on sustainable products.[20] These findings also suggest that Gen Zs, along with millennials, are the most likely group to make purchase decisions based on individual and collective values and principles related to social, economic, and environmental concerns. The social impact consultancy DoSomething reported that 75% of Gen Z respondents said they wanted to see that brands were ensuring employee and consumer safety.[21] The sentiment suggested, "If [brands] are not authentic, Gen Z will be the first to raise a red flag."[22]

Millennials as well as Gen Zs seek to combine purpose and profit, thus proving these two seemingly opposing elements are not in conflict with each other. When brands have an authentic purpose, share it with the world, and truly stick to it, people are more than willing to pay a small premium. Therefore, these next generations are encouraging brands to become more purpose- and value-driven. Young people are spending their money on brands with aligned values. With this money, they are fueling businesses' purpose and encouraging them to continue their path. Recently, young people named three things when it comes to trusting a company: purpose, honesty, and transparency.[23] Businesses that have a purpose customers can identify with, as well as being honest and transparent, generate thriving success.

56% OF GEN Z CONSIDER THEMSELVES CREATIVE, COMPARED TO 44% OF MILLENNIALS.[24]

Innovation is thus a defining characteristic of the Gen Z era, as advanced technology and talent generate the ideal environment for agile thinking and creative ideas.[25] This is hopeful, as we need innovative, moonshot thinking that delivers radical solutions using tech. Findings show that 56% of Gen Z consider themselves creative, compared to 44% of millennials.[26] They are often technologically driven and knowledgeable, and their curiosity creates a significant competitive advantage in modern business. Combining a Gen Z workforce with innovative technology and new ideas enables the acceleration of digital transformation. This is highly lucrative, as findings show that 80% of supply chain leaders are prioritizing digital transformation due to disruption from the COVID-19 pandemic.[27]

IN BUSINESS

STRIPE [28]

Initiative: Stripe Climate
Headquarters: Dublin, Ireland and San Francisco, California USA

Stripe describes itself as "financial infrastructure for the internet." Millions of companies of all sizes—from startups to Fortune 500s—use Stripe's software to accept payments, send payouts, and manage their businesses online. Stripe is amplifying the sustainable carbon economy by creating a market for removing CO2 from the atmosphere. With a vision to create a trillion dollar-a-year market on carbon-removal technologies, the company launched the Stripe Climate initiative and catapulted itself into the moonshot realm. Stripe's moonshot innovation is offering a solution for businesses to invest in climate mitigation efforts. Calling on its customers to join this grand-scale carbon-removal strategy by contributing a percentage of their digital sales that flow through Stripe's software, the company now has tens of thousands of businesses that are part of Stripe Climate.

Stripe Climate took a moonshot leap to create a market for ambitious carbon-removal technologies to help save the planet (SDGs 12,13). The company got a "surprisingly positive reaction from the carbon-removal community," said Nan Ransohoff, Stripe's Head of Climate.[29] Stripe routinely convenes panels of scientific experts to evaluate new tech and decide which companies it will back through Stripe Climate, and then pays a premium for these companies' services in an effort to help them scale and bring the cost down (SDG 8). More than 15,000 companies across 40 countries have joined in these efforts, thereby helping provide a critical demand signal for new technologies.[30]

One of Stripe Climate's notable initiatives include financing nearly 10% of Climeworks' new direct air capture facility named Orca, the world's largest direct air capture and storage plant that permanently removes CO2 from the air (SDG 9).[31] Also, Stripe was the first customer for Charm Industrial's novel process for permanently injecting carbon-containing liquid underground, which has sequestered more than 5,000 tons of carbon (SDG 7).[32] In April of 2022, Stripe teamed up with Alphabet, Meta, Shopify, and McKinsey to launch an initiative called Frontier, which plans to purchase nearly $1 billion worth of carbon removal by 2030 from nascent carbon removal companies in an effort to accelerate research and development (SDGs 16,17).[33]

NEXT GENERATIONS TAKE DECISIVE ACTION WITH THEIR WALLETS

Gen Z is inspiring older generations to buy responsibly sourced products, and Gen X is following suit. In a recent 2021 study, nearly the same share of Gen X buyers considers sustainability over brand as Gen Z, and 67% of Gen X prefers to buy from sustainable companies.[34] This is a 25% increase from the previous year. Gen Z influencers are leading the way to ensure sustainable supply chain practices are imperative for brands to keep in mind.

Understanding and acting on the new demands that Gen Z consumer behavior reflects will be paramount for sustainable business growth. Bloomberg estimates in the United States alone, the disposable income of Gen Z is $360 billion.[35] This means companies have a huge opportunity to grow their businesses alongside the rising of the Gen Z era. With more than 30% of the global population, Gen Z's domination of the next decade could lead to major profits for companies that prioritize environmental and social sustainability at all levels of their business, from corporate governance to logistics suppliers.

Protecting the environment is high on Gen Z's priority list, closely behind unemployment and healthcare or disease prevention.[36] Approximately 73% of this young age group is willing to pay more for expensive products "when [they are] ethically sourced," which is more than every other generation.[37] It is revealed that 66% of Gen Z and 57% of millennials agree that environmental concerns should take priority over economic growth, compared with 44% of baby boomers and 45% of Gen X.[38]

This is demonstrated in many companies launching sustainability campaigns and emphasizing green practices.[39] A recent survey by Deloitte shows that nearly half — 46% — of Gen Zs and millennials said that their personal ethics have played a role in their career choices.[40] Sustainably-oriented companies realize that these new generation growth numbers will only rise from this point on, as 90% of the incoming generation say they will switch brands in case a sustainable alternative arises.[41]

GEN Z IS REPORTED TO BE AN AGILE AND CREATIVE GENERATION.[42]

Companies looking to proactively recruit employees from Generations Y and Z gain an edge on competitors. In addition to embracing new technologies and software that help businesses acquire and keep new customers, millennials and Gen Zs are often at the heart of designing and implementing new strategies and systems.[43] One such tech company started by next gen business leaders is Canva (Case 73). Canva is an Australian graphic design platform that is used to create social media graphics and presentations. The tech startup has changed the way people design, both for work and personal projects, by putting its digital templates in everyone's hands. The app includes ready-made templates for users and the platform is free, with additional paid offerings such as Canva Pro and Canva for Enterprise for additional functionality.

IN BUSINESS

CANVA[44]

Initiative: Marketing and Branding Solutions for Tech Companies
Headquarters: Sydney, Australia

In May 2012, Australians Melanie Perkins and Cliff Obrecht, both in their mid-twenties, raised the first part of what would become a $3 million seed round from investors.[45] A year later, they launched the online design and publishing tool Canva. It is now one of the most influential design platforms on the planet, with 100 million monthly active users who create, on average, 150 designs every second. The company, which was valued at $40 billion in July 2022, is now exceeding $1 billion in revenue.[46]

By democratizing design—and challenging the unwritten rules around who gets to consider themselves a designer—Canva was recognized on Fast Company's 2022 cover as one of the most innovative companies (SDG 9). The service, which debuted as a free tool before adding a paid Pro tier, currently has over 5 million Pro customers. Over the past two years, it has rolled out features that allow for real-time collaboration across diverse companies (SDGs 8,17). An impressive 85% of the world's 500 largest companies are using Canva's platform.[47]

The tech innovator has created over 13 billion designs, of which sustainability plays a prominent role (SDGs 10,12). It is a platform to design anything and everything. "I mean it very literally, actually, we are continuously picking off the next, most critical strategic pillar that we believe is most important to our customers," says Perkins. "Maybe in 20 years' time, you can take your imagination as far as it will go. I have this very wildly optimistic belief that there is enough money and goodwill in the world to solve all of the world's problems."[48] At a time when communication channels are quickly evolving, Canva is more than keeping up. It is setting the pace with specific, targeted messaging for their clients' commitments to the SDGs as well. The company believes the more people who know about the SDGs, the better.

Therefore, to help bring awareness to business, Canva provides services related to the Global Goals that ensure communities stay active and governments are held accountable.[49] Important SDG-related actions include around 27 million teachers and students use Canva daily in over 190 countries, and since the launch of Canva Education, the program has attracted over 25 million users (SDG 4); the Canva team planted over 1 million trees through their one print, one tree program (SDGs 13,15); and a woman's ALS journey raised over $750,000 through the Team Drea Foundation using Canva for their designs to empower others to achieve goals they otherwise thought were impossible (SDGs 3,5).[50]

TECH FOR GOOD AS A GLOBAL MOVEMENT

Tech for Good is a defining term for business innovation acceleration. A quick online search for #TechforGood or #Tech4Good reveals the growing popularity surrounding the wider initiative driving the need to do good. But #TechforGood is much more than a hashtag, it is a global movement. The Tech for Good movement is composed of thinkers, scientists, startups, and mature, global companies as well as governments. They all share the vision that technology should serve society. Technology, as previously emphasized, needs collaboration among all stakeholders. The Tech for Good movement reflects this positive and powerful joining of forces.

Silicon Valley is known as the original tech headquarters area. Synonymous with big tech, Silicon Valley boasts established headquarters of tech giants like Apple, Google, HP, Intel, Adobe, eBay, and several other major players. These companies operate from the region with continued success, but there is growing awareness that big tech needs to repurpose and refocus on leveraging technology for the greater good. The Tech for Good movement is seeing tech giants diversify the regions in which they operate. As these tech innovators begin to spread out across the globe, they are seizing opportunities to serve not only direct shareholders and beneficiaries but society at large. Big tech will be increasingly required to scale initiatives and services to respond to a wider stakeholder group. While doing so, these companies will make a huge, positive difference on the business community and the planet.

#TECHFORGOOD IS MUCH MORE THAN A HASHTAG - IT IS A GLOBAL MOVEMENT.

Diversifying access is vital to accelerating tech innovations around the globe. Prominent regions outside of North America at the cutting edge of the Tech for Good movement include Europe and Asia. Consider the Tech for Good Summit in France, for instance.[51] Under the leadership of President Macron, France founded a true public-private partnership to increase cooperation and collaboration of actors of all sizes to put innovation, technology, and economics at the heart of humanity and the common good. Fifty CEOs joined in 2018, with many more following in the years after, and the French initiative became an impactful call to good. London is also an important incubator for Tech for Good startups. As the United Kingdom startup ecosystem matures, so does the opportunity to attract capital from all over, even from Silicon Valley.

Beyond Europe, the movement is gaining traction in many other regions. There are many more national tech movements in Canadian, Australian, and Asian countries. The Tech for Good initiative in Israel, for example, boasts an internationally renowned entrepreneurial ecosystem where investments in high-tech companies continue to grow. Delivering exciting technological innovations from several new businesses, Israel is known to some as the "Startup Nation."[52] Israeli unicorns and startups managed to raise over $10 billion in the first half of 2022 alone.[53] For instance, the Israeli company DriveNets, which builds communication networks on the cloud, raised $262 million in late August 2022.[54] This brings the total amount raised by the company to $587 million, with the its valuation now exceeding $2 billion.

TECH FOR GOOD AREAS

As Tech for Good becomes a wider field with broader applications, the related sustainable growth markets are being unlocked and discovered. As explained throughout each tech chapter, new sustainable tech areas are popping up and growing rapidly where solutions are urgently needed. Tech areas that were not tradtionally associated with sustainable objectives are now beginning to turn their focus toward Tech for Good. FinTech is an example. Although innovations have disrupted the financial sector, FinTech was originally not associated with purpose-driven business practices. Now it is becoming a global movement for change as part of the wider Tech for Good movement.

TECH FOR GOOD INNOVATORS AROUND THE WORLD

It is often said that Silicon Valley led the software revolution, but other regions around the globe are emerging at the forefront of the Tech for Good era.

Over the past decade, Asia has been the innovation hub for the travel and mobility tech sector, with half of all global venture capital funding in the sector flowing into Asian startups. This trend resulted in billions of dollars flowing to numerous tech unicorns, such as China's Didi, Singapore's Grab, Indonesia's Gojek, and India's Ola.[55] Southeast Asia's technology startups had a combined valuation of $340 billion in 2020, and they are anticipated to triple in value by 2025.[56] One is Grab, the Southeast Asian service Launched in 2012, which offers rides, food delivery, hotel bookings, and financial services. In 2018, it pushed Uber out of Southeast Asia and is now the most valuable Southeast Asian tech unicorn.

In 2021, One is Grab went public in New York following a $39.6 billion merger with a blank check company.[57] Another major player is Gojek, an Indonesian on-demand multiservice platform and digital payment technology group. Launched in 2010 as a call center, an app was then developed that originally offered only four services. But in 2021 Gojek merged with Tokopedia (an e-commerce company) and created the new holding named GoTo. In March 2022, GoTo Group raised $1.1 billion in one of the world's largest initial public offerings in 2022.[58]

In recent years, Latin America has established itself as one of the world's most promising regions for burgeoning tech talent and start-up activity. Venture capital investment in Latin American tech has been growing steadily over the past five years, doubling annually since 2016 before reaching a record high of $4.6 billion in 2019.[59] Over 60% of start-up investments in Brazil are concentrated in São Paulo, which is open referred to as Brazil's innovation powerhouse where tech giants such as Amazon, Uber, and Spotify have chosen the city as their Latin American base.[60] The city is home to a tech ecosystem which supports a number of local unicorns, as well as boasting more fintech start-ups than any other Latin American city.

Mexico City, with its strategic location between the American continents, attracts many big-name companies as well. Streaming giant Netflix, for example, has established a regional headquarters in North America's most populous city.

Although Europe might not have spawned a Google, Apple, or Facebook, the continent does find itself in a prime position to become a leader in Tech for Good. A growing number of entrepreneurs and investors are setting out to prove that Europe can create alternative models for tech innovation that are both profitable and good for society. In that sense, the region could set a new global standard by showing that best practices on environmental impact, diversity, and privacy are a driver for financial performance.

London has been named the best city in the region to develop and grow digital Tech for Good solutions that address social and environmental challenges, according to new research from global innovation foundation Nesta. The European Digital Social Innovation Index (EDSII) and the interactive map produced as part of the EU-funded DSI4EU project, show 60 European cities that are ranked on 32 indicators for digital social innovation (DSI) and Tech for Good.[61]

There is even a specific organization FinTech for Good which was founded in 2013 by a group of finance professionals, tech engineers, and economists who sought to show what could be possible if society pursues more human-centric, sustainable, and socially responsible systems for managing capital.[62] FinTech for Good was started ahead of its time and was a first-mover in sharing information and funding creative projects that showcase financial inclusion, social governance, and climate responsibility. Coordinating information around socially responsible finance, the participatory think-tank provides industry leadership and advocates for financial inclusion and climate responsibility. FinTech for Good is part of a wider network of communities advocating globally for financial democratization in tech including members such as Nesta, The Finance Innovation Lab, The Smart CSOs Lab, The New Economic Foundation, and many more. There are now several VC funds and startups around the globe investing in Tech for Good, such as a Brazilian FinTech company Solfácil that focuses on financing solar power systems in homes (Case 74).

FINTECH FOR GOOD IS PART OF A WIDER NETWORK OF COMMUNITIES ADVOCATING GLOBALLY FOR FINANCIAL DEMOCRATIZATION IN TECH.

FinTech collaborations are growing in numbers in an interesting way. HealRWorld, a social impact for profit ESG FinTech unveiled its new corporate debit card in late 2022.[63] In collaboration with Mastercard and its Priceless Planet initiative, RailSR, Toqio, and Penrose Digital, the HealRWorld corporate debit card is the first of its kind to reward sustainable businesses and promote their commitment to the SDGs.[64] The card is powered by HealRWorld's proprietary sustainability data on global small and medium-sized enterprises (SMEs), which is based on data signifying that businesses committed to ESG standards are on average three times more creditworthy than their peers.[65] The HealRWorld debit card was launched using Toqio's white-labeled digital finance SaaS plaXorm and RailsR provided the necessary payment tools to enable its SMEs to enjoy a unique experience. While linking a debit card and payment account to the unique Priceless Planet proposition, this FinTech collaboration allows users to give back to the planet by contributing towards planting a tree with each purchase.

TRADITIONAL AND NEW TECH AREAS ARE BEING REPURPOSED TO RESPOND TO THE TECH FOR GOOD MOVEMENT.

The broad spectrum of 4IR technologies reveals the pervasive nature of tech innovation throughout business sectors. Within the preceding chapters, many tech areas were identified as sustainable growth opportunities, often with disruptive benefits, like FinTech. Collaborations and joint ventures between companies with different competencies and sector knowledge are fruitful. Traditional and new tech areas are being repurposed to respond to the Tech for Good movement while seeking new growth and profit markets.

MANY OF THESE TECH AREAS, INCLUDING CARBONTECH, CLEANTECH AND CLIMATETECH, HAVE DIRECT TECH FOR GOOD OBJECTIVES THAT CLEARLY ADDRESS THE GLOBAL GOALS.

Many of these tech areas, including CarbonTech, CleanTech and ClimateTech, have direct Tech for Good objectives that clearly address the Global Goals. Examples of CleanTech, which refers to the product or service that reduces negative environmental impacts through significant energy effciency improvements and sustainable use of resources, are evident in several cases. EdTech, the technology supporting and transforming education, is also a highly beneficial tech area that has positive impacts across regions and communities. Yet some of these areas have continued to lack an obvious role in our sustainable journey are only now beginning to morph and repurpose. It is crucial, as we develop and apply 4IR technologies, that we choose to formulate these tech areas in an ethical, purposeful way.

IN BUSINESS

SOLFÁCIL[66]

Initiative: FinTech for Good financing residential solar
Headquarters: São Paulo, Brazil

Solfácil is a Brazilian FinTech online marketplace for financing solar power systems in homes. It connects residential consumers with multiple investors and installers of solar energy (SDGs 8,17). The company works with a credit line without the need for upfront investments from clients (SDG 10). The amount of funding raised is used for tech improvements, new credit lines (agribusiness), and expanding its partner network. As of December 2022, Solfácil raised $165 million over five funding rounds.[67] In an effort to make solar energy mainstream, the funds will be used to expand what Solfácil calls its "solar ecosystem" (SDGs 7,9). This includes a range of solutions that, besides the credit lines, also incorporate a marketplace for solar equipment and an IoT device built with proprietary technology to monitor and improve the productivity of solar power systems provided by integrators (partner companies that design and build solar panel projects for the end customer) (SDG 12).

When it entered the market in 2018, Solfácil aimed to make access to solar energy popular among Brazilians (SDG 13). With credit lines to finance solar energy panels for individuals, farmers, and small and medium businesses, the startup has already financed more than $230 million in "solar loans." Users can define the photovoltaic solar project they want on the basis of requirements and pay monthly installments (SDG 1). Solfácil is the third-largest financier for solar energy in Brazil, next to major banks BV and Santander. "Today we are more than a FinTech, we are a solar energy ecosystem. We have a FinTech to provide access to the solar energy system, a marketplace to sell the photovoltaic kit, which is a key part of the investment beyond the installation, and now the proprietary IoT that takes care of this solar system over 30 years of use that it will have in the customer's home," said Fábio Carrara, CEO and founder of Solfácil.[68]

Solfácil currently has a customer base of 40,000 and over 10,000 integrator partners connected to its platform all over Brazil (SDG 11).[69] The startup's marketplace features more than 5,000 products, such as solar panels and inverters, and connects partner integrators to a variety of distributors and brands. In this regard, the Solfácil marketplace solves two of the biggest issues of a market of high demand and unstable supply chain: the prices and availability of products. The startup reached the start of 2023 with a credit portfolio of approximately $600 million and over 100,000 customers served. A portion of the funds will be allocated to technology to improve the marketplace and to enhance the IoT device (SDG 16).

As one of the most pressing challenges, climate change will be at the forefront of boosting growth in areas like CarbonTech and ClimateTech. CarbonTech is attracting more and more interest from investors and governments lately. While concerns over global warming become stronger, the tech area has promoted and proliferated carbon capture.

Although the tech has been around for decades, it is only recently ramping up the ability to deliver on its promise. Now, a new cohort of carbon capture technologies and companies are emerging with their sights set on bridging the gap between the ongoing energy transition and the world's reliance on heavy emitting oil and gas industries. Aker Carbon Capture, Climeworks, and LanzaTech represent just a few of the innovative companies in the CarbonTech area.

TECH AREAS REPURPOSED

Several tech areas that help drive us toward a sustainable future are emerging around the world:
- AgriTech – effciency farming
- CarbonTech - productive use of CO2
- CleanTech – energy effciency
- ClimateTech – emissions reduction
- EdTech – augmented learning
- FinTech – streamlining financial services
- FoodTech – nutrient fortification
- GreenTech – reducing environmental impact
- HealthTech – enabled healthcare
- MedTech – medical advancements
- PropTech - greener buildings
- UrbanTech – improving city life

There are also examples of grand-scale, technologically advanced cities being built with these tech areas as a basis for rethinking urban planning. The Carbon Free City Neom in Saudi Arabia is one such initiative, progressively combining CarbonTech, ClimateTech, GreenTech, PropTech, and UrbanTech as an integral component of its design. The city will be a 26,500-square-km high-tech development on the Red Sea with several zones, including industrial and logistics areas, planned for completion in 2025.[70] With no roads, cars, or emissions, it will run on 100% renewable energy and 95% of the land will be preserved for nature.

PRIVATE INVESTMENT FIRMS ARE FOCUSING ON ACTIVE ENTREPRENEURIAL VALUE INVESTING ACROSS TECH AREAS AND GEOGRAPHIES.

The carbon capture and sequestration industry has been attracting major investor interest, as the market is expected to grow from $2.01 billion in 2021 to $7 billion by 2028 at an estimated CAGR of 19.5%.[71] In the UK alone, ClimateTech startups raised nearly $8 billion in 2022, which is double the entire $4 billion raised by the same firms throughout 2021.[72] Private investment firms are focusing on active entrepreneurial value investing across tech genres and geographies. G9CM is a forward-thinking business with offices around the world that invest in opportunities for unlocking untapped potentials arising from tech innovation. Their venture capital growth strategy identifies candidates that have developed a solid business model and are ready to scale globally. G9CM's selected investments start with a minimum equity volume of $250,000 with a maximum of $10 million in several tech areas including EdTech, FinTech, AgriTech, CarbonTech, HealthTech, SpaceTech, and others.[73]

THE CARBON CAPTURE AND SEQUESTRATION INDUSTRY HAS BEEN ATTRACTING MAJOR INVESTORS' INTEREST AS THE MARKET IS EXPECTED TO GROW FROM $2.01 BILLION IN 2021, TO $7 BILLION BY 2028 AT AN ESTIMATED CAGR OF 19.5%.[74]

LEADING THE TECH FOR GOOD MOVEMENT

The Tech for Good movement is gaining momentum as it is increasingly engaging stakeholders from all sectors and regions. When developing technology, businesses must take the lead to incorporate responsible practices and sound frameworks. While tech has been a major force for progress, it also has the potential to be abused and cause harm. From steam power to automobiles, history shows that technology is neither good nor bad in and of itself. It can be both beneficial and detrimental, depending on how it is used. Modern 4IR tech advancement, like that of the Internet and AI, is no different. Leadership in Tech for Good takes on different forms. Bold companies with vision and purpose are guiding us along a tech paradigm ship toward an imaginable and achievable sustainable future.

TECHNOLOGY CAN BE BOTH BENEFICIAL AND DETRIMENTAL DEPENDING ON HOW IT IS USED.

On one hand, tech connects us all. During the COVID-19 pandemic, digital services and the Internet kept us in touch with one another. In this regard, AI and machine learning are helping solve some of the world's most pressing problems. Tech has amazing capabilities to diagnose diseases, thwart cyberattacks, mitigate climate change, and much more. AI now powers everything from online searches to medical advancement to job productivity. On the other hand, if left unchecked, algorithms can also perpetuate biases, create digital divides, and compromise safety and privacy. Hidden algorithms may threaten cybersecurity and conceal bias, while opaque data can erode public trust. One case that solidifies this point is the BlenderBot 3 launched by Meta in August 2022.[75] The AI chatbot made anti-Semitic remarks and factually incorrect statements regarding the United States presidential election, and even asked users for offensive jokes.

"DURING THE PANDEMIC, DIGITAL TECHNOLOGIES HAVE KEPT SOCIETIES FUNCTIONING AND PEOPLE CONNECTED. BUT THE PANDEMIC HAS ALSO HIGHLIGHTED A YAWNING GAP IN ACCESS TO THESE TOOLS. THE WORLD ENTERED THE DIGITAL AGE DECADES AGO, BUT A CORE CHALLENGE REMAINS: CLOSING THE DIGITAL DIVIDE."[76] - UN SECRETARY-GENERAL, ANTONIO GUTERRES

In an effort to stave off these risks, business is taking action. The private and non-profit sectors have rallied behind the Tech for Good movement, which ultimately strives to "put the digital world and technology at the service of humanity."[77] In its most direct and sweeping form, Tech for Good promises technology can help the world achieve the UN's Global Goals. Investors are taking note and implementing responsible tech practices. There has been rapid proliferation and uptake of AI in recent years, where 75% of all businesses already include AI in their core strategies.[78] Technology is also at the forefront of portfolio management for private equity and venture capital investments. In 2020, AI accounted for 20%, or $75 billion, of worldwide VC investments.[79] McKinsey & Company has reported that AI could increase global GDP by roughly 1.2% per year adding a total of $13 trillion by 2030.[80]

THE SENTIMENT OF THE GLOBAL GOALS IS TIMELESS. BUT WE WILL BE REQUIRED TO UPDATE OUR COLLECTIVE STRATEGY FOR SUCCESS.

The accelerated pace at which tech advancement is moving forward has surpassed many of our current policies and financial structures. Strong business leadership is unlocking new markets and developments, while also creating space for all that tech has to offer. Much has changed in the decade since the SDGs were devised at the United Nations Conference on Sustainable Development held in Rio de Janeiro, Brazil, in 2012. In 2015, when the UN voted on 17 universal objectives to transform the world through 2030, many of the tech advancements we discuss in this book had not yet been imagined. The 17 Sustainable Development Goals are defined in a list of 169 SDG Targets and progress toward these Targets was agreed to be tracked by 232 unique Indicators. But the era in which the SDGs were designed is behind us and the 4IR is now upon us. Although the sentiment of the Global Goals is timeless, we will be required to update our collective strategy for success.

THERE WILL BE MORE THAN 500 BILLION MACHINES CONNECTED TO THE INTERNET BY 2030, WHICH IS MORE THAN 60 TIMES THE WORLD'S POPULATION.

Businesses are recognizing the need to shift with the times. They are taking action and leading the movement by changing their approach, thereby using the 17 Global Goals as a framework for where they want to go next. Although the Goals remain relevant, many of the Targets and Indicators may need to be rethought and revised as we move into uncharted territory. Consider the implementation of the 6G network, for instance. Many of the specific components of SDGs will need to be updated and modified to include elements of the unknown technological advancements to come. Because there will be more than 500 billion machines connected to the Internet by 2030, which is more than 60 times the world's population, businesses must take on a leadership role in devising new systems for these machines that have a host of different technical requirements beyond simply connecting people.[81] Our visions of science-fiction will become reality once 6G is commercialized. Tech giant Samsung is leading the way in the all-new connectvity ship to a 6G future. In the case of 6G dissemination for the entire planet, Samsung will address all 17 Global Goals indirectly from the next generation tech perspective (Case 75).

THE GLOBAL GOALS ARE NOT MEANT TO BE RESTRICTIVE OR LOCK US INTO A PATTERN OF STALLED PROGRESS.

Bold business leadership is driving the Tech for Good movement. Companies that are nimble and take decisive action can quickly redirect and accelerate forward progress on the 17 SDGs. The Global Goals are a vision for the world. We all own them, together as a collective body, and therefore each of us own the responsibility of achieving them. Let us not, however, forget that the UN's framework is fluid and serves primarily as a roadmap to direct our journey.

The path to our destination is not linear. Forward-thinking businesses have the power to take charge, devise a plan that serves both profit and purpose, and lead the way in the Tech for Good movement.

IN BUSINESS

SAMSUNG[82]

Initiative: 6G of the Future
Headquarters: Seol, South Korea

In May 2022, Samsung Electronics released its vision for leadership securing global frequency bands for 6G, the next generation of communications technology. The company's report, 6G Spectrum: Expanding the Frontier, discusses ways to obtain the spectrum needed to achieve the 6G vision.[83] "We have started on our journey to understand, develop and standardize the 6G communications technology," said Sunghyun Choi, Executive Vice President and Head of the Advanced Communications Research Center at Samsung Research.[84]

This next gen tech is set to bring about a new era of connectivity. It will enhance sustainable services across all facets of society by supporting the tech ecosystems that address several global challenges (SDGs 1,2,3,5,6,14,15). With connectivity speeds up to 1 Tbps (one trillion bits per second) data transmission rate, 6G will enable real-time conversations with people on the other side of the world via holograms (SDGs 4,8,10). In addition, the 6G connected networks will support vehicles, robots, and even home appliances all around the globe (SDGs 9,11,12). Samsung stands to grow its business exponentially, as the comprehensive 6G Market is expected to create a revenue pocket surpassing $340 billion and expand at 58.1% CAGR during the forecast period 2031 to 2040.[85]

Whereas 5G requirements are mainly focused on performance aspects, 6G services are defined by three categories – performance, architecture, and trustworthiness. Examples of 6G performance requirements are a peak data rate of 1,000 Gbps (gigabits per second) and an air latency of less than 100 microseconds (µs), which is 50 times the peak data rate and one-tenth the latency of 5G. The architectural requirements of 6G include resolving the issues arising from the limited computation capability of mobile devices, as well as implementing AI right from the initial phase of technology development and enabling the flexible integration of new network entities. The trustworthiness requirement addresses the security and privacy issues arising from the widespread use of user data and AI technologies.

6G would require spectrum with ultra-wideband contiguous bandwidth to enable new services such as high-fidelity mobile holograms and truly immersive XR that are characterized by ultra-high-speed communications and a large amount of data. Samsung also capitalizes on AI to minimize energy consumption at the base station, without affecting network performance (SDGs 7,13). In a real data-based replicated simulation of base stations, Samsung applied its AI energy innovation tech to demonstrate energy savings of more than 10%.[86] In addition, it notes that research on forward-looking regulations and technologies on spectrum utlization is essential to provide efficient and flexible support of 6G. Samsung is committed to taking the lead and sharing its findings to spread the vision to bring the next hyper-connected experience to the world (SDGs 16,17).

PREREQUISITES FOR SCALING TECH FOR GOOD

In scaling Tech for Good to reach its full potential, there are overarching risks to identify, conditions to be met, and gaps to be filled. We have explored the major risks to address together and hurdles to overcome in every tech chapter. Two of the most fundamental conditions to propel Tech for Good are simply training people and investing money. Rapid advances in technology development and adoption require significant human skills and expertise as well as financial investments.[87] If not adequately addressed, these gaps in these areas will become significant scaling risks or even blockers.

The current pool of workforce expertise in the tech area is too small and unequal to develop the correct technological systems at scale. Around three-quarters of IT decision-makers worldwide claim to be facing critical skills gaps across tech departments, according to research by Skillsoft.[88] After questioning around 9,300 IT workers, the EdTech company found that 76% of IT leaders have skills gaps in their departments, a significant increase of 145% since 2016.[89] This refers to tech skills in general, not specifically Tech for Good. Michael Yoo, general manager of technology and developer at Skillsoft, said in an interview in ComputerWeekly: "Gaps in skills don't just disappear, they only grow wider if not properly addressed."[90]

MANY NEW TECHNOLOGIES REQUIRE SIGNIFICANT TECHNOLOGY EXPERTISE AND TOOLS.

Many new technologies, including AI and robotics operations, require significant technology expertise and tools. There is an urgent need to address this skill gap. For many companies, their survival is at stake. Digital transformation is stalling due to lack of job-ready digital talent. Recent research shows that nearly 60% of employers self-report that not having enough skilled employees has a major or moderate impact on their business.[91] Further, 50% of employers report that digital transformation initiatives are held back due to lack of employee adoption or engagement.

There is also the investment scaling hurdle, as already explored in my previous book The Trillion Dollar Shift. The UN estimates a funding gap of $5 to $7 trillion per year to meet the Global Goals, with an annual investment gap in developing countries of about $2.5 trillion.[92] This number refers to the finance gap to achieve the SDGs in general, but can also be applied to a tech gap. This investment gap, along with inadequate financing models, is a risk for achieving the SDGs, especially in instances when projects are not directly linked to private-sector markets. Traditional finance has a strong focus on centralized and capital-intensive infrastructure. Digital and decentralized technologies, however, often require a different financing model.

THE UN ESTIMATES THAT THERE IS A FUNDING GAP OF $5 TO $7 TRILLION PER YEAR TO MEET THE GLOBAL GOALS, WITH AN ANNUAL INVESTMENT GAP IN DEVELOPING COUNTRIES OF ABOUT $2.5 TRILLION.[93]

Digital assets are generally smaller amounts and tend to be more geographically dispersed. With an additional layer of complexity, the necessary financial tools and structures have not fully adapted to the needs of decentralized and distributed emerging technologies. There is currently a lack of the innovative public, private, and blended investment arrangements that are often required to scale the right 4IR digital infrastructure in order to support these new technology solutions.

BRIDGING THE TECH GAP

No tech better exemplifies the "leapfrog" phenomenon than the mobile phone. The widespread adoption of the handheld device has allowed even the most underserved communities to entirely forgo the need to implement traditional telecommunications infrastructures like wire networks and landline capabilities. Over 90% of the world's population owns mobile phones.[94] Of the 1.7 billion people that remain unbanked, 1.1 billion are reported to have access to a mobile phone. For these people, their first experience with financial services will likely happen on decentralized infrastructure.[95]

Decentralized finance (DeFi) technology, like mobile phones, has the potential to be a leapfrog technology. By enabling the underbanked to bypass traditional finance and gain access to digital services and assets that were previously unavailable, mobile phones as a DeFi tech help to bridge the tech gap. In less than five years, decentralized finance has become a billion-dollar industry with a market valued at an all-time high of more than $180 billion in 2022.[96] From January 2020 to today, the number of users on DeFi has increased from under 100,000 to over six million.[97]

The lack of a clear business case for investment in Tech for Good has also been challenging. Across several Global Goals, the short-term return on investment is low. A higher risk of investment for many technology solutions due to either being unproven at scale, or because the underlying technology is rapidly changing, is also identified as a major hurdle. Assets can quickly become obsolete, which is evident where tech solutions are public sector-led or heavily regulated. Finally, a lack of incentives for robust financing is a major setback in the Tech for Good movement.

A World Economic Forum assessment identified that Goals 1, 5, 14, and 15 have the lowest number of tech applications and therefore they generate the lowest amount of financial capital. Further analysis of specific technology applications under these Global Goals revealed that, for specific social ventures tied to public goods, markets are lagging or are virtually nonexistent.

Finance mechanisms of all types are a positive force to stimulate new market solutions. They are particularly critical to enable scaling of 4IR solutions where market failures exist, there is a challenging investment climate, or the benefits are largely public goods. More broadly, by staying ahead of the latest tech trends, governments, public finance institutions, companies, and investors have the opportunity to back and scale new technology solutions that help countries leapfrog traditional systems.

WE HAVE
IMAGINED

We have imagined what was, until recently, thought to be unimaginable. We have pictured a world in which technology's purpose is to solve our greatest challenges. When we put our mind, heart, soul, investment, and perseverance into realizing our goals, we can achieve anything. If we dare to imagine the impossible to be possible, if we reach beyond what we believe to be our boundaries, there are no limits to what we can accomplish.

Within the preceding tech chapters, we traveled throughout the exciting landscapes of the 4IR. Along our journey we experienced coral reefs restored via 3D printing, skies cleaned by smog-eating advanced materials, manufacturing lines enhanced with robots, energy savings on the blockchain, and augmented crop yields thanks to AI. And we imagined the 6G network bringing us new realities that lead to a greater universal existence.

Tech for Good is here now. We are immersed in it. It is no longer a theoretical concept on the distant horizon. While imagining the 4IR, the blending of digital and physical technologies creates a vast and expansive landscape of Tech for Good innovations. As we have only just begun this journey, countless technological advancements are still to come on the road ahead. Throughout our tech journey, we have seen that technology, when really applied with a purpose for good, makes a significant contribution to our Global Goals. We must continue imagining, adapting, and discovering as we scale to unprecedented heights.

The #TechforGood movement requires a collective, global effort. Imagine if tech companies, governments, industry, civil society, and researchers alike joined in to unlock the potential of technologies to address the SDGs. We have imagined a world that moves beyond celebrating a few brilliant business cases and enters the realm of unlimited potential. We must put our imagination into action and invest money, time, and expertise into this agenda. Not only will we be required to find new ways of working together to unlock innovations, but humanity must accelerate #TechforGood with impactful and sustainable solutions.

If we truly want to achieve the Global Goals, businesses must be action-driven by leveraging technologies to reach their full potential. Demonstrating how Tech for Good can achieve the Global Goals while creating commercial business opportunities was ultimately my personal purpose for this book. It was my mission to inspire the reader to see the vast possibilities, rather than accept the status quo. Tech for Good ultimately teaches us we do not have to accept this. Along with business, and the global community, let's first imagine, then work toward creating, a sustainable, thriving world.

Join the Tech for Good movement today.